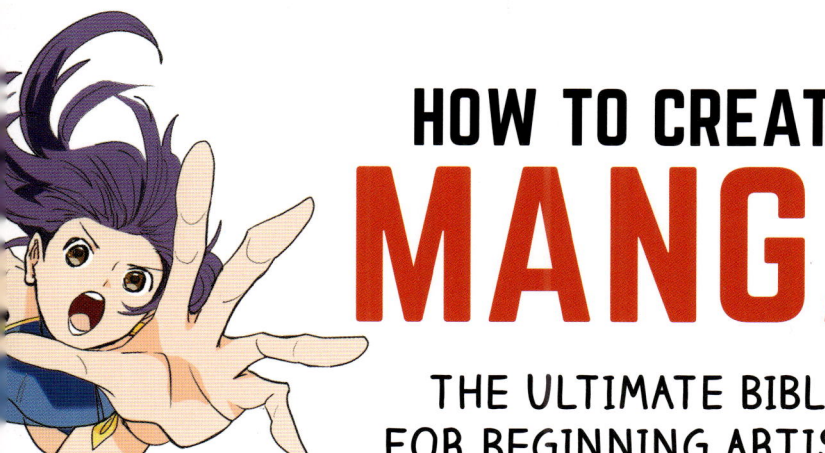

HOW TO CREATE
MANGA

THE ULTIMATE BIBLE FOR BEGINNING ARTISTS

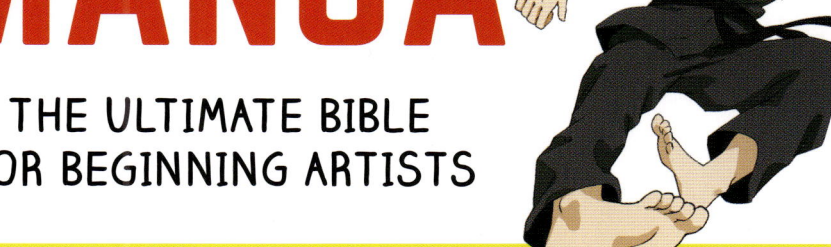

DRAWING DYNAMIC HAND & BODY MOVEMENTS

SIDERANCH

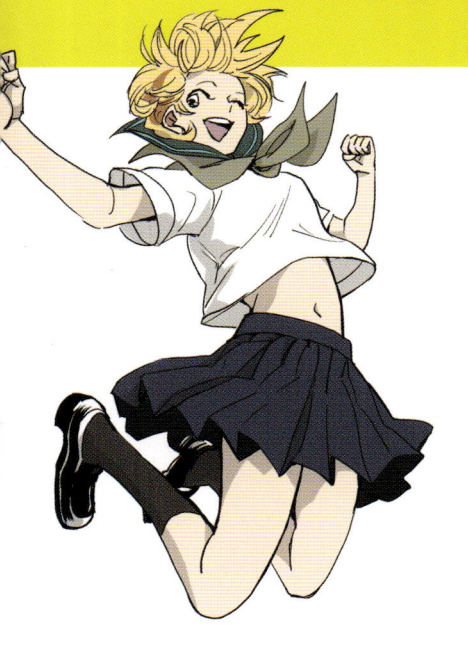
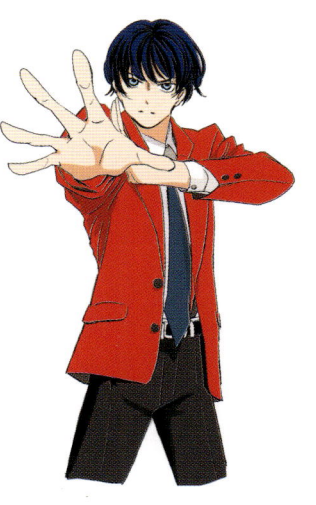
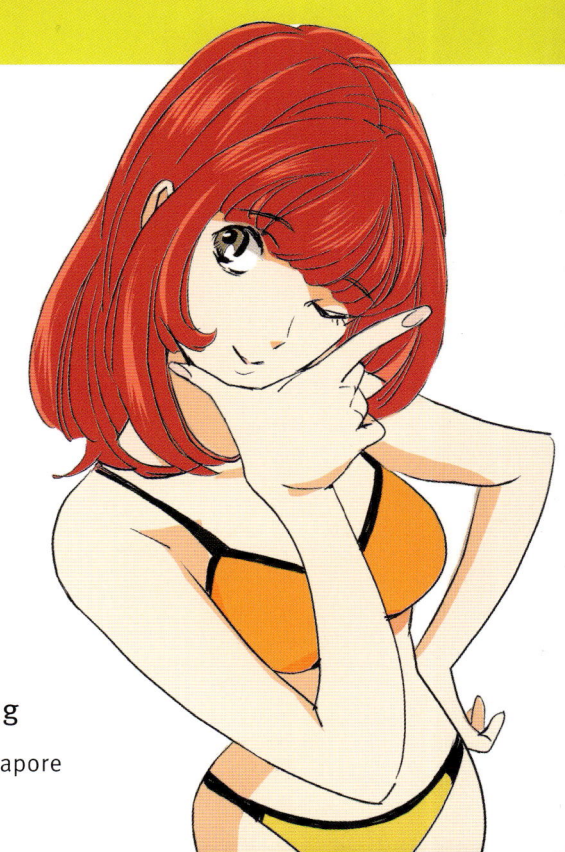

TUTTLE Publishing

Tokyo | Rutland, Vermont | Singapore

Contents

Why We Wrote This Book 6 / How to Use This Book 8

PART 1 Drawing Amazing Characters: The Basics 9

How to Think About Poses 10 / How to Think About Composition 12 / Angles 14 / Three-dimensionality 15

PART 2 Dynamic Hand Movements 19

One Hand Extended 20 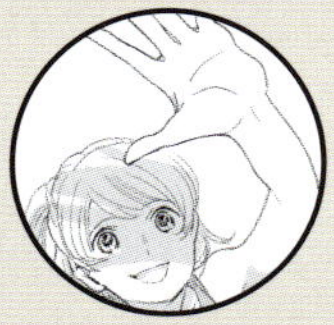
Both Hands Extended 22 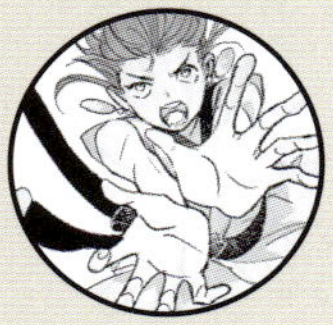
Pointing 24 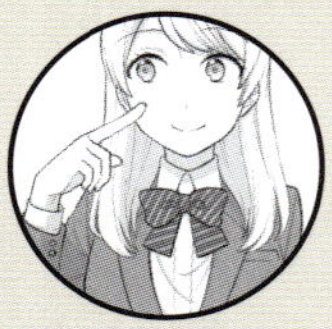
Blowing a Kiss 26 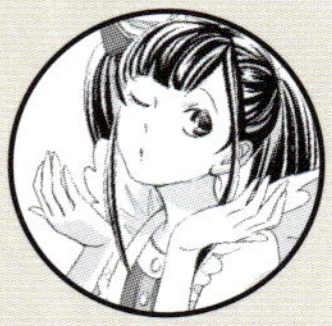
Peace Sign 28

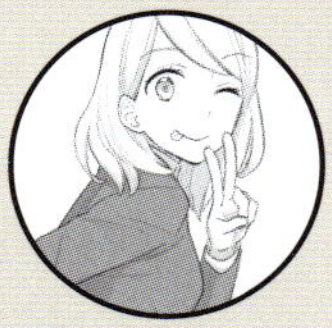

Warm Greetings 30 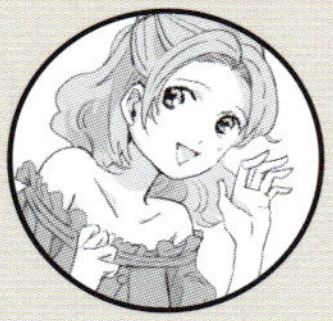
Laughing 32 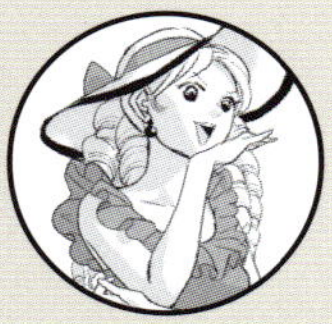
Resting on the Chin 33 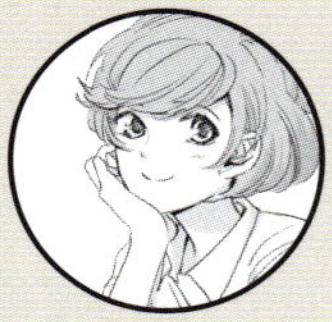
Finger to the Lips 34 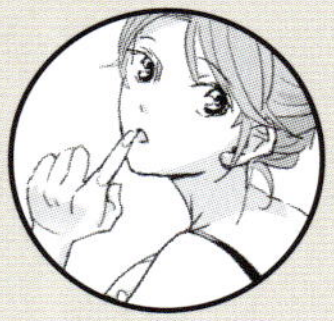
Fist Pumps 36

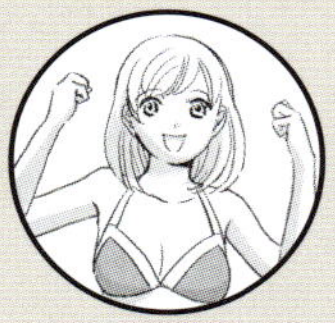

Lost in Thought 38 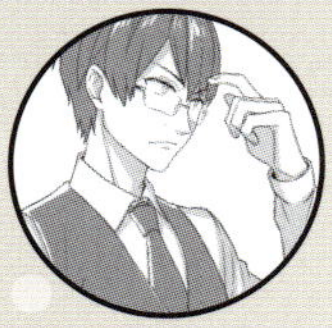
Simulating a Gun 40 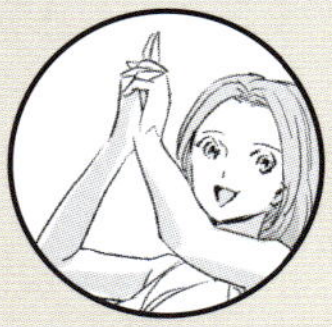
Wiping Away Tears 42 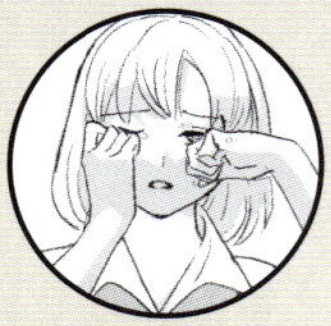
Pointing to One's Self 43 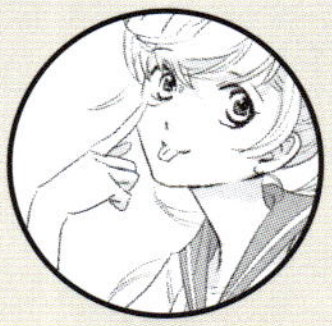
Looking into the Distance 44

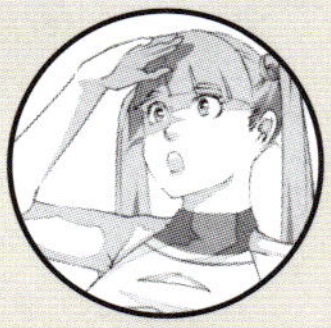

Expressing Shyness 45 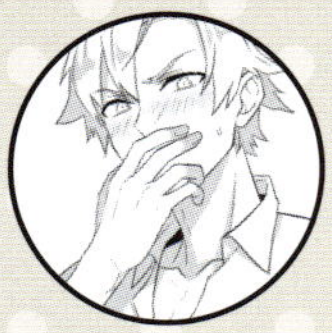
Touching the Head 46 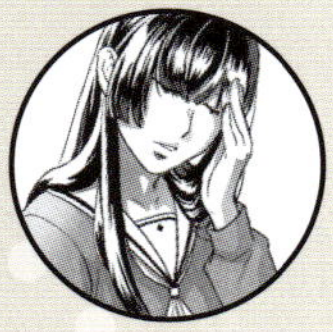
Beckoning Motions 47 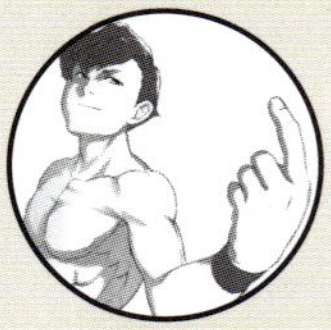
Imitating Animals 48 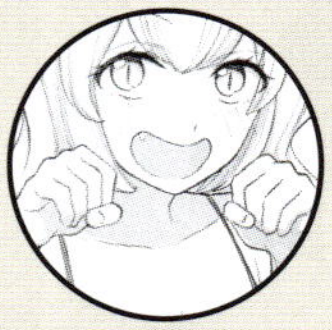
Affirmative Gestures 50

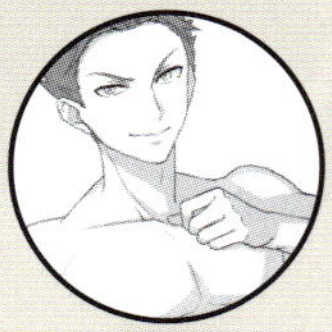

Salutes 51 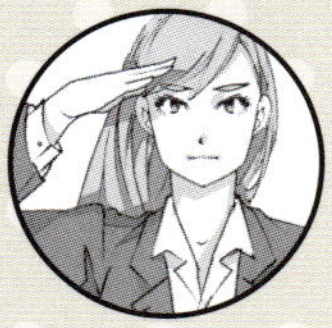
Heart Hands 52 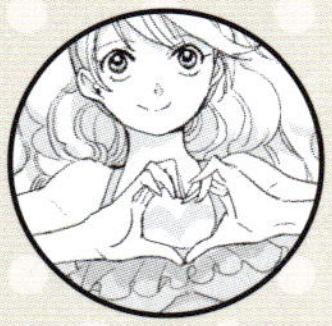
Praying 53 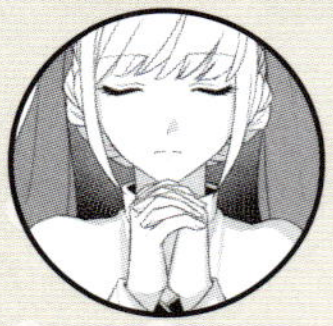
Putting the Hands Together 54 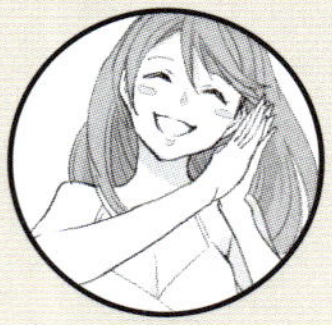
Chin in Hands 55

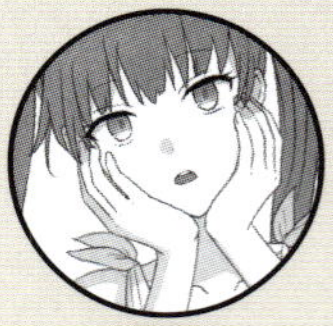

Expressing Surprise 56
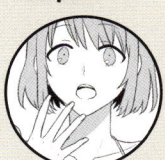

Open Stance 57
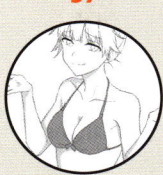

Arms Folded 1 58
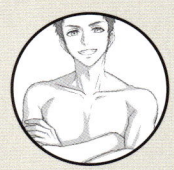

Covering the Ears 59
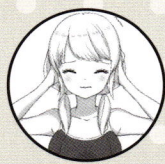

Arms Folded 2 60
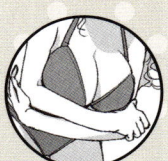

Self-Embrace 61
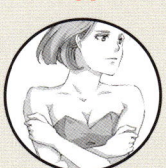

Playing with Hair 62
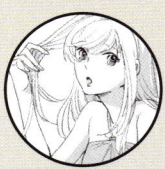

Tucking Hair Behind the Ears 63
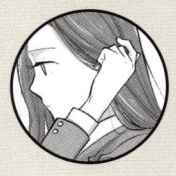

Touching the Hair 64
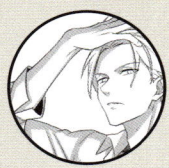

Tying Back Hair 65
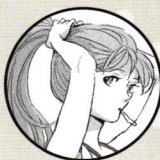

Covering the Face 66
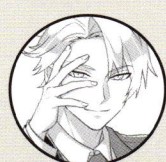

Fingers Near the Mouth 67
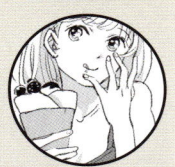

Index Fingers Pointed 68
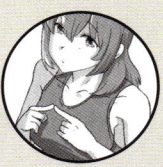

PART 3 Dynamic Full-Body Movements 69

Standing 70
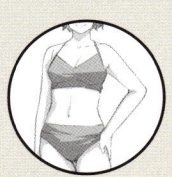

Arms Crossed, Legs Apart 71
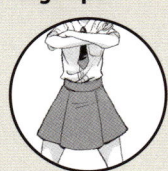

Looking Back 72
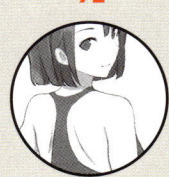

Raising the Arms 74
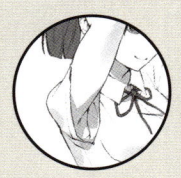

Bending Down 75
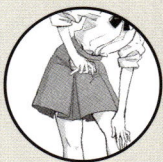

Standing on One Leg 76
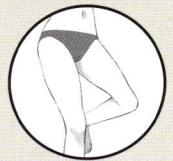

Kneeling 78
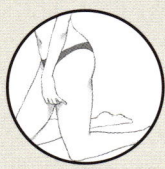

Down on One Knee 80
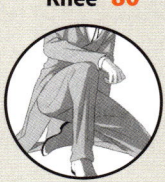

Crouching 81
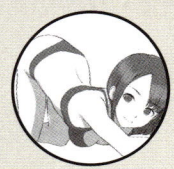

Lying on the Back 82
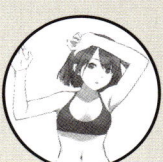

Arching Back 83
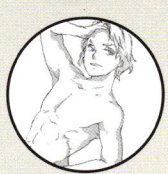

Lying on the Stomach 84
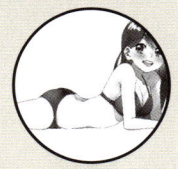

Lying on the Side 85
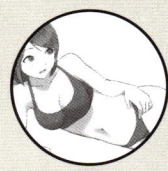

Fetal Position 86
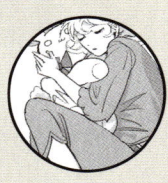

Sitting Crosslegged 87
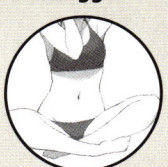

Squatting 88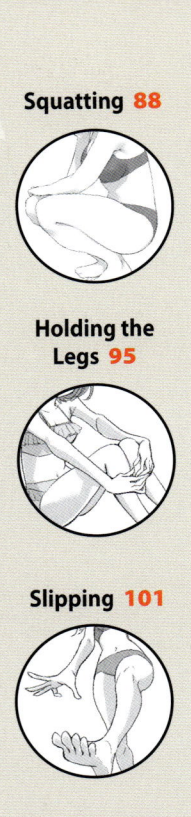

Sitting Down 90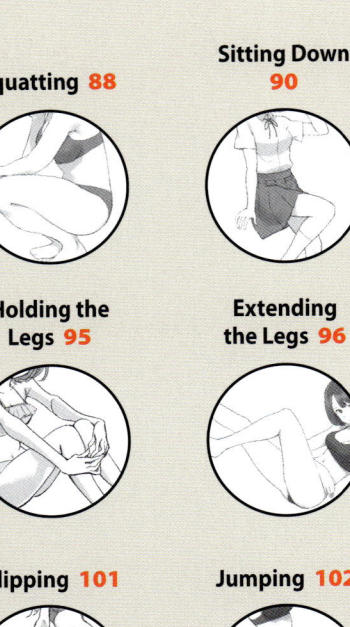

Crossing Legs 92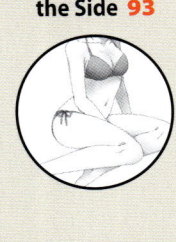

Sitting to the Side 93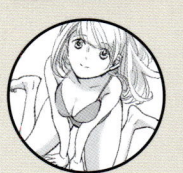

Kneeling, Viewed from Above 94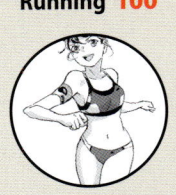

Holding the Legs 95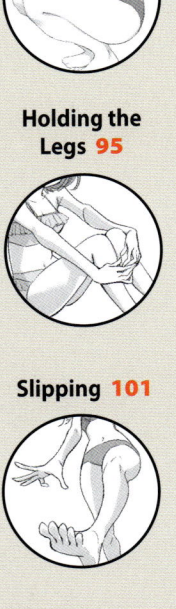

Extending the Legs 96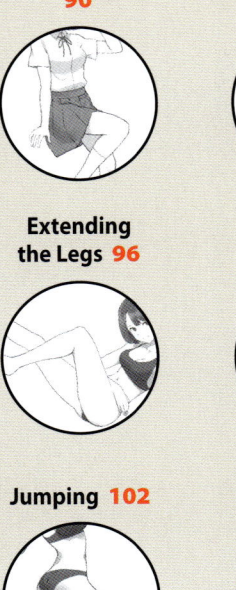

One Knee Raised 97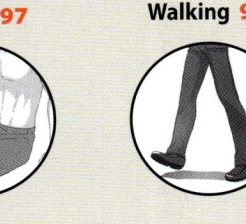

Walking 98

Running 100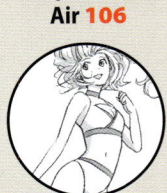

Slipping 101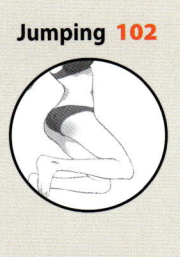

Jumping 102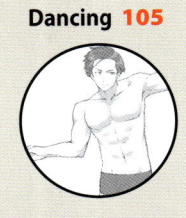

Landing 105

Dancing 105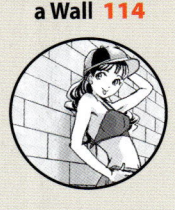

Suspended in Air 106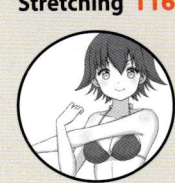

Sparring 108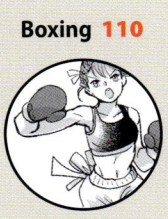

Boxing 110

Kicking 112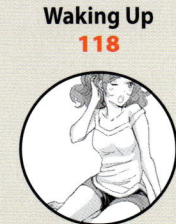

Leaning Against a Wall 114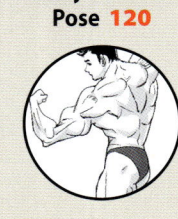

Stretching 116

Working Out 117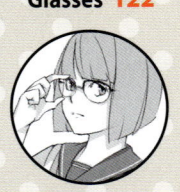

Waking Up 118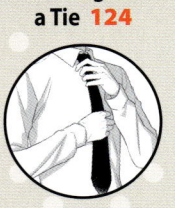

Doing Ballet 119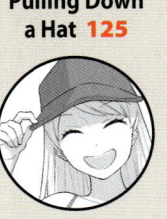

Bodybuilder's Pose 120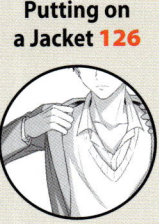

PART 4   Using Objects and Accessories 121

Pushing Up Glasses 122

Putting on a Tie 124

Pulling Down a Hat 125

Putting on a Jacket 126

Fixing a Skirt 128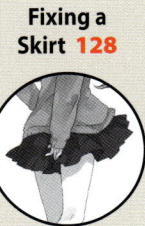

Tightening a Hairbow **130** 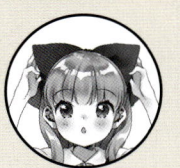	Pulling off Gloves **131** 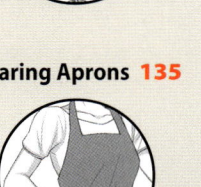	Adjusting a Shoe **132** 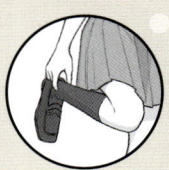	Fixing the Fit **133** 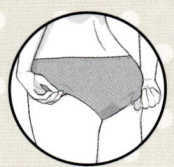	Putting on Lipstick **134** 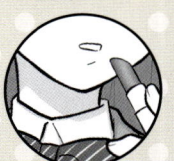
Wearing Aprons **135** 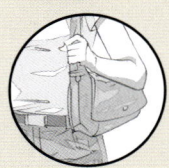	Serious and Studious **136** 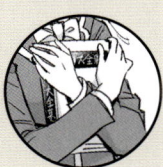	Holding a Bouquet **137** 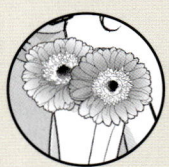	Holding a Phone **138** 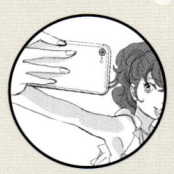	Taking a Picture **139** 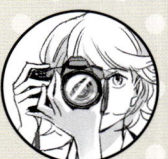
Holding a Bag **140** 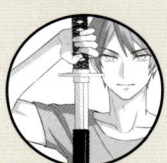	Holding an Umbrella **142** 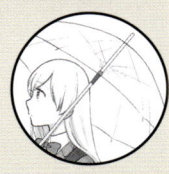	Leaning on a Desk **144** 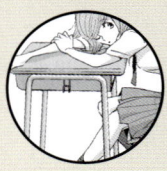	Sitting with Legs Crossed **147** 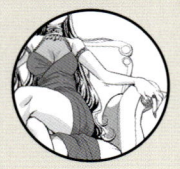	Wielding a Sword **148** 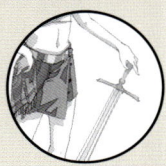
Drawing a Katana **150** 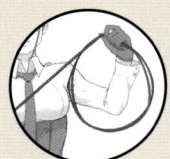	Holding a Gun **152** 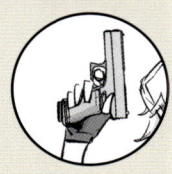	Using a Bow **155** 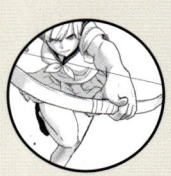	Holding a Curved Blade **156** 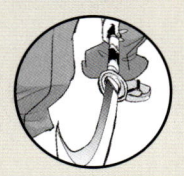	Casting a Spell **158** 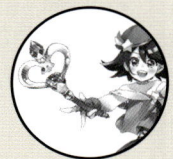
Using a Whip **159** 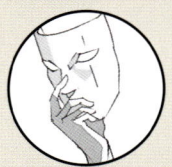	Eating **160** 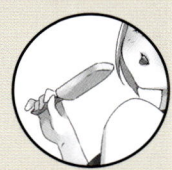	Drinking **162** 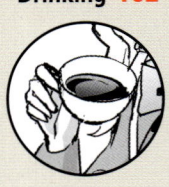	Smoking **164** 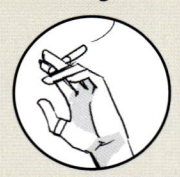	Wearing Handcuffs **165** 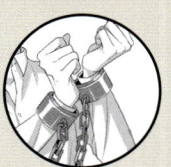
Using a Mask **166** 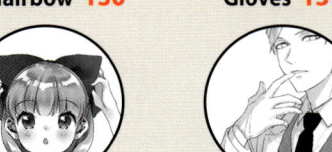	Holding a Megaphone **167** 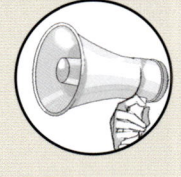	Conducting **168** 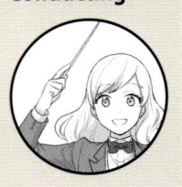	Listening to Music **169** 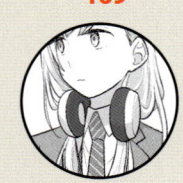	Holding a Guitar **170** 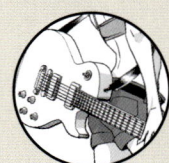

Singing **172**

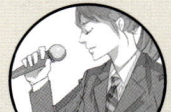

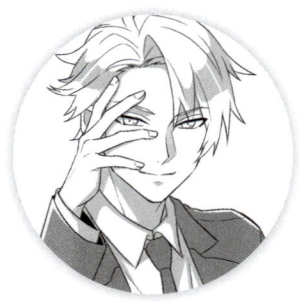 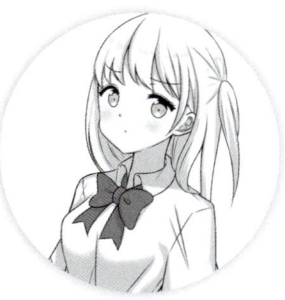 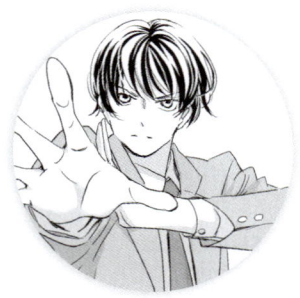 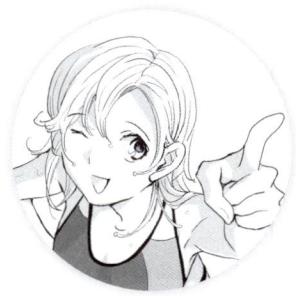

Why We Wrote This Book

Are you ready to imbue your characters with new dynamic dimensions, signature poses and a more compelling physicality and presence? Then this is the book for you. It's essentially a compendium of poses—480 of them in all!—that are ideal for anime, manga or any form of illustration you're pursuing. Do you need to find that perfect gesture to capture the emotions of first love? Or maybe your character is the cool type in need of the perfect sneer or pout? From slinky and seductive to the intricacies of combat and action scenes, the right pose not only makes your characters more memorable, it also sends essential information to your viewers about what exactly is going on in the story you're trying to tell. Details of setting, plot, personality and attitude are all accurately captured and conveyed in the perfect pose, posture or gesture.

    With so many possible poses, to make it easier for you to find that essential one, we've grouped the options into three categories: hand-based gestures and poses, postures and stances involving the entire body and, finally, poses and positions involving objects.

    Part 1 is all about the hands, key appendages when it comes to character development and conveying action. Here we've collected everything from common gestures, such as the peace sign, to expressions using hands and arms, such as fist pumps and

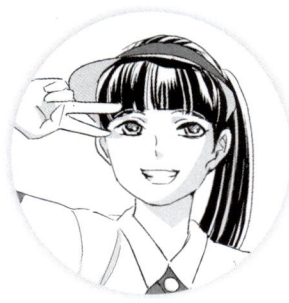 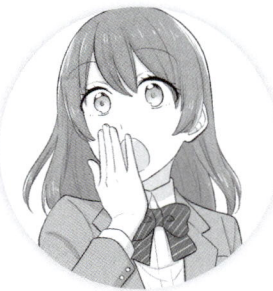 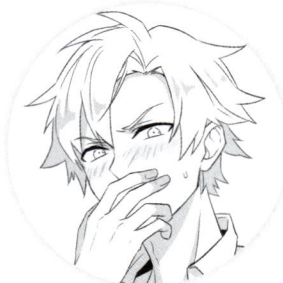 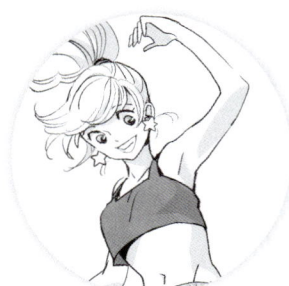

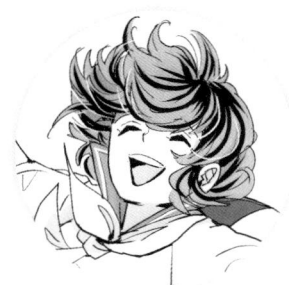 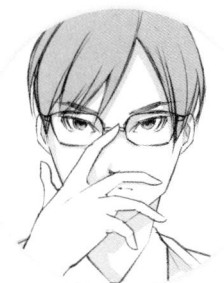 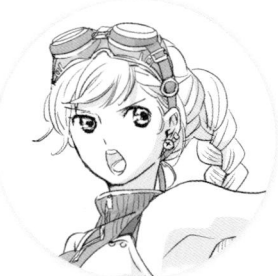 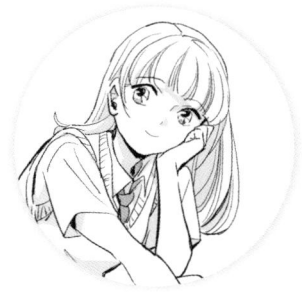

salutes. In particular, we've included poses that are easy to reproduce, even for compositions that only involve the upper body.

In Part 2, the focus shifts to the bigger picture of the entire body. This section features characters in a variety of poses essential to your storytelling: standing, sitting and lying down, along with a range of variations and permutations. In addition, you'll find more complex compositions here, including martial arts action poses and dynamic dance poses.

Part 3 concludes this guide with a deep dive into the world of objects. Your characters will need to come in contact with an endless array of items, accessories and garments. The poses here include everything from putting on a jacket to demurely licking an ice cream cone. There's also a wide variety of standard-issue illustrated items, such as weapons and musical instruments, that will eventually pop up in your own manga and anime illustrations.

Are you ready to make your characters leap off the page? Have you been struggling to capture dynamic details in your characters' physicality? So what are you waiting for, the answers await in the three sections ahead. Thanks for taking the time to learn with us and, oh yeah, happy posing!

—**Sideranch**

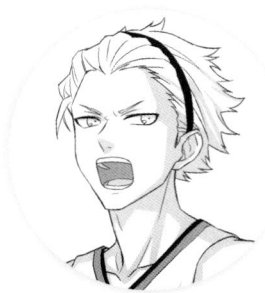 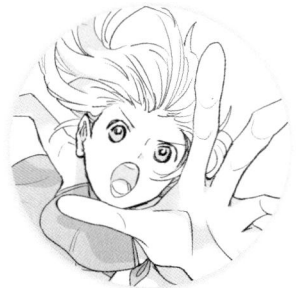 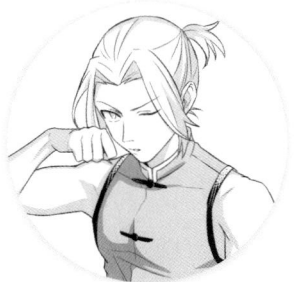 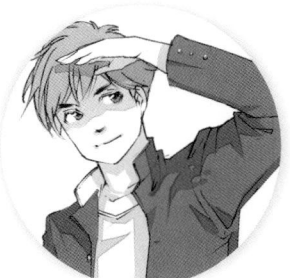

How to Use This Book

POSE REFERENCES: PARTS 1-3

We'll show examples of poses for each category and explain their characteristics and main points.

Category
Specific type of pose.

ANGLES
Here we look at perspective and recommended angles.

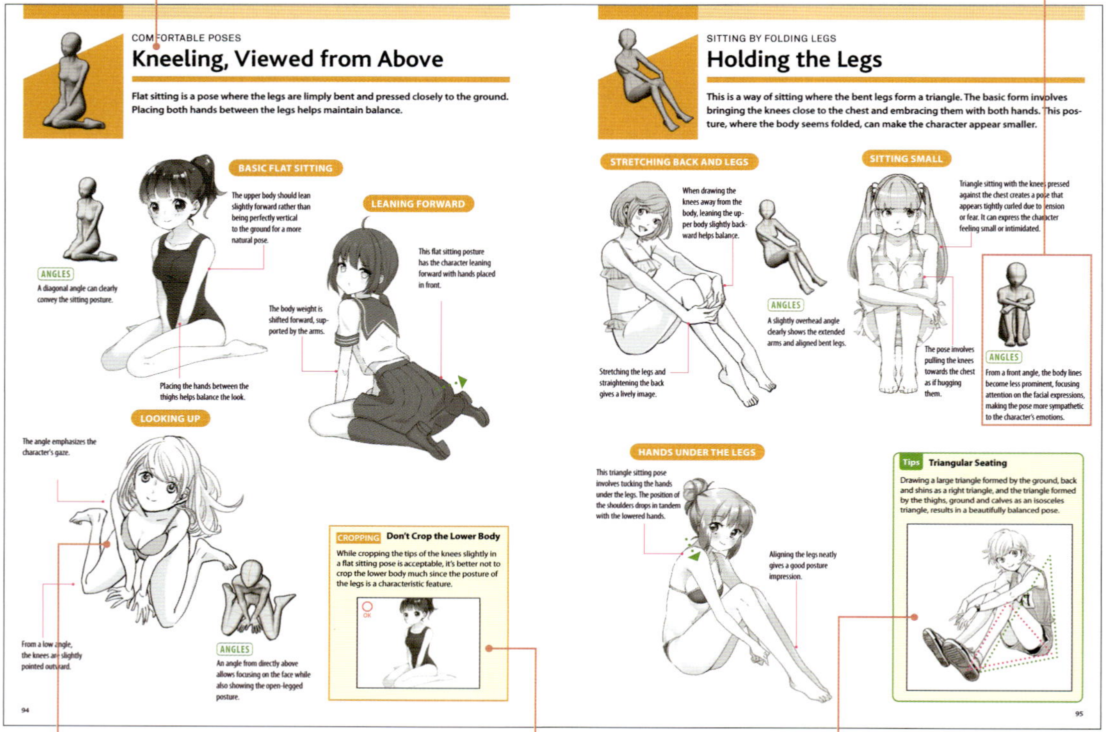

Pose Examples
We explain the features and main points of each example.

CROPPING
This section explains things to keep in mind when cutting out part of an illustration image.

Tips
These sidebars take a closer look at key details or offer additional tips and advice.

BASIC KNOWLEDGE: PART 1

This page explains basic knowledge that's useful to know about poses.

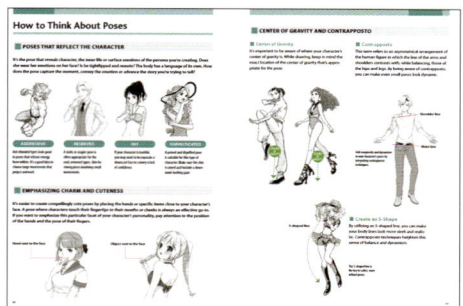

EXCEPT FOR THE FACE, THE ILLUSTRATION IS WORKING

■ If you wish to use the poses in this book for your own work, please refrain from tracing or copying the faces. Drawings of the body that do not include the face can be used for tracing or copying, whether for commercial or private purposes. There is also no need to include credit for this book in the work you create.

■ Feel free to copy these drawings as part of your practice. You may publish copies of the illustrations in parts 1 to 3 on social media such as Twitter and Instagram. When publishing copies that include drawings of faces, please clearly cite this book as the source of the illustration.

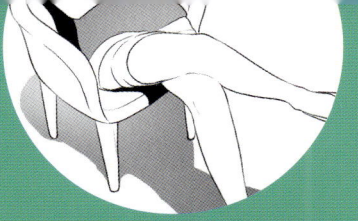
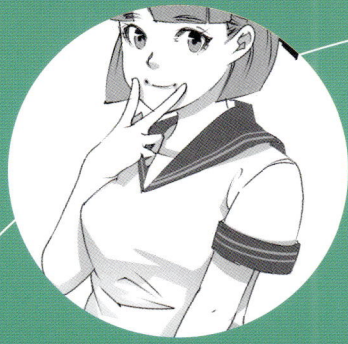
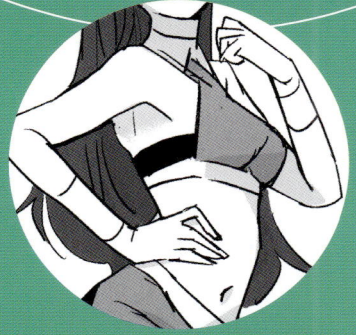
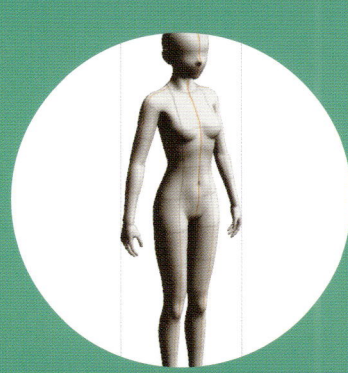
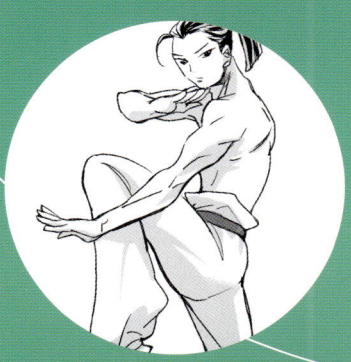
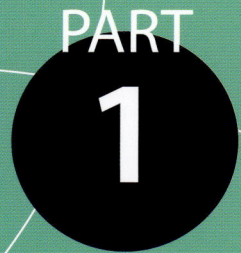

PART 1

Drawing Amazing Characters: The Basics

It's time to learn the basics of dynamic poses, positions and gestures. What are some things to keep in mind when creating effective and indelible poses and scenes?

How to Think About Poses

How to Think About Composition

Angles

Three-Dimensionality

How to Think About Poses

POSES THAT REFLECT THE CHARACTER

It's the pose that reveals character, the inner life or surface emotions of the persona you're creating. Does she wear her emotions on her face? Is he tightlipped and remote? The body has a language of its own. How does the pose capture the moment, convey the emotion or advance the story you're trying to tell?

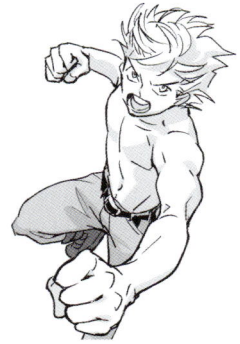
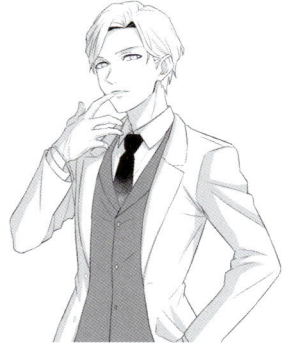
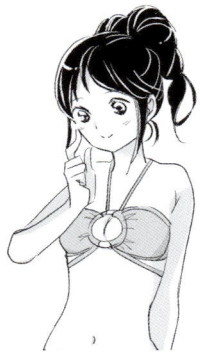
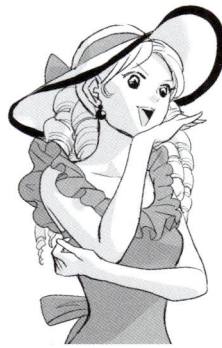

AGGRESSIVE

Hot-blooded types look good in poses that release energy from within. It's a good idea to choose large movements that project outward.

RESERVED

A static or stagier pose is often appropriate for the cool, removed types. Aim for strong poses involving small movements.

SHY

If your character is bashful, you may want to incorporate a downcast face to convey a lack of confidence.

SOPHISTICATED

A poised and dignified pose is suitable for this type of character. Make sure the chin is raised and include a downward-looking gaze.

EMPHASIZING CHARM AND CUTENESS

It's easier to create compellingly cute poses by placing the hands or specific items close to your character's face. A pose where characters touch their fingertips to their mouths or cheeks is always an effective go-to. If you want to emphasize this particular facet of your character's personality, pay attention to the position of the hands and the pose of their fingers.

Hand next to the face

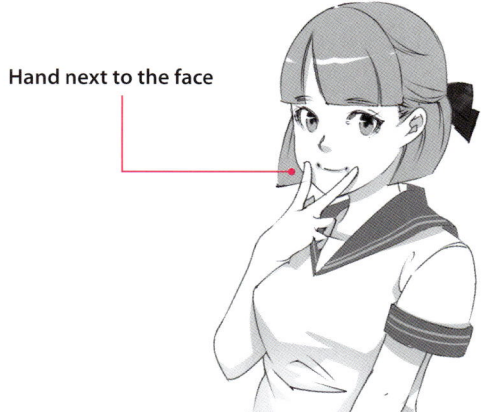

Object next to the face

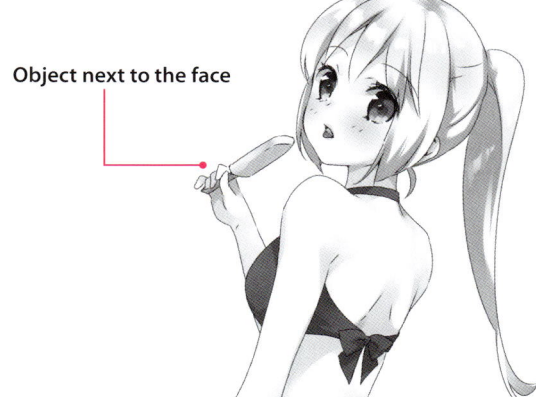

CENTER OF GRAVITY AND CONTRAPPOSTO

■ Center of Gravity

It's important to be aware of where your character's center of gravity is. While drawing, keep in mind the exact location of the center of gravity that's appropriate for the pose.

■ Contrapposto

This term refers to an asymmetrical arrangement of the human figure in which the line of the arms and shoulders contrasts with, while balancing, those of the hips and legs. By being aware of contrapposto, you can make even small poses look dynamic.

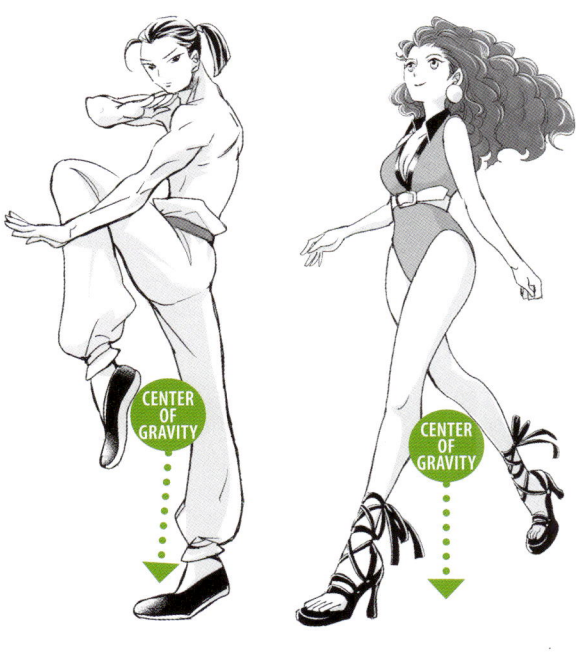

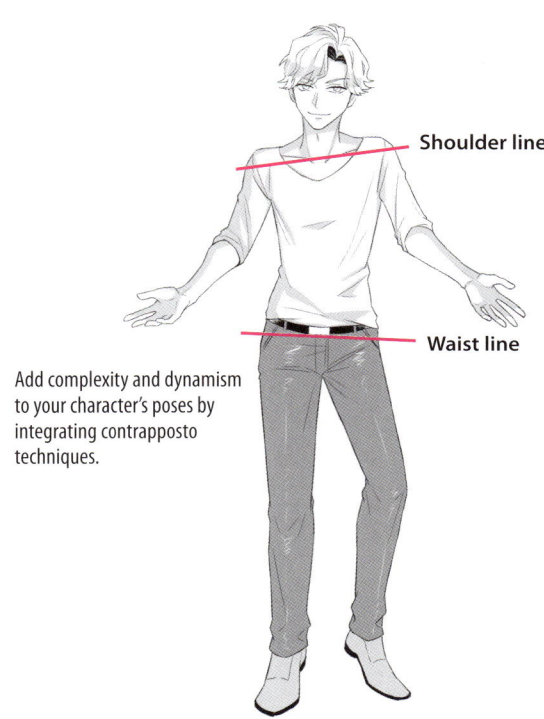

Add complexity and dynamism to your character's poses by integrating contrapposto techniques.

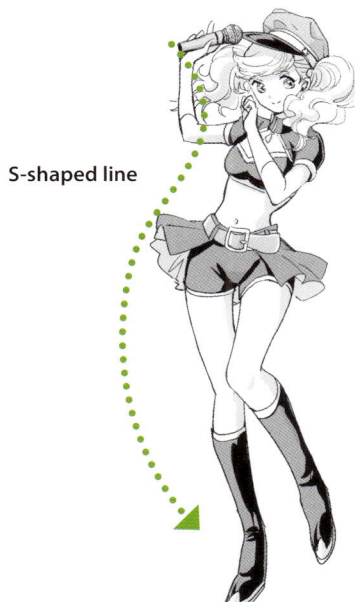

S-shaped line

■ Create an S-Shape

By utilizing an S-shaped line, you can make your body lines look more sleek and realistic. Contrapposto techniques heighten this sense of balance and dynamism.

The S-shaped line is the key to softer, more refined poses.

How to Think About Composition

■ FROM CLOSEUPS TO FULL-BODY SHOTS

It's important from the outset to decide how much of the character fits on the screen. Are we seeing a portion or the entire view? Choose the appropriate pose to pair with the perspective and immediacy you're looking for.

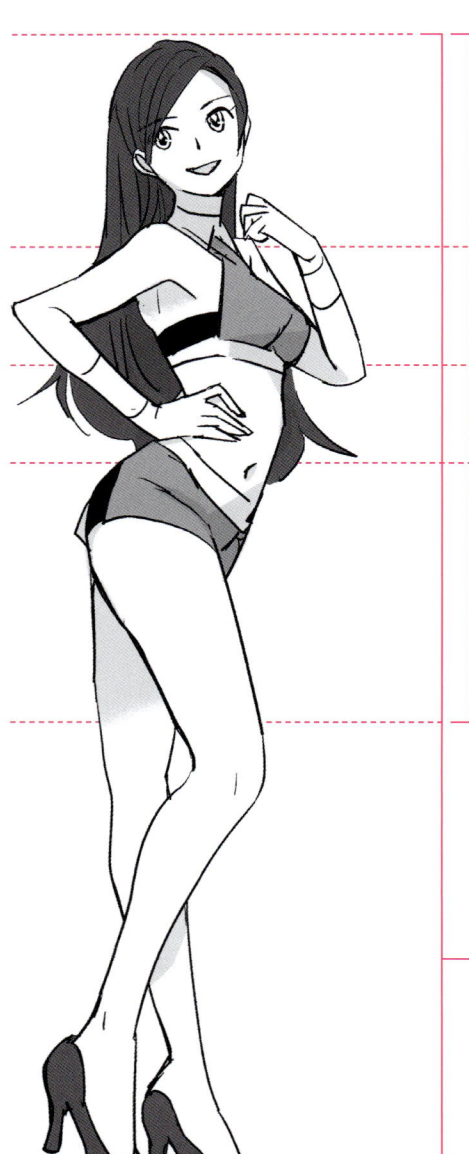

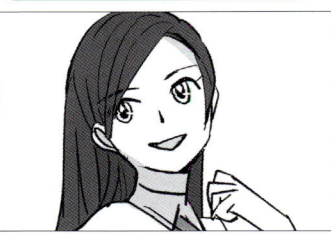
CLOSEUP

Closeup
By showing a large section of the face, you can highlight subtle facial expressions.

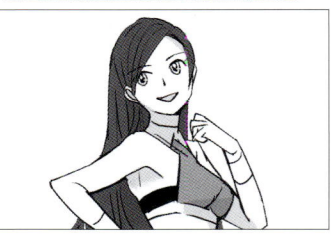
UPPER-BODY SHOT

Upper-Body Shot
The focus of this compositional mode is from the chest up, by which you can make the facial expressions and hand gestures look bigger.

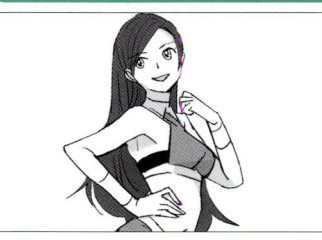
WAIST OR HALF-BODY SHOT

Waist or Half-Body Shot
Composing from the waist up allows you to show off the pose and proportions of the upper body.

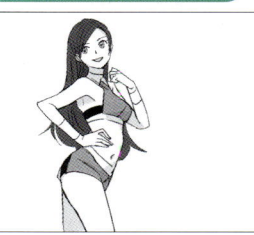
THREE-QUARTERS SHOT

Three-Quarters Shot
With this option, you can highlight proportions and especially facial expressions because the face is larger than in a full-body shot.

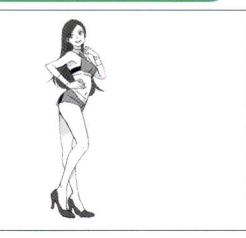
FULL-BODY SHOT

Full-Body Shot
This mode shows the whole body within the frame, allowing you to clearly show the movement of the whole body more effectively than the other options.

AREAS THAT ATTRACT ATTENTION

The eye tends to be drawn to the area slightly above the center of the composition. So position your characters while keeping in mind the areas that stand out. Depending on the scene you're drawing, you can determine where the viewer's gaze will go. In general, people tend to scrutinize faces and hands. However, the eyes, in particular, are where most of the attention goes.

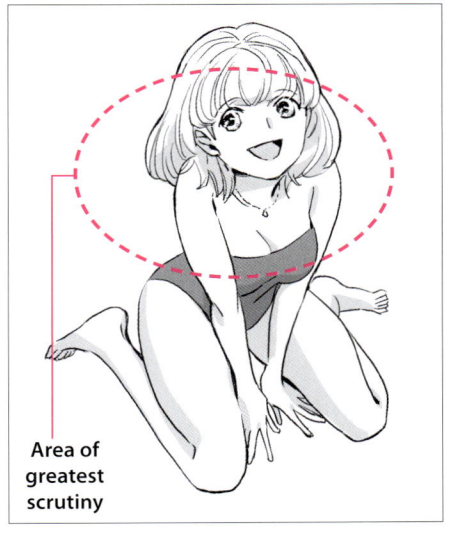

Area of greatest scrutiny

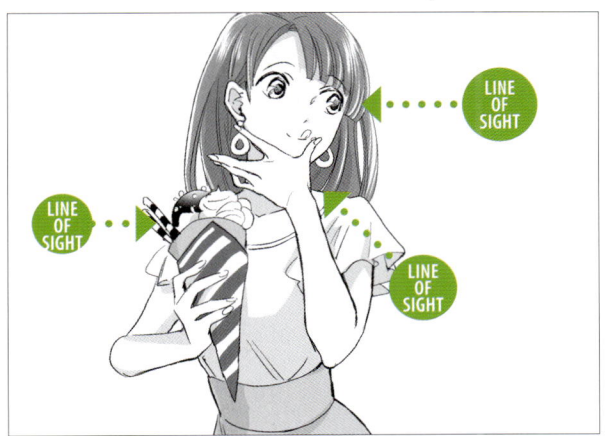

The eyes are the most visible part. In general, any feature or item that stands out is an area where it's easy to attract attention.

EDITING AND REVISING YOUR ILLUSTRATION

Cropping means cutting out unnecessary parts of an image. For closeups and upper-body shots, you may need to crop some parts of the body offscreen. When trimming, be sure not to cut off the figure at the joints.

AVOID BEHEADINGS

A composition that cuts off at the neck gives off an oddly disembodied impression. Unless you have a specific intention, it's best not to create a floating head effect.

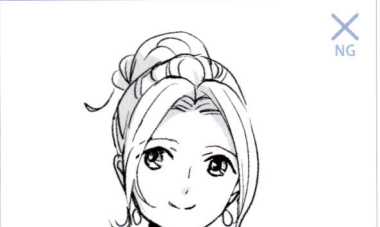
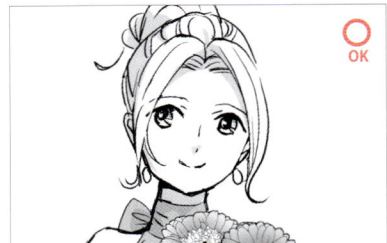

DON'T CUT OFF AT THE JOINTS

This is a practice to be avoided as well. If you cut at the wrist, the composition tends to be unnatural and draw attention to the area beyond.

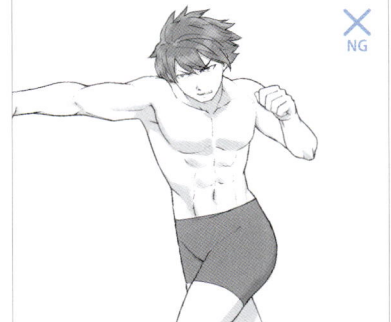
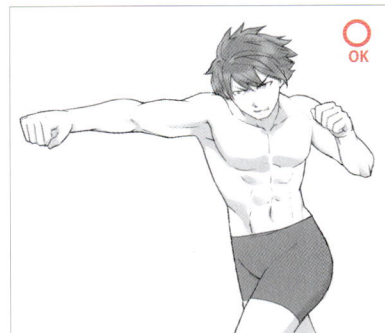

Angles

ANGLES THAT SUIT THE POSE

The way the pose looks changes depending on the angle. You can effectively show off prominent parts such as hands and faces, or make the features look more impressive by finding the right angle for the pose.

Frontal Views

The front angle has the strength of a direct appeal. If you want to strongly convey the character's intentions and emotions, consider a frontal angle.

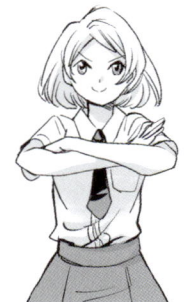
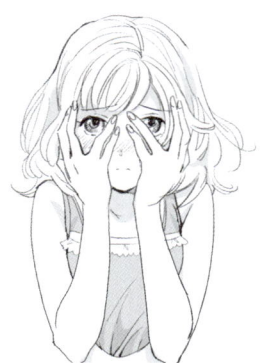

The front angle gives the stronger impression.

Upward Angles

This perspective is created by looking up from a ground-level view. This has the effect of making the motif appear larger. Use this option to express strength or arrogance.

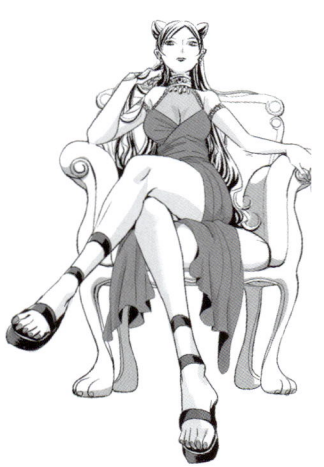
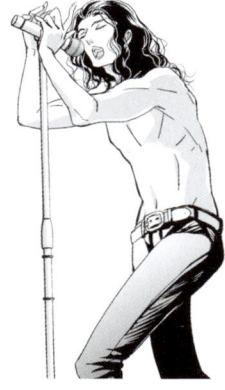

The tilt makes it easy to create a more dramatic impression, so it's suitable for highlighting the character's presence.

Diagonal Angles

This perspective makes it easier to see proportions than a frontal view, so it's effective when you want to make your body lines look lithe and sleek. It also gives a natural and casual impression, making it a strong choice for everyday poses.

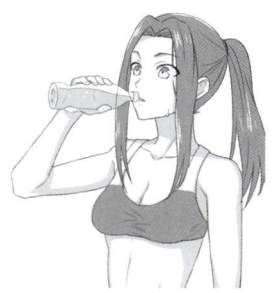
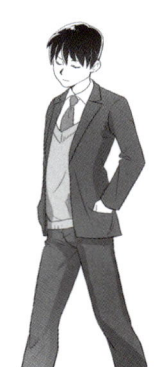

If you want to draw casual everyday gestures, the diagonal angle is a safe bet.

Bird's-Eye Views

In the case of character illustrations, viewing the action from above has the advantage of making it easier to fit the whole body into the screen. Draw the face larger to compensate for this extreme perspective.

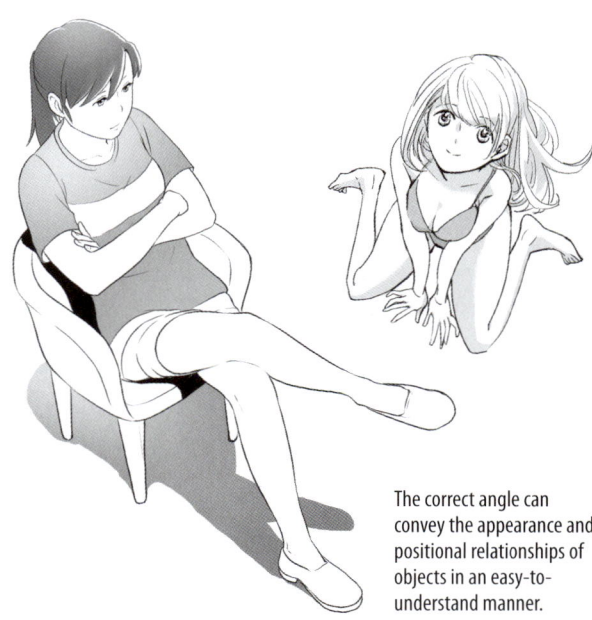

The correct angle can convey the appearance and positional relationships of objects in an easy-to-understand manner.

Three-Dimensionality

STEP 1 PASTE AND SELECT

The 3D functionality of your preferred digital illustration software can be used to sketch different angles and poses.

Pasting Three-Dimensional Characters

These figures can be made using the [Material] palette. You can paste it by dragging and dropping. The pasted 3D drawing figure is displayed on the [Layer] palette.

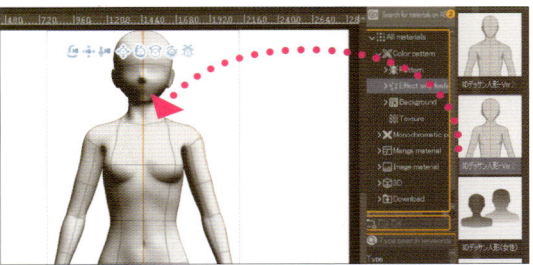

MATERIAL PALETTE

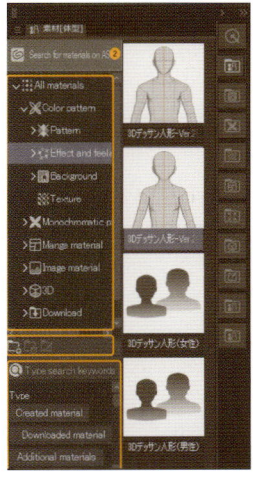

Choose the Type
There are two types of 3D drawing templates: you can choose between male and female types. You can adapt these basic forms to create nontraditional characters.

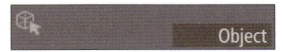

Select with the Object Tool
By selecting the 3D drawing figure using the [Operation] tool → [Object], you can perform various editing operations.

STEP 2 ADJUSTING THE POSITION

Using the movement manipulator displayed above the 3D drawing figure, you can change the camera angle and move/rotate the 3D drawing figure. To use it, click the icon you want to use, activate it and drag it across the canvas.

MOVING MANIPULATOR

1. Rotates the camera
2. Translates camera in parallel.
3. Moves the camera forward and backward
4. Moves the 3D drawing figure up/down/left/right.
5. Rotates the 3D drawing figure based on the camera's viewpoint.
6. Rotates a 3D drawing figure in a plane.
7. Rotates the 3D drawing figure so that it's parallel to the base/ground in 3D space.
8. Absorbs movement while adhering to the material.

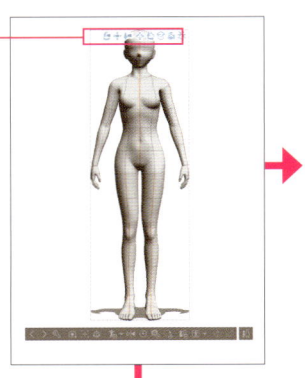

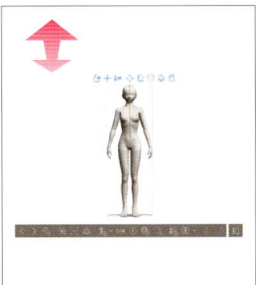

Adjusting Frame Size
You can adjust the frame size of the 3D drawing figure by moving the camera closer or farther away using [Move camera forward/backward].

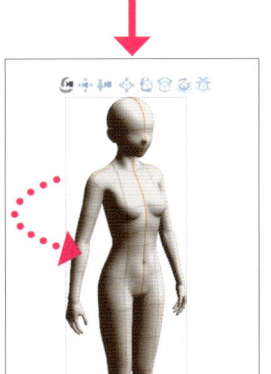

Adjusting the Angle
The basic idea is to change the angle by rotating the camera.

STEP 3 CHANGING BODY SHAPES

3D drawing dolls can change their body shapes. Click [Change body shape] in the object launcher at the bottom to display the [Sub tool details] palette, where you can adjust the body shape.

SUB TOOL DETAILS PALETTE

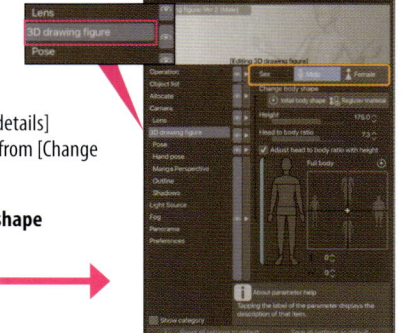

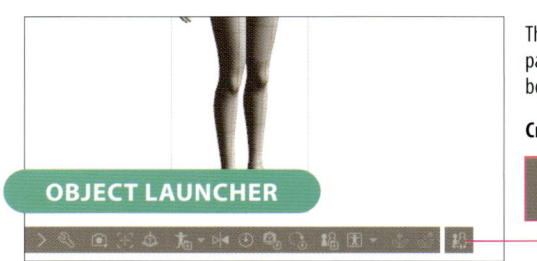

The [Sub tool details] palette opens from [Change body shape].

Create body shape

■ Height and Head/Body Adjustments

You can set your height using the [Height] bar. [Head] adjusts the head and body of the 3D drawing doll. When [Adjust head and body to match height] is on, the head and body will automatically change according to the [Height] value.

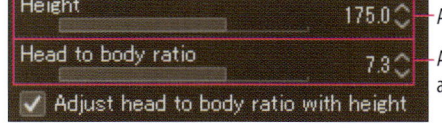

- Adjust the height.
- Adjust the body and head.

■ Adjusting the Entire Body Shape

Use the [Body type] category on the [Sub tool details] palette to adjust the body shape by moving a slider. The higher you move up, the more muscular or voluptuous the body becomes. The more you move it to the right, the thicker it becomes, and the more you move it to the left, the thinner it becomes.

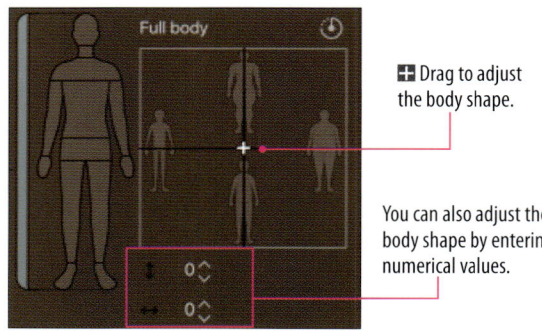

- Drag to adjust the body shape.
- You can also adjust the body shape by entering numerical values.

Initial state　　**Muscular**　　**Flat body shape**　　**Thick body shape**　　**Thin body shape**

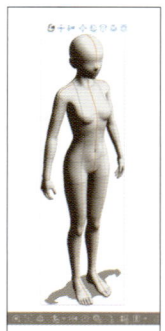 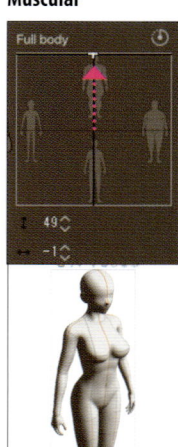 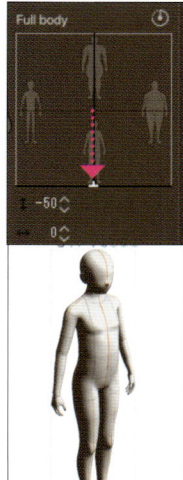 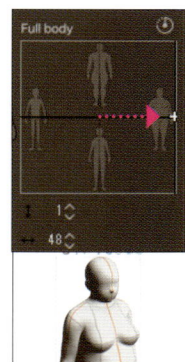 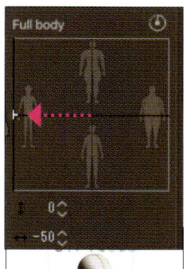
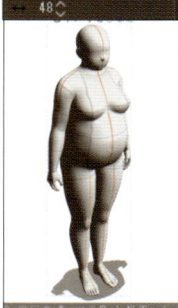 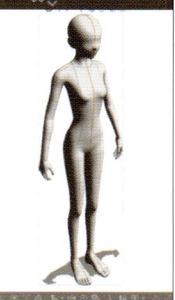

■ Adjusting Thickness and Length

By selecting parts of the human body diagram, you can also make adjustments to individual parts. For example, you can make only the arms thicker or only the legs longer.

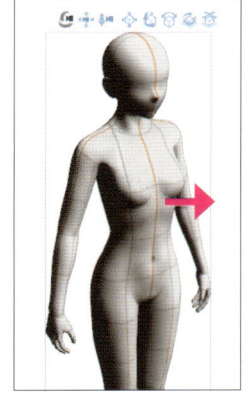
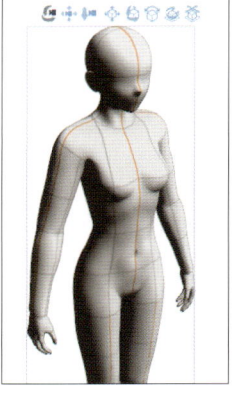
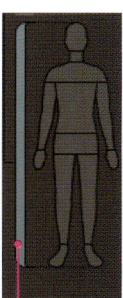

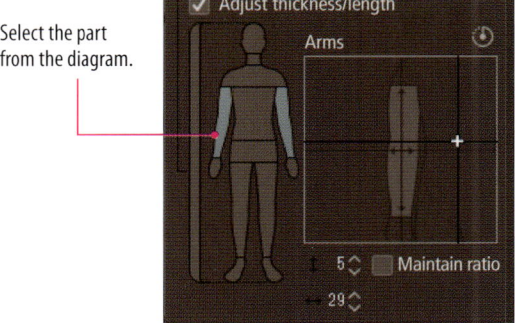

Select the part from the diagram.

➕ Drag to change the thickness and length of the part. Adjust. The more you move it up, the longer it becomes, and the farther right you move it, the thicker it becomes.

If you want to return to the whole body template, press the bar on the left.

■ STEP 4 POSES

■ Move Parts by Dragging

You can move a specific part by grabbing and dragging it. However, other parts also move from the same area simultaneously.

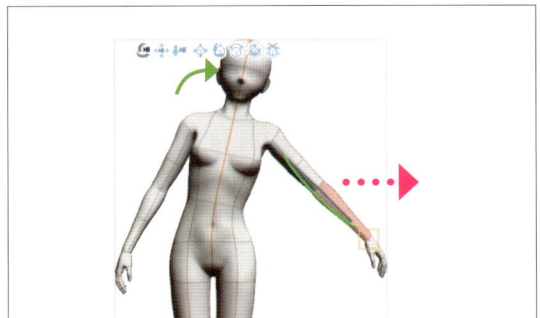

■ Fixing Joints

You can fix the joint by right-clicking. When you drag and move the part, the part beyond the fixed joint will not move.

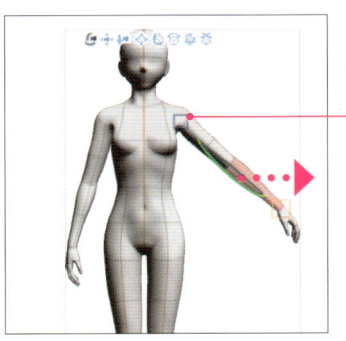

Lock the Joints

For example, if you right-click on the left shoulder and then pull the left arm, nothing beyond the shoulder will move.

■ Moving with the Manipulator

When you click on a part to select it, a ring-shaped manipulator that is color-coded in the direction of movement will appear, and when you drag it, the joint will move. When moving a joint with a manipulator, other parts don't move even if the joint isn't fixed.

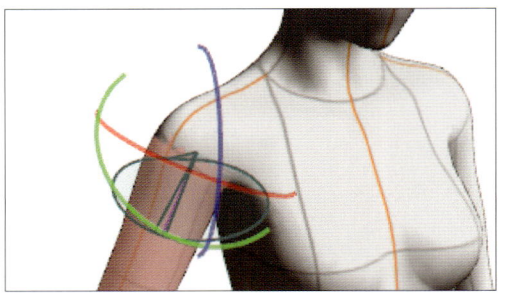

| Tips | **Add Power with Manga Perspective** |

If you turn on the [Tool Property] palette → [Manga Perspective] while selecting a 3D drawing figure with the [Object] tool, you can enlarge a part of the 3D drawing figure to create a manga-like effect.

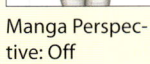

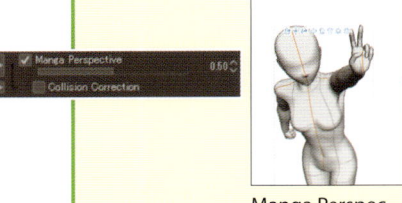
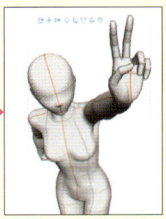

Manga Perspective: Off

Manga Perspective: On / The area closest to the camera will be displayed larger.

17

STEP 5 CHANGING HAND GESTURES

The setup when you want to change the hand gesture.

❶ Select the hand whose gesture you want to change.

❷ Next go to [Pose] on the [Tool Property] palette.
➕ Click to display the hand setup.

❸ Lock the fingers you don't want to move.

❹ ➕ Drag and move the fingers to create a pose.

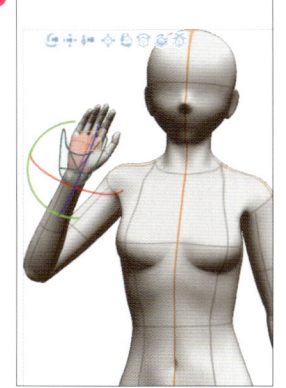

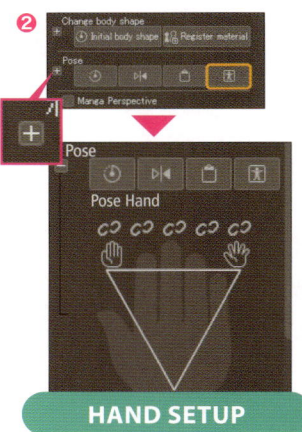

HAND SETUP

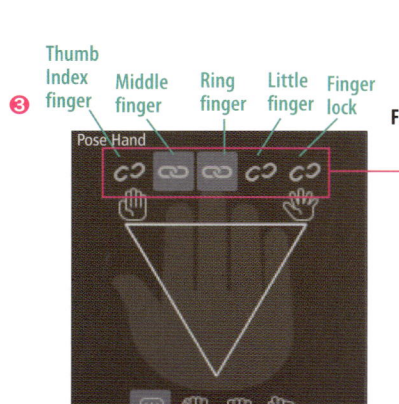

Thumb / Index finger / Middle finger / Ring finger / Little finger / Finger lock

Finger Menu

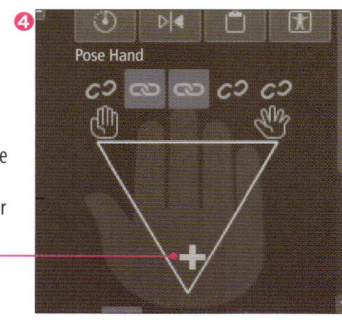

➕ Move the symbol up to open the hand and move down to grip it. Also, the more you move it to the right, the wider the space between your fingers will be.

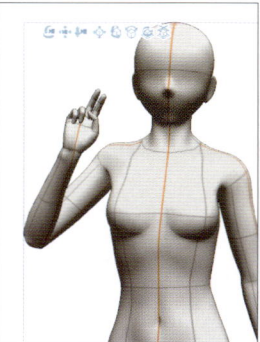

STEP 6 REGISTER A POSE AS A MATERIAL

The created pose can be registered as a pose material.

❶ Select [Register whole body pose as material] on the object launcher.

❷ The [Material Properties] window will open, so select the material name and save location, and press [OK] to complete the registration. The registered pose material can be selected from the [Material] palette, and when you want to use it, drag it onto the 3D drawing figure on the canvas.

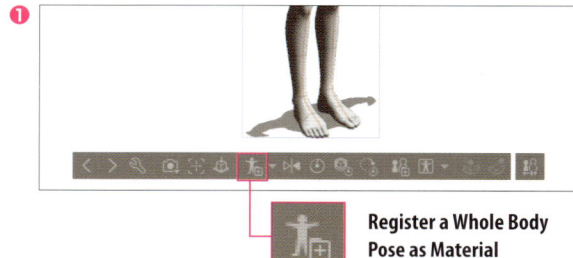

Register a Whole Body Pose as Material

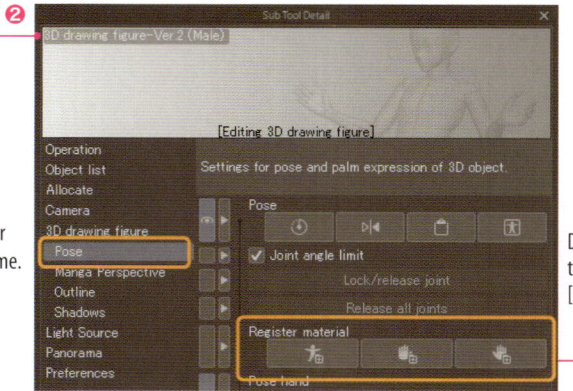

Decide and enter the material name.

Decide where to save it in the [Material] palette.

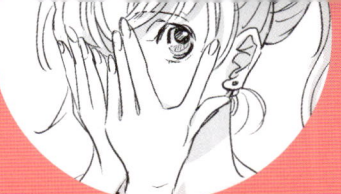
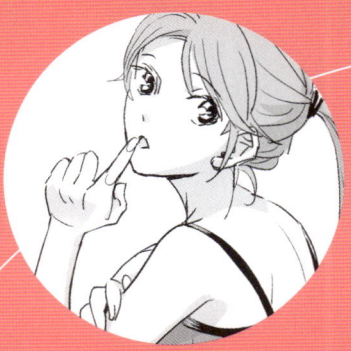
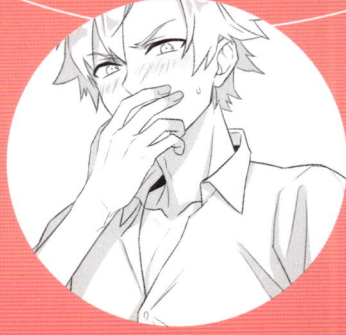
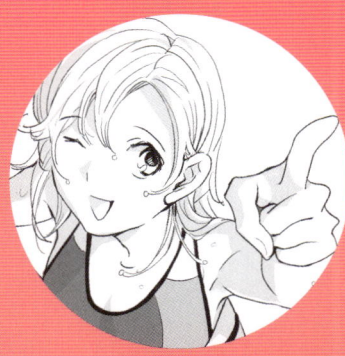
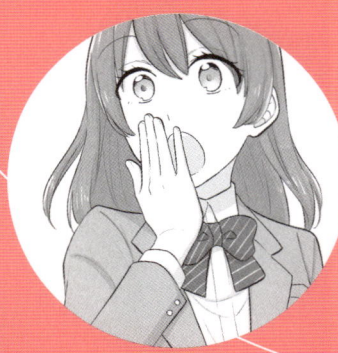

PART 2

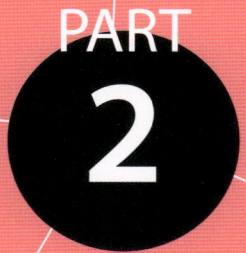

Dynamic Hand Movements

We use our hands all the time, to point, to gesture and even to talk. Mastering this key part and its expressive possibilities is essential to creating memorable movements and dynamic poses.

One Hand Extended
Both Hands Extended
Pointing
Blowing a Kiss
Peace Sign
Warm Greetings
Laughing
Resting on the Chin
Finger to the Lips
Fist Pumps
Lost in Thought
Simulating a Gun
Wiping Away Tears
Pointing to One's Self
Looking into the Distance
Expressing Shyness
Touching the Head
Beckoning Motions
Imitating Animals
Affirmative Gestures

Salutes
Heart Hands
Praying
Putting the Hands Together
Chin in Hands
Expressing Surprise
Open Stance
Arms Folded 1
Covering the Ears
Arms Folded 2
Self-Embrace
Playing with Hair
Tucking Hair Behind the Ears
Touching the Hair
Tying Back Hair
Covering the Face
Fingers Near the Mouth
Index Fingers Pointed

A DYNAMIC POSE
One Hand Extended

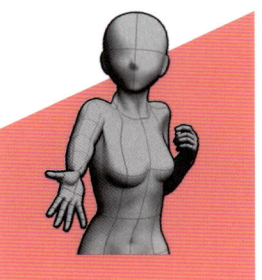

A pose with one hand out in front, with the fingers open, gives the impression of invitation or welcome. It's also a useful gesture to express a character's strong will, such as trying tenaciously to grasp hold of something.

REACHING OUT

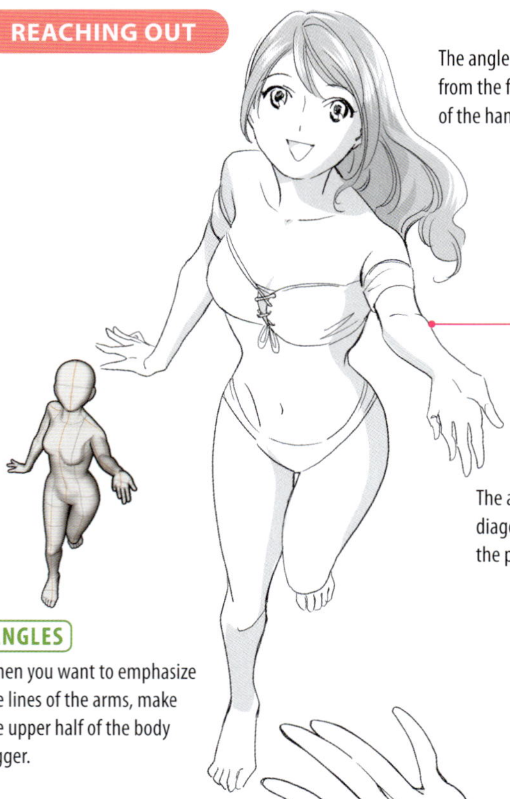

The angle shows the hand outstretched from the front, emphasizing the sense of the hand being extended toward you.

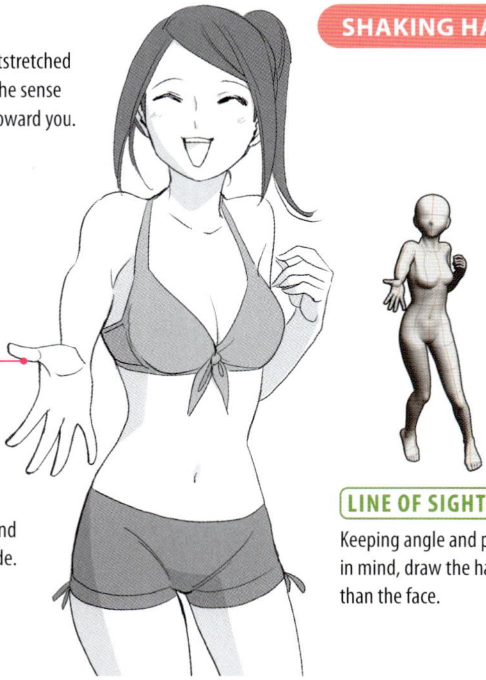

The arms are extended diagonally downward, and the palms are spread wide.

ANGLES

When you want to emphasize the lines of the arms, make the upper half of the body bigger.

SHAKING HANDS

LINE OF SIGHT

Keeping angle and perspective in mind, draw the hands larger than the face.

RAISED PALM

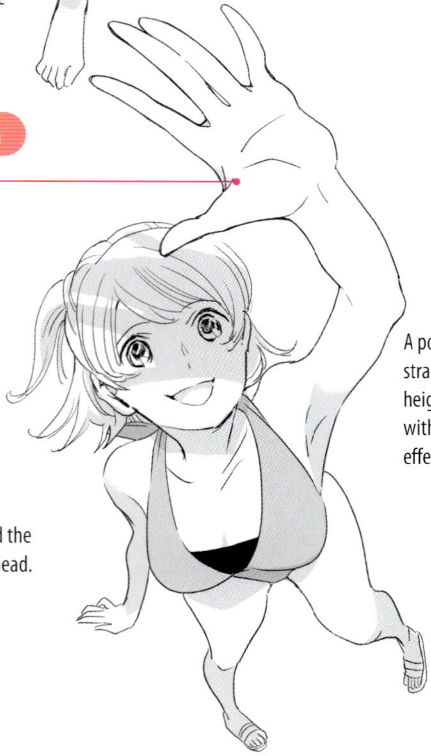

The fingers are spread, and the arm is extended over the head.

PALM EXTENDED STRAIGHT FORWARD

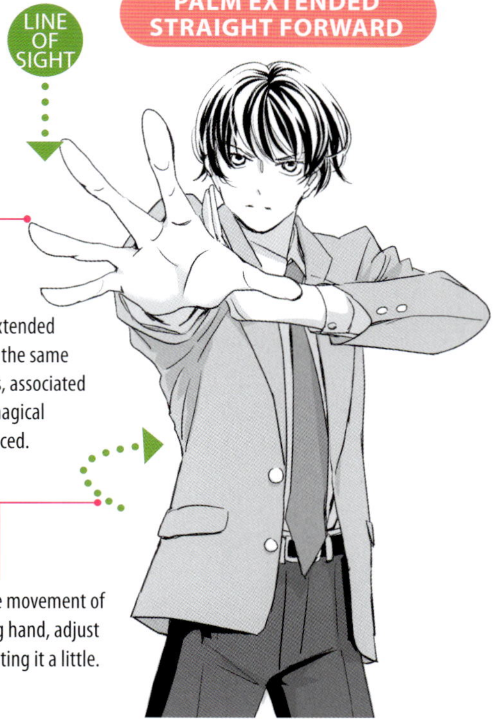

LINE OF SIGHT

A pose with one arm extended straight out in front, at the same height as the shoulders, associated with scenes in which magical effects are being produced.

To support the movement of the protruding hand, adjust the body, twisting it a little.

HAND HELD TO THE FRONT

The body twists naturally and the other hand is extended backward to create a sense of movement.

HAND HELD TO THE SIDE

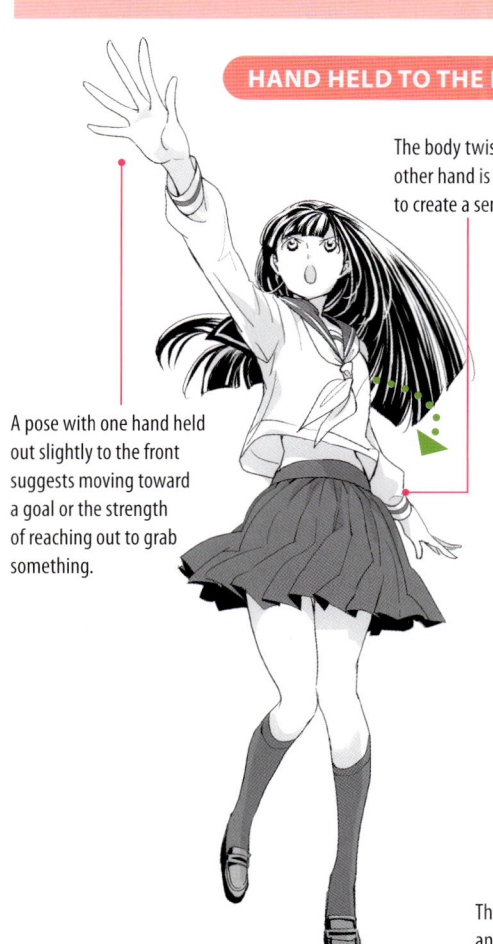

A pose with one hand held out slightly to the front suggests moving toward a goal or the strength of reaching out to grab something.

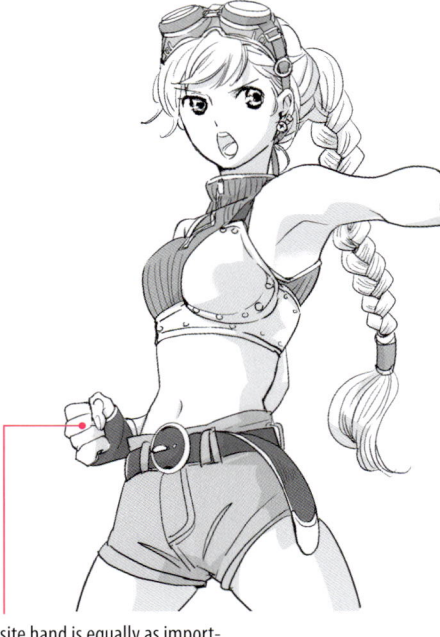

By holding one hand out to the side and spreading the fingers wide, you create a more dynamic composition.

The opposite hand is equally as important here. By clenching the fist, you can suggest or conjure a strong will.

REACHING OVER THE HEAD

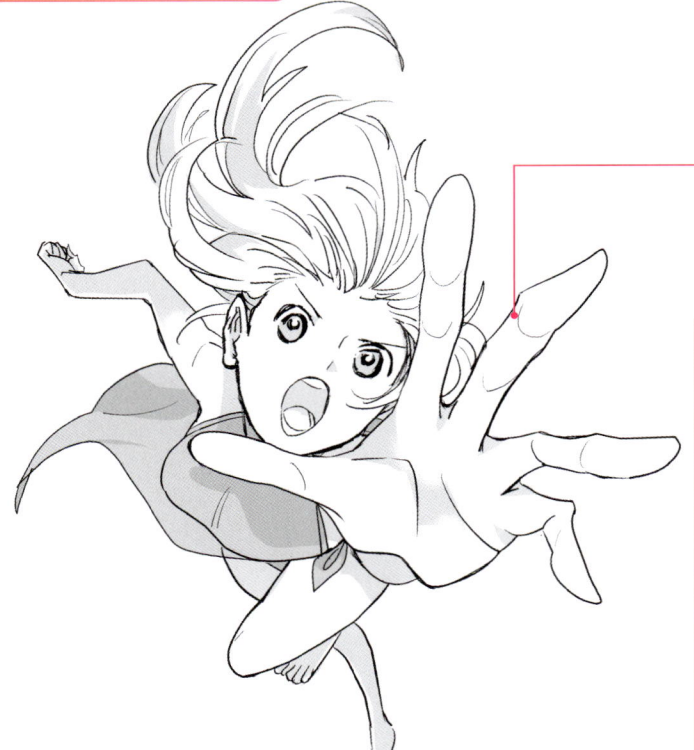

A pose where one hand with its fingertips spread wide is aligned with the face. Combined with the urgent expression, it creates a realistic feeling of someone desperately trying to grasp something.

CROPPING — Staging the Gesture

It's best not to crop the hand that's being so demonstratively asserted, as it naturally becomes the focal point of the pose.

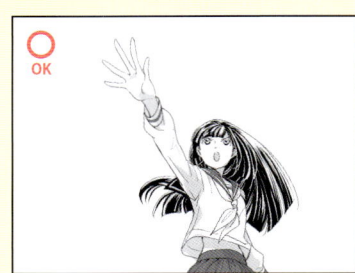

OK

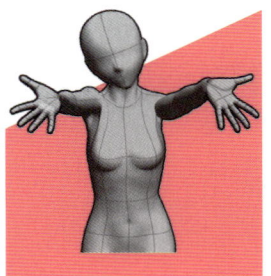

A WELCOMING POSE
Both Hands Extended

Spreading both hands forward can suggest welcoming, joy or openness. Poses using both hands can create dynamic, memorable illustrations and characters. In some cases, the character is directly reaching out, inviting the viewer into the illustration.

SPREADING BOTH HANDS

A pose with hands widely spread to both sides, expressing joy and a sense of liberation.

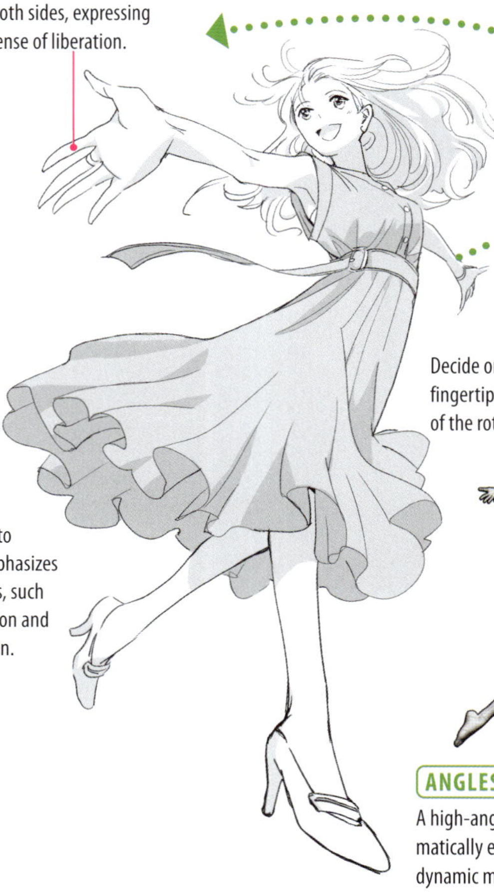

Draw the palms large as they extend straight into the foreground.

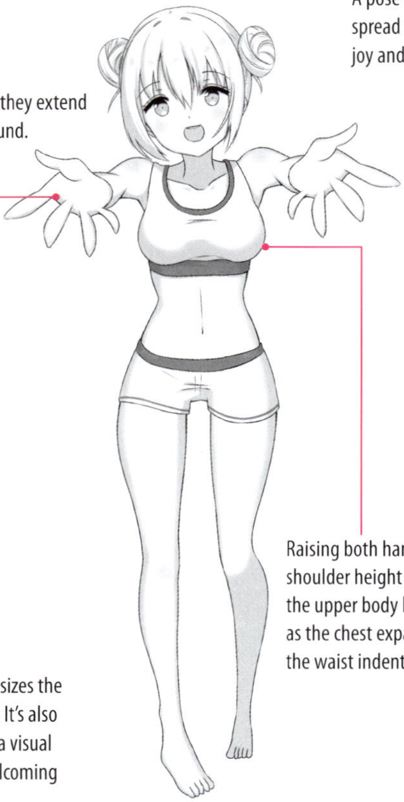

Raising both hands to shoulder height emphasizes the upper body lines, such as the chest expansion and the waist indentation.

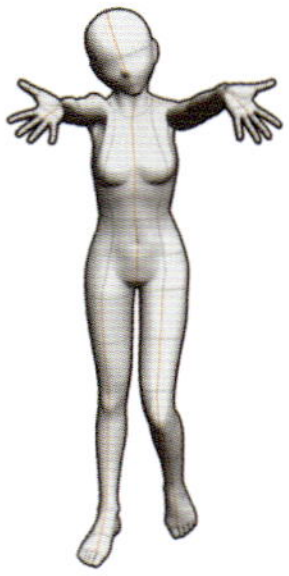

ANGLES
A low-angle shot emphasizes the character's youthfulness. It's also effective in establishing a visual relationship with the welcoming subject.

SPREADING HANDS TO BOTH SIDES

Decide on the angle of the fingertips and the direction of the rotating face.

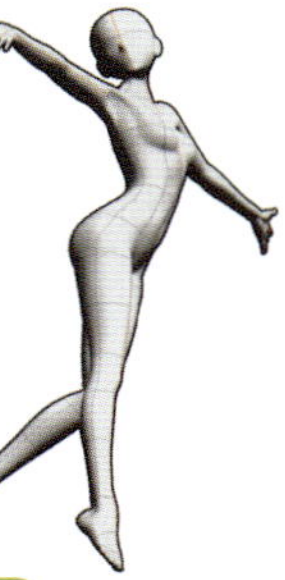

ANGLES
A high-angle shot can dramatically enhance a pose's dynamic movements.

SHOWING BOTH PALMS

Open the hands near the face to suggest flowers blooming.

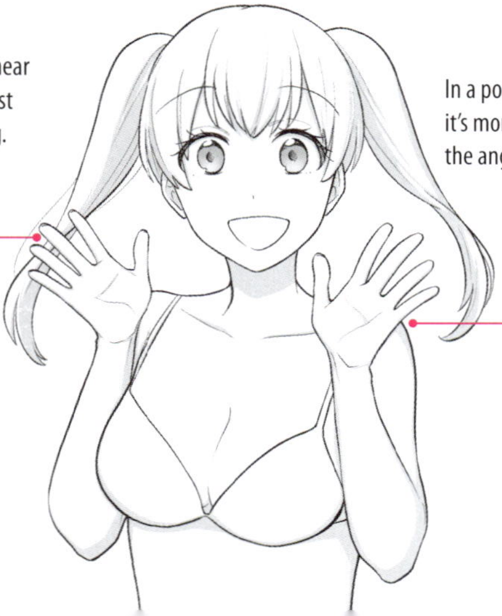

In a pose showing both palms, it's more natural not to align the angles of both hands.

CROPPING Cut to Preserve Movement

When cropping drastically and eliminating parts of the body, be cautious as it can limit the sense of movement.

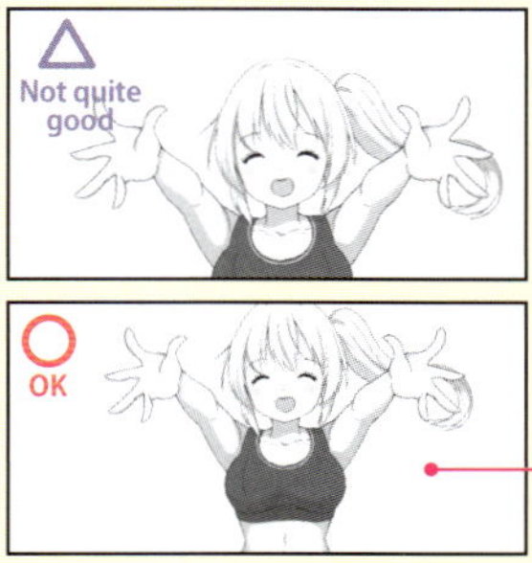

△ Not quite good

Including more of the upper body enhances the sense of dynamism.

○ OK

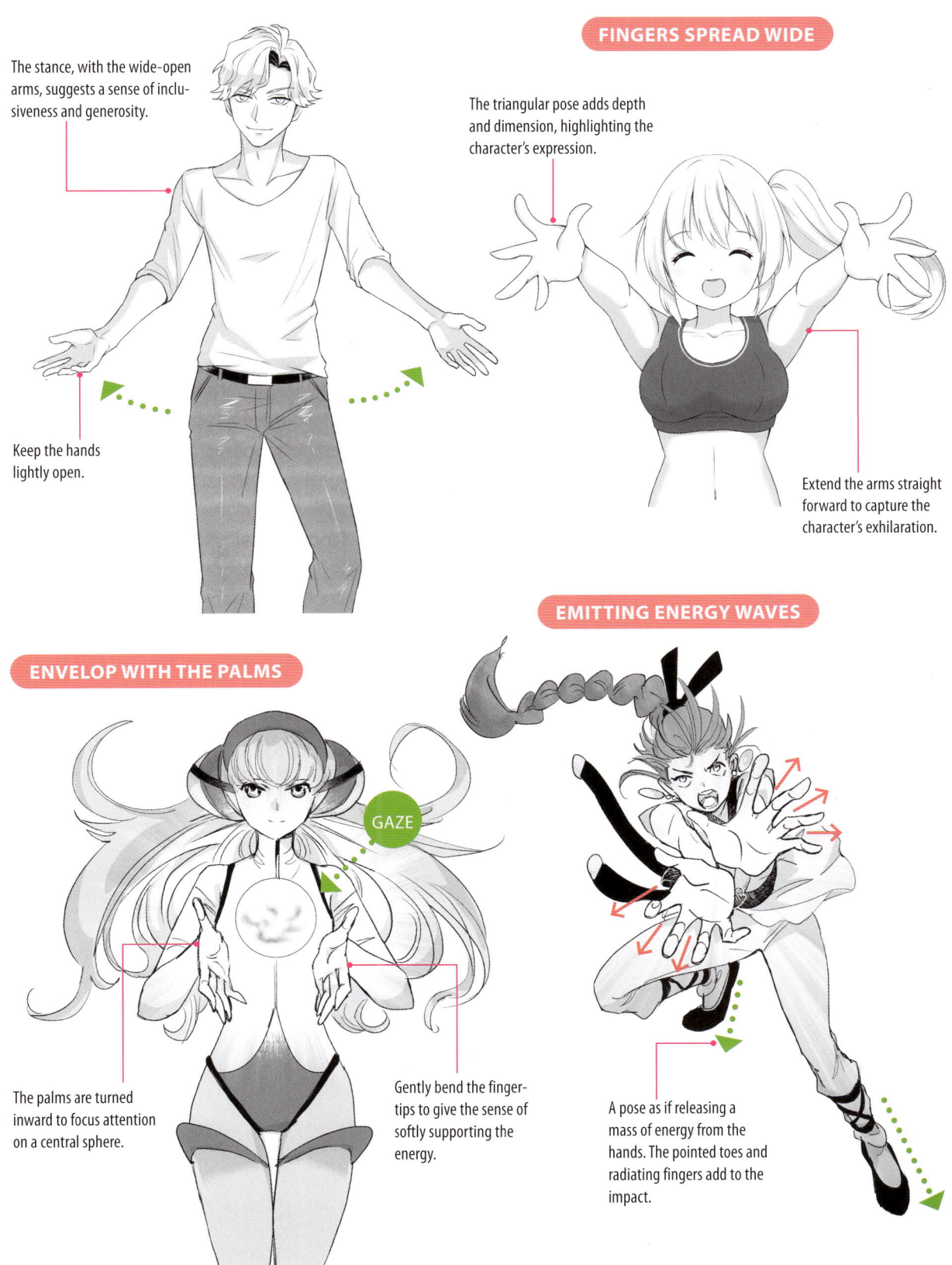

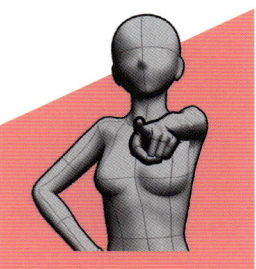

VERSATILE GESTURES
Pointing

This pose grabs attention or directly engages the viewer. It projects decisiveness and confidence and can enhance a character's appeal by highlighting his or her features.

POINTING FORWARD

The hand on the hip suggests the character's haughty attitude.

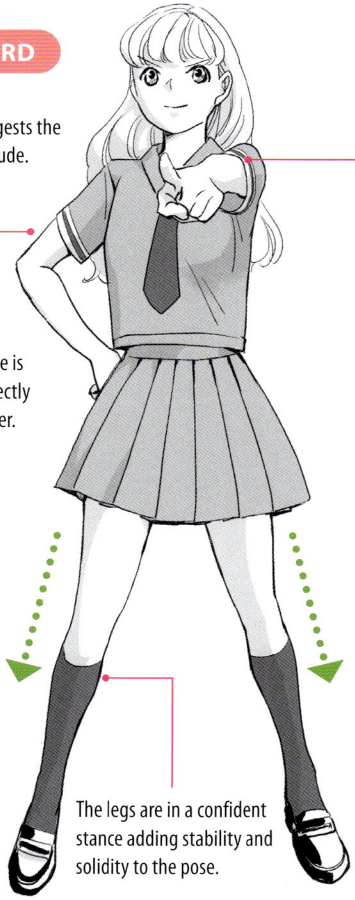

The index finger pointing directly forward is suitable for strong-willed characters.

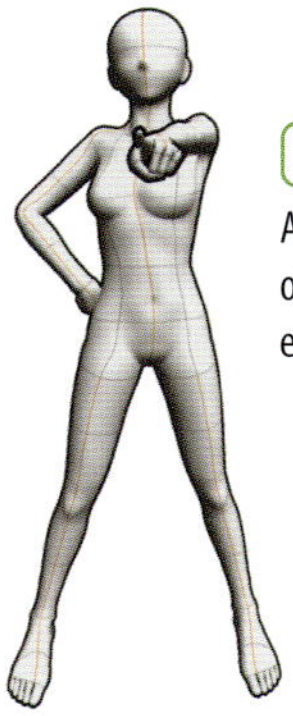

ANGLES
A front-facing angle is often effective, directly engaging the viewer.

The legs are in a confident stance adding stability and solidity to the pose.

POINTING UP

In a pose where the fingertips are directed upward, slightly bending them adds movement.

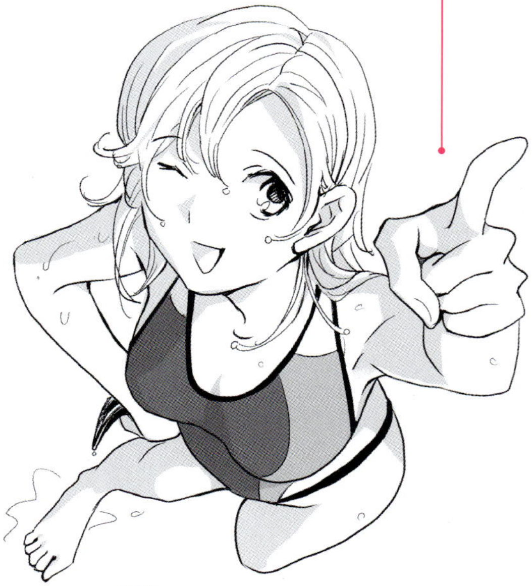

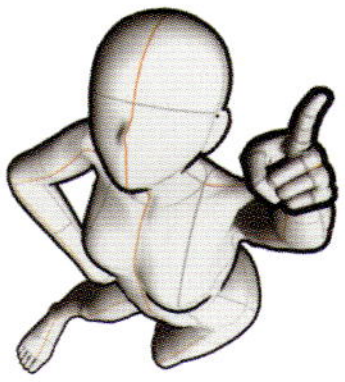

POINTING TO SIDE

One arm is naturally lowered to capture a relaxed demeanor.

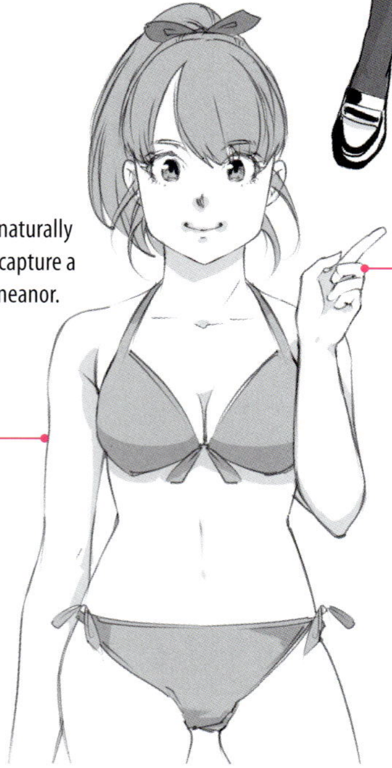

With a pose used to draw attention to the fingertips, turning the fingers outward embellishes the character's charm.

ANGLES
An overhead angle gives an even more dramatic immediacy to the pose.

ARM STRETCHED STRAIGHT

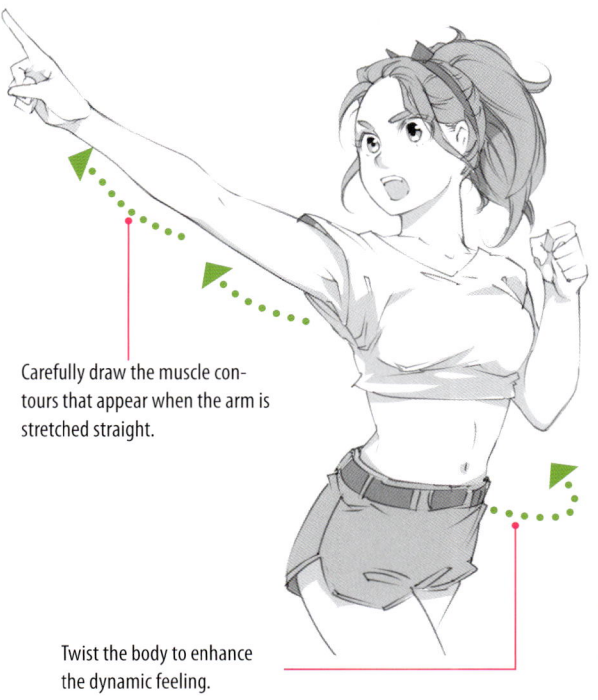

Carefully draw the muscle contours that appear when the arm is stretched straight.

Twist the body to enhance the dynamic feeling.

FINGERTIP TOUCHING THE CHEEK

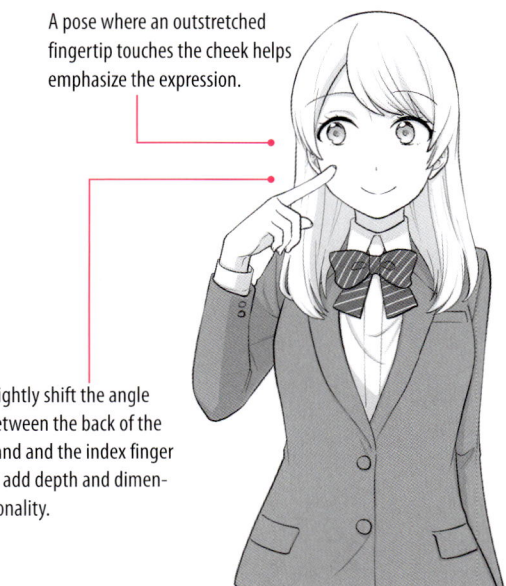

A pose where an outstretched fingertip touches the cheek helps emphasize the expression.

Slightly shift the angle between the back of the hand and the index finger to add depth and dimensionality.

POINTING FORWARD

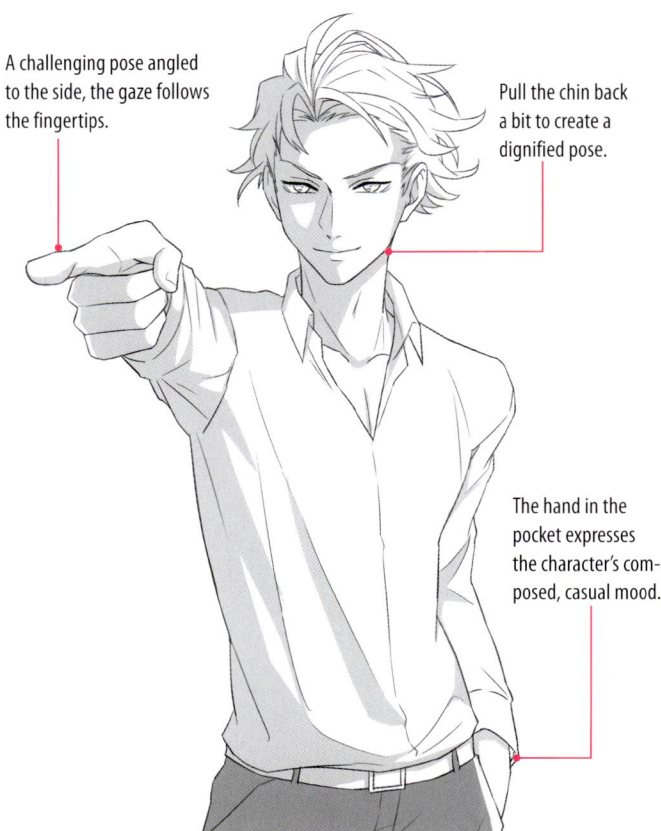

A challenging pose angled to the side, the gaze follows the fingertips.

Pull the chin back a bit to create a dignified pose.

The hand in the pocket expresses the character's composed, casual mood.

CROPPING — Prominently Placed Fingertips

When cropping for a waist shot or upper-body shot, placing the finger around the center of the frame maintains the assertive feel of the pose.

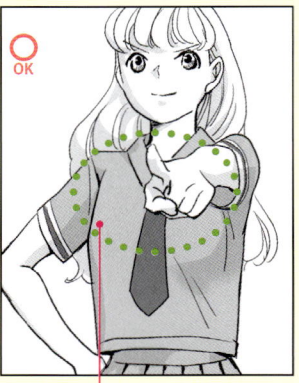

OK

The pointing gesture is placed in a prominent area, slightly above the center of the screen.

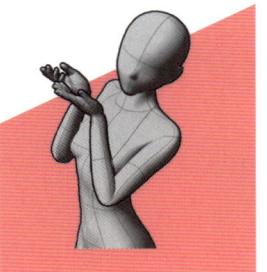

FLIRTY POSES
Blowing a Kiss

This is a pose that immediately conveys a character's charm and appeal. It can be combined with expressions, like a wink, that convey affection. The viewer can be directly engaged or a character that's outside the frame of the illustration.

GESTURE OF BLOWING ON THE PALM

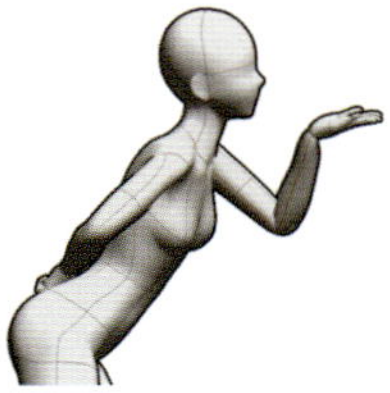

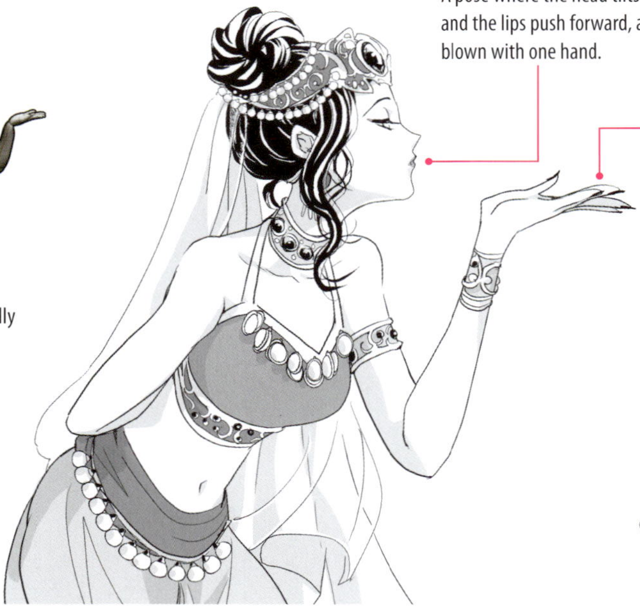

A pose where the head tilts back and the lips push forward, a kiss is blown with one hand.

The hand should be drawn as if it's directing the blown kiss.

ANGLES
A side angle beautifully showcases the facial expression and the pose of the hand.

TWO-HANDS POSE

ONE-HAND POSE

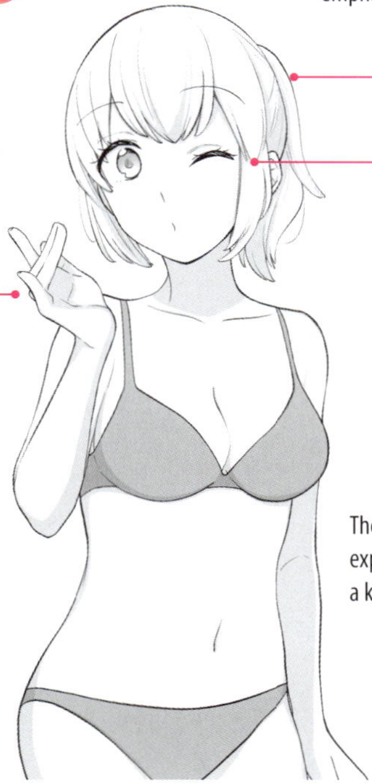

Tilt the head slightly to emphasize the expression.

Bring one hand close to the mouth, as if throwing a kiss with the middle and ring fingers.

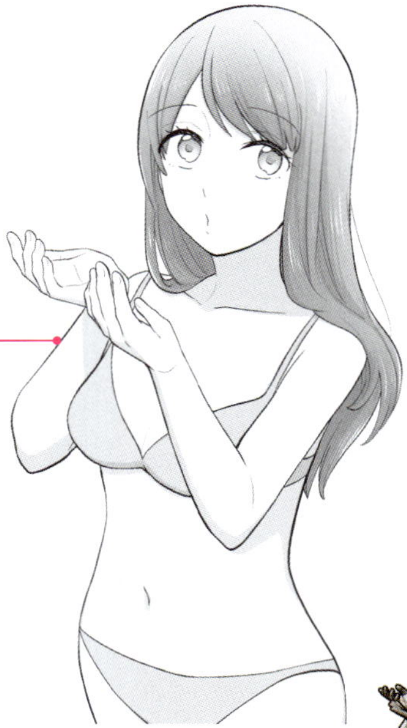

Gently extend both hands, as if enveloping the blown kiss with the palms. Compared to one hand, this suggests a greater degree of affection.

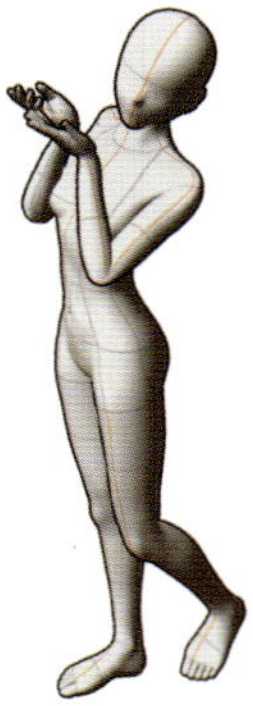

The typical facial expression for blowing a kiss includes a wink.

ANGLES
A slightly overhead angle allows for a compelling upward-looking expression.

HAND BY THE MOUTH

The two splayed fingers and winking eye add distinctive details, drawing the viewer's attention and curiosity.

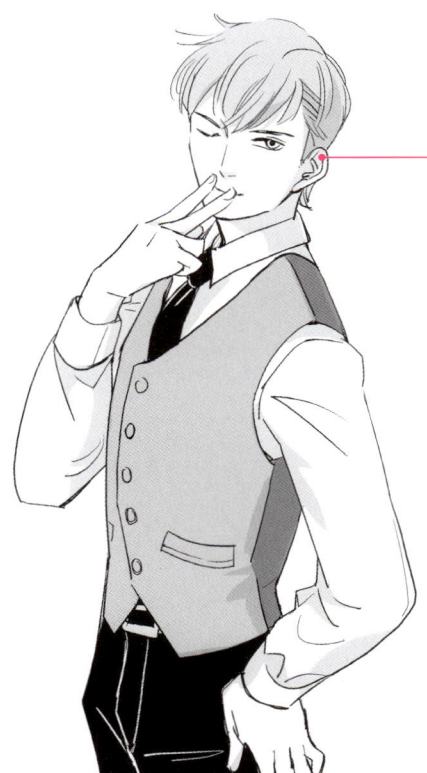

BLOOMING LIKE A FLOWER

By widely spreading both hands at the mouth, the expression is given a natural framing device.

Curving the hands creates a gentle sense of movement.

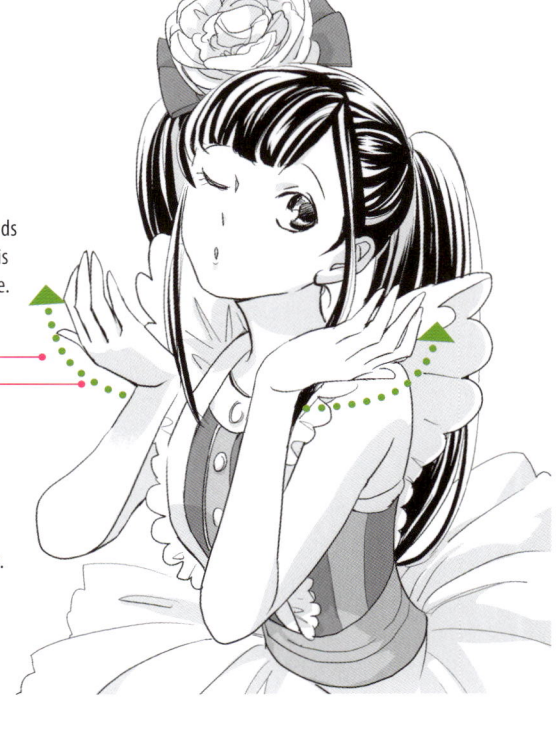

ADDING MOVEMENT TO THE BODY

This soft and friendly pose integrates the peace sign.

By bending the hips, the pose suggests motion and intimacy at the same time.

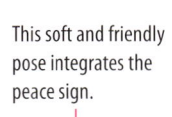

CROPPING — **Cropping Arms Looks Unnatural**

A blown kiss is successful as long as the mouth and hands are visible. However, depending on the pose, cropping the arms can result in an unnatural, cramped composition.

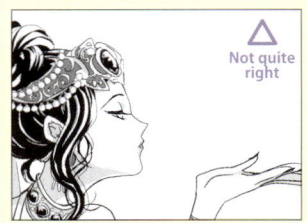

⚠ Not quite right

Due to cropping the arms, in the revised illustration, it became unclear as to whom the hand belongs to.

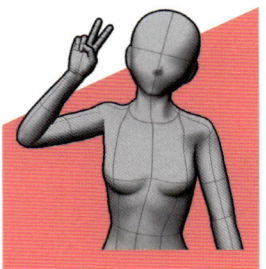

A UNIVERSAL SYMBOL
Peace Sign

While smiling, making a V-shape with fingers is a standard pose for photo shoots. Besides peace signs made near the face or with an outstretched arm, there are variations that add complexity and a heightened sense of movement to the pose.

PEACE SIGN AT EYE LEVEL

This is a traditional pose from a frontal angle, making the peace sign near the face.

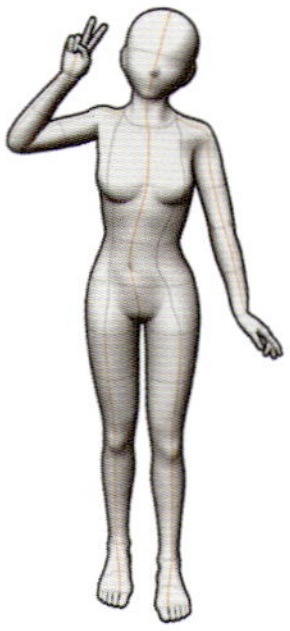

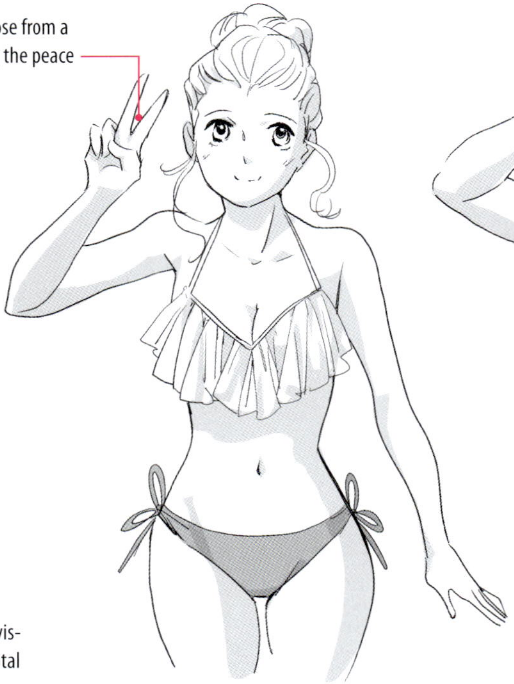

ANGLES

An angle where the peace sign is easily visible is best, so a frontal or slightly overhead angle is effective.

SIDEWAYS PEACE

Place the tilted peace sign beside the eye. It's also an effective pose when you want to highlight the eyes.

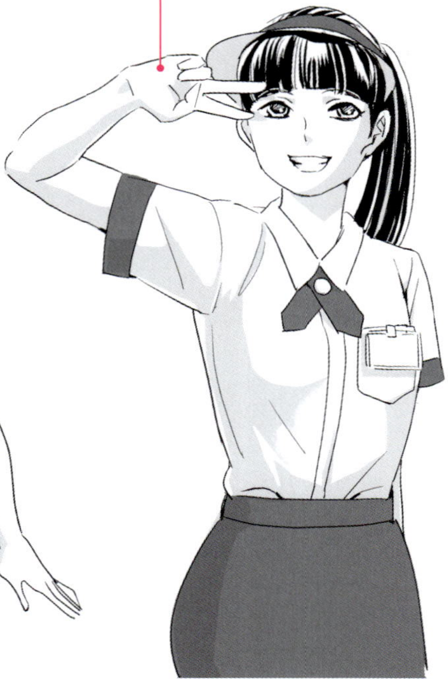

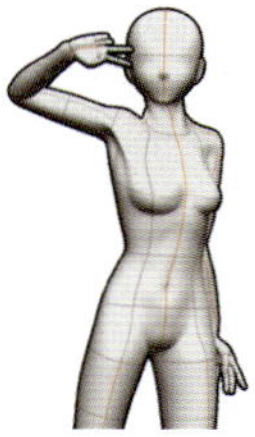

ANGLES

It's a slightly diagonal angle, but placing the face and hands toward the front makes the expression and gesture more prominent.

PUSHED FORWARD

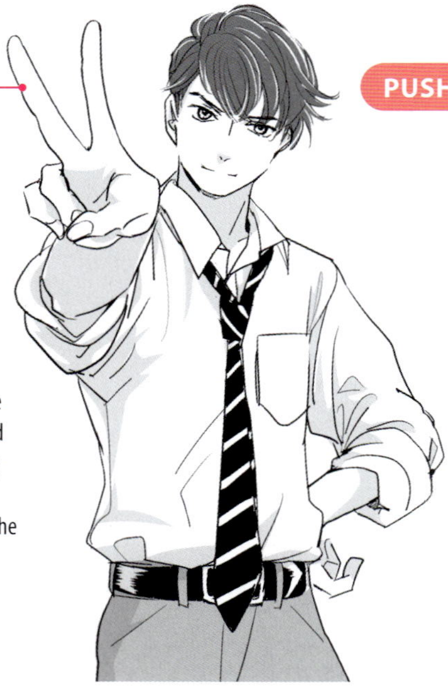

A bold composition where the peace sign is extended in front of the body. Using perspective to make the hand appear larger than the face adds impact.

CROPPING When Is It O.K. to Crop the Arms?

When cropping a peace sign pose, it's better not to remove the arms as they add movement; but a close-up shot with the arms completely cropped can be effective if the hands are close enough to the face.

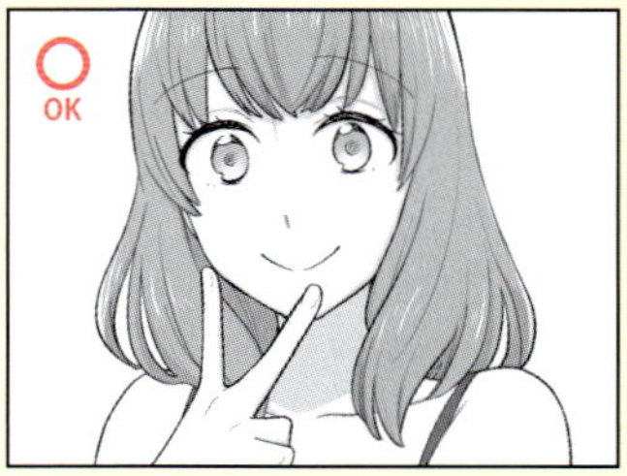

OK

SENDING A SILLY SIGN

Instead of from the front, a peace sign turned around adds a playful touch when combined with the right facial expression.

REVERSE PEACE

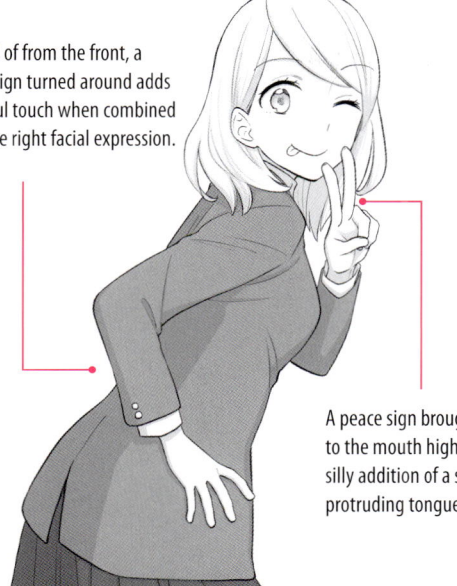
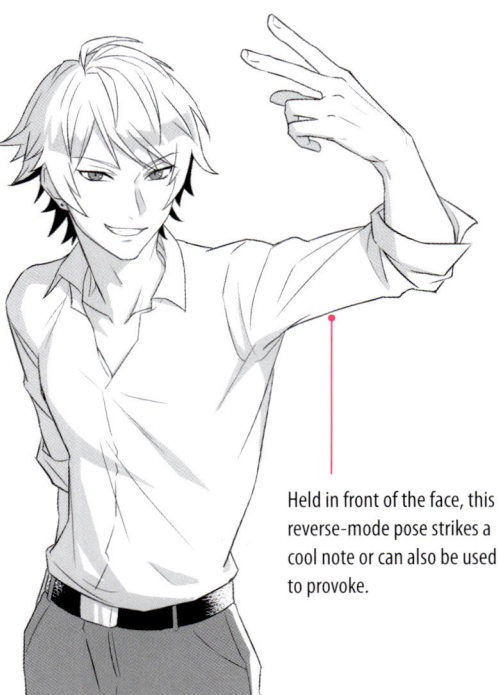

A peace sign brought close to the mouth highlights the silly addition of a slightly protruding tongue tip.

Held in front of the face, this reverse-mode pose strikes a cool note or can also be used to provoke.

BRINGING IT TO THE MOUTH

DISPLAYING EASE

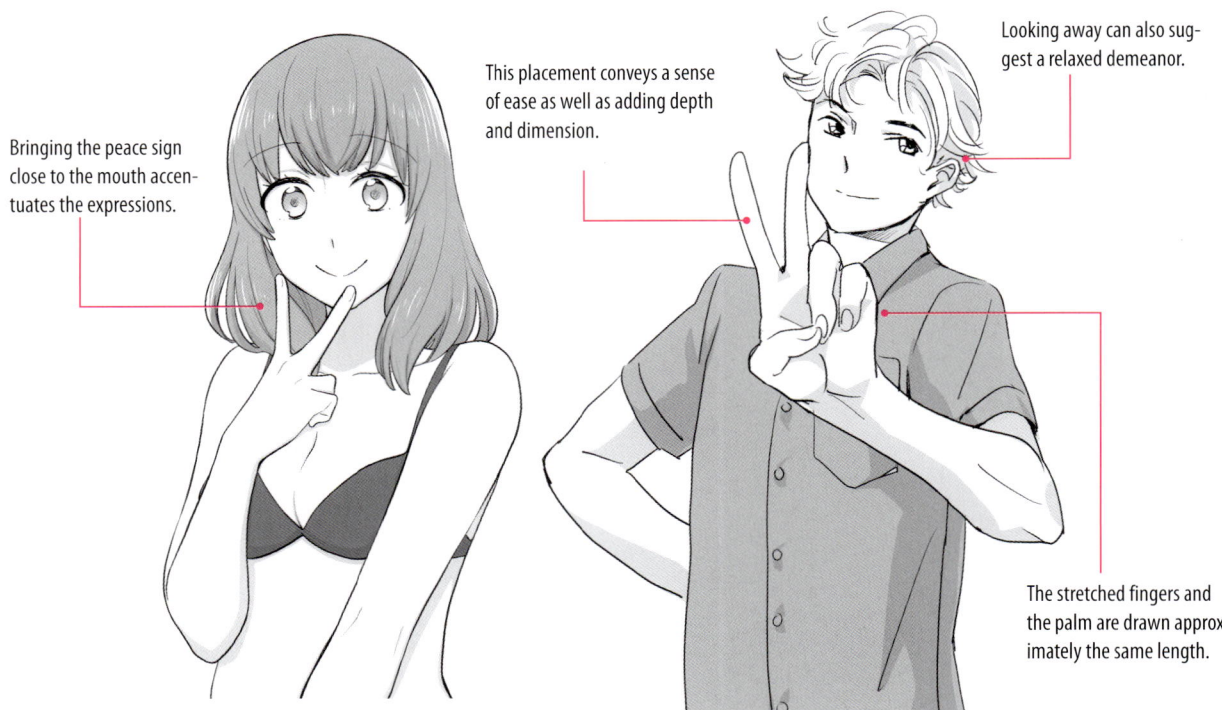

Bringing the peace sign close to the mouth accentuates the expressions.

This placement conveys a sense of ease as well as adding depth and dimension.

Looking away can also suggest a relaxed demeanor.

The stretched fingers and the palm are drawn approximately the same length.

ENERGETIC AND ELEGANT POSES
Warm Greetings

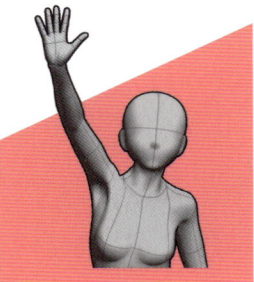

When using hands and arms to capture a greeting, the nature of the expression changes with the extent of the movements. Pay attention to the direction of the character's gaze in relation to the position of the person being greeted.

ENERGETIC GREETING

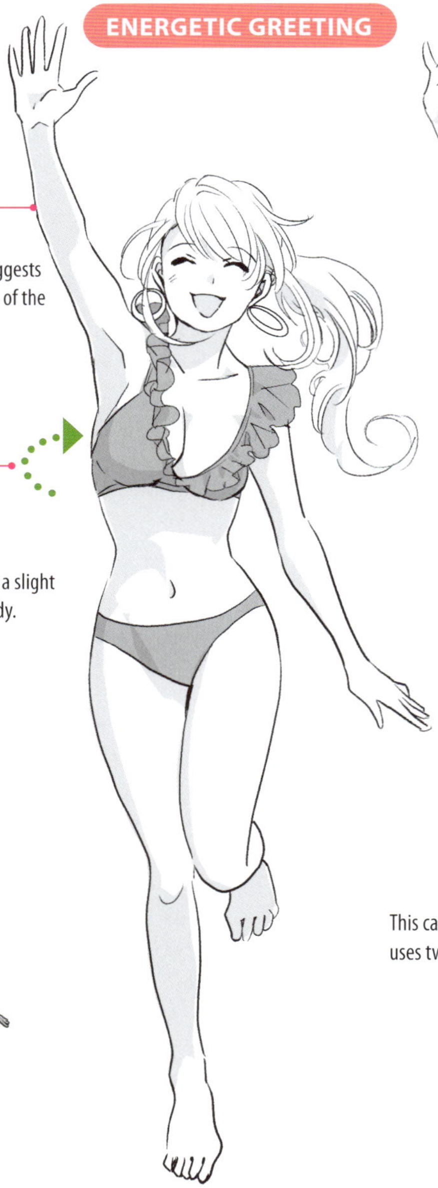

Raising the hand suggests the energetic nature of the character.

Raising one arm adds a slight twist to the upper body.

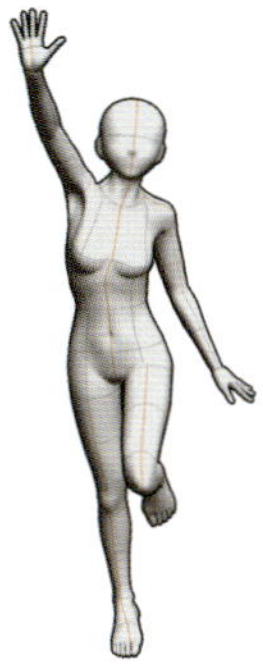

ANGLES
A frontal angle directly engages the viewer.

GREETING FROM A DISTANCE

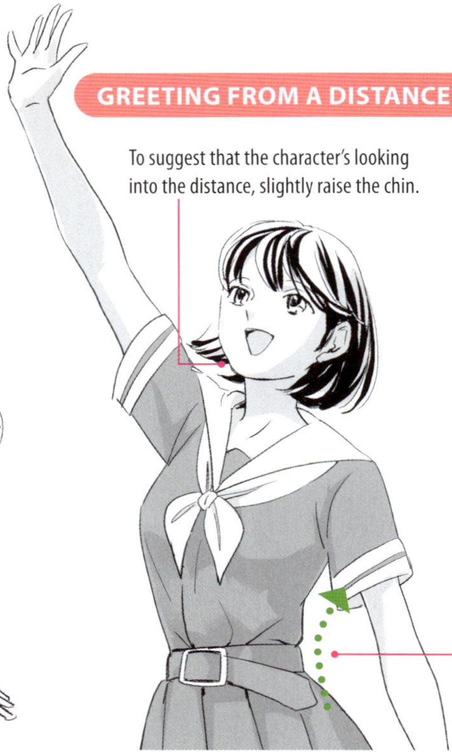

To suggest that the character's looking into the distance, slightly raise the chin.

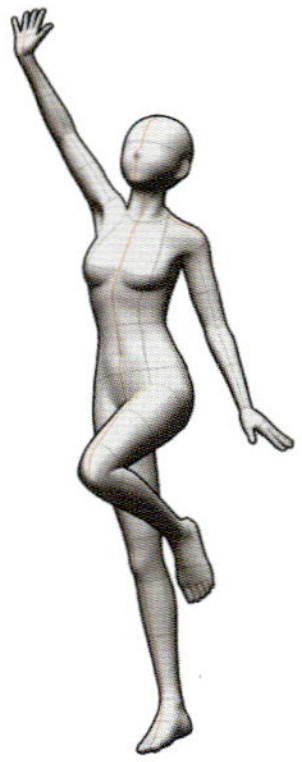

ANGLES
A diagonal angle clearly highlights the posture, as does the movement of the extended hand.

In a pose greeting someone far away, the back is slightly arched.

CASUAL GREETING

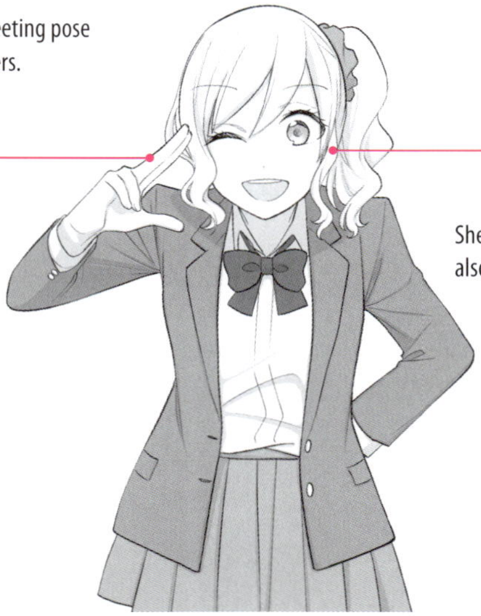

This casual greeting pose uses two fingers.

She leans forward, the face also pushed forward.

SMALL GREETING

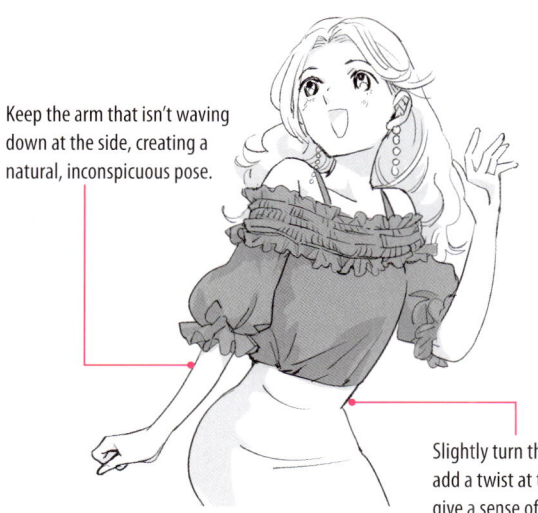

Keep the arm that isn't waving down at the side, creating a natural, inconspicuous pose.

Slightly turn the body and add a twist at the waist to give a sense of movement.

HAND NEAR FACE

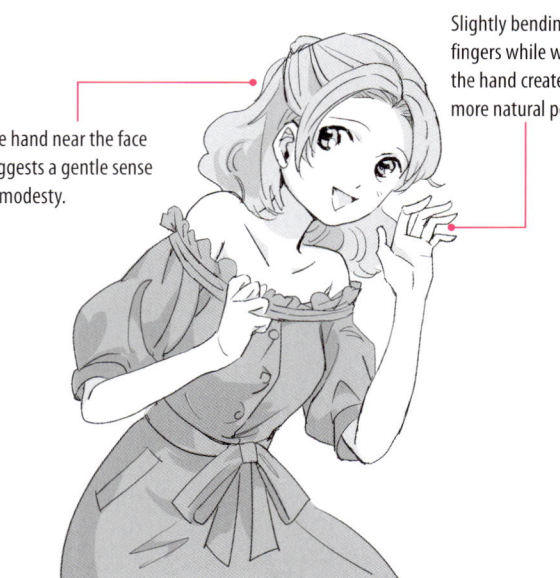

Slightly bending the fingers while waving the hand creates a more natural pose.

The hand near the face suggests a gentle sense of modesty.

HANDS CLASPED IN FRONT

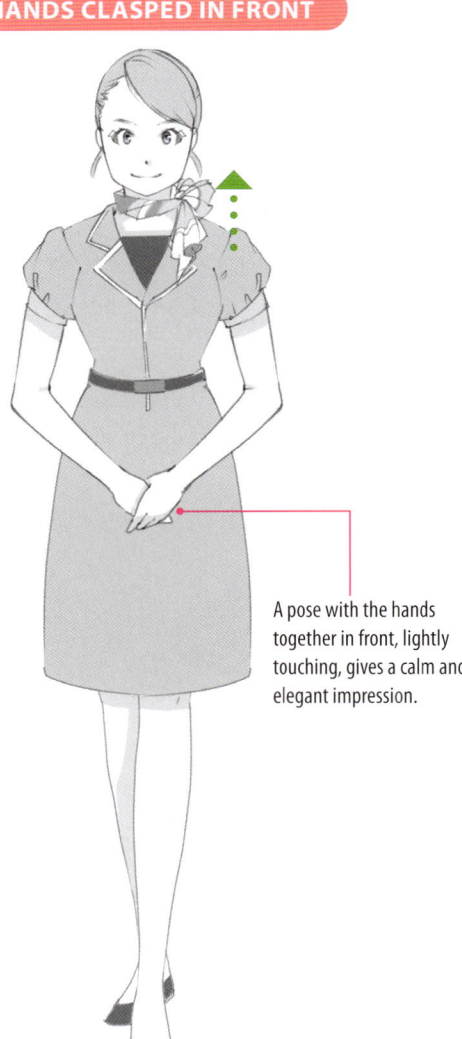

A pose with the hands together in front, lightly touching, gives a calm and elegant impression.

HOLDING THE SKIRT

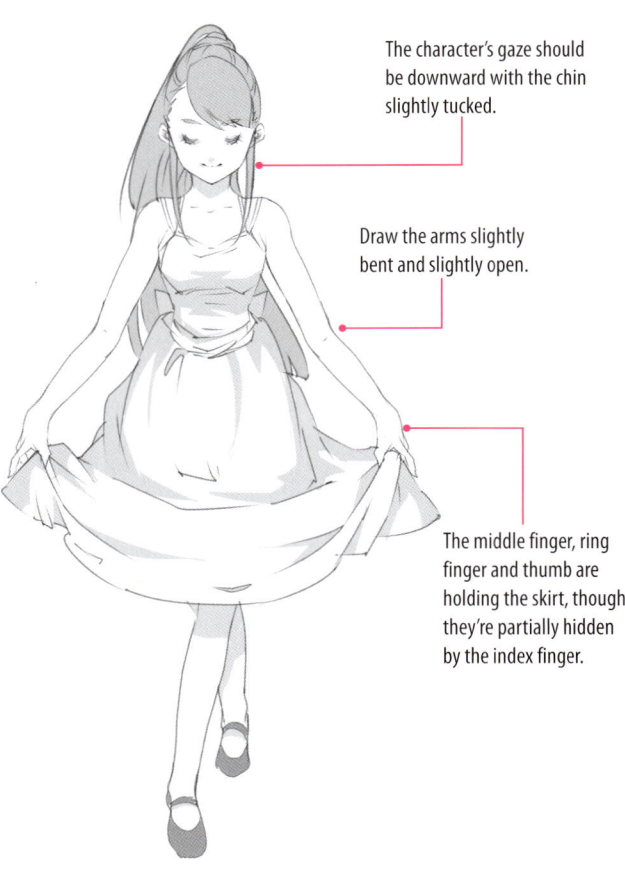

The character's gaze should be downward with the chin slightly tucked.

Draw the arms slightly bent and slightly open.

The middle finger, ring finger and thumb are holding the skirt, though they're partially hidden by the index finger.

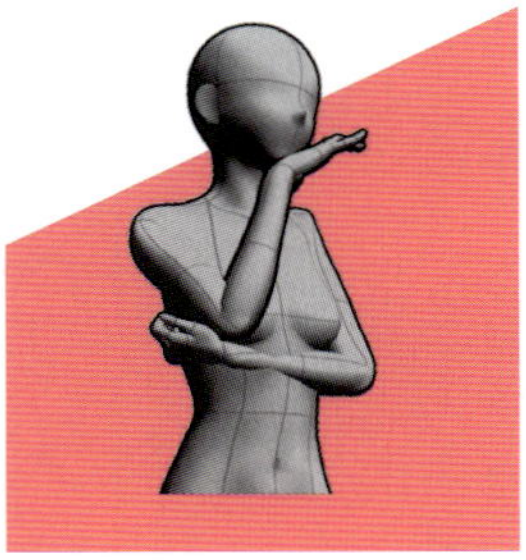

A HAND HELD TO THE MOUTH
Laughing

For a spontaneous burst of laughter, some characters naturally bring their hands to their mouths and faces. Choose a pose that fits the character's personality, the hand gesture drawing the viewer's gaze to the dynamic expression.

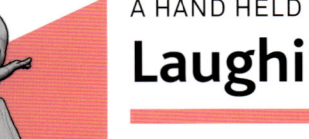

LOUD LAUGH

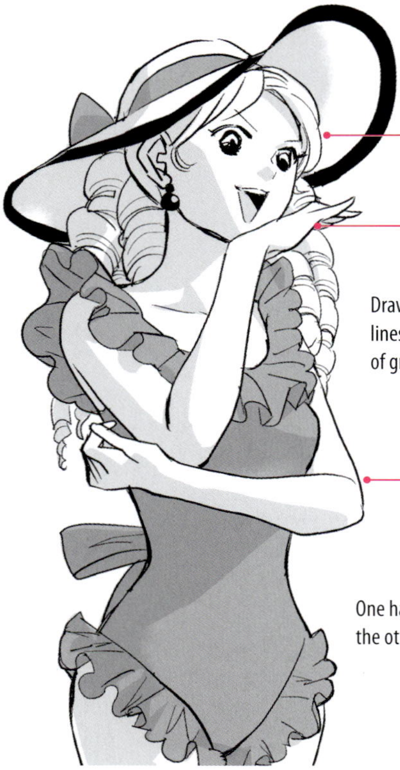

The key is to tilt the face as if the character is looking downward.

Draw the hand with smooth lines to give the impression of graceful movement.

One hand should support the other arm.

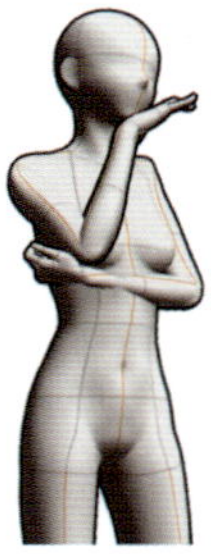

ANGLES
A low-angle shot is suitable for portraying an imposing character.

ELEGANT LAUGH

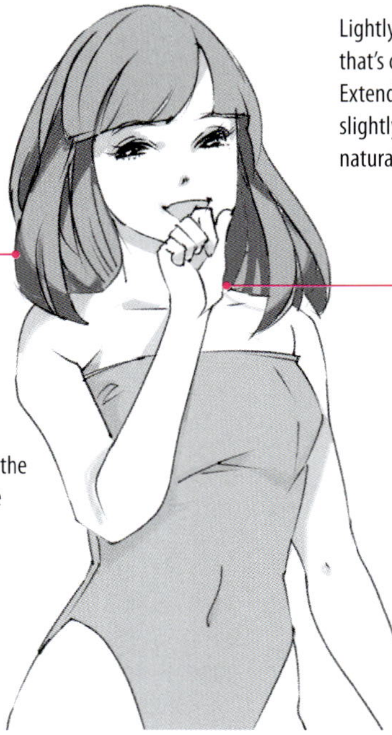

Lightly clench the hand that's covering the mouth. Extending the index finger slightly can help achieve a natural shape.

Create movement in the hair to show that the body is in motion.

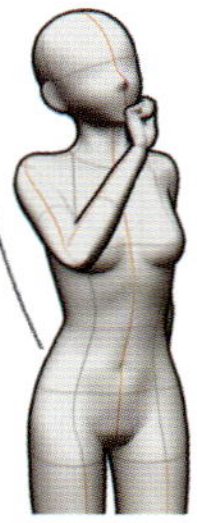

ANGLES
A diagonal angle can naturally showcase subtle gestures.

GIGGLING

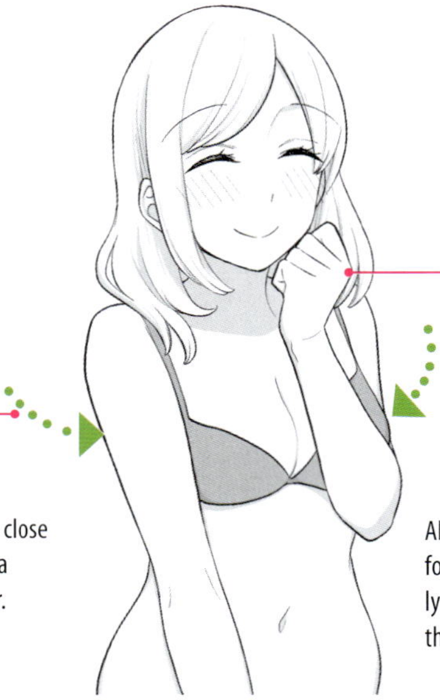

A pose with arms close to the body suits a demure character.

Although covering the mouth is standard for an elegant laugh, if you want to clearly show the mouth, create a pose where the hand is held slightly to the side.

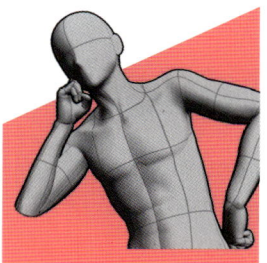

RELAXED POSES
Resting on the Chin

Support the weight of the head with the hand, creating a relaxed posture. This pose allows you to depict a character in a relaxed and unstrained manner. Placing a hand near the face can also result in a charmingly appealing pose.

RESTING BOTH CHEEKS IN HANDS

Encircle the face with both hands.

The shoulders will rise slightly.

Resting both cheeks in the hands makes the face appear smaller.

ANGLES
For illustrations where the character is gazing while resting their cheek in hand, use a frontal angle to emphasize facial expressions.

RESTING ONE CHEEK IN HAND

Lightly rest the face on one hand.

Place the other arm on the desk for a relaxed posture.

RESTING CHEEK IN CLENCHED HAND

Lightly clench the hand and place it against the cheek to support the head.

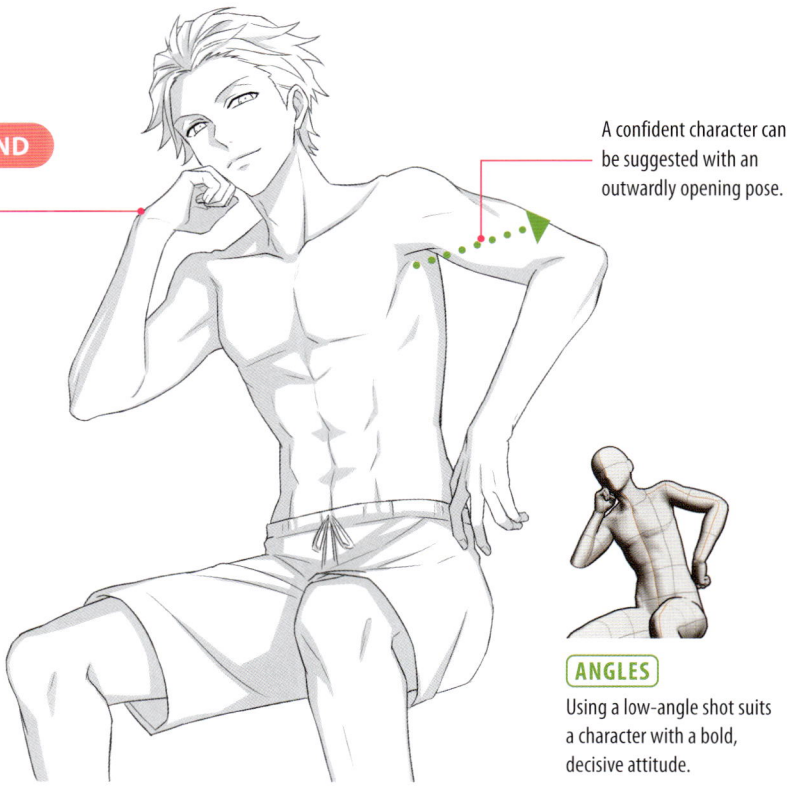

A confident character can be suggested with an outwardly opening pose.

CROPPING **Effective Even in Closeup**

Resting the cheek on an upturned palm can fully convey the atmosphere even in a closeup composition.

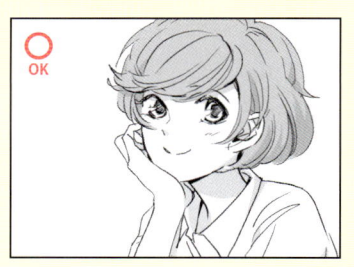
OK

ANGLES
Using a low-angle shot suits a character with a bold, decisive attitude.

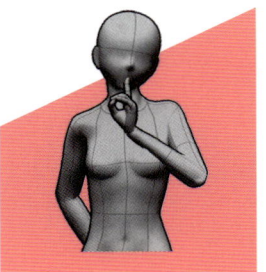

A FLEXIBLE GESTURE
Finger to the Lips

Placing a finger on the lips can evoke a sense of youthfulness and charm. In addition to being an effective gesture for signaling silence, it also matches an introspective or contemplative character mulling life's possibilities.

QUIET DOWN

Drawing the body lines with smooth contours makes the pose more realistic and dynamic.

Positioning the hand so the side of it shows while placing a finger to the lips signals for silence.

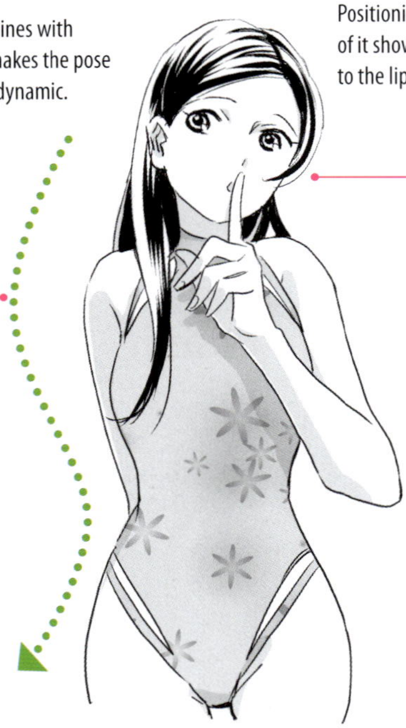

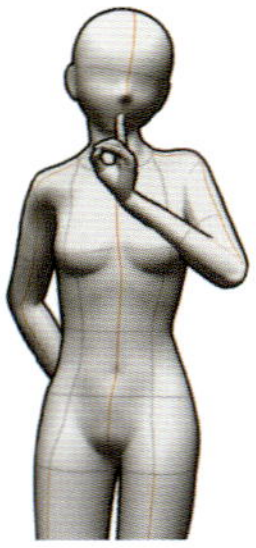

ANGLES
A frontal angle can clearly highlight small movements.

A SENSE OF CAUTION

The same gesture can convey different impressions based on the posture. With a sidelong glance and a hand on the hip, this pose takes on a cautioning tone.

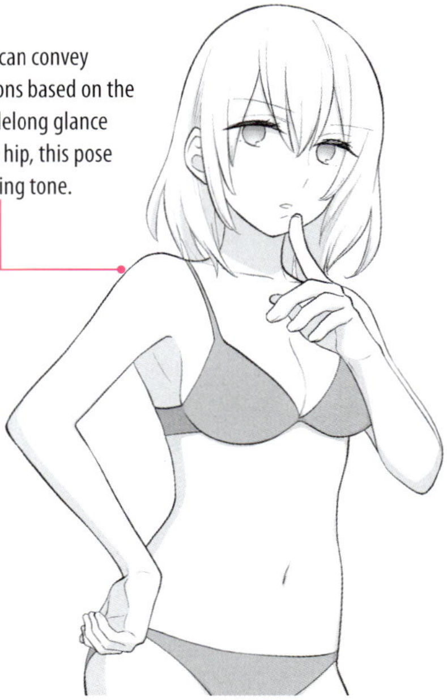

LONGING LOOK

Placing a finger on the lips and adding an upward gaze suit a distracted or contemplative look.

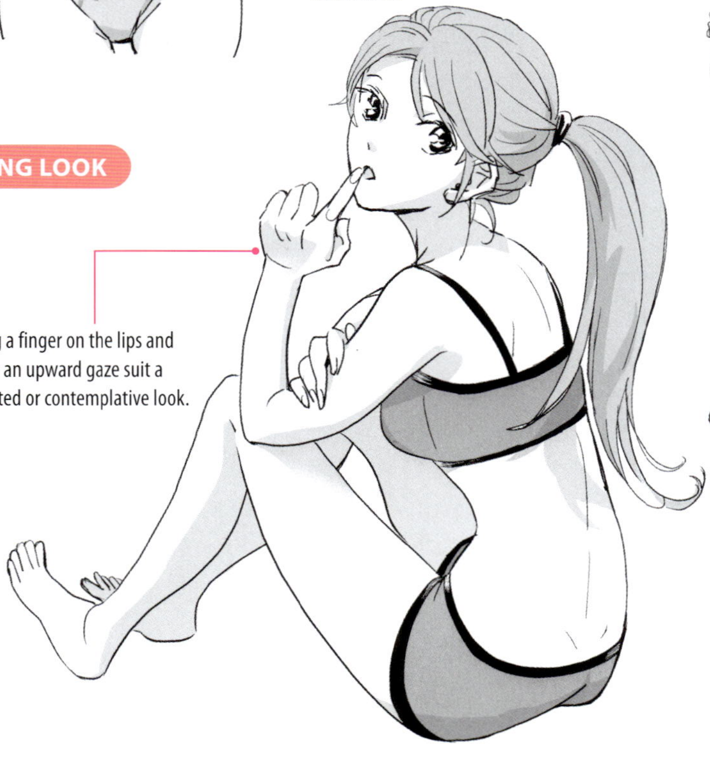

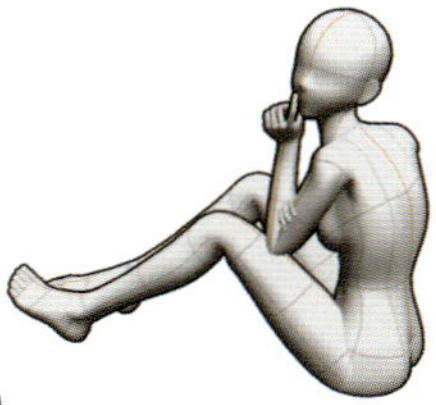

ANGLES
An overhead angle highlights the coiled pose.

SHOWING THE PROFILE

Positioning the body in profile, with a hand covering the mouth, suggests sharing a secret.

The index finger is pointed straight up.

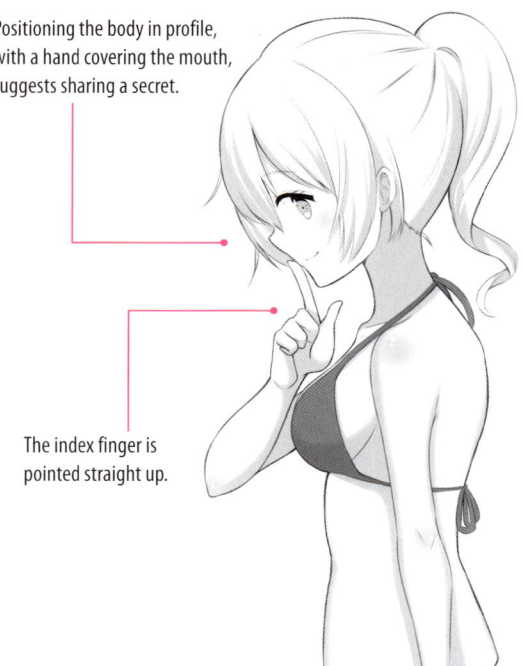

TURNING BACK WHILE SILENCING

This pose involves turning back and giving a sideways glance.

Puff out the chest to create a confident impression and convey a sense of composure.

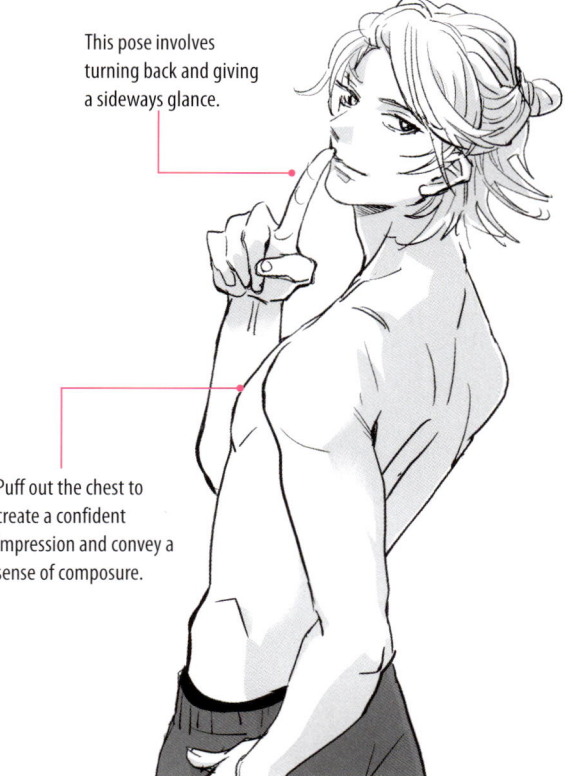

ENVIOUS

This pose can convey a feeling of envy or childish petulance.

The back of the hand should be pointed outward, similar to how a child might suck on a finger.

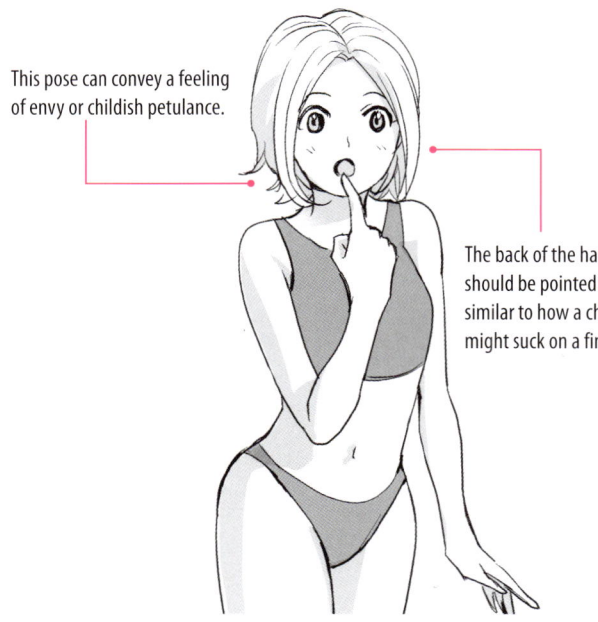

SURPRISED

This is a pose of surprise, instinctively covering the mouth with a hand.

Open the eyes wide to underscore the sense of shock.

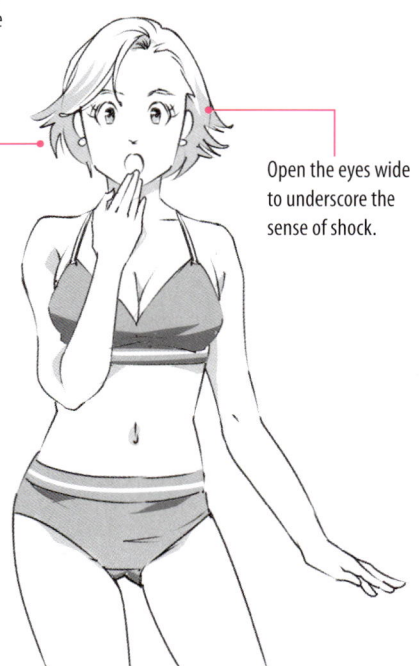

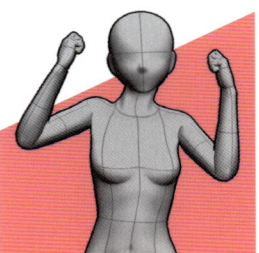

EXPRESSING MOTIVATION AND JOY

Fist Pumps

This pose is used to express the joy of victory or the satisfaction of wishes being fulfilled. The character's sense of achievement allows you to create bold facial expressions and use definitive arm movements.

RAISING BOTH HANDS

Gently bend the arms without spreading them too wide.

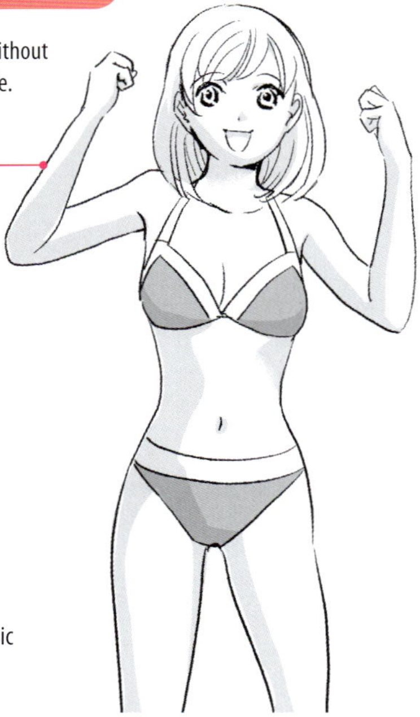

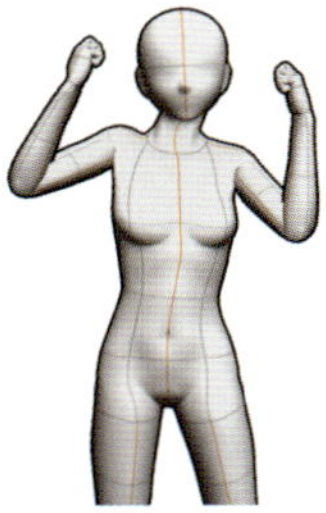

Spread the arms wide and swing them up.

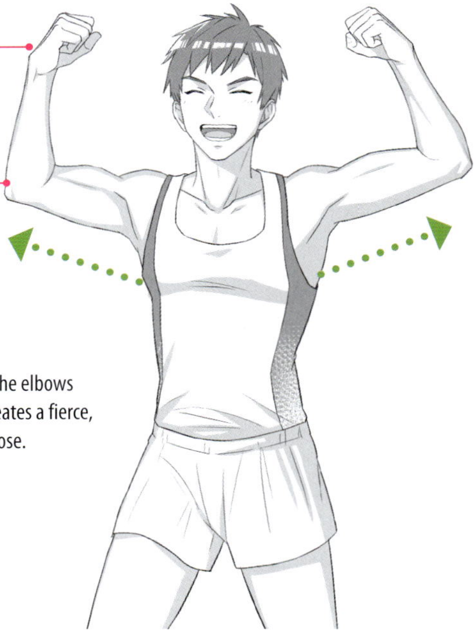

SPREADING THE ARMS WIDE

Extending the elbows outward creates a fierce, definitive pose.

ANGLES
A frontal angle is classic for poses that convey emotional strength.

Raising one arm straight up is the key to this distinctive pose.

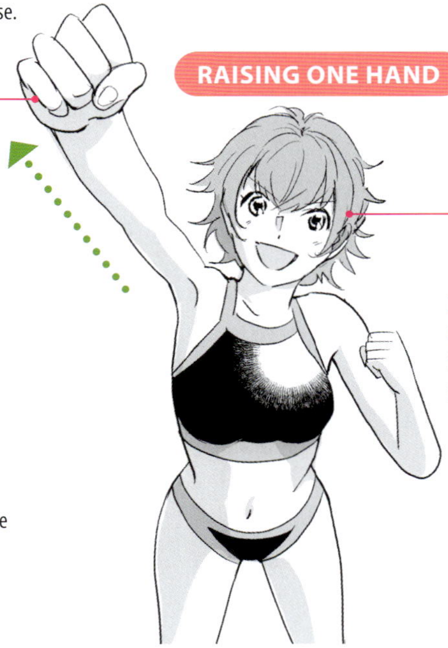

RAISING ONE HAND

Direct eye contact can also effectively convey the character's strong motivation.

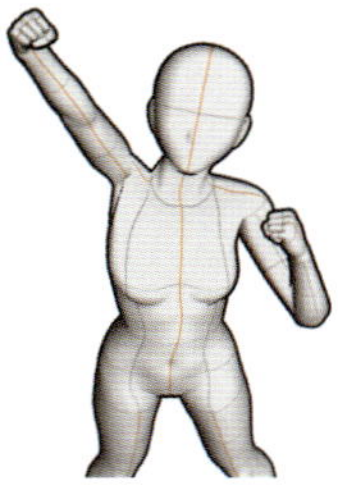

ANGLES
When you want to emphasize the extended hand and make it look larger, an overhead angle often works best.

36

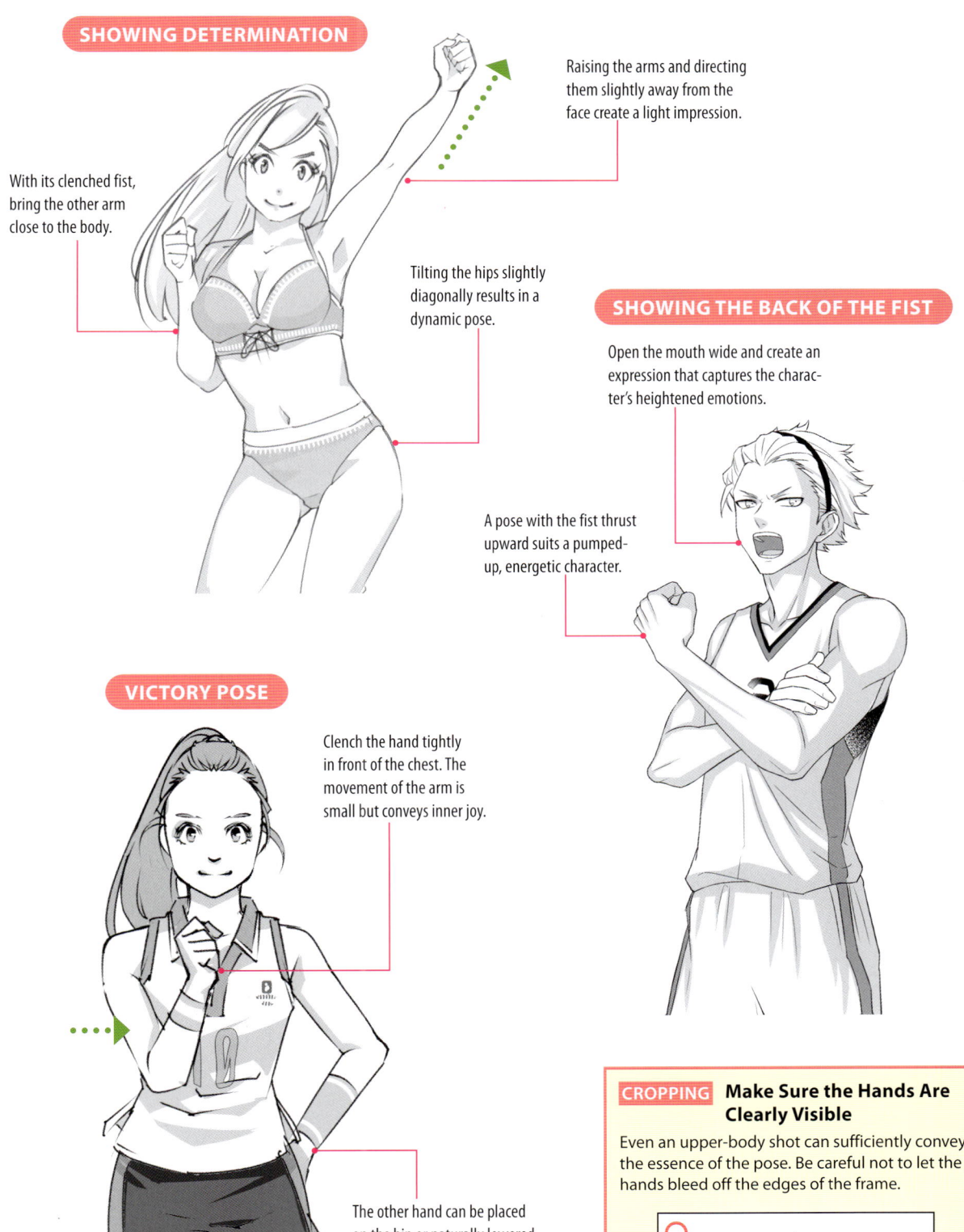

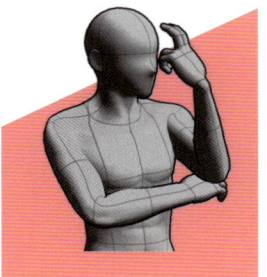

CONTEMPLATIVE GESTURES
Lost in Thought

The placement of the hands and the movement of the fingertips can help indicate the degree and seriousness of thought. Pay attention to the movement of the mouth and the furrowing of the brows to convey the character's inner distraction or turmoil.

INDEX FINGER BETWEEN EYEBROWS

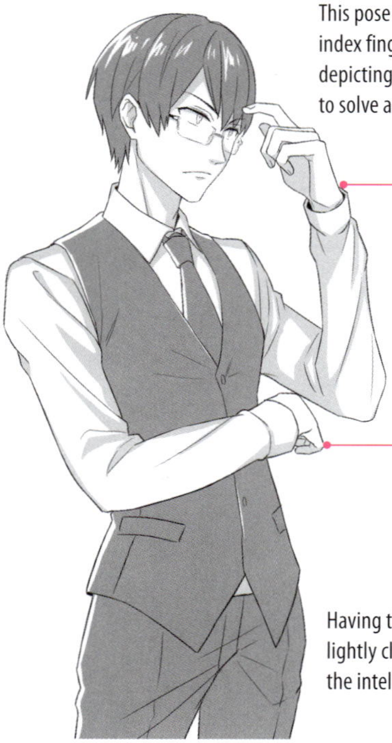

This pose involves placing the index finger between the eyebrows, depicting deep thought or the effort to solve a difficult problem.

Having the other hand lightly clenched add to the intellectual image.

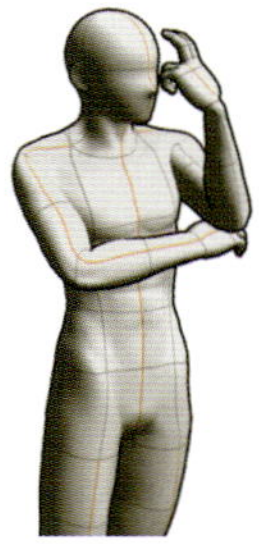

RESTING CHIN ON HAND

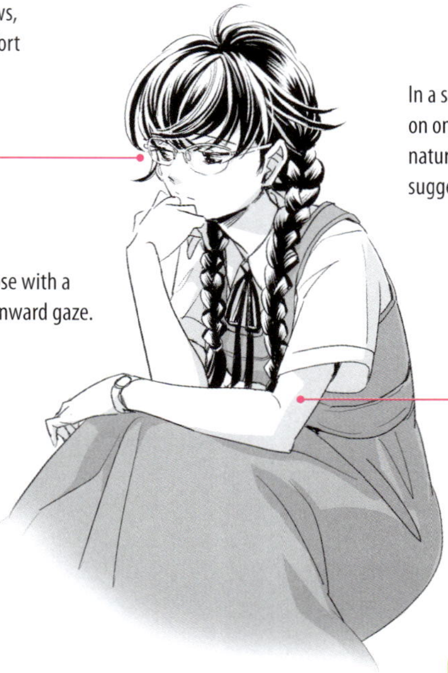

In a seated position, rest the chin on one hand, with the other arm naturally placed on the thigh, suggesting a reflective mood.

Draw this pose with a slightly downward gaze.

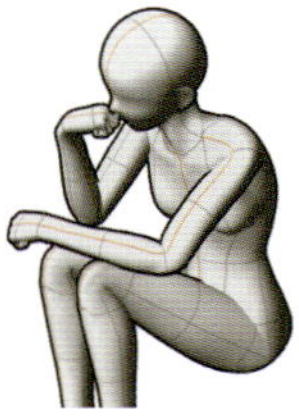

ANGLES
A seated pose shown from an overhead angle enhances the downward angle and the contemplative mood.

ANGLES
A diagonal angle allows for a clear view of the shape of the bent arm.

INDEX FINGER ON CHIN

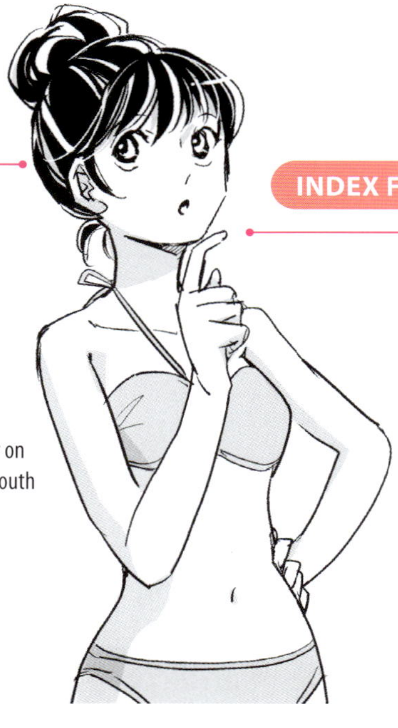

Position the index finger on the chin and have the mouth slightly opened.

With the other hand placed on the hip, adding dynamism to the subtle movements, this pose suggests the character is trying to recall something.

RESTING THE HAND ON THE CHIN

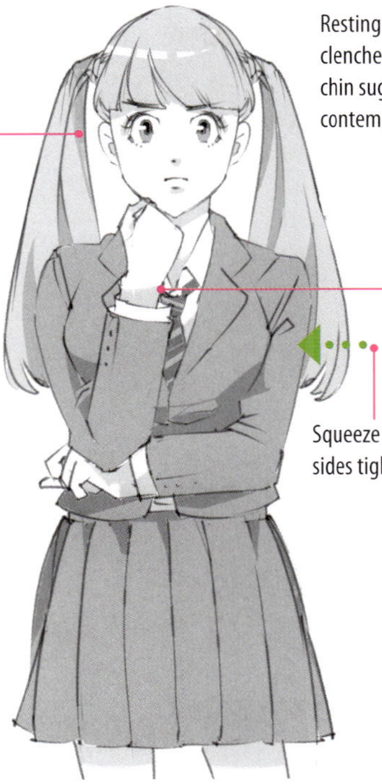

Resting the lightly clenched hand on the chin suggests serious contemplation.

Furrowed eyebrows and wide eyes add to the sense of deeply concentrating on a problem.

Squeeze the sides tightly.

POINTING WITH THE INDEX FINGER

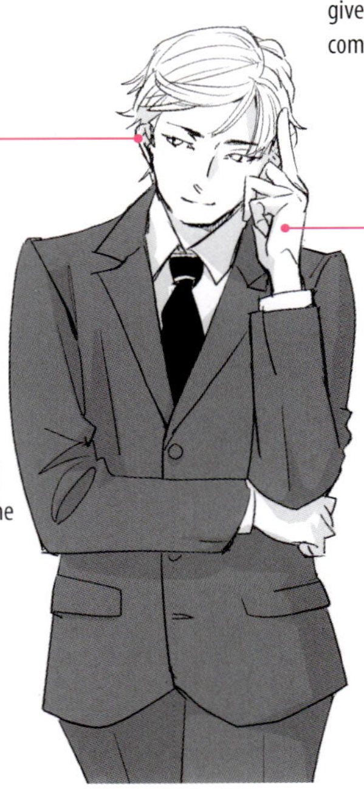

Pointing straight up can give the sense of having come up with a great idea.

The head is slightly tilted toward the direction of the finger.

THINKING WITH A CHEEK PROP

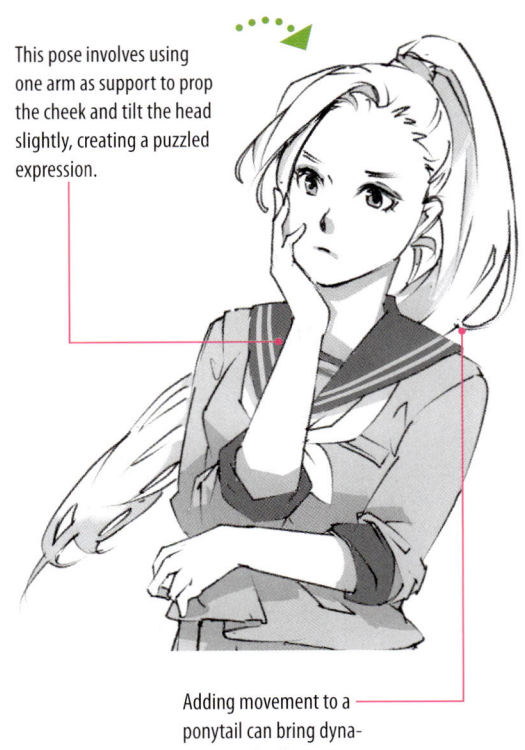

This pose involves using one arm as support to prop the cheek and tilt the head slightly, creating a puzzled expression.

A downward gaze gives an impression of serious contemplation.

Adding movement to a ponytail can bring dynamism to the illustration.

INDEX FINGER ON THE TEMPLE

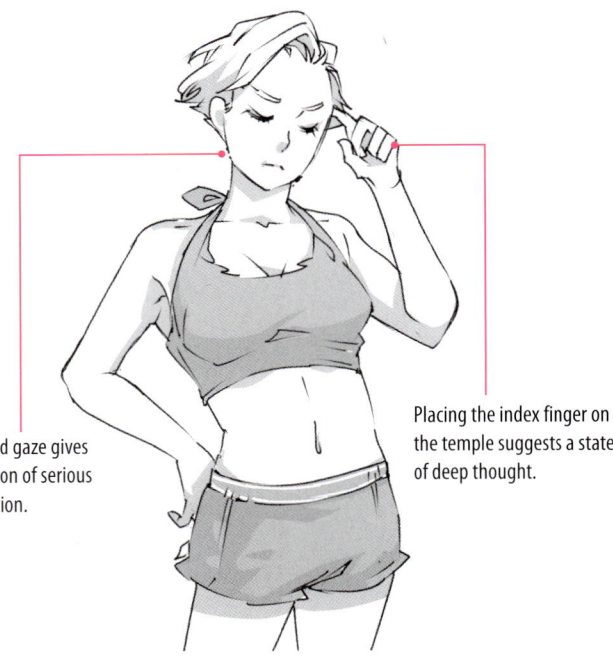

Placing the index finger on the temple suggests a state of deep thought.

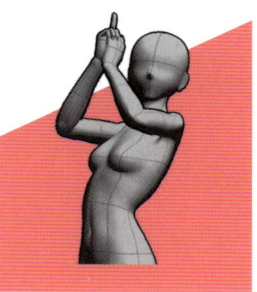

PRETENDING TO SHOOT WITH A FINGER PISTOL

Simulating a Gun

The finger pistol is a classic pose used for cute and playful characters. It can be varied as well to give it a more menacing or aggressive impression when desired.

FRONT-FACING PISTOL

A pose with the gaze and fingertips directed toward the viewer can strongly emphasize the character's presence.

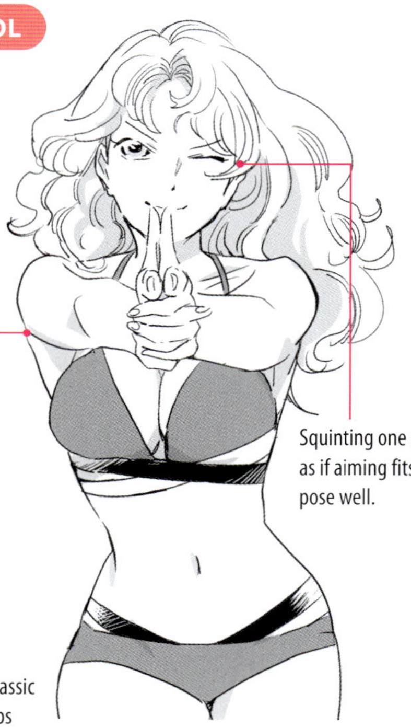

Squinting one eye as if aiming fits this pose well.

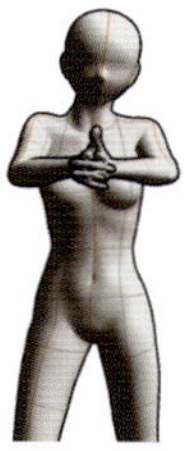

ANGLES
The front-facing angle is classic for poses with the fingertips pointed toward the viewer.

EMPHASIZING THE LINES OF BOTH ARMS

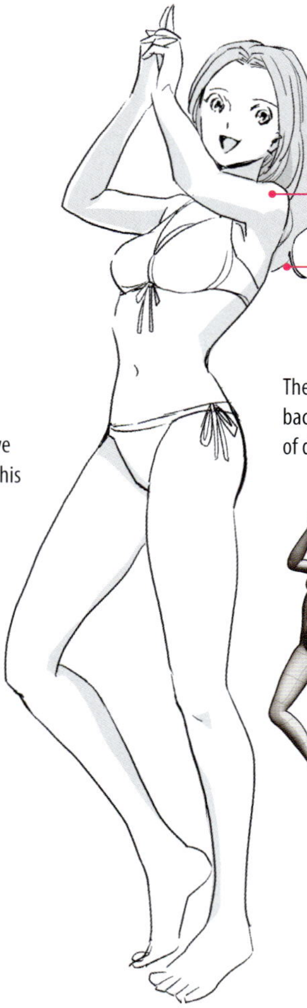

This pose clearly shows the lines of both arms, leading to the upraised hands.

The long line of the back can create a sense of dynamism.

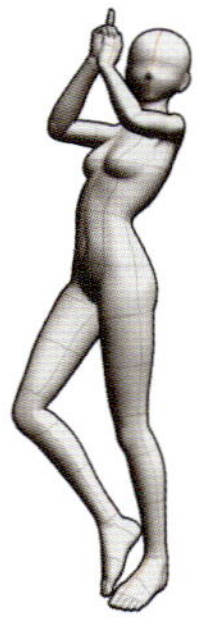

ANGLES
An angle slightly from the side with a low-angle shot can clearly suggest an aiming stance.

PLAY-SHOOTING

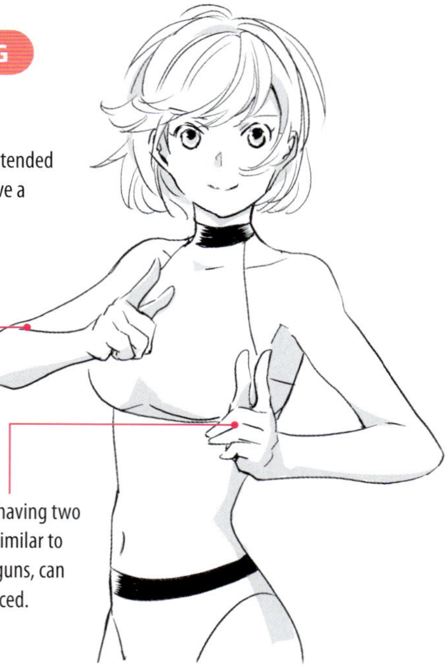

The hands are not extended too far forward to give a playful impression.

Variations like having two finger pistols, similar to wielding dual guns, can also be introduced.

CROPPING Don't Crop the Fingertips

Even if you crop the image to focus on the upper body, the pose will still retain its power and charm, but be careful that the key elements are not cut off.

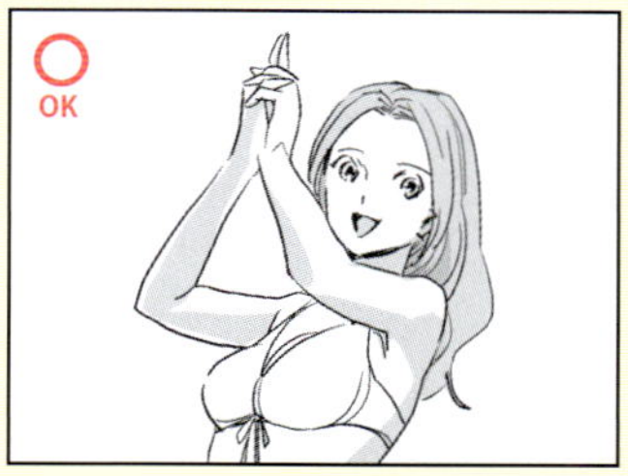

OK

40

ONE-HANDED PISTOL

With this pose's diagonal tilt, the hand displaying the finger pistol is emphasized.

A one-handed finger pistol can give a less playful and more aggressive impression compared to using both hands.

SHOOTING AT THE TEMPLE

Aiming the finger pistol at the temple carries a somewhat edgy, off-blanced image and suits dark characters.

The hand not forming the finger pistol should be in a relaxed, natural pose.

EMPHASIZING THE FACE

Encircling the chin emphasizes the character's face, drawing the viewer's gaze not to the fingers but to the face.

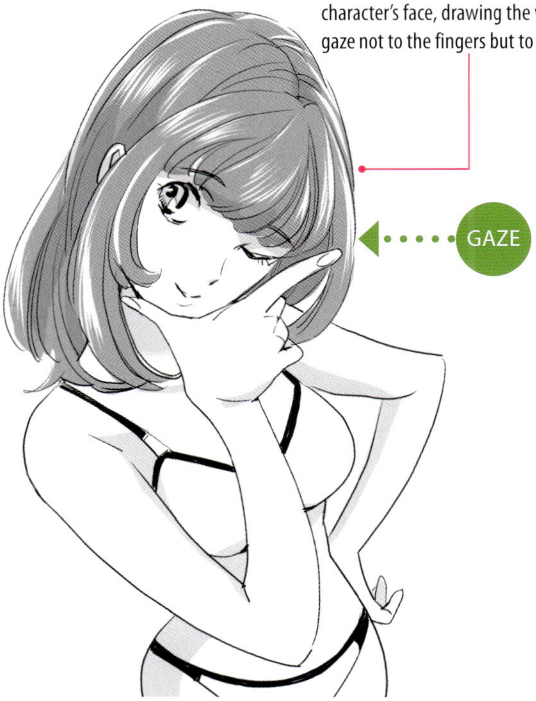

GAZE

BLOWING ON THE BARREL

Blowing on the fingertips/barrel is effective when the character is playfully impersonating a gunslinger.

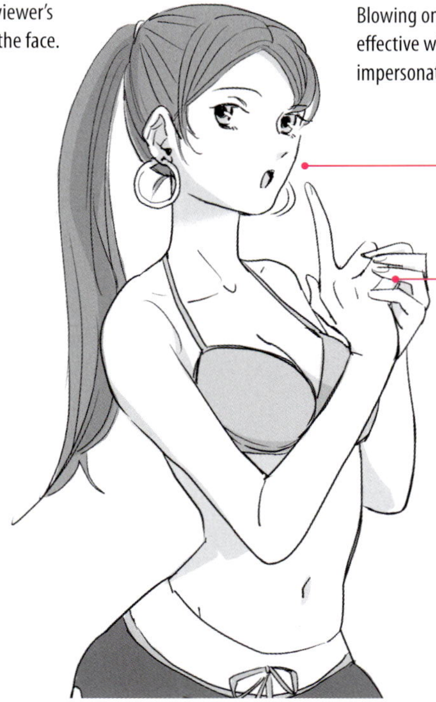

Here, use a side or diagonal angle and clearly show the fingertips.

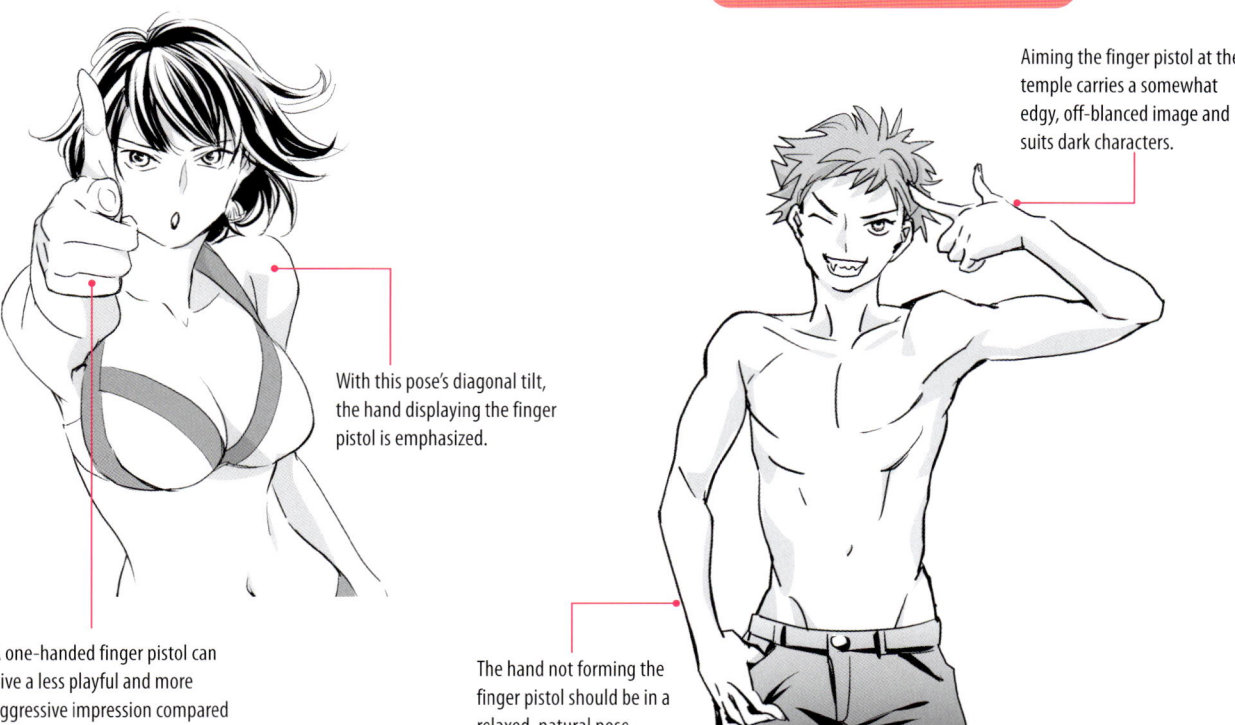

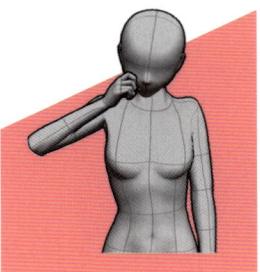

AN OVERFLOW OF EMOTION
Wiping Away Tears

It's that moment when emotions intensify and tears overflow. The hand wiping the tears primarily uses the index finger. This is a nuanced pose that can express a character's delicate nature or the turbulent emotions of adolescence.

WIPING TEARS WITH BOTH HANDS

The face is usually tilted slightly downward. Drawing tears emphasizes sadness.

This pose involves lightly clasping both hands to wipe away tears. In this case, the more the sides expand, the more it conveys the impression of sobbing uncontrollably.

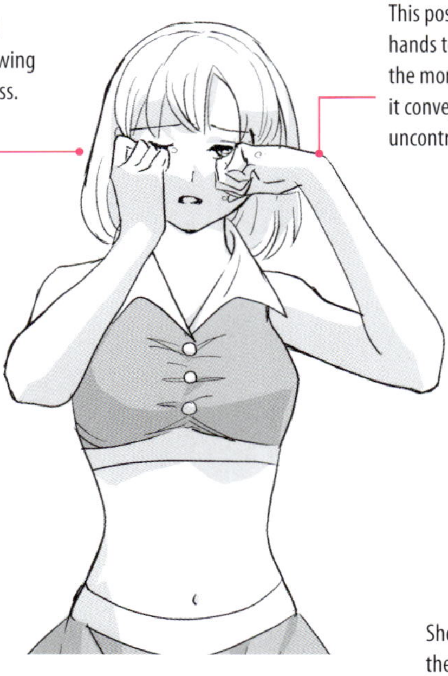

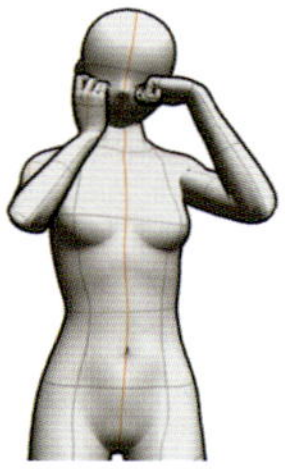

ANGLES
A slightly low-angle view gives the impression of looking up at a crying face.

POUTING

The mouth pouts slightly as if sulking.

Shoulders are raised, and the sides are tightly closed, making the body shrink.

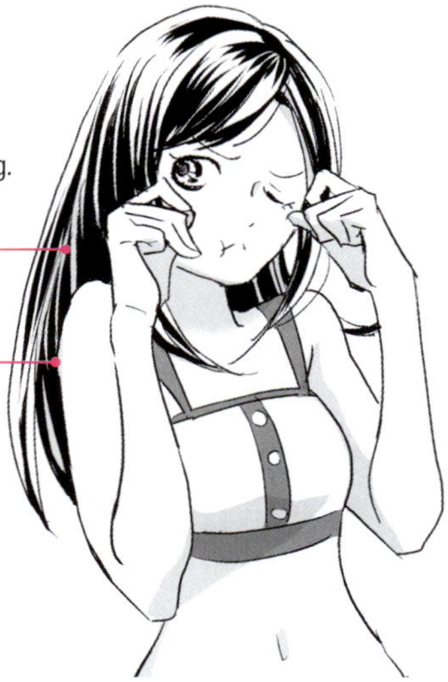

WIPING TEARS WITH THE INDEX FINGER

Tears that seem about to spill are wiped away with the knuckle of the index finger.

The other arm hangs limply, giving the impression that the person had been holding back tears until now.

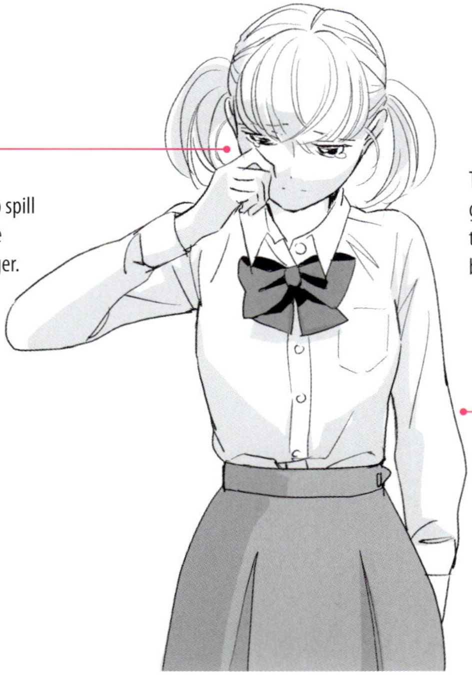

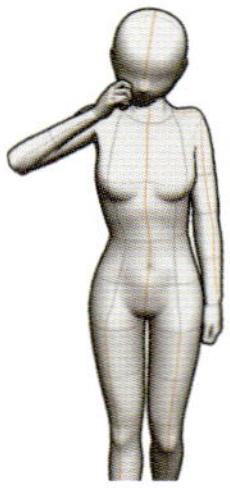

ANGLES
A slightly high-angle view can enhance the impression that the character is feeling down.

42

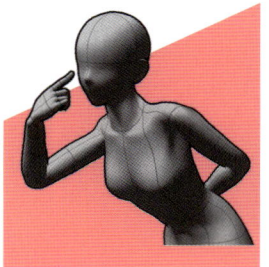

POSES THAT DRAW OUT PLAYFULNESS
Pointing to One's Self

This is an especially playful pose where the lower eyelid is pulled down with the index finger and the character sticks out her tongue. It can suggest a playful relationship or the close intimacy associated with fooling around with friends.

TURNING AROUND PLAYFULLY

This is a playful pose where the character slightly pulls down the lower eyelid with the index finger. Facing sideways gives a more realistic, three-dimensional impression.

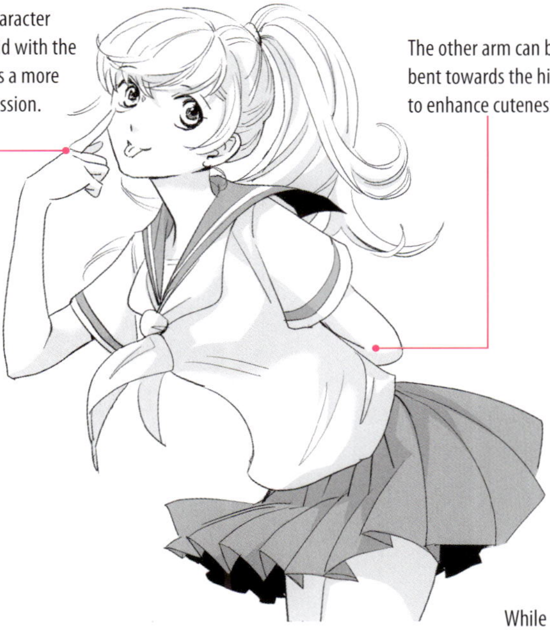

The other arm can be bent towards the hip to enhance cuteness.

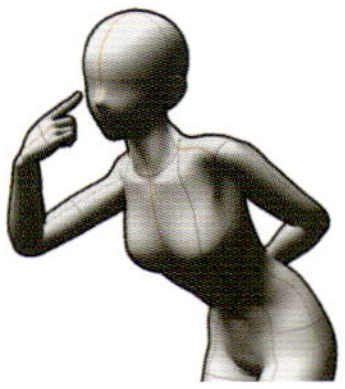

MAKING A FUNNY FACE

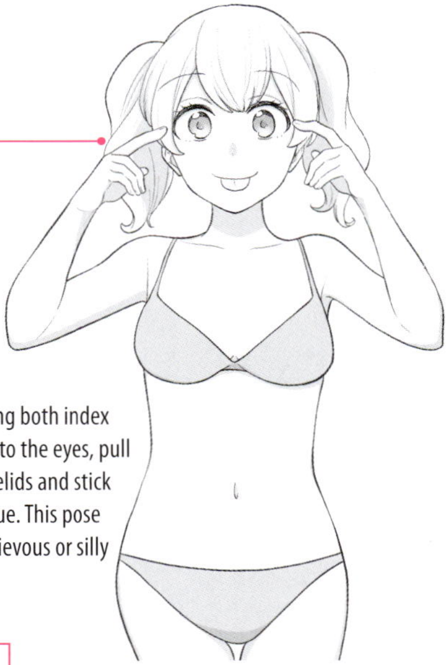

While bringing both index fingers close to the eyes, pull down the eyelids and stick out the tongue. This pose suits a mischievous or silly character.

ANGLES
An angle that shows the shape of the arms from the side is recommended.

MISCHIEVOUSLY STICKING OUT THE TONGUE

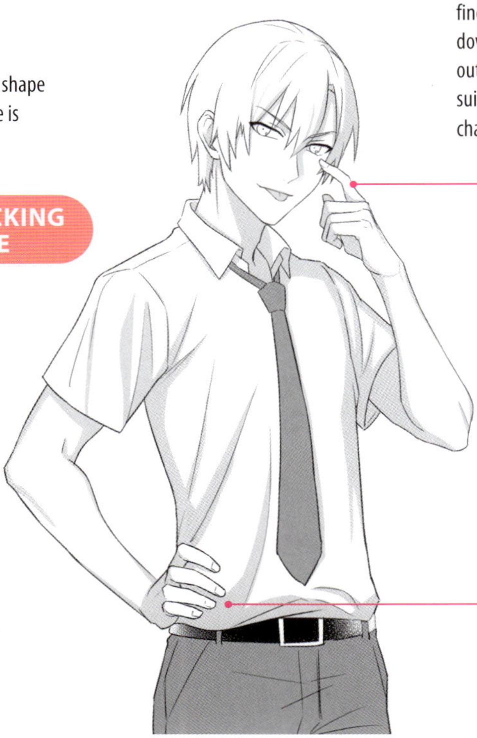

The index finger is just placed near the eye area without showing the underside of the eyelid, and the tongue is stuck out.

Placing the other hand on the hip can create an arrogant character vibe.

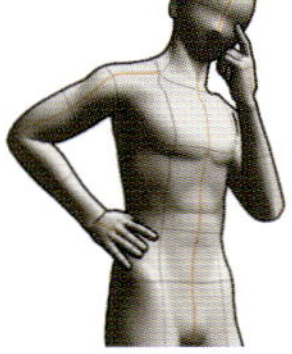

ANGLES
A diagonal angle can also express the dishonest nature of a defiant character.

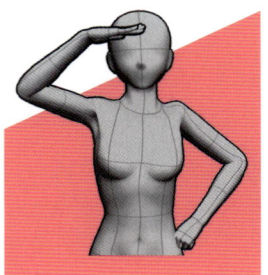

A HAND SHADING THE EYES

Looking into the Distance

The key to this pose is combining the hand gesture with a gaze directed far into the distance. It draws your viewer's attention outside the frame of the illustration, adding depth, complexity and quite possibly a note of mystery.

RAISING ONE HAND

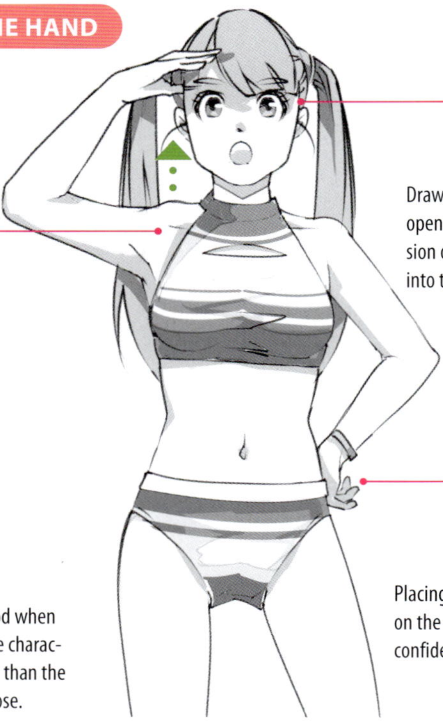

Raising the hand also slightly lifts the shoulder.

Drawing the eyes wide open gives the impression of intently looking into the distance.

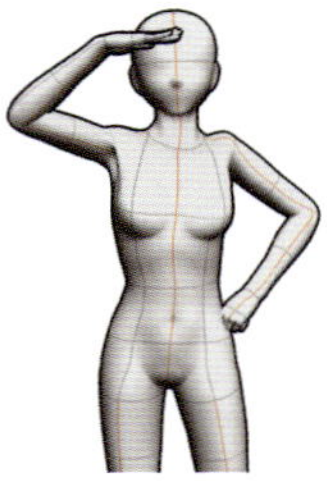

ANGLES
A frontal angle is good when you want to show the character's expression more than the atmosphere of the pose.

Placing the other hand on the hip creates a confident impression.

RAISING BOTH HANDS

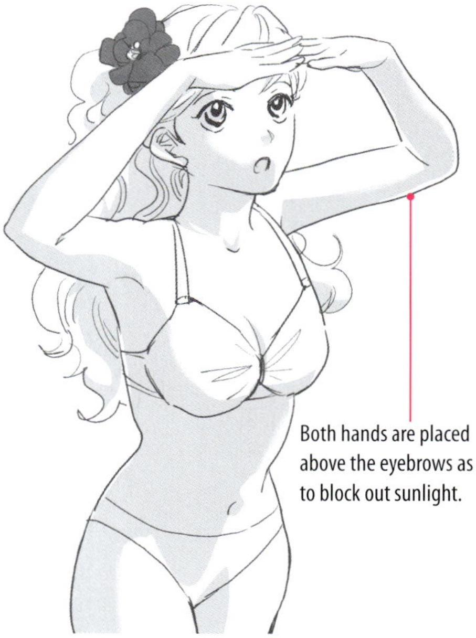

Both hands are placed above the eyebrows as if to block out sunlight.

ARCHING THE UPPER BODY

Slightly arching the upper body matches the character's far-away glance.

The raised hand should create an opposing line to the shoulder line, mindful of the contrapposto effect.

ANGLES
A diagonal and low-angle view helps to convey the feeling of looking into the distance by making the viewer aware of the wide background space.

CROPPING Leave Space in Front of the Face

The pose of looking into the distance can work even in a close-up shot of the face. When using a diagonal angle, it's good to leave space in front of the face to include the raised hand.

OK

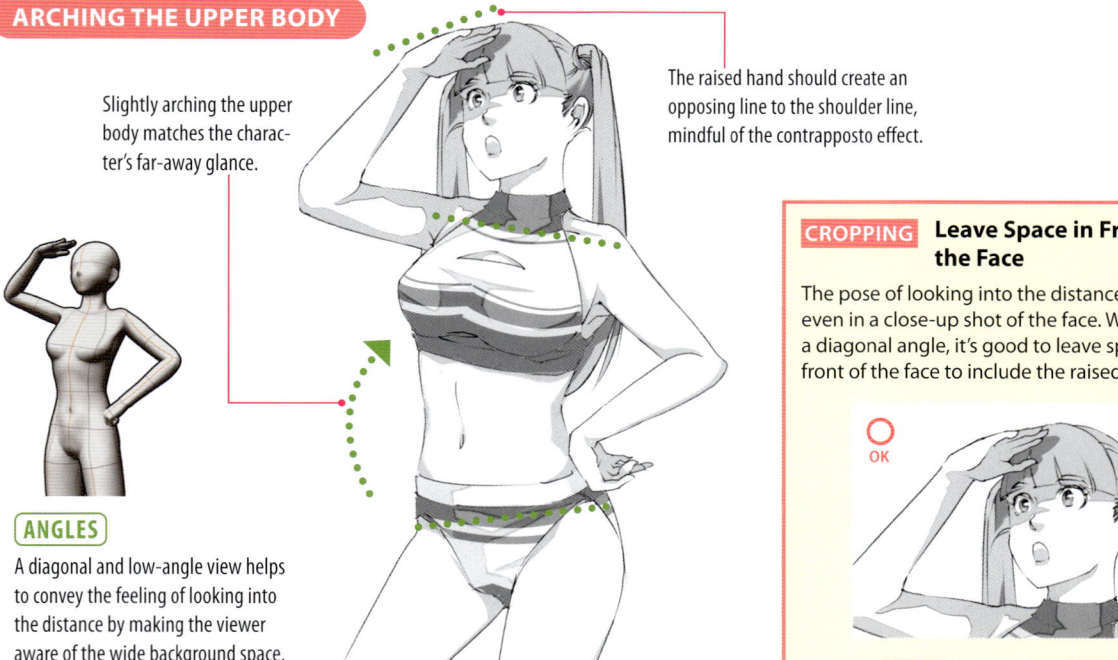

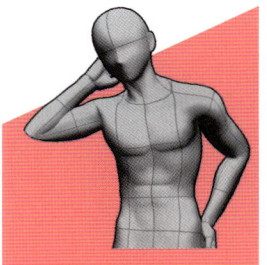

HIDING TRUE FEELINGS
Expressing Shyness

To hide true feelings or to express embarrassment or joy, these poses and gestures have a wide range of applications. They allow for the expression of complex emotions and subtly hint at the character's true intentions.

HIDING THE EXPRESSION

A pose where the mouth is covered to hide the expression indicates a psychological desire to keep one's true feelings hidden.

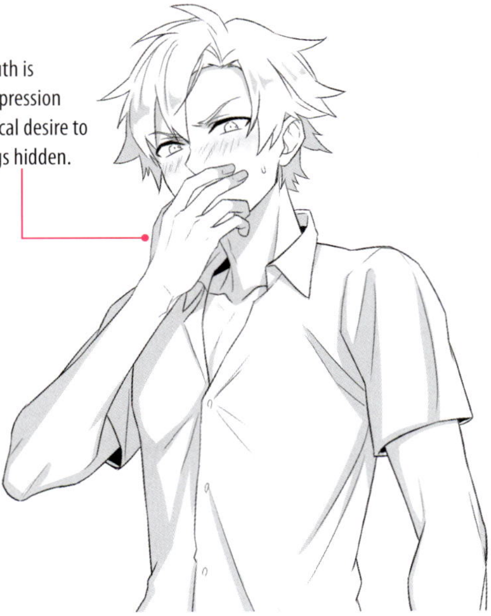

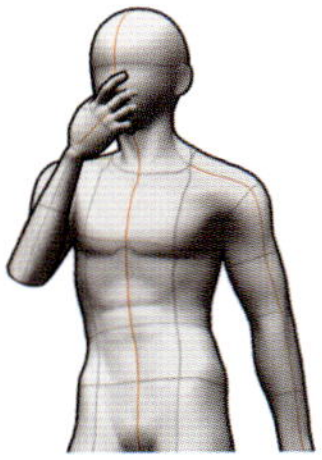

ANGLES
A slightly low-angle view can create a dramatic scene.

SCRATCHING THE CHEEK

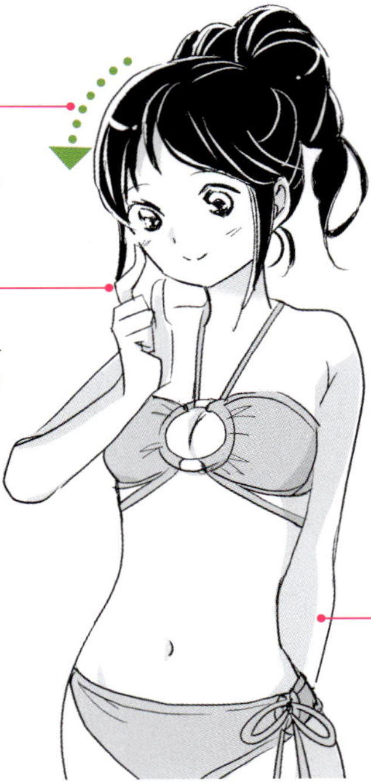

Slightly pull back the chin and look down.

The gesture of scratching the cheek with the index finger suggests an attempt to conceal embarrassment.

The other arm is wrapped behind the back, expressing the personality of a character.

SCRATCHING THE HEAD

A pose where one hand scratches the back of the head can express a troubled mind or unsettled, worried mood.

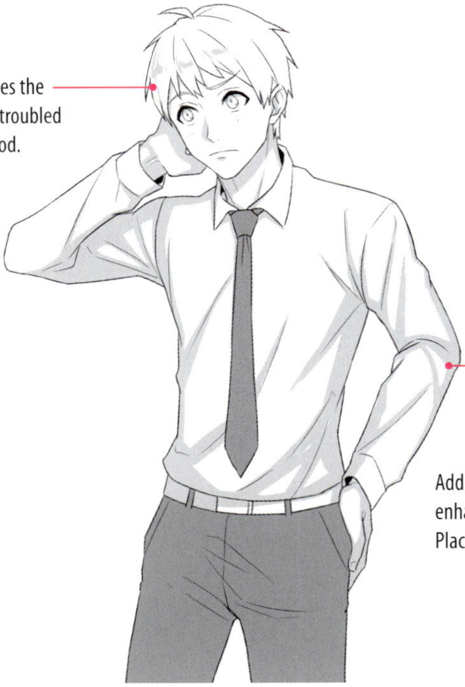

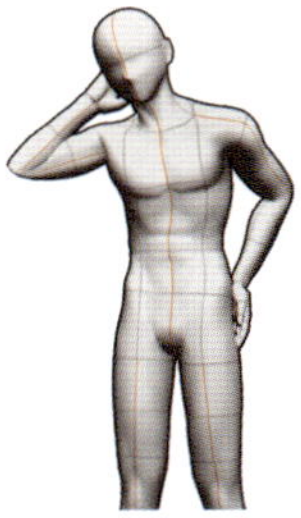

ANGLES
An angle viewed from the side at about eye level creates a casual and natural atmosphere.

Adding movement to the opposite hand enhances the troubled atmosphere. Placing it on the hip looks natural.

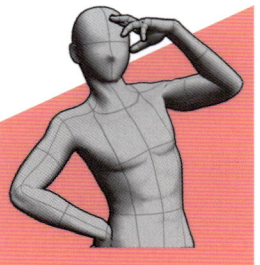

DEEP IN THOUGHT OR A TROUBLED MIND
Touching the Head

Holding or supporting the head while glancing downward can convey a sense of exasperation, a feeling of unease or dizziness. Alternately, it can be transformed into a pretentious pose, a thinking character lost in deep thoughts.

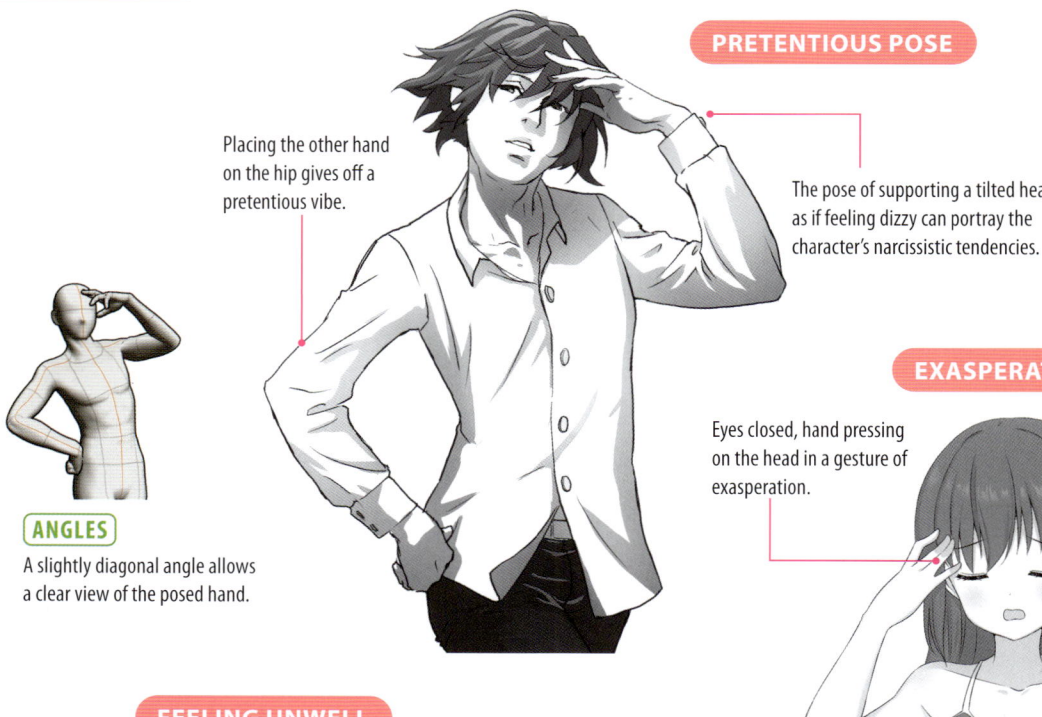

PRETENTIOUS POSE

Placing the other hand on the hip gives off a pretentious vibe.

The pose of supporting a tilted head as if feeling dizzy can portray the character's narcissistic tendencies.

ANGLES
A slightly diagonal angle allows a clear view of the posed hand.

EXASPERATION

Eyes closed, hand pressing on the head in a gesture of exasperation.

FEELING UNWELL

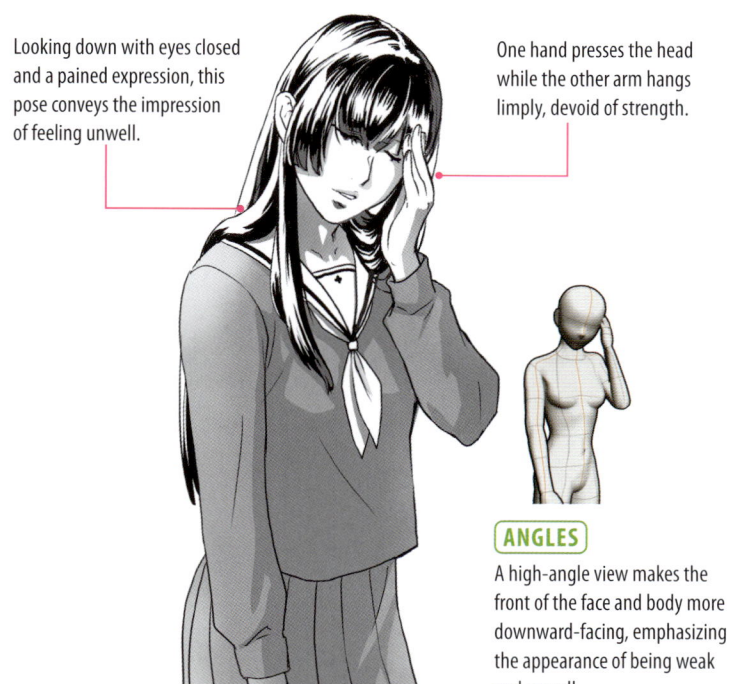

Looking down with eyes closed and a pained expression, this pose conveys the impression of feeling unwell.

One hand presses the head while the other arm hangs limply, devoid of strength.

ANGLES
A high-angle view makes the front of the face and body more downward-facing, emphasizing the appearance of being weak and unwell.

CROPPING   **From the Shoulders Up**

This pose works with just the tilted head, the supporting hand and the shoulders visible, so it's fine to crop from the chest down.

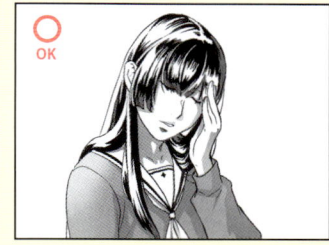

○ OK

46

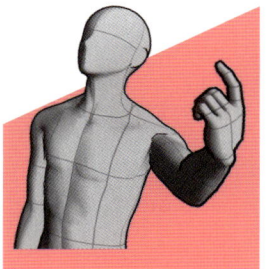

ENTICING OR PROVOKING AN OPPONENT
Beckoning Motions

This pose is used in action or fight scenes to provoke or guide an opponent. The back of the hand or the index finger is directed toward the opponents, drawing them in and calling them closer. It suits a character brimming with confidence.

PROVOKING WITH A FINGER

The pose of pointing a single index finger at the opponent has a high degree of provocation and emphasizes a demeanor overflowing with confidence.

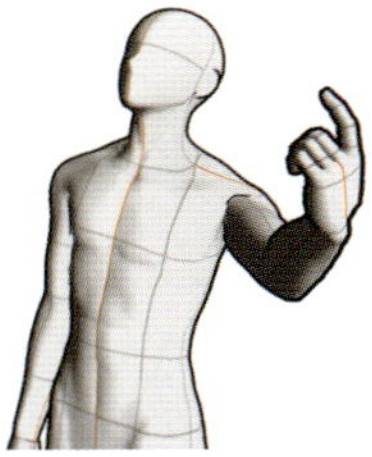

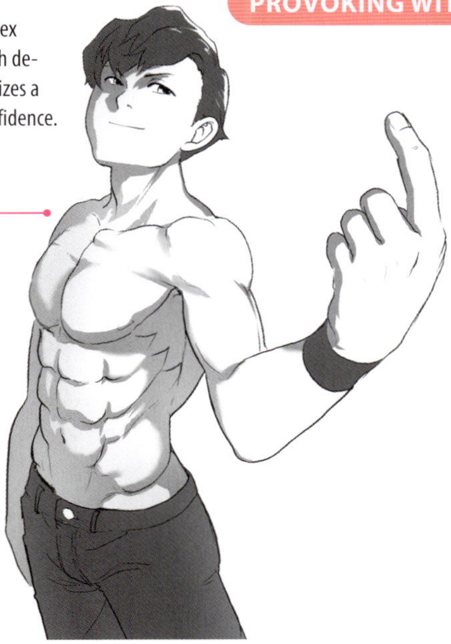

ANGLES
Position the extended hand prominently in the foreground while displaying a well-toned physique.

BOLDLY BECKONING

Aligning all four fingers neatly gives off a polite yet imposing air.

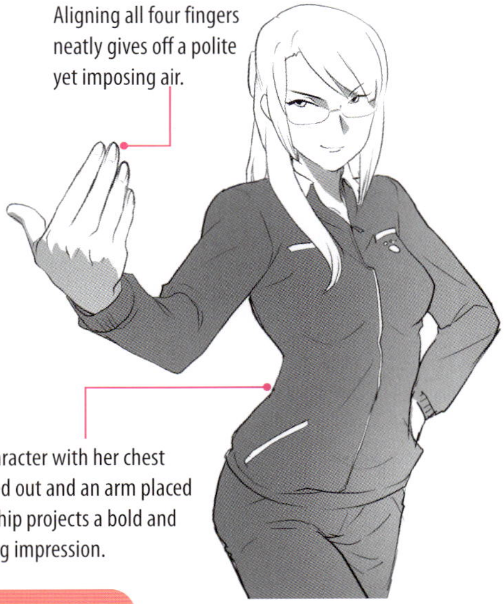

A character with her chest puffed out and an arm placed on a hip projects a bold and strong impression.

SUBTLE FINGER BECKONING

This is a minimalistic gesture to call someone over. The motion of the index finger gives it a comical impression.

Although beckoning with the index finger raised, choosing an angle that does not emphasize the hand conveys a relaxed situation.

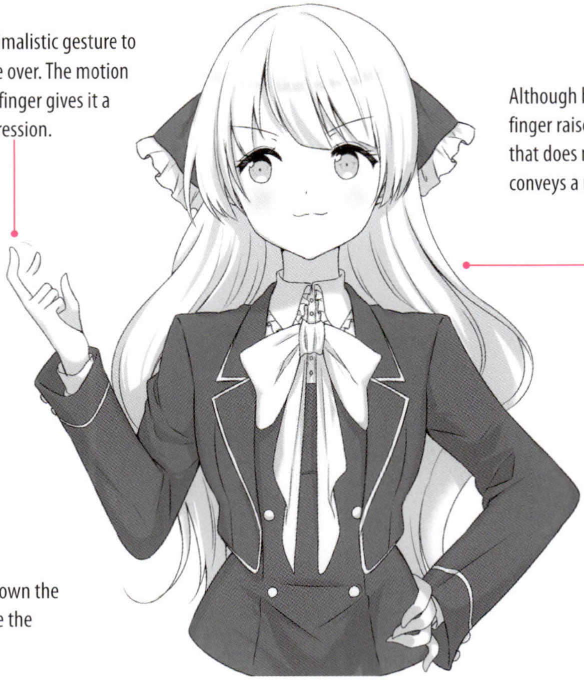

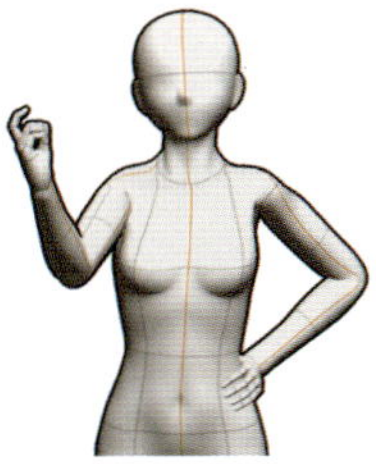

ANGLES
A frontal angle can tone down the dramatic feel and enhance the comical impression.

47

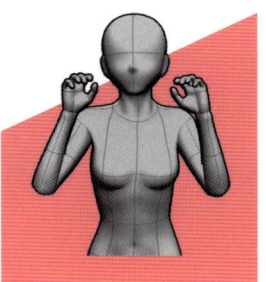

PLAYFUL KAWAII POSES
Imitating Animals

These poses are associated with kemonomimi (or "cat-girl" characters). They involve simulating paws or creating the appearance of rabbit ears by opening both hands above the head. The posed hands are typically placed near the face.

Spread the elbows to the side and move both wrists while making fists.

CAT HANDS

Winking enhances the sense of playfulness.

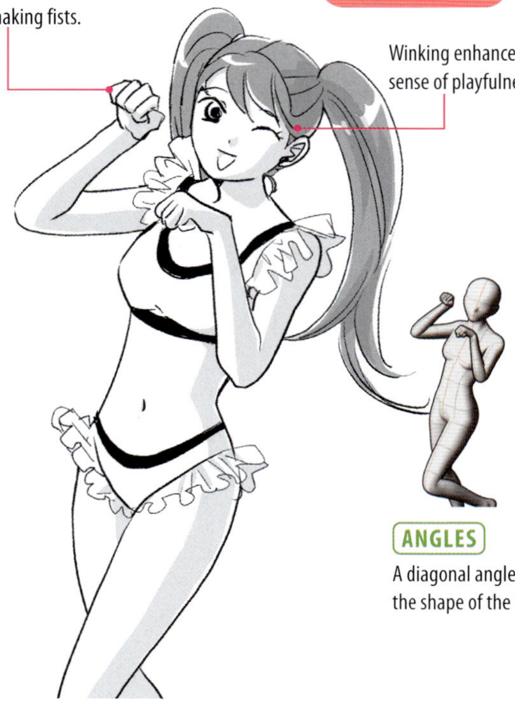

CUTE ATTACK

Loosely bending the fingers gives a claw-like impression, like a bear roaring and pouncing.

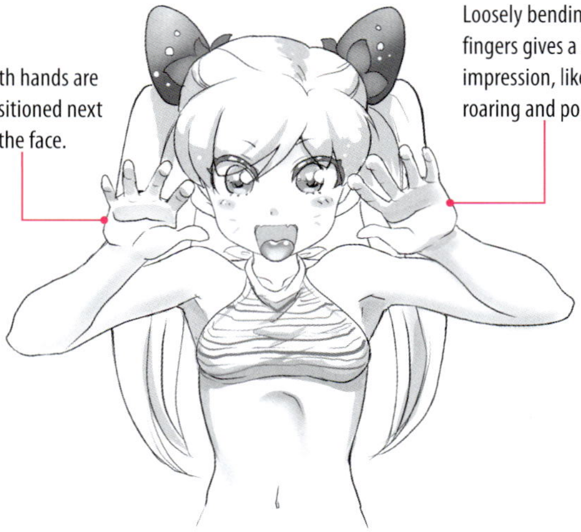

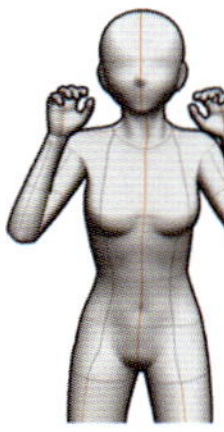

Both hands are positioned next to the face.

ANGLES
A diagonal angle clearly conveys the shape of the hand pose.

ANGLES
A frontal angle can create the feeling that the character is coming towards you.

MODEST CAT HANDS

A small movement with the elbows close to the sides gives a reserved impression.

CROPPING Show the Shape of the Arms

While this pose can be charming even in a close-up of the face, when cropping, it's good to include the arms in the frame to some extent.

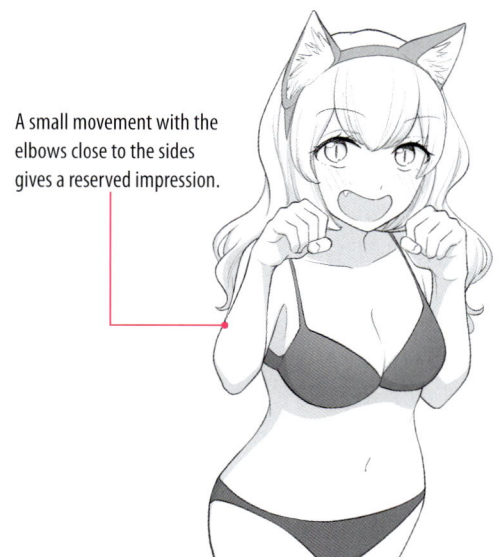

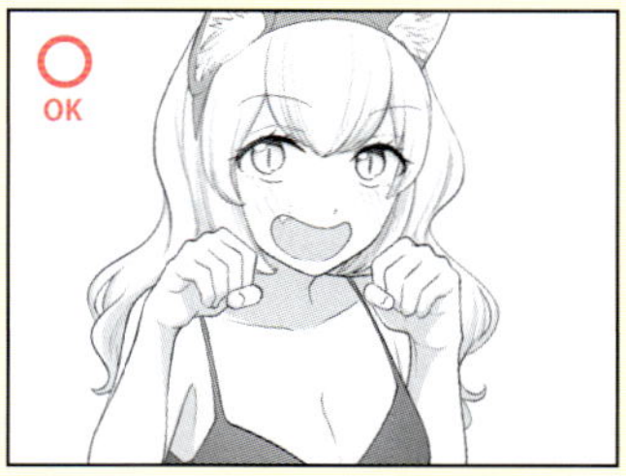

OK

BEAR HANDS

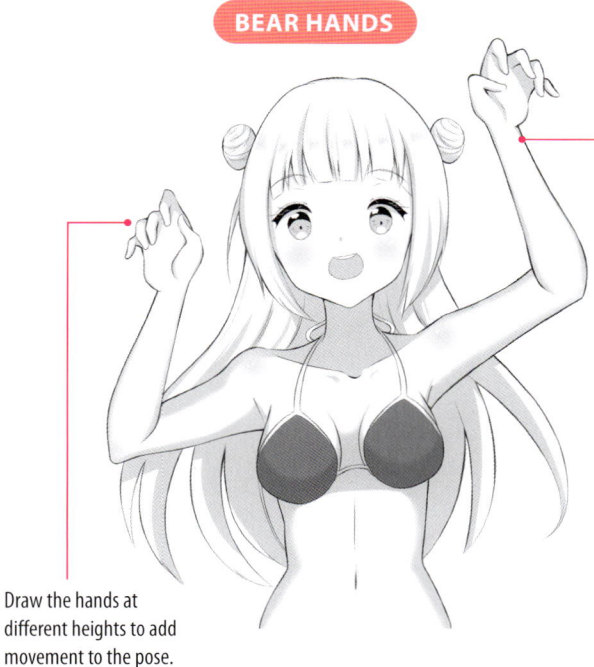

A pose with both hands gently bent and raised, lifting the hands away from the face gives an exaggerated impression, like a large bear rearing.

Draw the hands at different heights to add movement to the pose.

BECKONING CAT HANDS

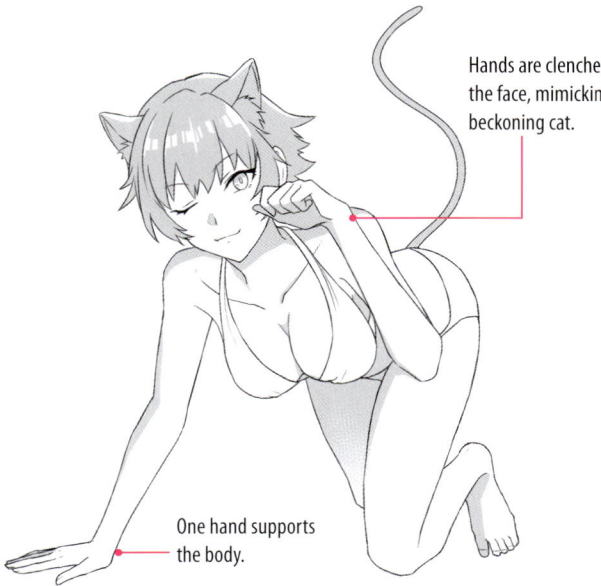

Hands are clenched near the face, mimicking a beckoning cat.

One hand supports the body.

SHOWING THE BACK OF THE HAND

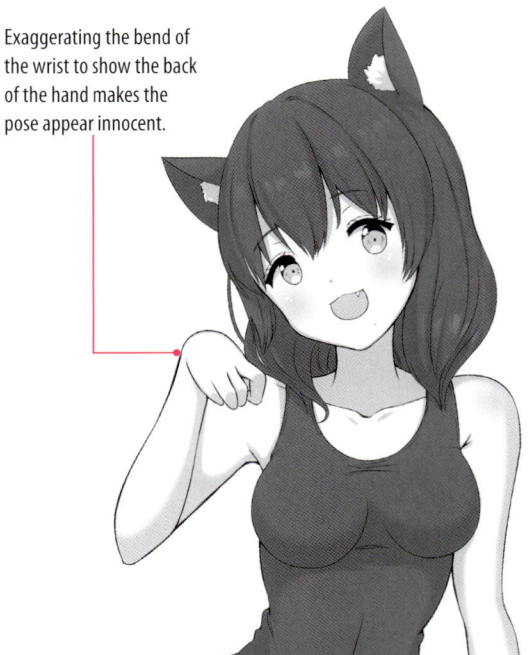

Exaggerating the bend of the wrist to show the back of the hand makes the pose appear innocent.

RABBIT HANDS

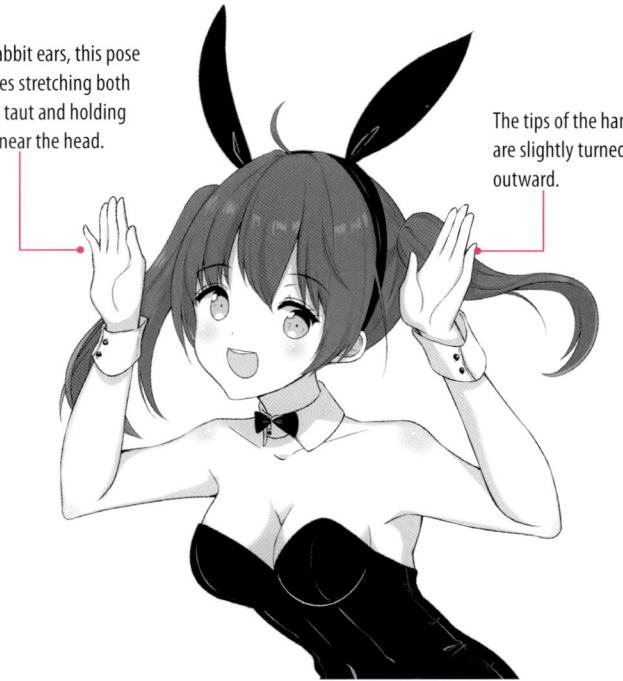

Like rabbit ears, this pose involves stretching both hands taut and holding them near the head.

The tips of the hands are slightly turned outward.

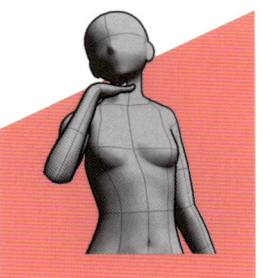

GIVING A THUMBS UP
Affirmative Gestures

Thumbs up, affirmative, everything's O.K.: we know the range of gestures well. The pose might involve placing a hand on the hip to counterbalance the pronounced gesture of the affirming hand.

PUNCHING THE CHEST WITH A FIST

A fist placed on the chest as if to say "I've got this!" can express bravery.

The other hand is placed on the hip, emphasizing a feeling of full confidence.

ANGLES
A nearly frontal angle ensures that the hand punching the chest is centered in the frame, making it stand out clearly.

HAND OPEN ON THE CHEST

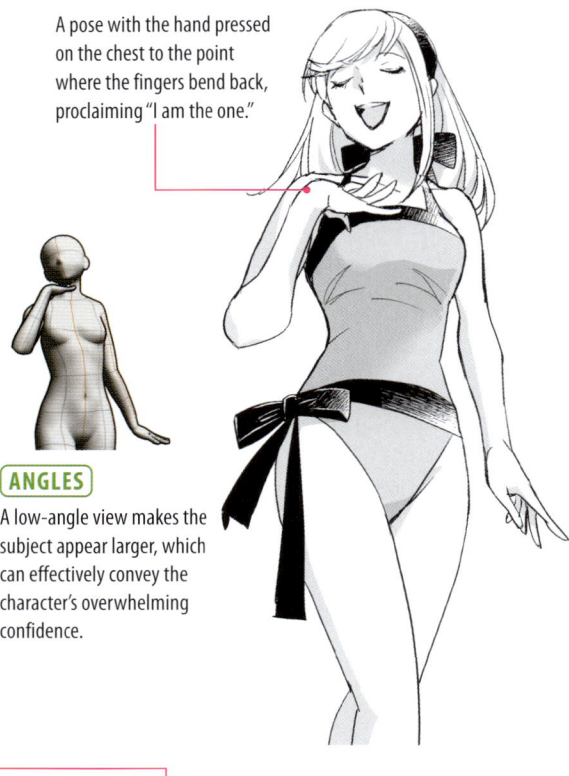

A pose with the hand pressed on the chest to the point where the fingers bend back, proclaiming "I am the one."

ANGLES
A low-angle view makes the subject appear larger, which can effectively convey the character's overwhelming confidence.

THUMBS UP

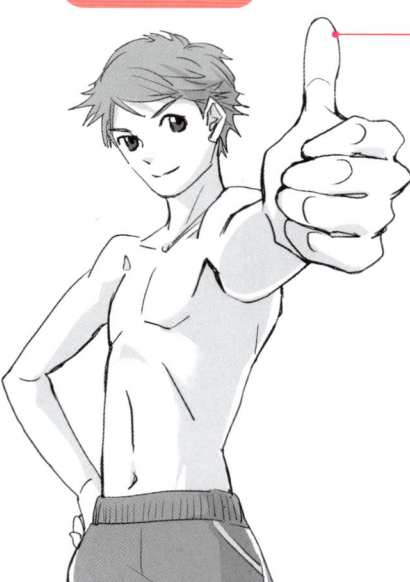

Pushing the thumb-up hand forward emphasizes the character's enthusiastic agreement.

CROPPING The Upper Body's Atmosphere is Important

Including the upper body without cutting it off makes it easier to convey the character's movements and fully communicates the atmosphere of a character saying "Leave it to me."

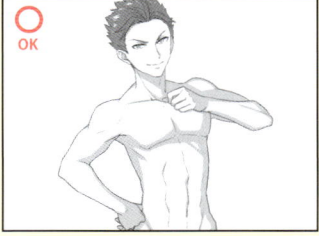
OK

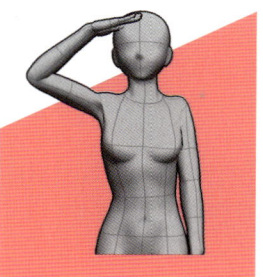

RESPECT OR ACKNOWLEDGMENT

Salutes

A salute that shows respect involves extending the hand rigidly, while a playful salute involves a more relaxed and loose motion. You can vary the pose and style based on the character or situation.

HAND TO FOREHEAD

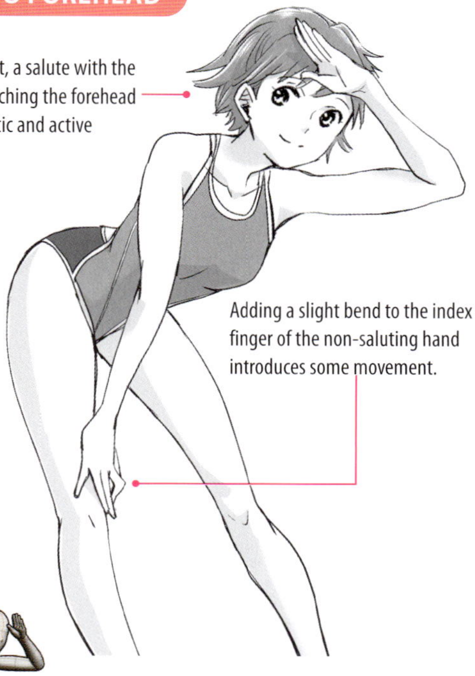

With elbows out, a salute with the hand firmly touching the forehead suits an energetic and active character.

Adding a slight bend to the index finger of the non-saluting hand introduces some movement.

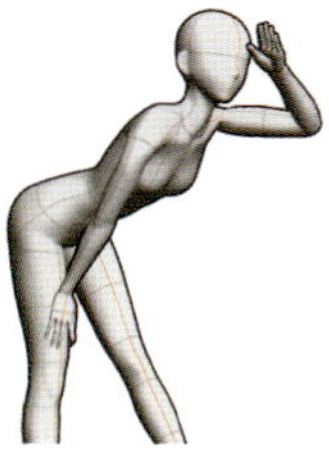

ANGLES

A diagonal angle can make the form of the salute appear more three-dimensional.

DEMONSTRATING RESPECT

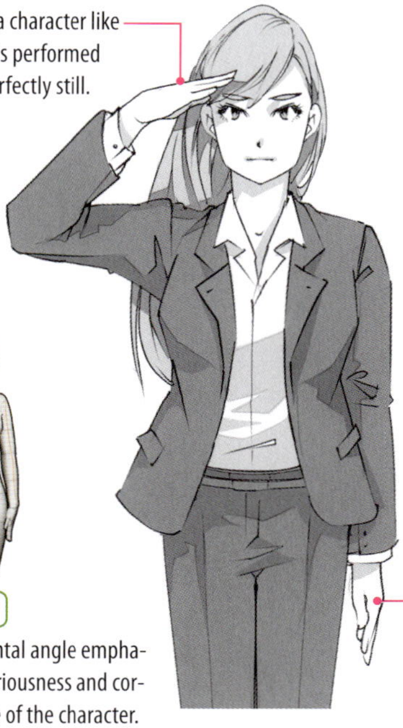

A salute by a character like a detective is performed standing perfectly still.

The other arm is also extended straight down to the fingertips.

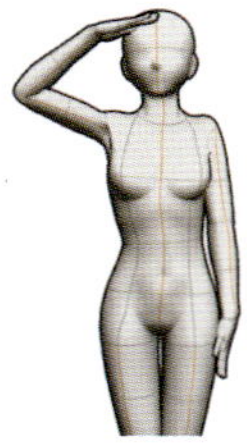

ANGLES

A direct frontal angle emphasizes the seriousness and correct posture of the character.

PLAYFUL ACKNOWLEDGMENT

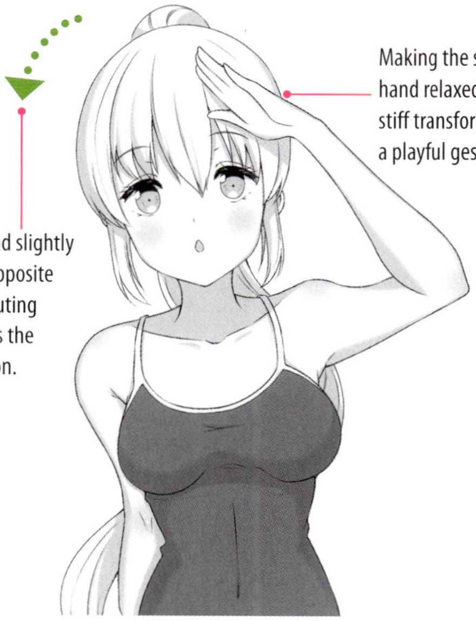

Tilting the head slightly towards the opposite side of the saluting hand increases the sense of motion.

Making the saluting hand relaxed and not stiff transforms it into a playful gesture.

RELAXING THE HAND

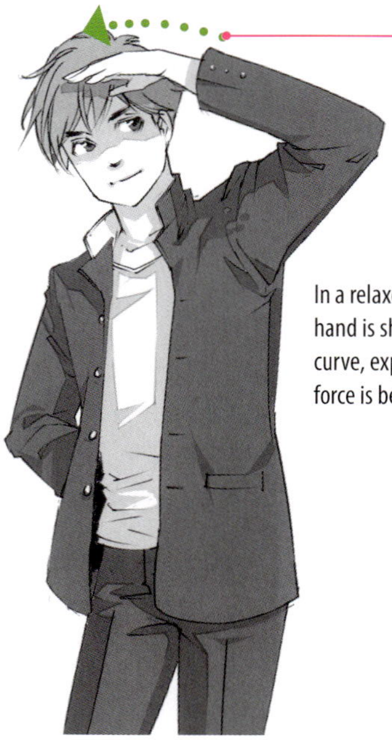

In a relaxed salute, the hand is shaped with a loose curve, expressing that no force is being exerted.

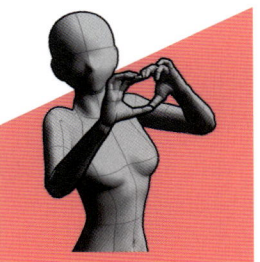

A NEW UNIVERSAL SYMBOL
Heart Hands

The heart pose, where the index fingers and thumbs of both hands are joined together, conveys affection. The position and size of the heart can be adjusted to create variations and to fit the atmosphere.

BESIDE THE FACE

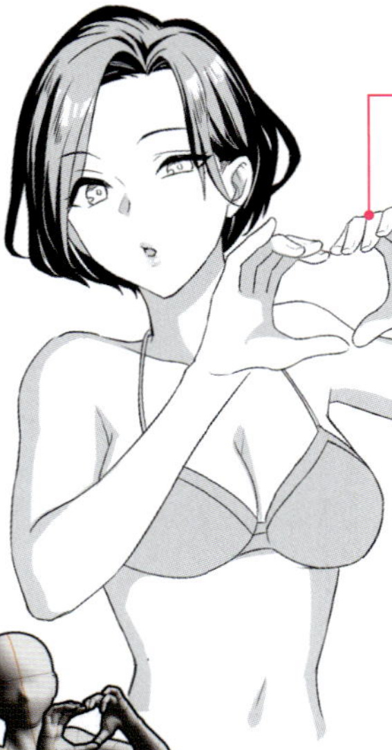

Placing the heart beside the face emphasizes the character's expressions.

Drawing each finger delicately and in detail gives an elegant feel.

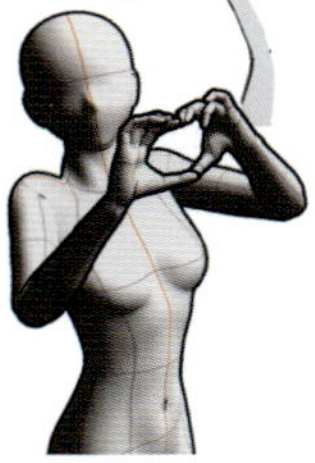

ANGLES
A diagonal angle is good for clearly showing the lines of the arms and emphasizing their movement.

AT THE CHEST

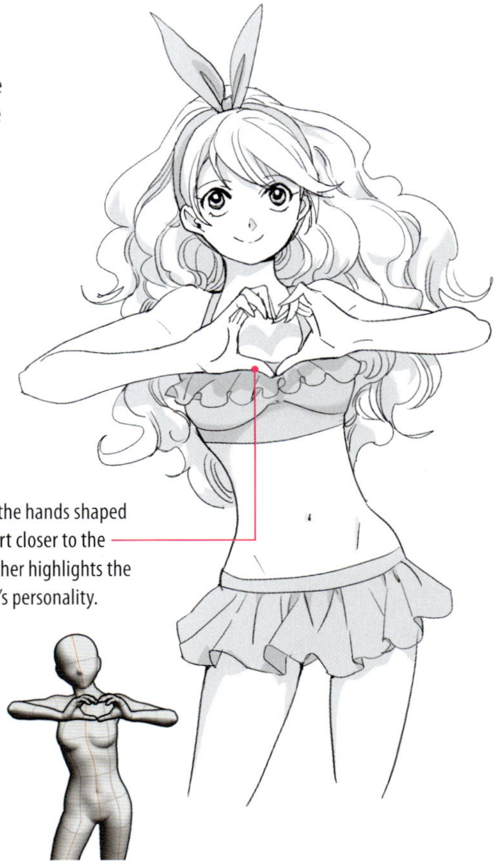

Bringing the hands shaped like a heart closer to the chest further highlights the character's personality.

ANGLES
If you want to show the shape of the heart clearly, use an angle that views the heart-shaped hands from the front.

UNDER THE CHIN

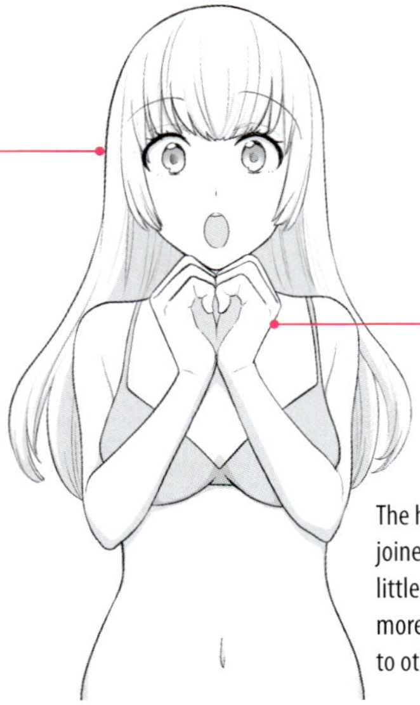

With eyes wide open and a surprised expression, this pose can convey a feeling of being thrilled.

The hands are made into fists and joined together, with the bend of the little fingers forming a heart, giving a more subdued impression compared to other heart poses.

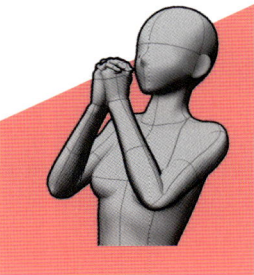

PETITIONS FOR DIVINE INTERVENTION

Praying

This pose involves closing the eyes and clasping the hands in front of the chest or face. The serious expression is used not only to capture the intensity of prayer but also in scenes where characters are fervently hoping their wishes come true.

OFFERING PRAYERS TO THE HEAVENS

This pose involves facing upward and lifting clasped hands in front of the face as if offering prayers to the heavens.

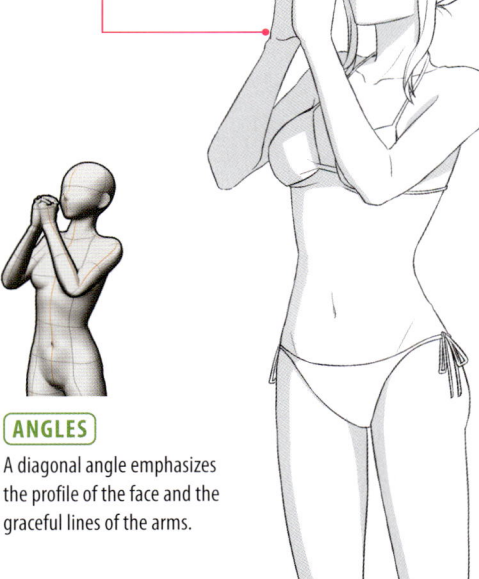

ANGLES

A diagonal angle emphasizes the profile of the face and the graceful lines of the arms.

BASIC PRAYER POSE

The basic prayer pose involves clasping the hands without opening the arms wide and placing them near the chest with eyes closed.

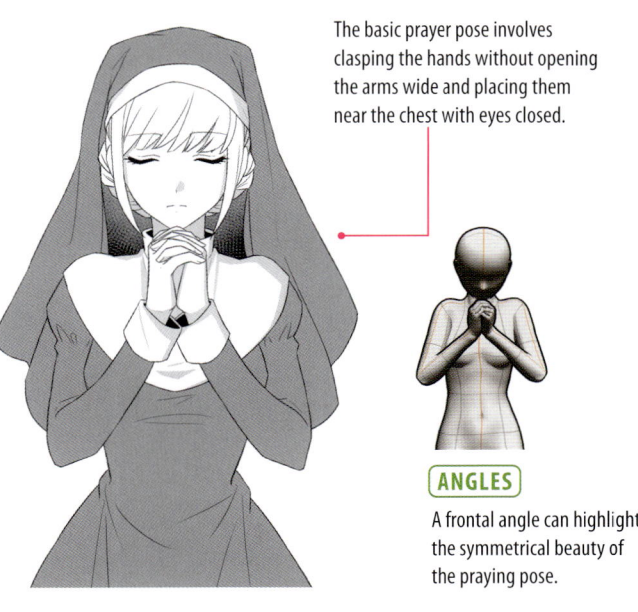

ANGLES

A frontal angle can highlight the symmetrical beauty of the praying pose.

PRAYING WITH ABANDON

The pose includes slightly bending the body forward with clasped hands placed near the mouth, praying.

Closing the eyes and looking downward creates a sense of deep devotion in prayer.

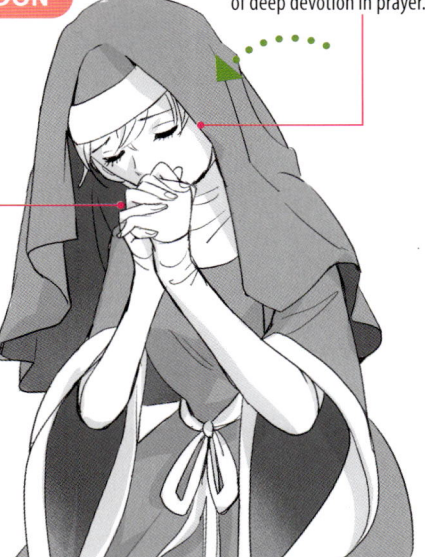

Tips — **Showing the Background**

The choice of angle can also be based on how the background is incorporated. Using a low angle in the prayer pose can create a composition where the camera seems to be pointing up towards the sky (or the ceiling if indoors), emphasizing the 'heavens' to which the prayers are directed.

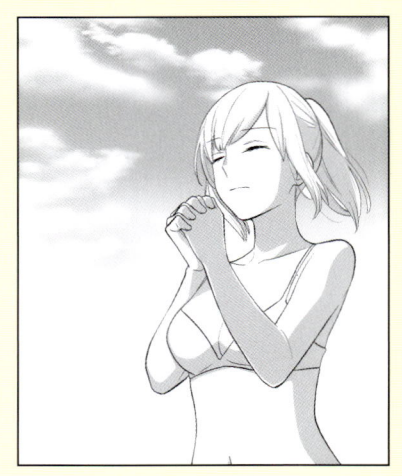

53

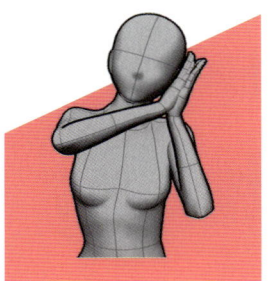

EVERYDAY GESTURES
Putting the Hands Together

Tented fingers or the palms placed against each other, this gesture tightens the sides and makes the body appear more compact. Is your character feeling cutesy, contemplative or chilled through? These varied poses have a range of applications.

EXPERT IN APPEALING

This pose represents expressions like "Thank you!" or "You saved me!" by bringing the hands together.

Tilting the joined hands slightly and positioning them beside the face creates an impression of being good at appealing.

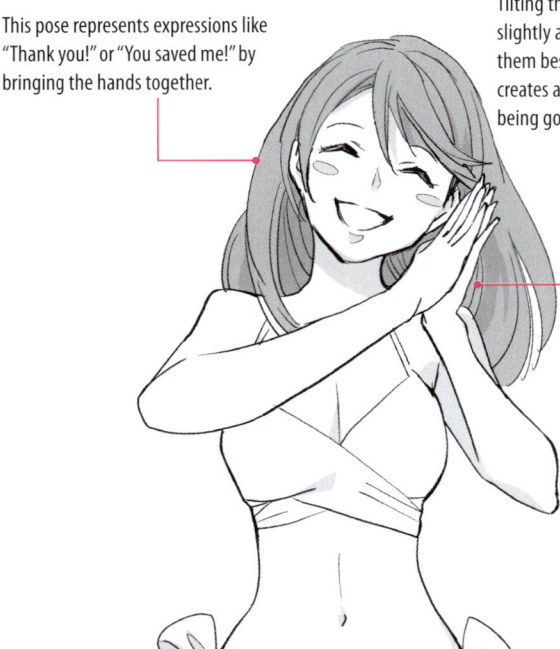
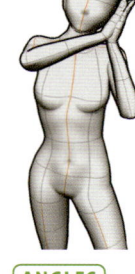

JOINING HANDS IN FRONT OF THE BODY

ANGLES
Use a frontal angle when you want to show the facial expression.

Bringing the hands together in front of the body with fingertips touching creates a pose that suggests hesitation or readiness, as if saying "Well" or "Let's see."

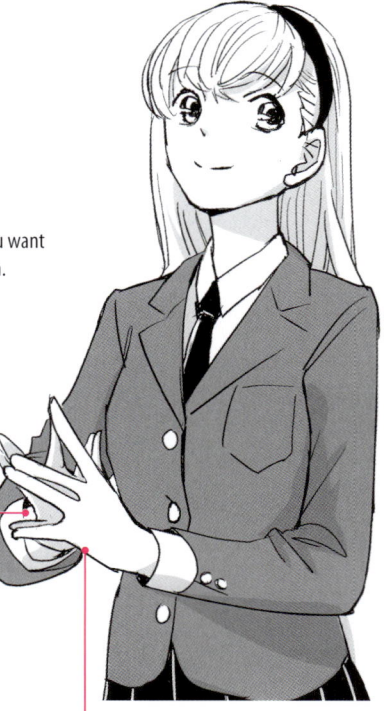

Carefully balance the openness of the fingertips when drawing.

WARMING HANDS WITH BREATH

This pose involves joining the fingertips of both hands in front of the mouth to warm fingers chilled by the cold with breath.

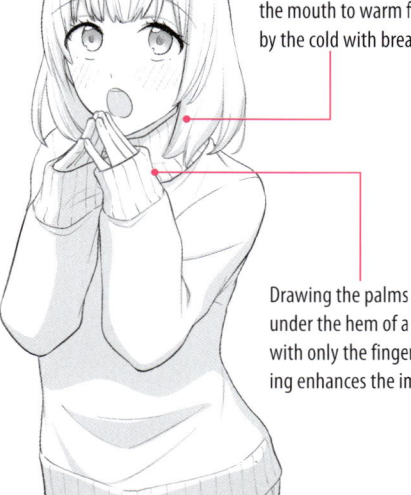

Drawing the palms hidden under the hem of a sweater with only the fingertips showing enhances the image.

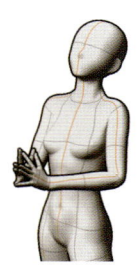

ANGLES
A diagonal angle might be easier for drawing the hands joined in the pose described above.

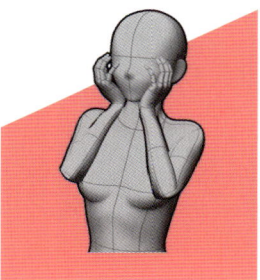

CRADLING THE FACE
Chin in Hands

Cradling the chin and cheeks with both hands along the lines of the face is the very essence of striking a pose, deliberately evoking cutesy charm. It's also suitable for moments when a character is feeling startled or shy.

WHILE TILTING

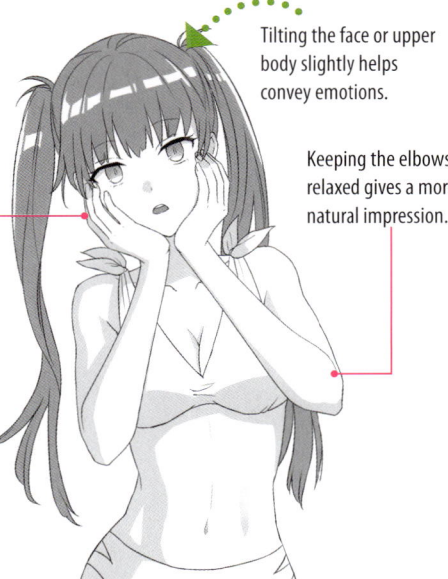

The pose of encircling the chin and cheeks with both hands emphasizes the face, making the character's gaze and expressions stand out more.

Tilting the face or upper body slightly helps convey emotions.

Keeping the elbows relaxed gives a more natural impression.

Closing the arms and tightly pressing the face can convey an atmosphere of savoring happiness.

TIGHTLY PRESSING THE FACE

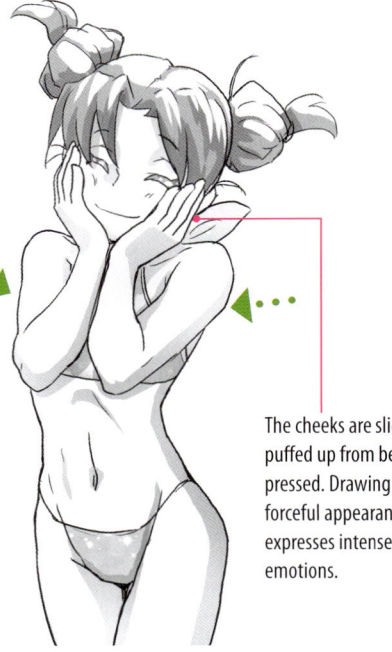

The cheeks are slightly puffed up from being pressed. Drawing this forceful appearance expresses intense emotions.

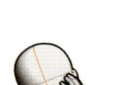
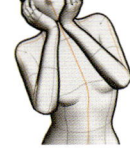

ANGLES
A frontal angle clearly shows the tilted posture.

LIGHTLY CRADLING THE FACE

A pose that lightly cradles the face with both hands. When you want to show the face, position the hands so they do not obscure it.

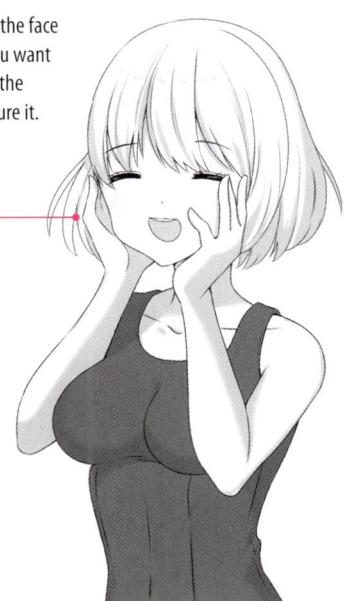

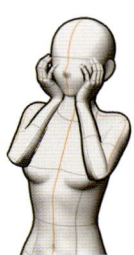

ANGLES
As in the example, a diagonal angle can emphasize various features and expressions.

55

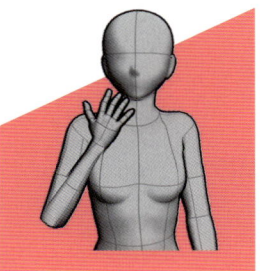

WIDE-EYED, OPEN-MOUTHED SHOCK
Expressing Surprise

Have you ever gasped in surprise? This pose is for moments when a character discovers or witnesses something shocking. Placing one or both hands near the gasping mouth a gasp captures the jolt and equally grabs your viewer's attention.

BASIC SURPRISE

TWO HANDS

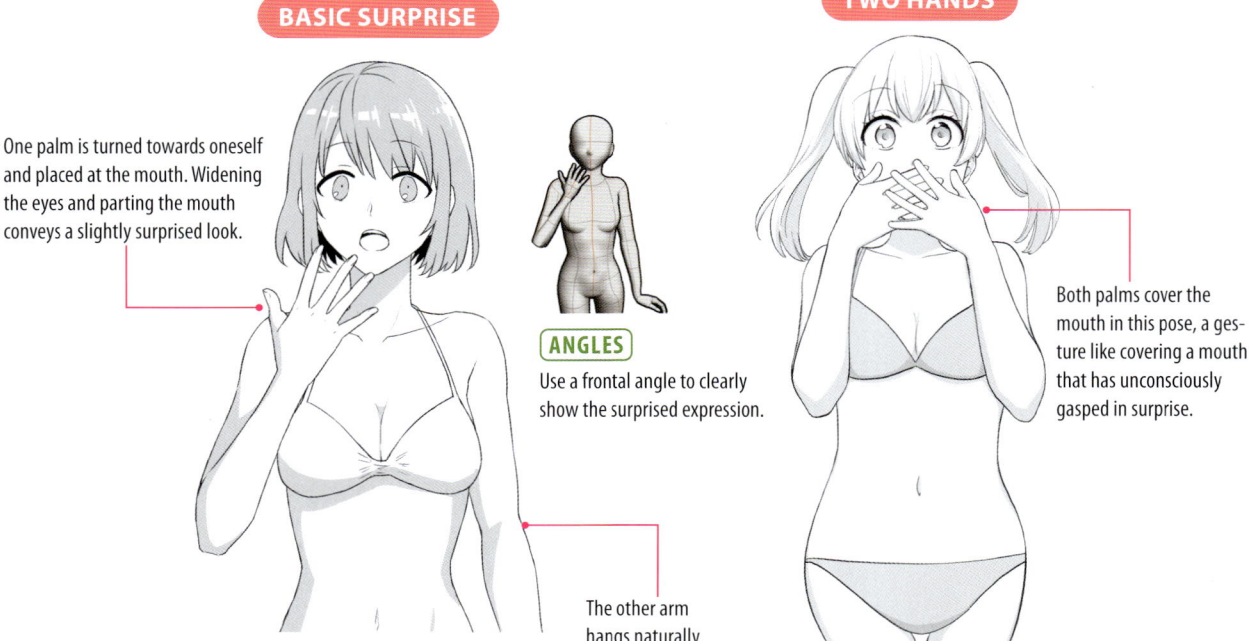

One palm is turned towards oneself and placed at the mouth. Widening the eyes and parting the mouth conveys a slightly surprised look.

ANGLES
Use a frontal angle to clearly show the surprised expression.

The other arm hangs naturally.

Both palms cover the mouth in this pose, a gesture like covering a mouth that has unconsciously gasped in surprise.

COVERING THE MOUTH WITH ONE HAND

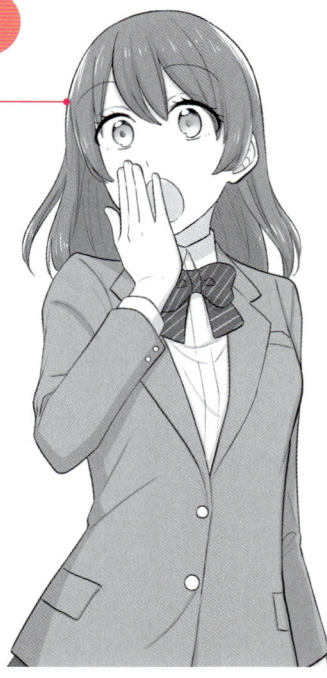

This pose involves covering the mouth with one hand while the eyes are wide open.

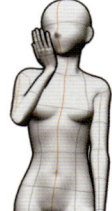

ANGLES
For a dramatic portrayal of surprise, a slightly low-angle view can be effective. Even with the mouth covered by the hand, a diagonal angle allows the degree of mouth opening to be visible.

CROPPING **Expression Conveys It All**

A surprised face, characterized by raised eyebrows and wide-open eyes and mouth, conveys emotion effectively. This can be achieved not only in a bust-up shot but also in a close-up of the face alone. Cropping focused on showing the expression can make the portrayal more impactful.

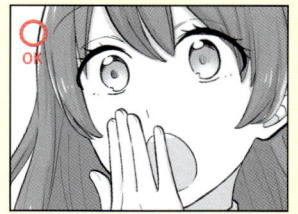

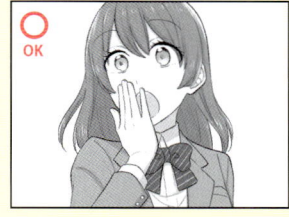

A GESTURE OF SURRENDER
Open Stance

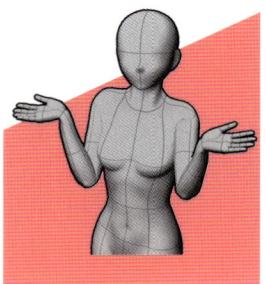

Turning the palms up to signify surrender, defeat or general confusion is a common pose. Exaggerating the gesture can also emphasize a playful situation and can be an effective addition to romance manga.

BOTH HANDS UP

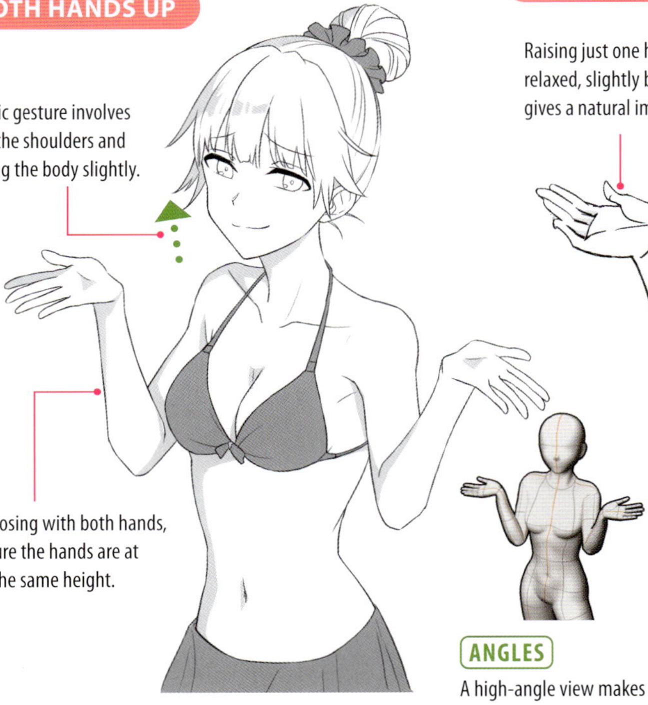

The basic gesture involves raising the shoulders and shrinking the body slightly.

When posing with both hands, make sure the hands are at nearly the same height.

ONE HAND UP

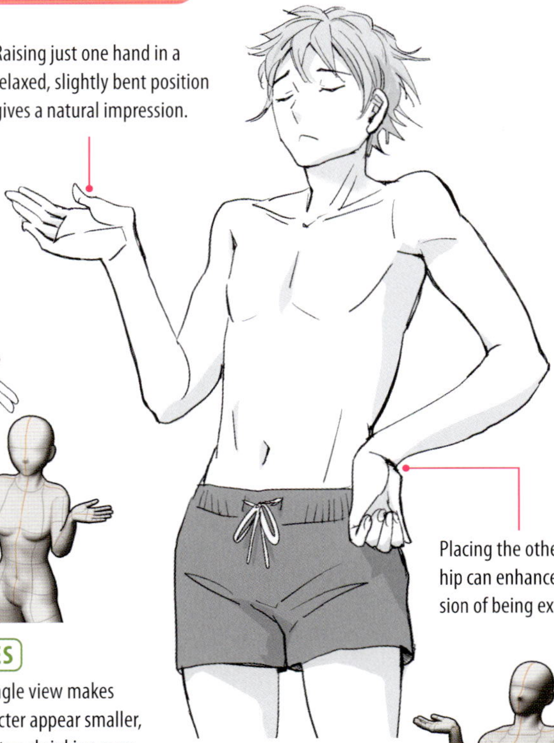

Raising just one hand in a relaxed, slightly bent position gives a natural impression.

Placing the other hand on the hip can enhance the impression of being exasperated.

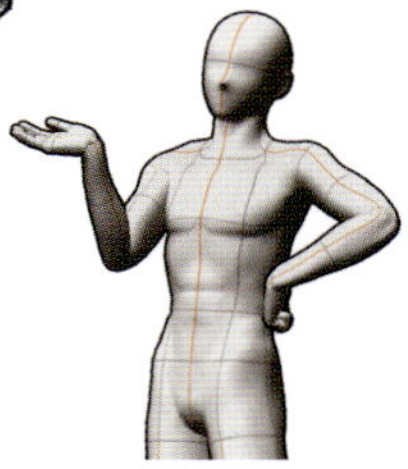

ANGLES
A high-angle view makes the character appear smaller, which suits a shrinking pose.

ARCHING THE UPPER BODY

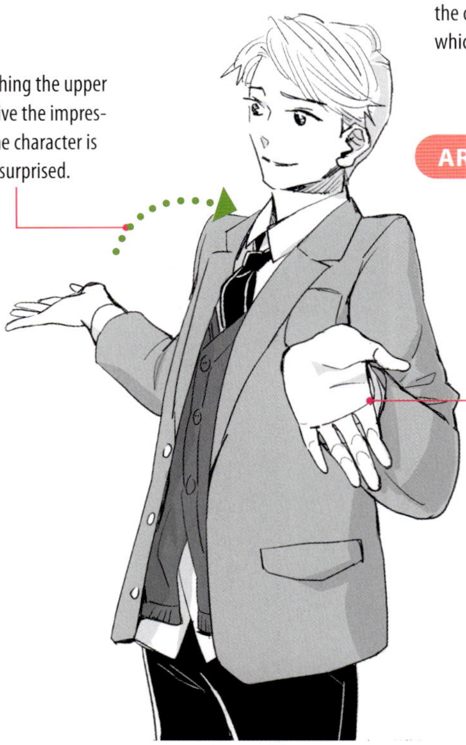

Slightly arching the upper body can give the impression that the character is somewhat surprised.

Showing the palms facing upward can demonstrate an exaggerated reaction.

ANGLES
In scenes where there isn't a significant emotional shift, a casual diagonal angle works well.

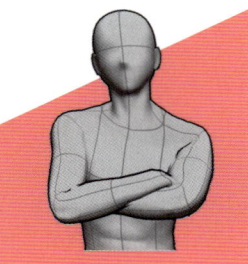

CONFIDENT POSES
Arms Folded 1

Having a character cross both arms in front of the chest can express a state of relaxation or being deep in thought. Alternately, the stance can be used to emphasize a character's arrogant or haughty demeanor.

NATURAL FORM

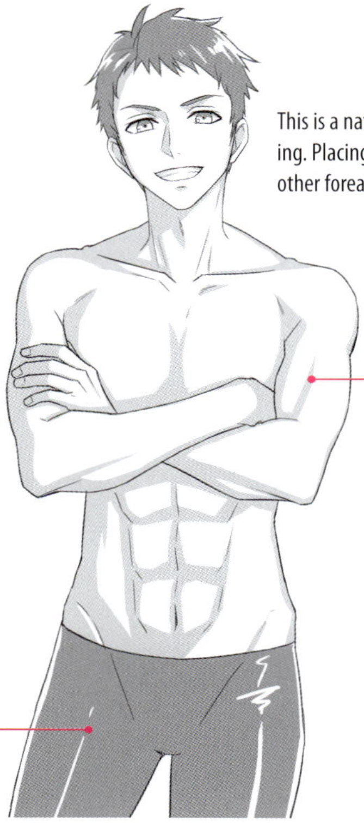

This is a natural form of arms crossing. Placing one arm under the other forearm gives a natural feel.

You can create movement by slightly spreading the legs.

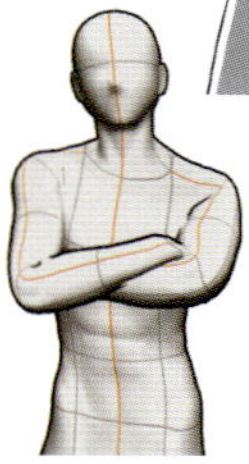

LEANING ASKEW

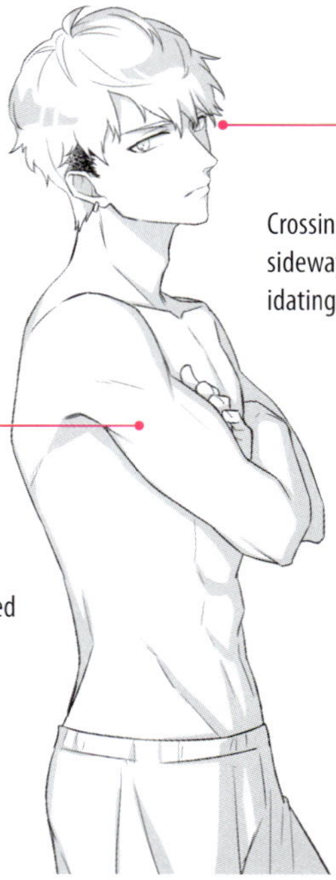

Crossing arms while giving a sideways glance can give an intimidating feel.

The muscles in the crossed forearms should be emphasized.

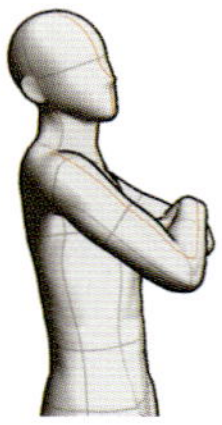

ANGLES
From a side angle, the character can create a glaring expression.

ANGLES
When you want to clearly show the form of the crossed arms, use a frontal angle.

VIEW FROM BEHIND

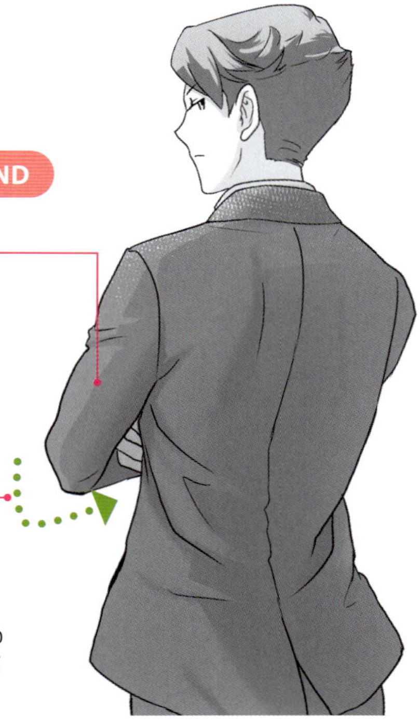

The left arm will appear slightly raised because the right arm is interposed.

From the back, only part of the crossed arms is visible, so pay attention to the angle of the bending elbows.

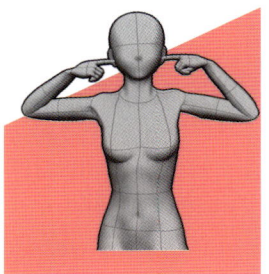

BLOCKING OUT SOUND
Covering the Ears

Either a sound is too loud or a character simply doesn't want to listen. This gesture involves blocking both ear openings with hands to stop an offending sound. A character who's being scolded or annoyed might resort to this active, memorable pose.

COVERING WITH THE INDEX FINGER

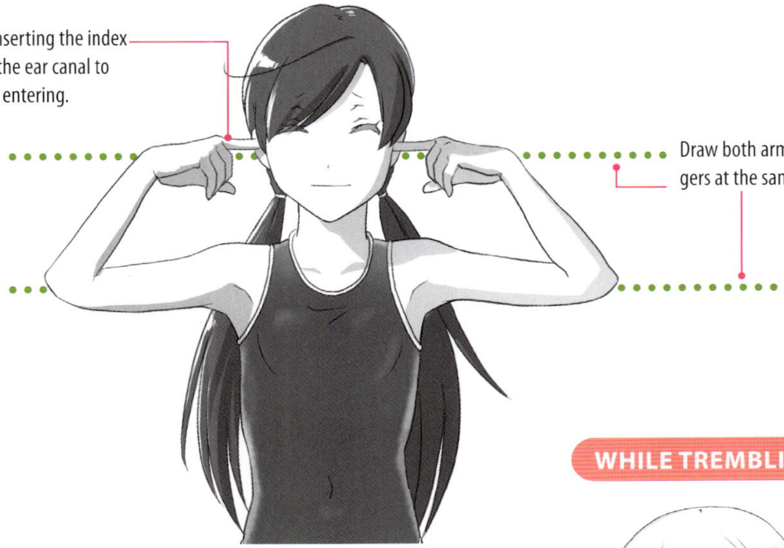

This pose involves inserting the index finger straight into the ear canal to prevent sound from entering.

Draw both arms and fingers at the same height.

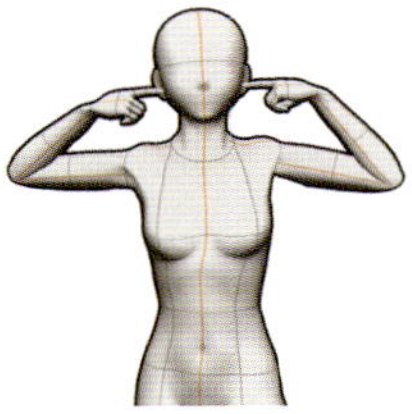

ANGLES
A symmetrical pose viewed from the front angle can give a humorous impression.

WHILE TREMBLING

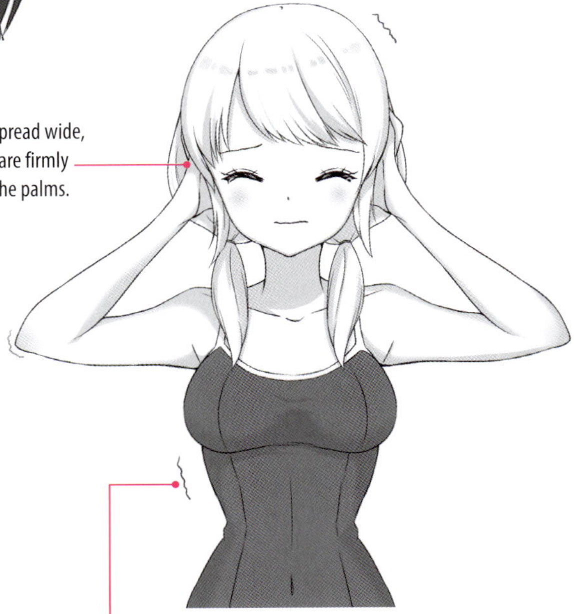

The arms are spread wide, and both ears are firmly covered with the palms.

ENGROSSED

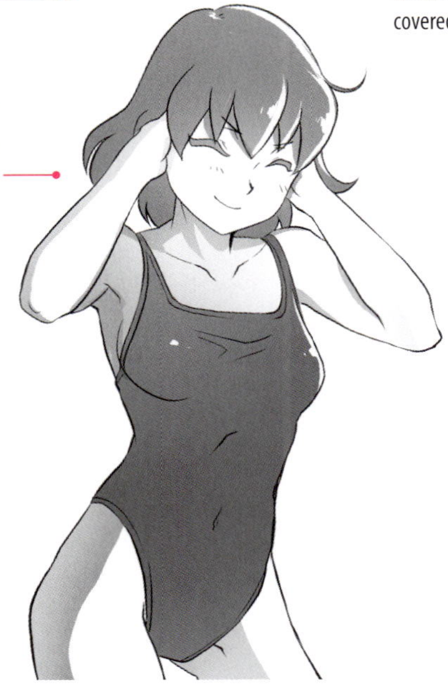

While the arms are slightly closed and the ears are firmly covered with both hands, the expression is cheerful, giving the impression of enjoying being engrossed.

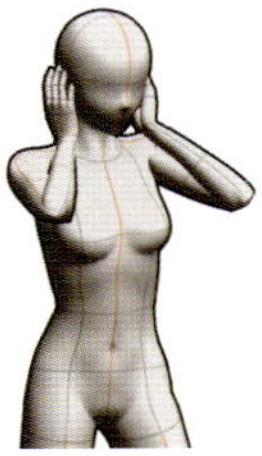

ANGLES
An angle slightly from above and diagonal clearly shows the hands covering the ears.

Drawing the body trembling can be a rather exaggerated expression. It conveys extreme fear or anxiety.

59

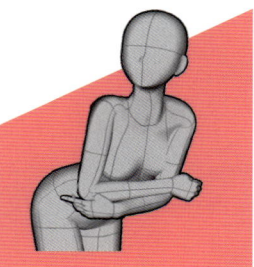

MAKING THE POSE LOOK NATURAL
Arms Folded 2

This is a pose used to capture a casual, offhand moment as suggested by the languid, relaxed positioning of the upper body. Using slight variations changes the mood and impression of the illustration.

HOLDING WITH BOTH ARMS

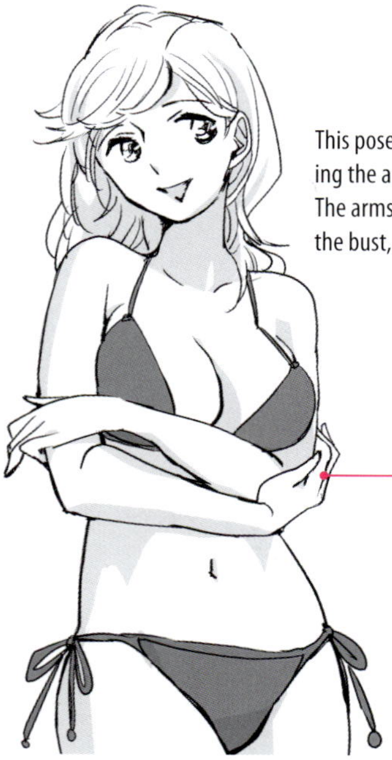

This pose involves lightly crossing the arms under the bust. The arms create a frame around the bust, emphasizing it.

LEANING FORWARD

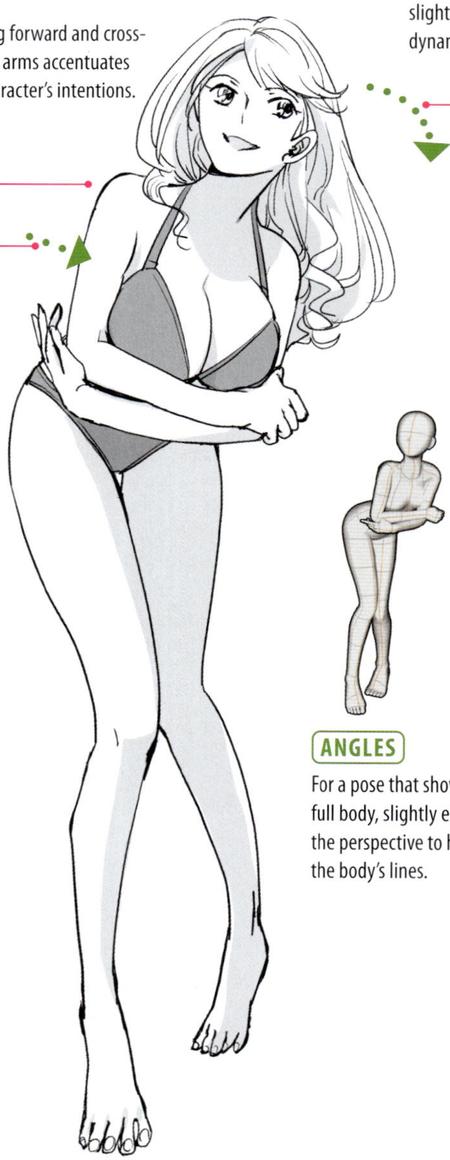

Leaning forward and crossing the arms accentuates the character's intentions.

Tilt the upper body slightly to create a dynamic pose.

The pose adds depth, dimension and complexity.

ANGLES

For a pose that shows the full body, slightly elevate the perspective to highlight the body's lines.

CROSSING ONE ARM

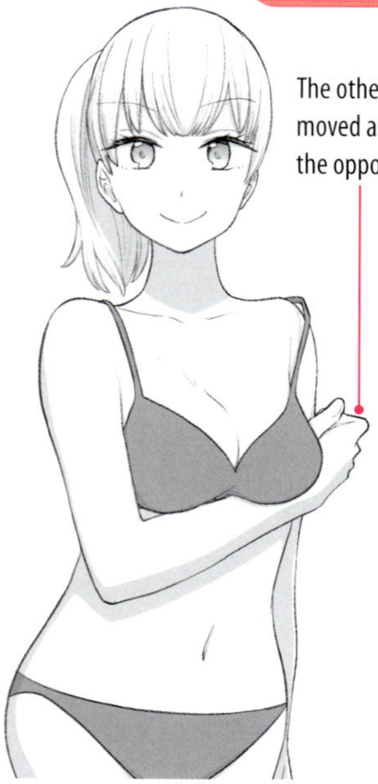

The other arm is moved as if grabbing the opposite arm.

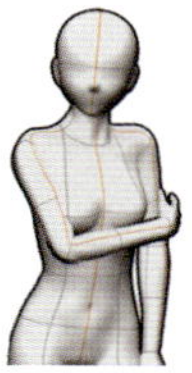

ANGLES

A diagonal angle allows the line of the arm to be accentuated.

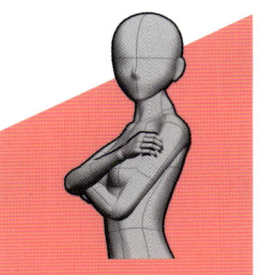

A PROTECTIVE SENTIMENT
Self-Embrace

Here, the body is hugged or cradled with one's own arms. The self-embrace can be used to generate warmth from the cold or to offer comfort during a vulnerable moment or trying time.

AVERTING THE GAZE

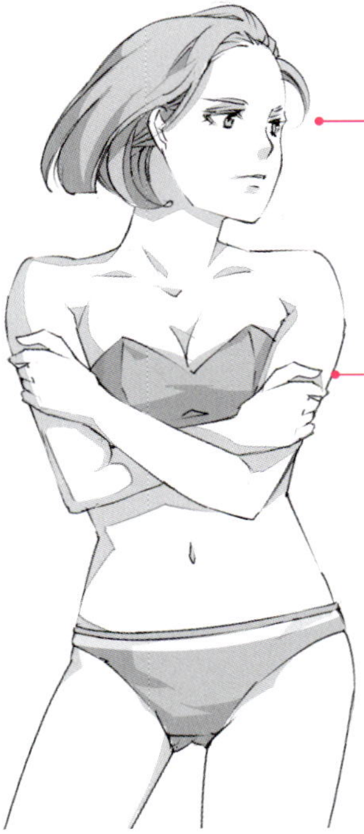

Turning sideways and deliberately averting the gaze expresses a contemplative mood.

Changing the position of the hands that are pressing on the upper arms adds a sense of movement.

LOOKING BACK

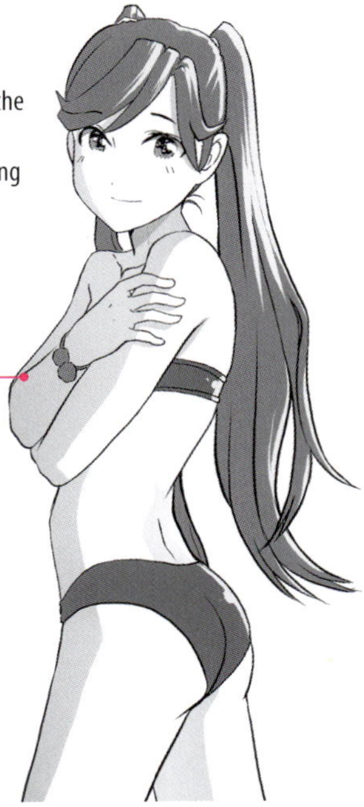

While the body faces sideways, the gaze directed at the camera makes it appear as though the arms are covering and shielding the chest.

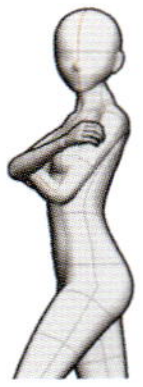

ANGLES
Create a scene with a side angle where the pose appears to hide the chest.

SHOWING THE BACK

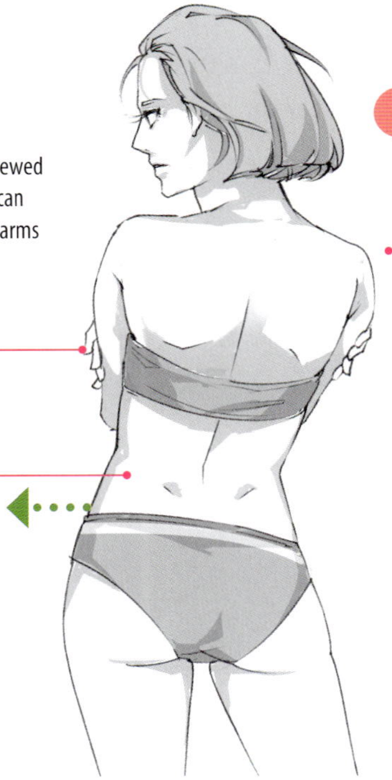

In a self-embrace viewed from the back, you can slightly see the forearms and fingertips.

A pose showing the back is suitable for conveying a character's reticent psychology or sadness.

Shifting the waist sideways emphasizes the waistline.

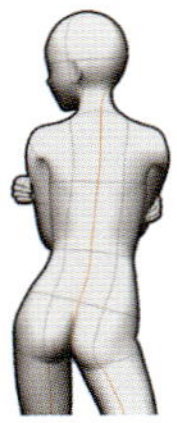

ANGLES
From a rear angle, the arms are mostly hidden, but the position of the arms can be inferred from the way the sides are closed.

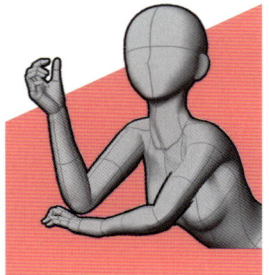

PLAYFUL POSES
Playing with Hair

When characters play with their hair while listening absentmindedly to someone or when they have nothing else to do, it appears natural if portrayed as an unconscious action. Wrap the hair around a finger as a visually compelling variation.

PLAYING WITH HAIR

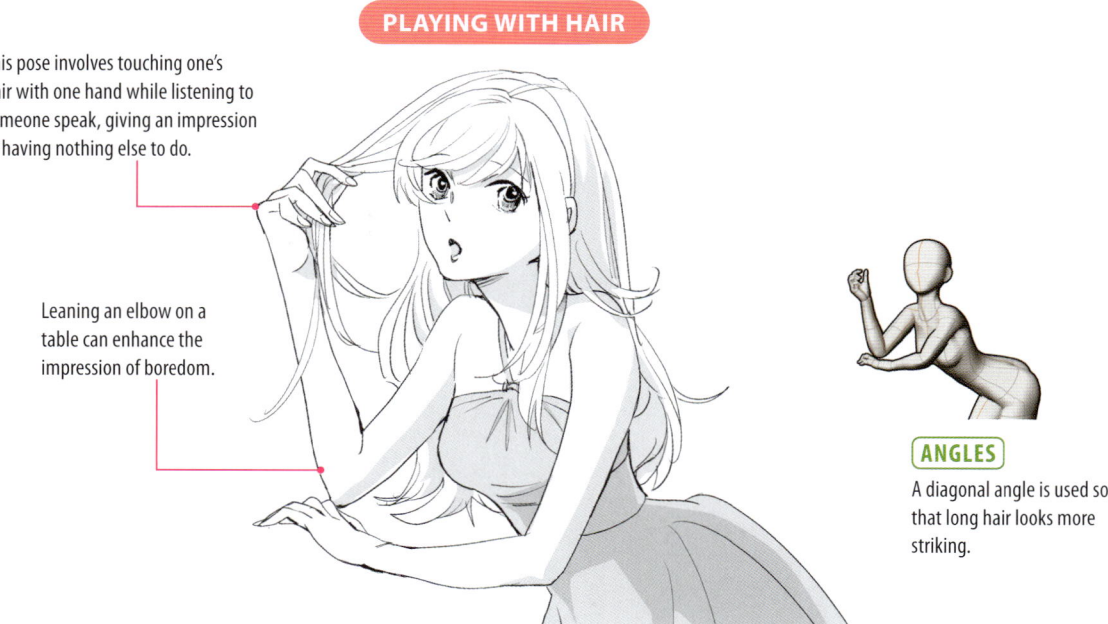

This pose involves touching one's hair with one hand while listening to someone speak, giving an impression of having nothing else to do.

Leaning an elbow on a table can enhance the impression of boredom.

ANGLES
A diagonal angle is used so that long hair looks more striking.

TWIRLING HAIR AROUND A FINGER

Playing with hair by twirling it around a finger suits characters with curly or wavy hair.

GRABBING AND MAKING PIGTAILS

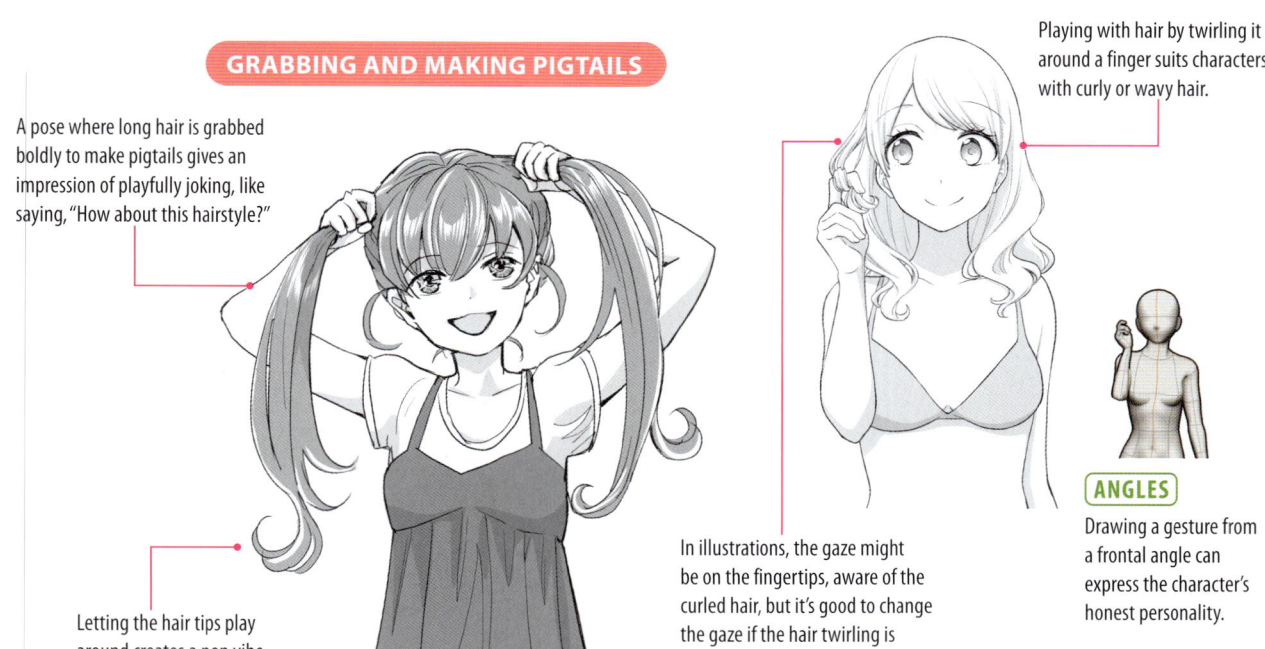

A pose where long hair is grabbed boldly to make pigtails gives an impression of playfully joking, like saying, "How about this hairstyle?"

Letting the hair tips play around creates a pop vibe.

In illustrations, the gaze might be on the fingertips, aware of the curled hair, but it's good to change the gaze if the hair twirling is meant to be unconscious.

ANGLES
Drawing a gesture from a frontal angle can express the character's honest personality.

COMMON GESTURES

Tucking Hair Behind the Ears

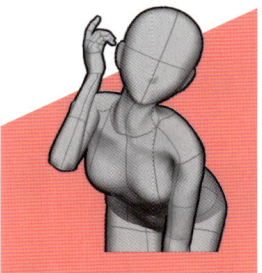

Tucking hair behind the ear is a pose common in everyday scenes. By bringing the hand near the ear, it draws the viewer's gaze to the face and enhances the impression of the expression. The action is typically performed with the index finger.

IN A PHOTOGENIC STYLE

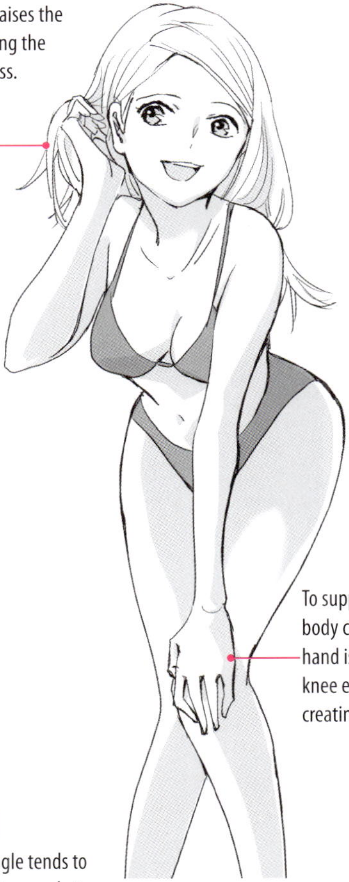

The hand naturally raises the hair to the ear, making the pose appear effortless.

To support the leaning upper body comfortably, the left hand is placed on the left knee extended forward, creating a relaxed posture.

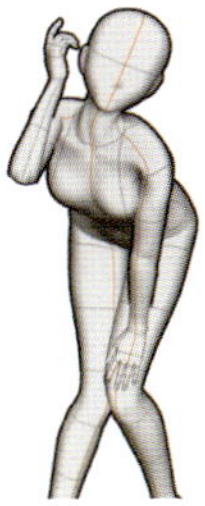

ANGLES

The frontal angle tends to be flat, but this pose, being in a leaning position, is three-dimensional, avoiding monotony.

SHOWING THE PROFILE

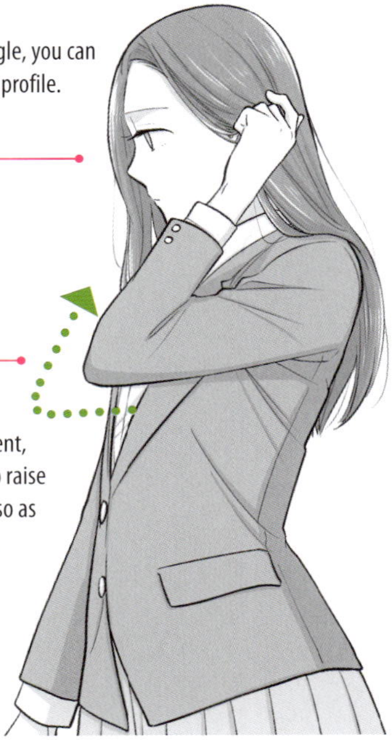

From a side angle, you can emphasize the profile.

The arm is deeply bent, but be careful not to raise the elbow too high so as not to hide the face.

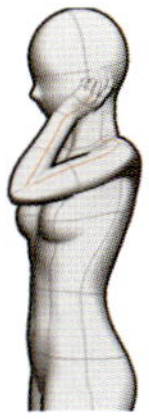

ANGLES

This angle clearly shows the pose of the arm tucking the hair behind the ear.

BLOWN BY THE WIND

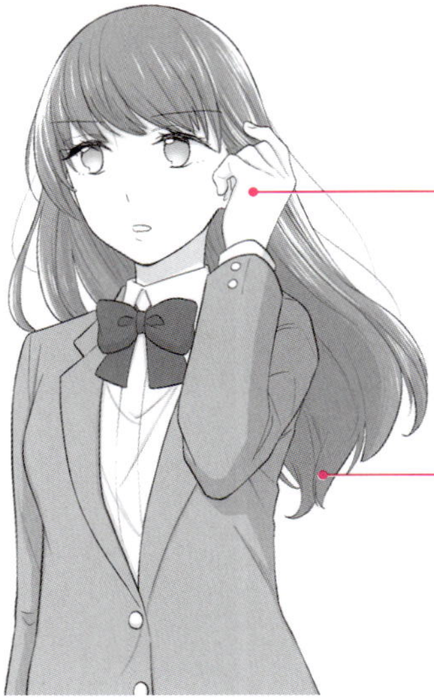

From a diagonal angle, the side of the hand is visible from the little finger side.

Creating a sense of hair being blown by the wind adds movement to the illustration.

EVERYDAY ACTIONS
Touching the Hair

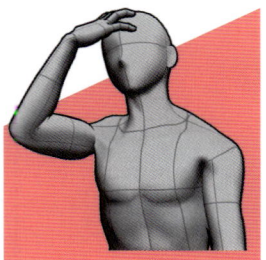

Sweeping hair up or back can suggest a casual, relaxed atmosphere, depending on the gaze and the way the arm is raised. Adjusting the hand position according to the thickness of the hair is advisable.

CASUALLY

When sweeping up short hair, position the hand above the forehead.

Separate the little finger slightly from the other fingers to avoid a monotonous alignment of fingers.

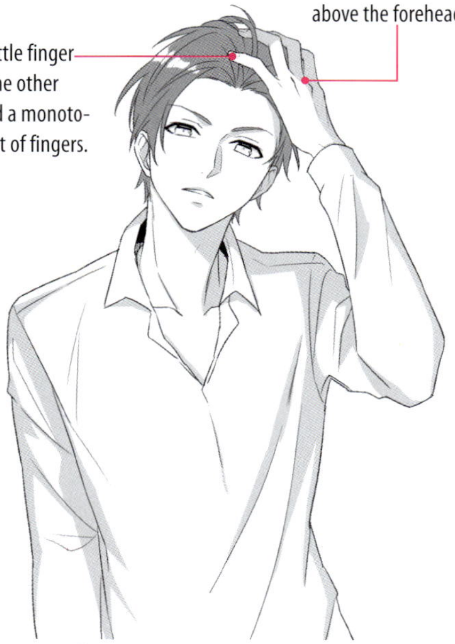

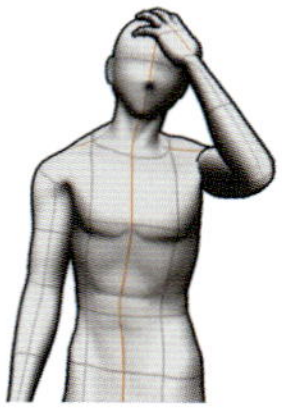

WILDLY

Allowing some hair to peek through the fingers makes the act of tousling the hair with the fingers appear more rugged and wild.

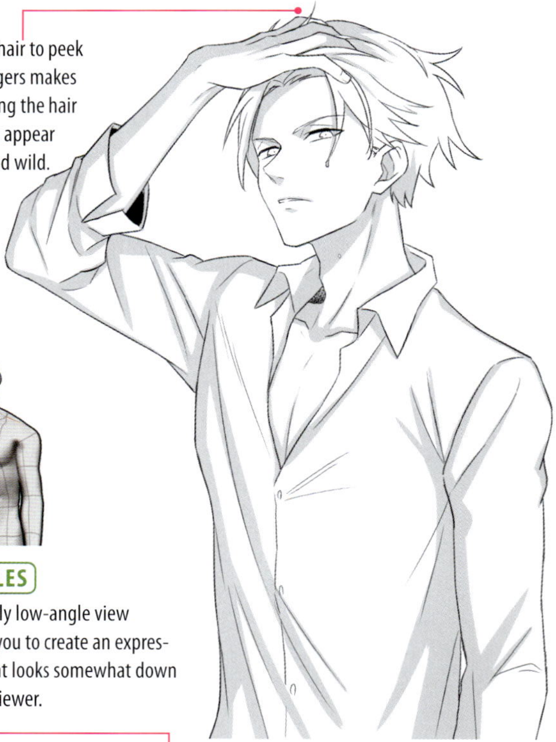

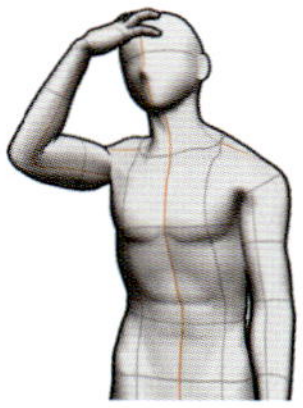

ANGLES

A slightly low-angle view allows you to create an expression that looks somewhat down at the viewer.

ANGLES

From a frontal angle, direct eye contact and the expression's impact become stronger.

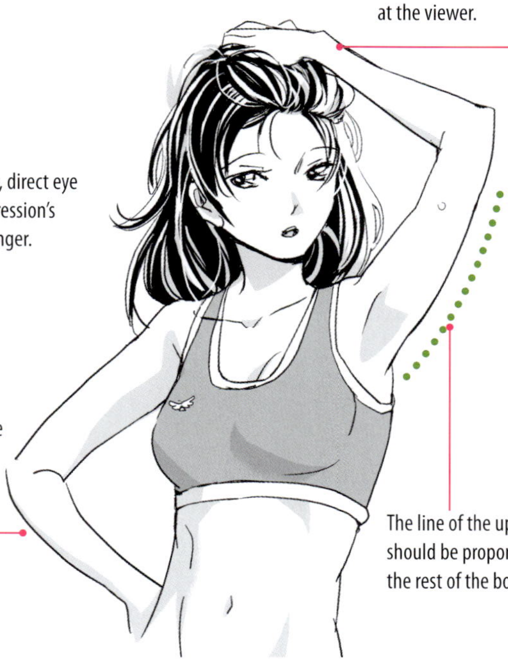

Lift the arm that sweeps the hair up high, and place the other arm on the hip to balance the posture of both arms.

For long hair, positioning the sweeping hand higher than for short hair makes the expression more realistic.

SWEEPING LONG HAIR UP

The line of the upper arm should be proportional to the rest of the body.

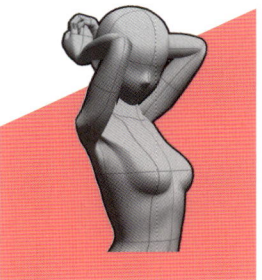

GESTURE OF TYING A PONYTAIL
Tying Back Hair

This pose is typicaly best shown from a side angle, which highlights the lines of the raised arms and the curve from the back to the buttocks.

ARMS RAISED

The pose of tying hair at the back results in an arched upper body and a posture that thrusts the chest forward.

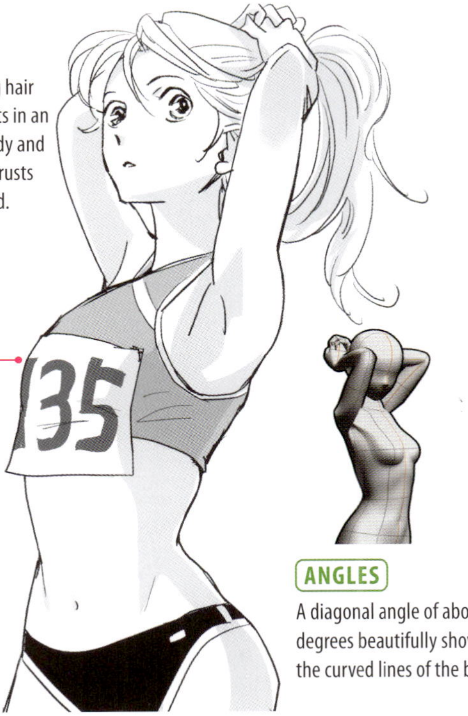

ANGLES
A diagonal angle of about 45 degrees beautifully showcases the curved lines of the body.

HOLDING THE HAIR TIE IN MOUTH

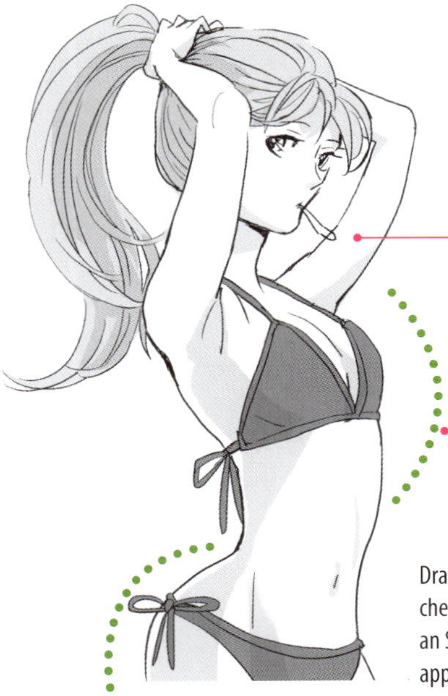

Holding a hair tie in the mouth can add a sense of relatability.

Drawing the lines of the chest and buttocks to form an S-shape makes the figure appear more elegant.

BACK VIEW OF TYING HAIR

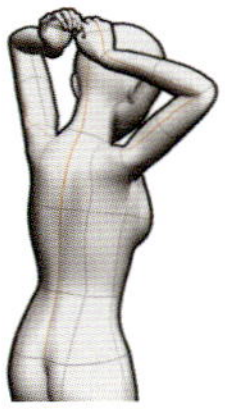

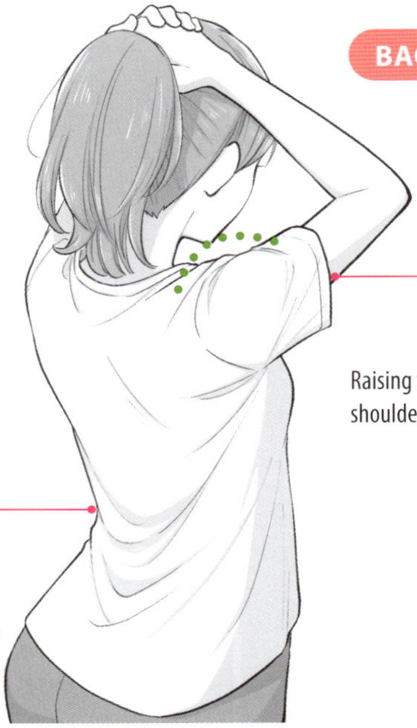

Raising the arms causes the shoulders to lift.

ANGLES
The angle from behind can convey the gesture of tying the hair and the beauty of the nape of the neck.

As the back is emphasized, the waistline should be drawn accurately.

Covering the Face

SEEN THROUGH SPLAYED FINGERS

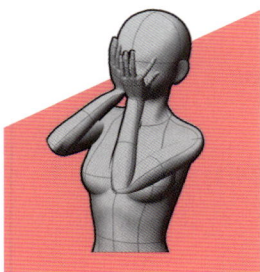

There are various situations when characters cover their faces: a moment of embarrasement or seeing something scary. Adjust the spacing between the fingers while keeping an eye on the balance of the expression visible through the gaps.

MYSTERIOUSLY

This pose covers the face with the hands like a mask, suitable for a mysterious character.

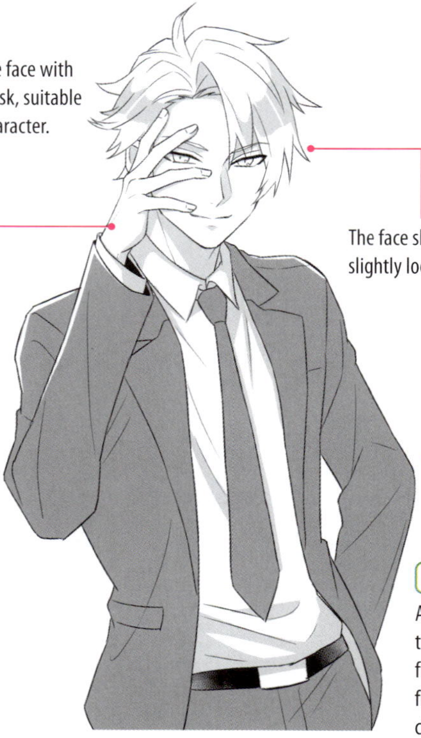

The face should be drawn slightly looking downwards.

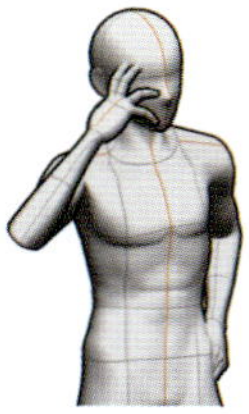

ANGLES

An angle slightly diagonal to the body rather than from the front is more fitting for a mysterious character.

EMBARRASSING MOMENT

Even while covering the face with both hands, troubled eyes and blushing cheeks are visible through the gaps between the fingers. This pose reflects embarrassment by covering the face.

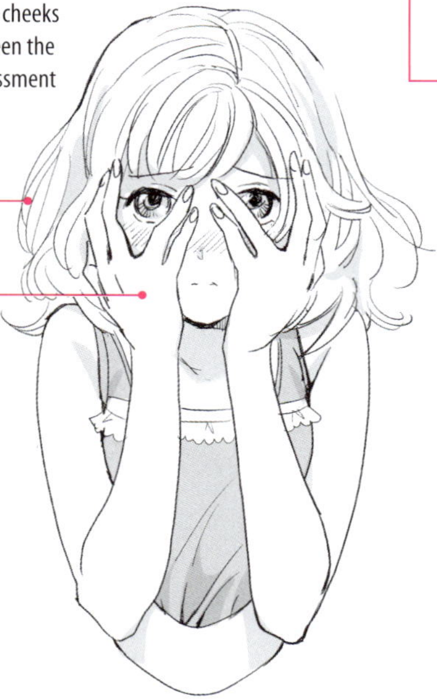

Keep the spacing between the fingers on both sides nearly the same to maintain balance.

CURIOSITY DESPITE FEAR

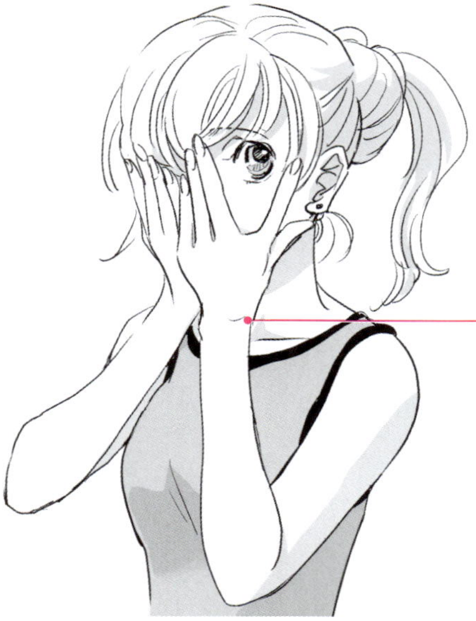

The eyes peeking through the fingers while covering the face with both hands convey the sentiment of wanting to see despite it being hard to look directly.

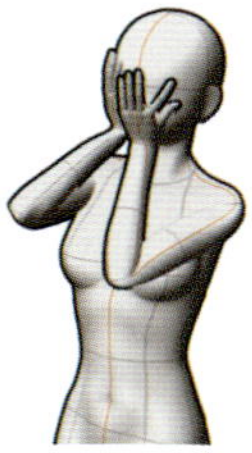

ANGLES

An angle where the body is positioned diagonally enhances the portrayal of being scared.

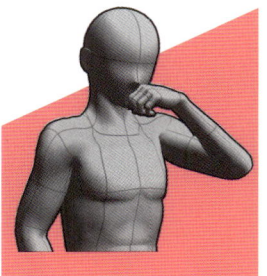

WIPING THE LIPS

Fingers Near the Mouth

Wiping the mouth certainly works for food-related scenes; it's a motion that can easily emphasize a character's charm or appeal. Alternately, it's a powerful gesture that shows strength of resolve or the making of a critical decision.

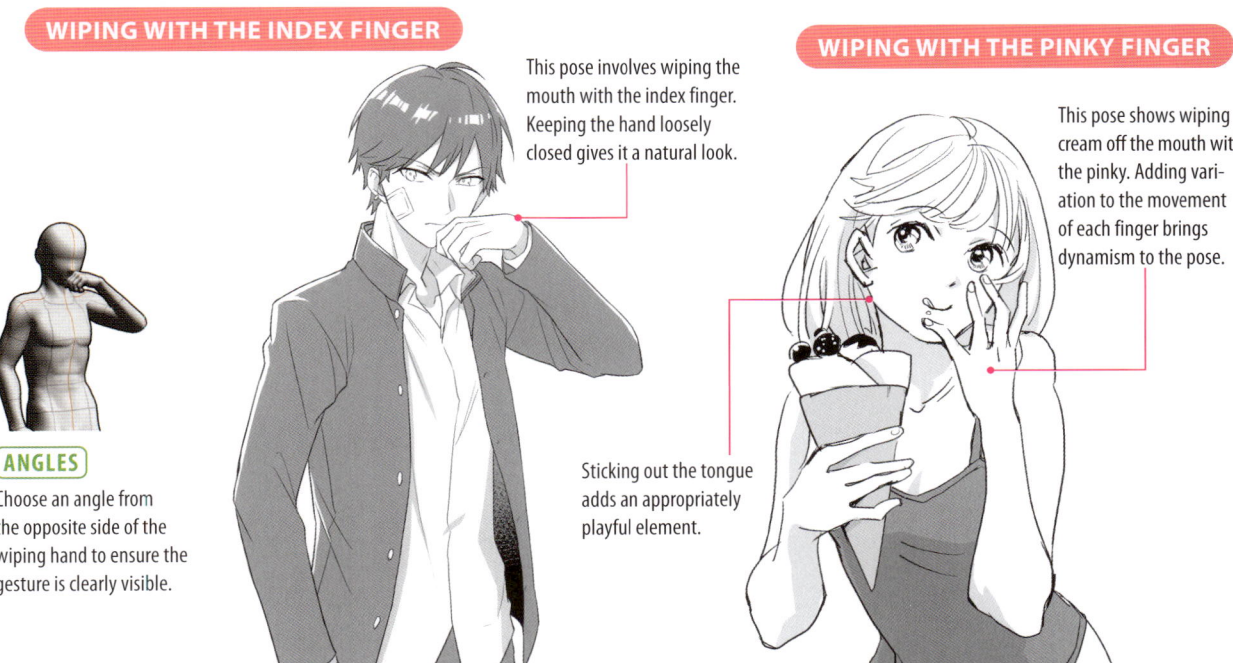

WIPING WITH THE INDEX FINGER

This pose involves wiping the mouth with the index finger. Keeping the hand loosely closed gives it a natural look.

ANGLES
Choose an angle from the opposite side of the wiping hand to ensure the gesture is clearly visible.

WIPING WITH THE PINKY FINGER

This pose shows wiping cream off the mouth with the pinky. Adding variation to the movement of each finger brings dynamism to the pose.

Sticking out the tongue adds an appropriately playful element.

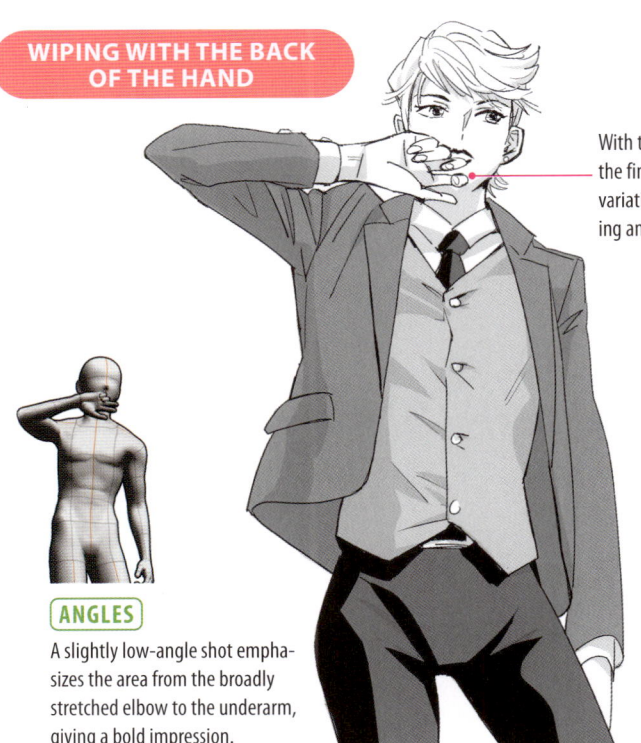

WIPING WITH THE BACK OF THE HAND

With the palm facing outwards, the fingertips are visible, adding variation to each finger's bending and stretching.

ANGLES
A slightly low-angle shot emphasizes the area from the broadly stretched elbow to the underarm, giving a bold impression.

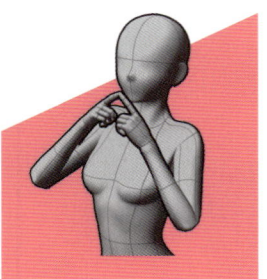

SULKING, BORED OR IN NEED OF A FAVOR
Index Fingers Pointed

Is your character bored, sulking or seeking a huge favor from a friend? Then this might be the pose you're after! Lightly touching, the fingertips should be slightly bent rather than straight to avoid a stiff impression.

ASKING A FAVOR

The index fingers of both hands are touching. Small movements using just the fingers add specificity and detail to the scene.

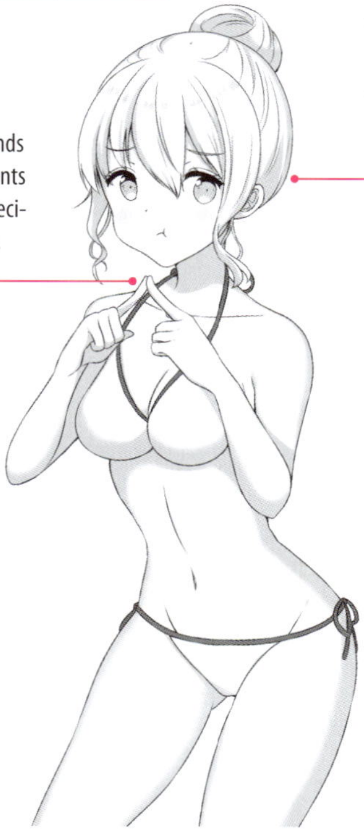

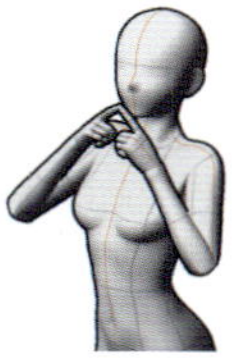

The gaze is directed at the person the character wants to make a request to.

ANGLES
A diagonal, orthodox angle allows for a clear view of the arm's shape.

WRITING ON THE GROUND

The gesture of writing something on the ground with a finger is a typical bored pose.

The gaze is directed toward the ground.

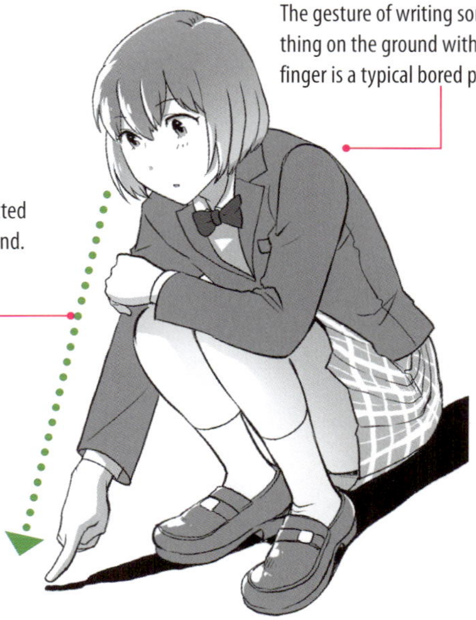

LOOKING UP WHILE SULKING

The fingertips meet in the center of the body, creating a symmetrical pose.

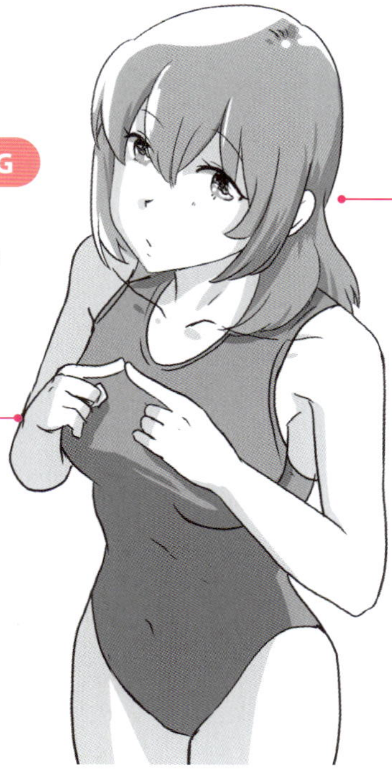

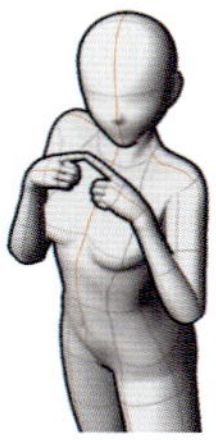

A sulking pose with an upward gaze conveys an atmosphere of wanting to say something.

ANGLES
A low-angle shot makes the face look downward, expressing a downhearted impression.

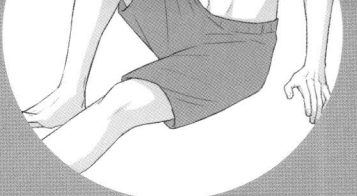
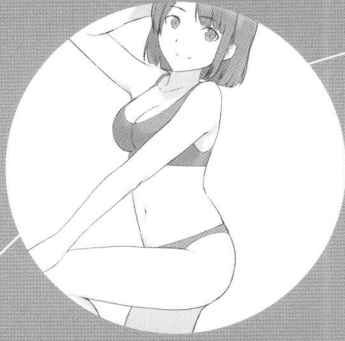
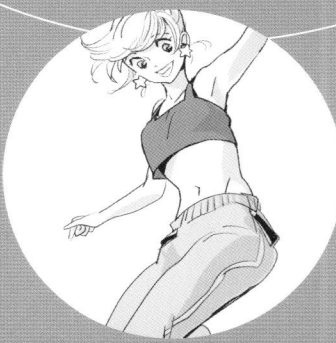
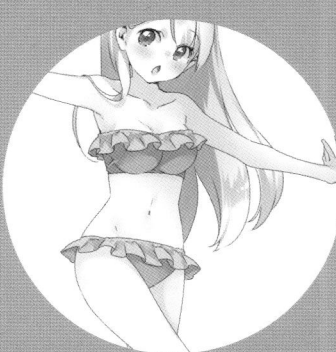
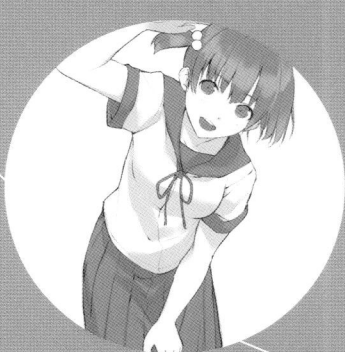

PART 3

Dynamic Full-Body Movements

Now we'll focus on poses that use the whole body.

Standing
Arms Crossed, Legs Apart
Looking Back
Raising the Arms
Bending Down
Standing on One Leg
Kneeling
Down on One Knee
Crouching
Lying on the Back
Arching Back
Lying on the Stomach
Lying on the Side
Fetal Position
Sitting Crosslegged
Squatting
Sitting Down
Crossing Legs
Sitting to the Side
Kneeling, Viewed from
 Above

Holding the Legs
Extending the Legs
One Knee Raised
Walking
Running
Slipping
Jumping
Landing
Dancing
Suspended in Air
Sparring
Boxing
Kicking
Leaning Against a Wall
Stretching
Working Out
Waking Up
Doing Ballet
Bodybuilder's Pose

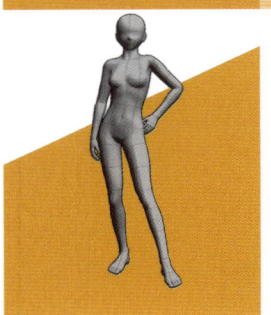

BASIC POSES
Standing

Placing the weight on one leg and resting a hand on the hip yields a strong standing posture, as commonly seen in fashion models. It's good to use when you want to clearly display the whole body or when you want to highlight the lines of the body.

SPREAD THE LEGS

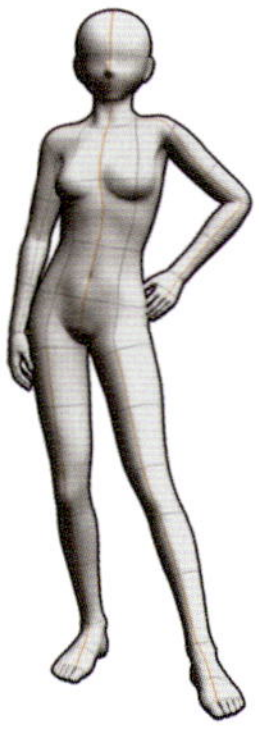

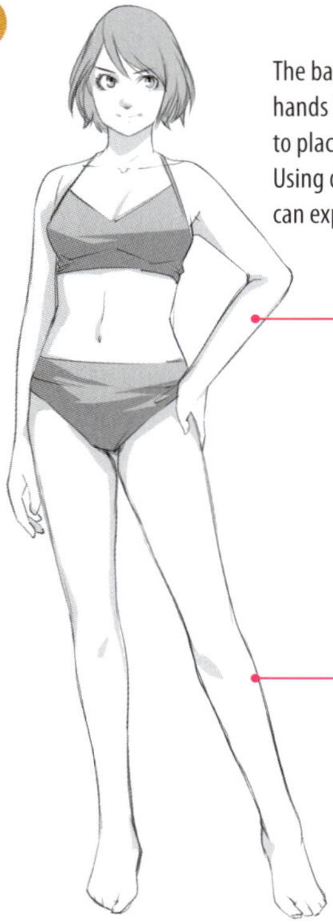

The basic form is to let the hands hang naturally or to place them on the hips. Using different hand poses can expand the variations.

EMPHASIZE THE BODY LINE

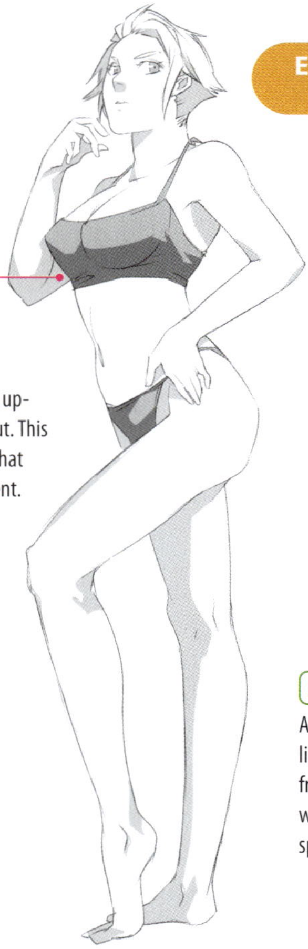

The posture should be upright with the chest out. This pose suits characters that are strong and confident.

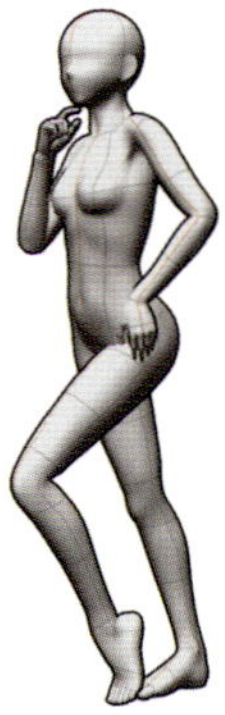

ANGLES
The basic frontal angle can clearly convey the silhouette of the character.

It's fundamental to slightly advance one leg to show the line of the legs.

ANGLES
A diagonal angle shows the body lines that are difficult to detect from the front. It's recommended when you want to emphasize specific areas of the body.

CROSS THE LEGS

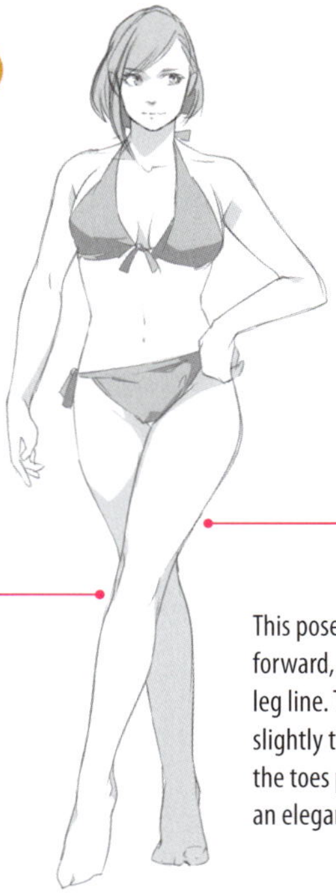

A model stance with crossed legs can give a more dynamic impression than a stance with legs apart.

This pose, with one leg forward, emphasizes the leg line. The legs should be slightly turned inward, with the toes pointed outward for an elegant look.

CROPPING — Showing Proportions

The basic composition for a model stance shows the entire proportion without cropping. However, if you need to make the character appear larger or when cropping is necessary, it is recommended to cut above the knees.

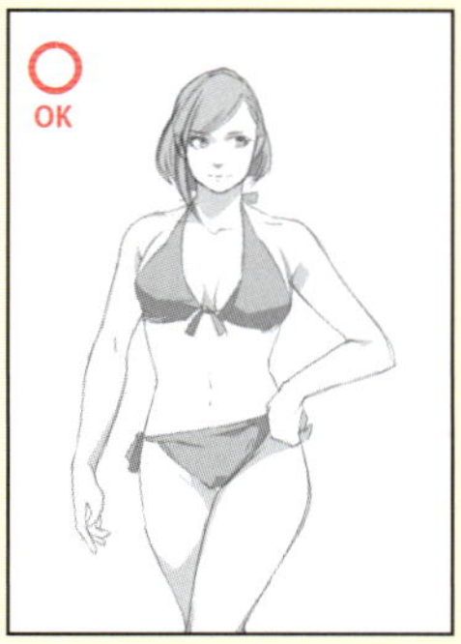

OK

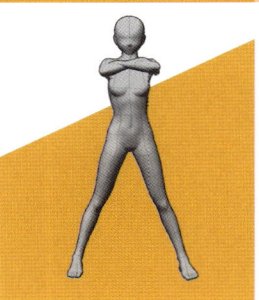

EXPRESSING STRENGTH WITH SIMPLE POSES

Arms Crossed, Legs Apart

This pose is used to emphasize strength and size. This involves spreading the legs, crossing the arms to showcase the arm muscles or placing the hands on the hips and puffing out the chest. Maintaining a confident facial expression is also crucial.

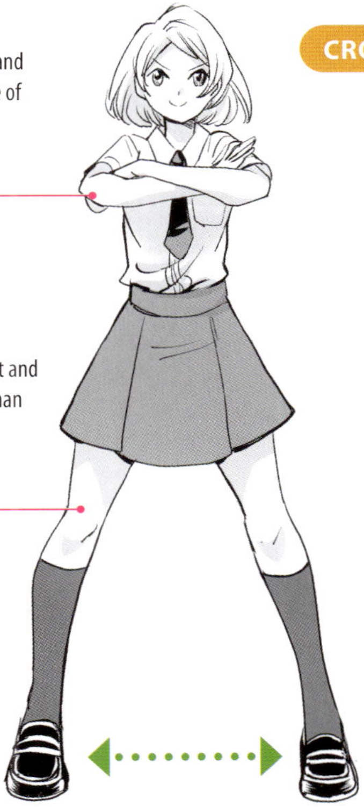

Crossing arms suits this pose. By crossing the arms slightly higher and stretching the elbows out, a sense of exertion is suggested.

CROSSING ARMS

Keep the legs straight and spread them wider than the shoulders.

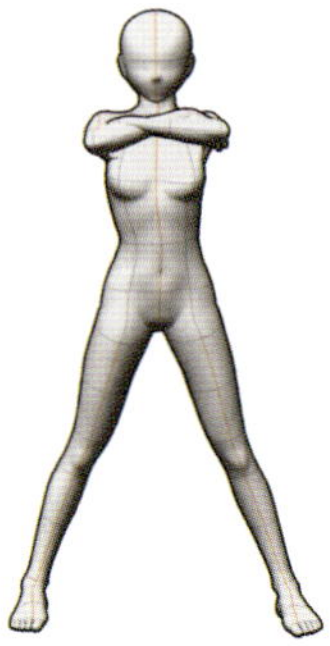

ANGLES

If you want a more imposing stance, a frontal angle works best. This straightforward perspective suggests confidence.

CROSSING ARMS BELOW THE CHEST

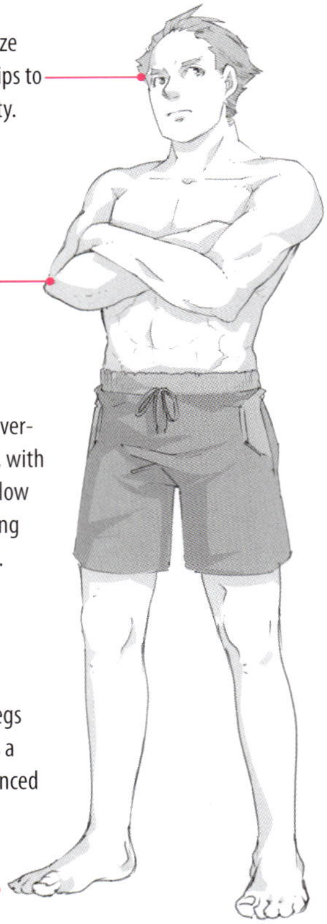

Sharpen the gaze and purse the lips to convey authority.

This is a relaxed version of the pose, with arms crossed below the chest, creating a natural stance.

Spreading the legs outward creates a solid, more balanced impression.

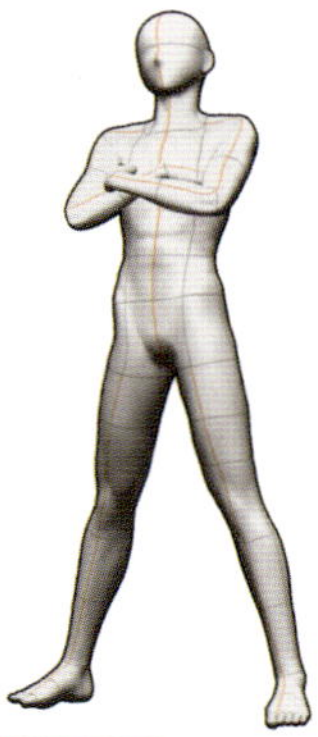

HANDS ON HIPS

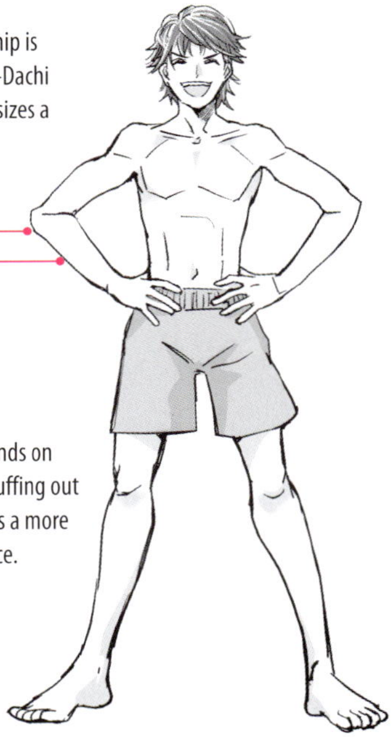

Placing a hand on the hip is also classic in the Nioh-Dachi pose. It further emphasizes a pompous impression.

Putting the hands on the hips and puffing out the chest yields a more imposing stance.

ANGLES

Choose a diagonal angle to show off the body line. If you want to portray a character with strong power, choose a low-angle shot to make the subject appear larger.

71

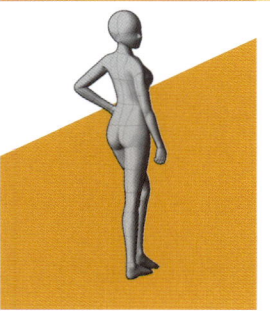

VERSATILE POSES
Looking Back

The pose of looking back adds movement and showcases the body's lines. By changing the angle, you can dramatically emphasize areas you want to highlight, such as the buttocks, waist and legs, with a sense of dynamism.

BASIC POSE

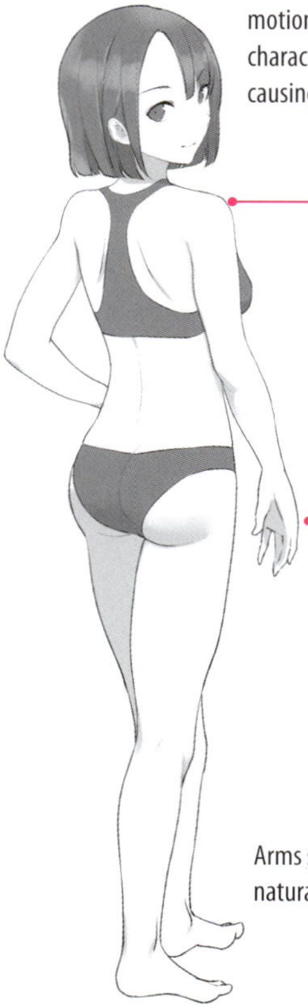

The basic pose involves a motion as if someone calls the character's name from behind, causing her to turn around.

Arms should hang naturally by the sides.

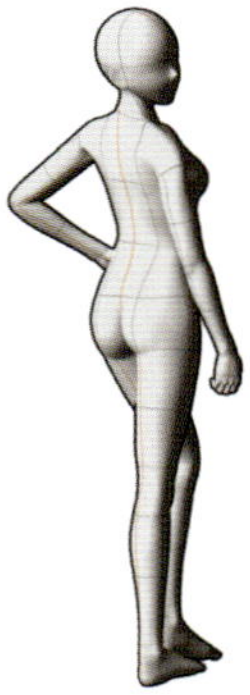

ANGLES
An angle slightly from the side rather than directly from behind makes it easier to create a composition that shows the face.

TURNING TO THE SIDE

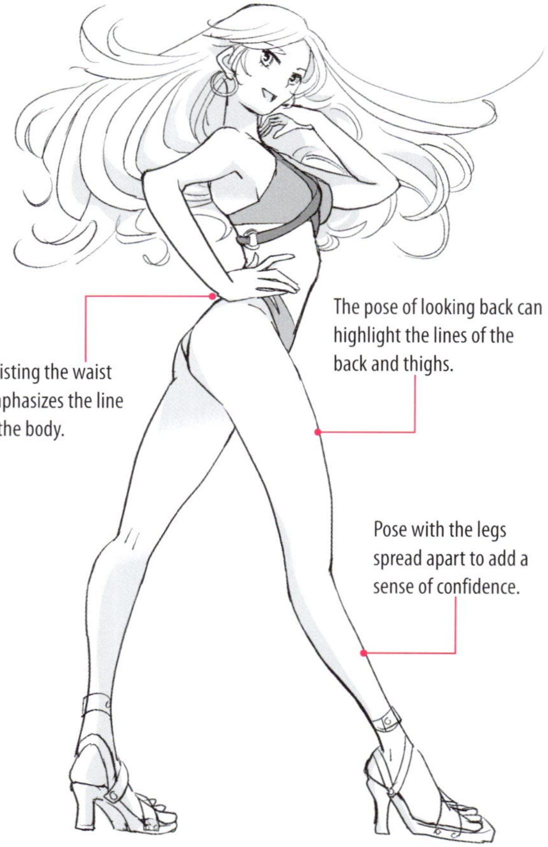

Twisting the waist emphasizes the line of the body.

The pose of looking back can highlight the lines of the back and thighs.

Pose with the legs spread apart to add a sense of confidence.

EMPHASIZING THE BUTTOCKS

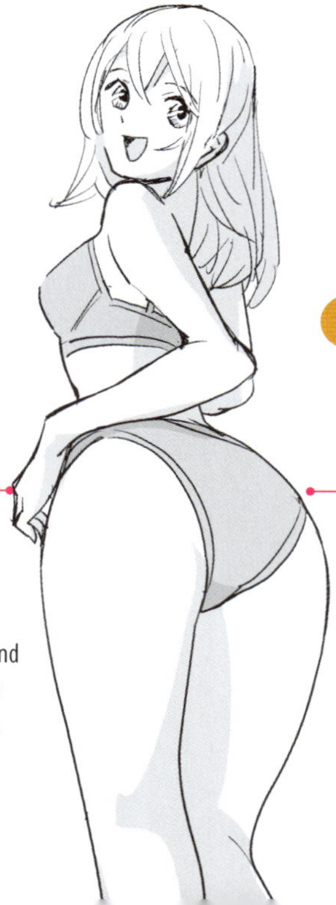

Placing a hand around the waist makes the pose more dynamic.

With this perspective, be careful to create realistic proportions.

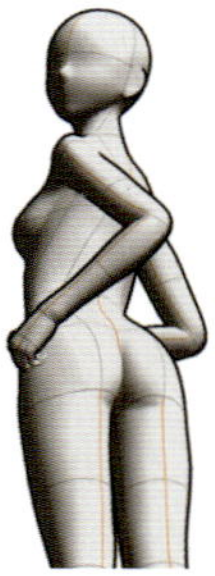

ANGLES
An angle from below can emphasize power or strength.

72

TURNING ONLY THE FACE

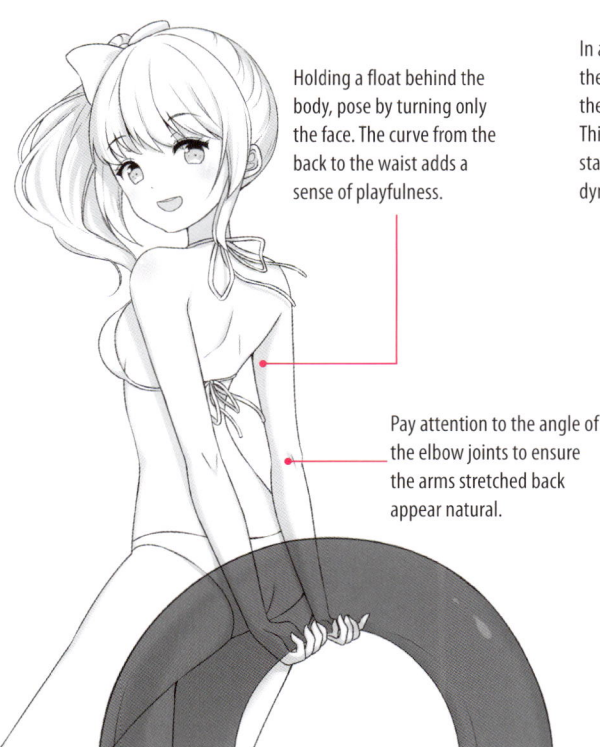

Holding a float behind the body, pose by turning only the face. The curve from the back to the waist adds a sense of playfulness.

Pay attention to the angle of the elbow joints to ensure the arms stretched back appear natural.

TURNING FROM A LYING POSITION

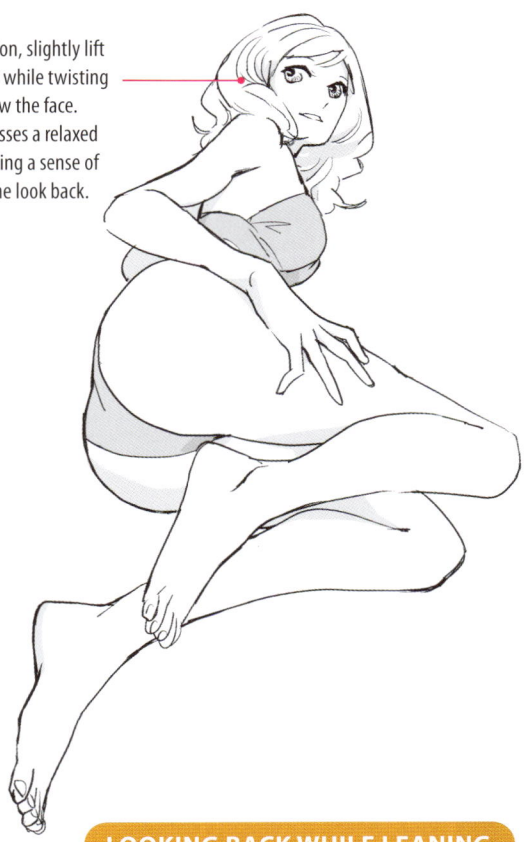

In a lying position, slightly lift the upper body while twisting the neck to show the face. This pose expresses a relaxed state while adding a sense of dynamism to the look back.

SHOW OFF THE BACK

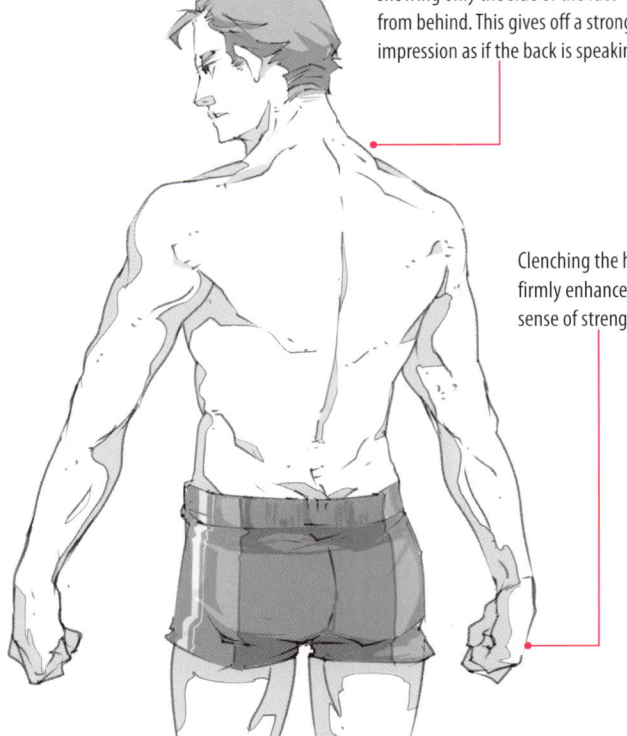

Pose as if just before turning back, showing only the side of the face from behind. This gives off a strong impression as if the back is speaking.

Clenching the hands firmly enhances the sense of strength.

LOOKING BACK WHILE LEANING

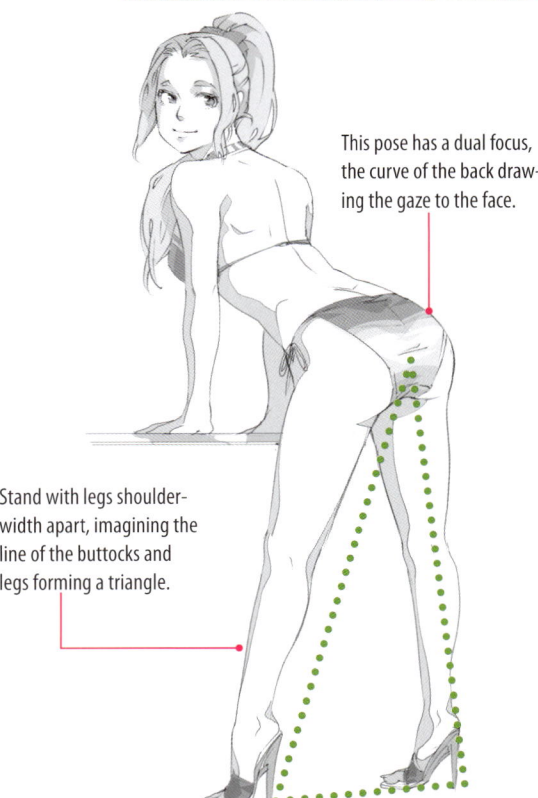

This pose has a dual focus, the curve of the back drawing the gaze to the face.

Stand with legs shoulder-width apart, imagining the line of the buttocks and legs forming a triangle.

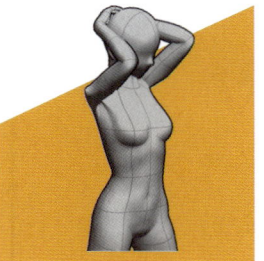

AN UPPER-BODY FOCUS
Raising the Arms

For a dynamic and complex pose, have your characters lift or raise their arms. Whether mimicking a model's stance or highlighting a quiet, everyday moment, these poses showcase the lines and contours of the body.

EVERYDAY MOVEMENTS

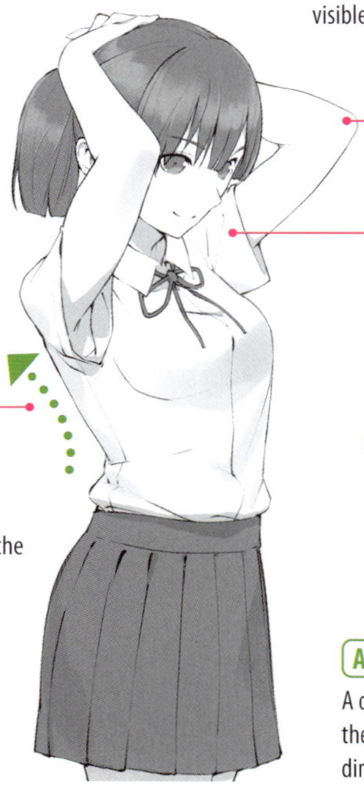

The gesture of tying the hair is a classic pose where the arm lines are visible during everyday movements.

To create a sense of everyday life, the face is slightly lowered, and the arm pose is kept from being exaggerated.

Raising both arms and placing hands behind the head arches the back.

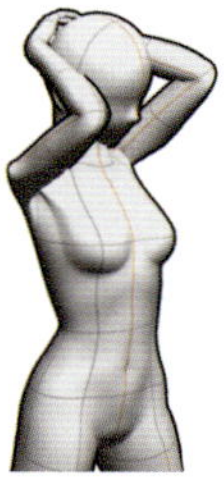

ANGLES
A diagonal angle clearly delineates the arm lines, offering a three-dimensional view of the character.

FRONTAL VIEW

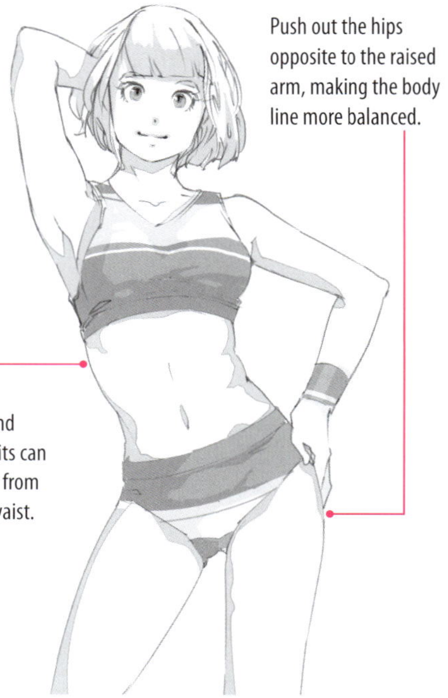

Push out the hips opposite to the raised arm, making the body line more balanced.

Raising the arms and exposing the armpits can emphasize the line from the armpit to the waist.

SHOWN FROM THE SIDE

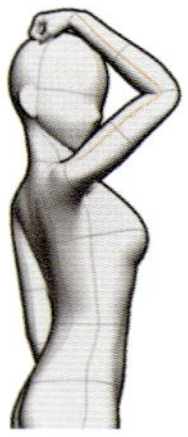

ANGLES
A side view angle can show the armpits while displaying the body lines.

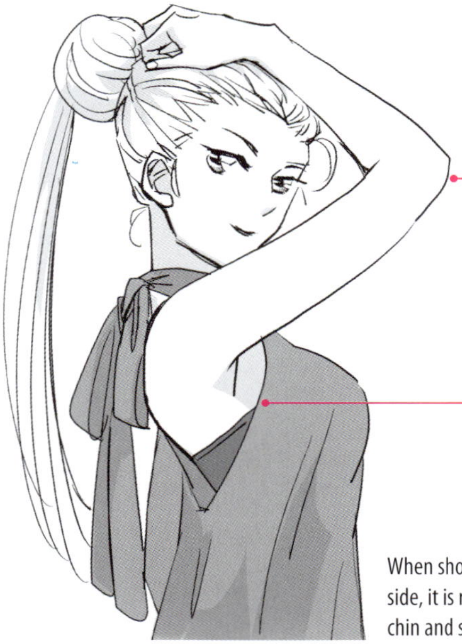

A pose that frames the face with the arms can enhance the impression of facial expressions.

When showing the armpits from the side, it is recommended to tuck in the chin and slightly straighten the back.

STANDING POSE VARIATIONS
Bending Down

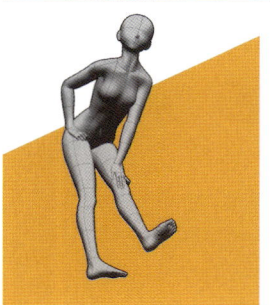

Leaning the upper body forward or tilting it to the side can bring out a sense of the character's energy and dynamism. Adding subtle movements to the hands or feet can make the pose look more natural.

RAISING THE TOES

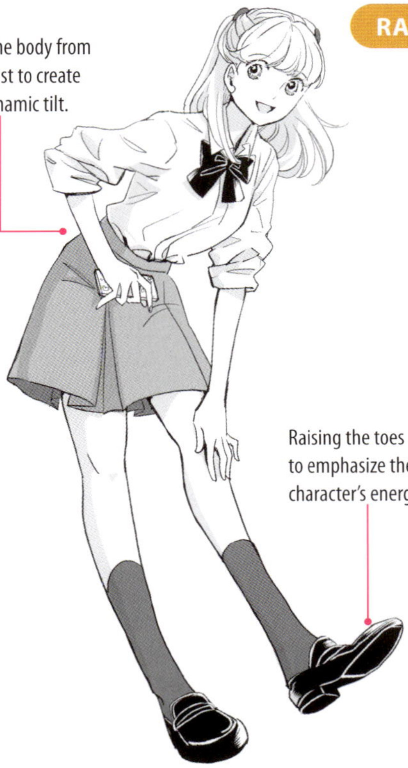

Bend the body from the waist to create this dynamic tilt.

Raising the toes to emphasize the character's energy.

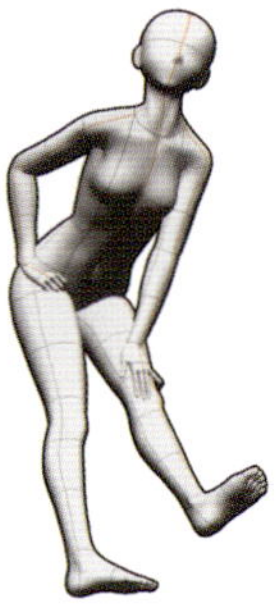

ANGLES

A slanted angle allows you to clearly show the entire body as well as the character's face.

CROUCHED DOWN

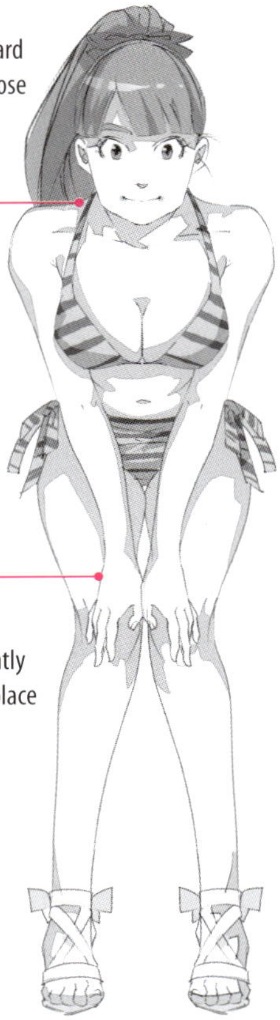

Leaning the upper body forward and tucking in the arms is a pose often seen in photography.

Keep the legs slightly pigeon-toed and place the hands on the knees for stability.

PEEKING FROM BELOW

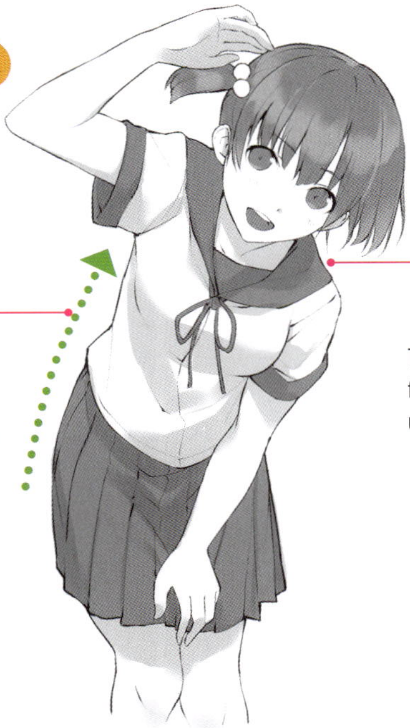

The muscles on the side with the raised hand stretch.

The character leans forward as if peeking under something.

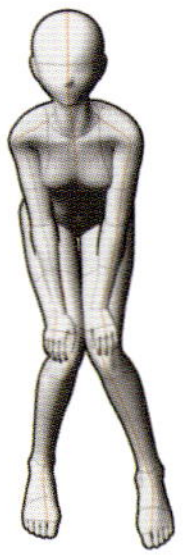

ANGLES

A frontal angle allows you to clearly show a facial expression as if the character is peeking at you.

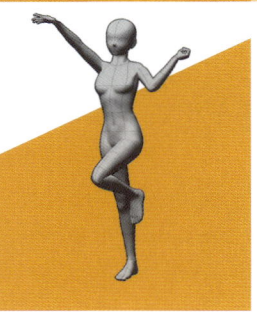

SHOWING MOVEMENT BY RAISING THE LEGS

Standing on One Leg

To avoid a standing pose looking too stiff, have the character stand on one leg to add a sense of movement. Since this creates an unstable stance, it's important to balance with the hands or align the weight-bearing foot with the body's center line.

RAISING ONE LEG WITH PIGEON-TOED STANCE

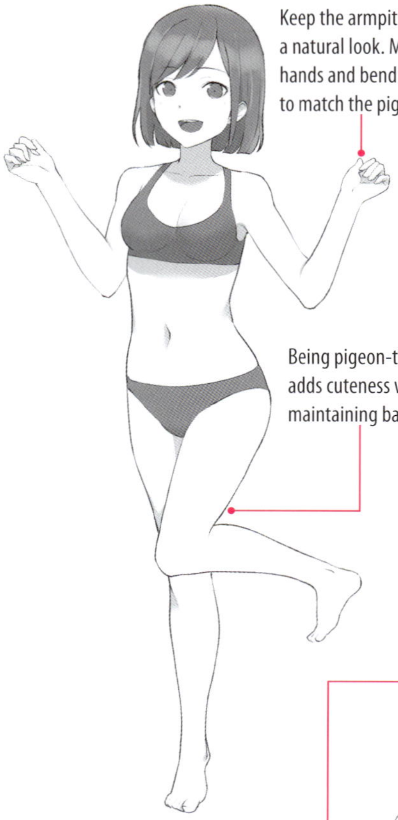

Keep the armpits slightly open for a natural look. Make fists with the hands and bend the arms slightly to match the pigeon-toed stance.

Being pigeon-toed adds cuteness while maintaining balance.

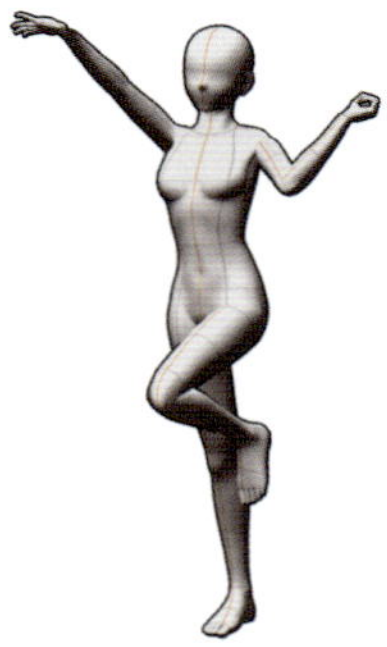

BALANCING WITH HANDS

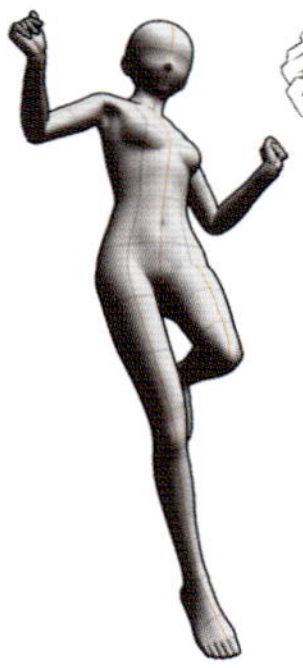

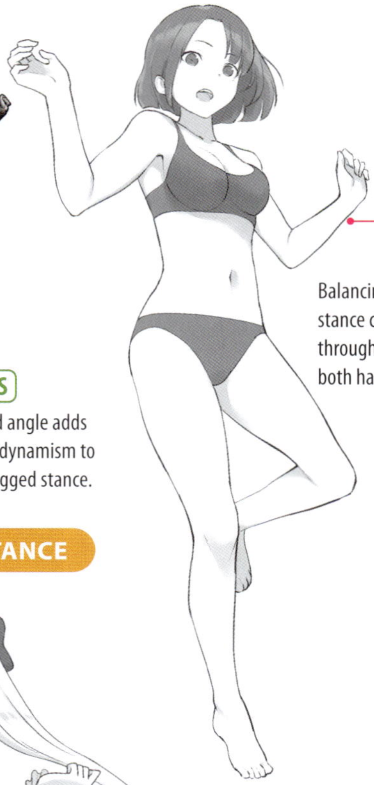

Balancing in an unstable stance can be expressed through the depiction of both hands.

ANGLES

An upward angle adds a sense of dynamism to the one-legged stance.

IDOL ONE-LEGGED STANCE

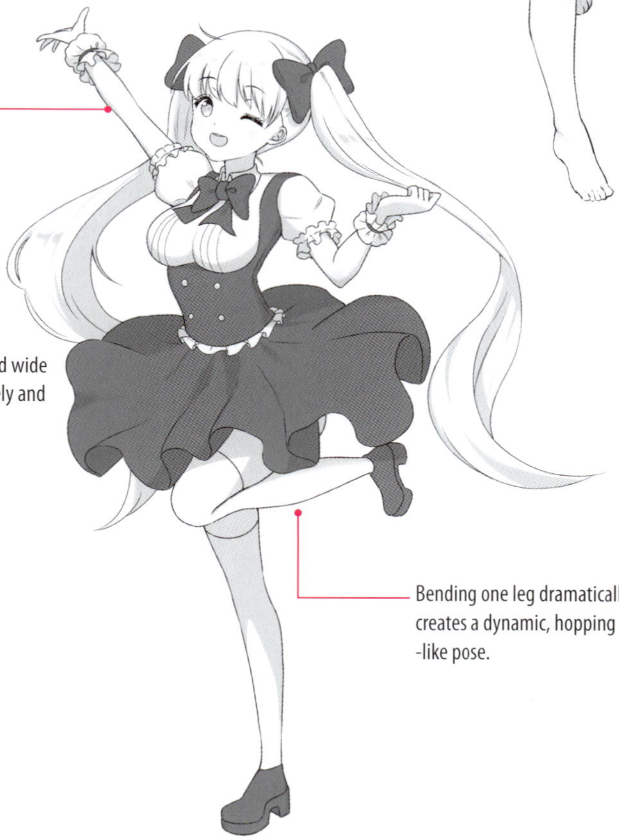

Arms are spread wide to convey a lively and energetic feel.

Bending one leg dramatically creates a dynamic, hopping-like pose.

ANGLES

A diagonal angle makes it easier to show the bent leg in a one-legged stance.

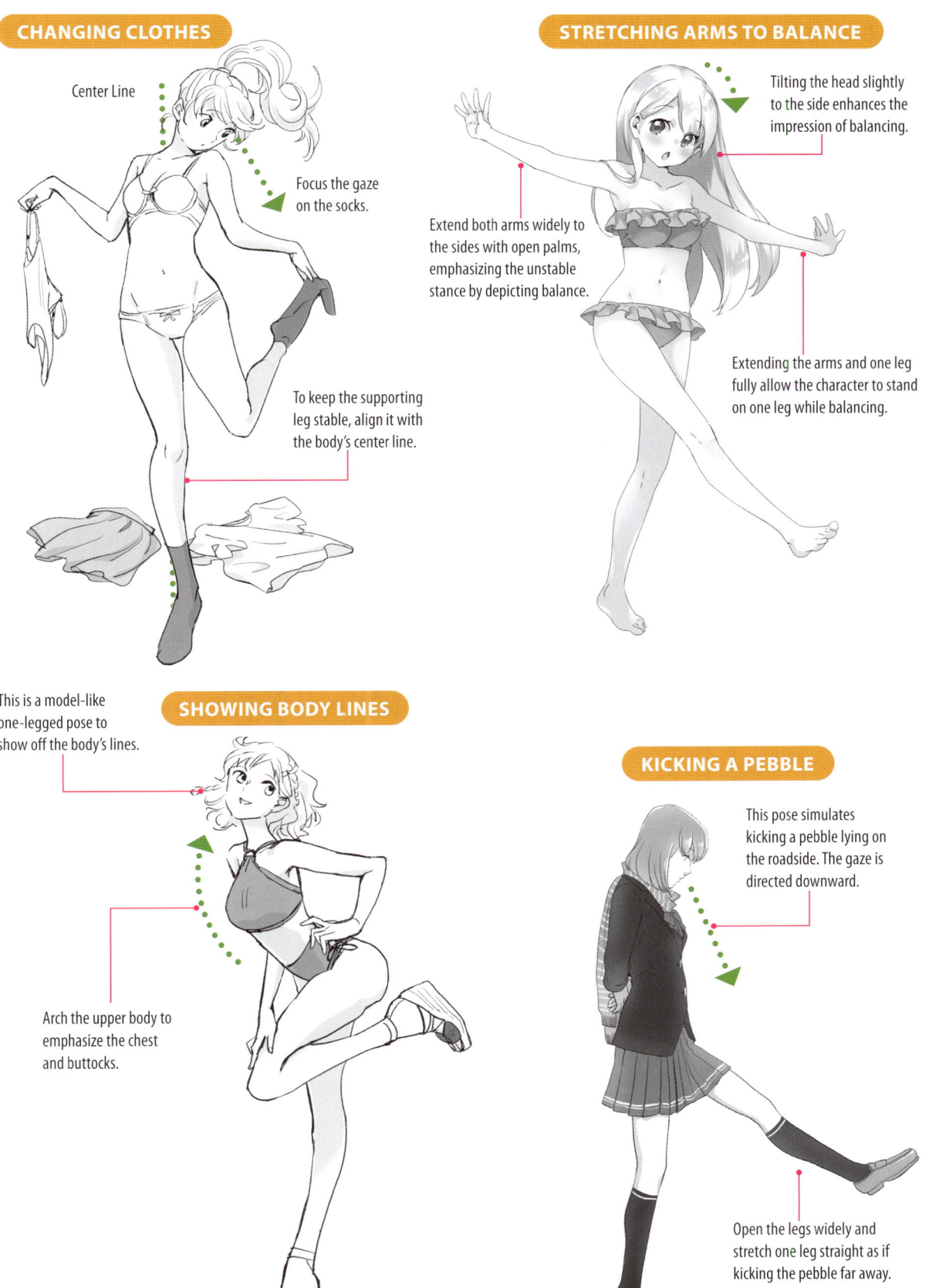

CLASSIC POSES
Kneeling

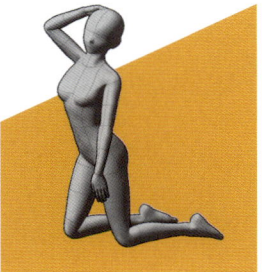

Kneeling is a familiar pose that allows for a compact presentation of the body's contours and lines. Unlike most standing or full-body poses, this option makes it easier to fit the entire frame into the illustration.

TWISTING THE WAIST

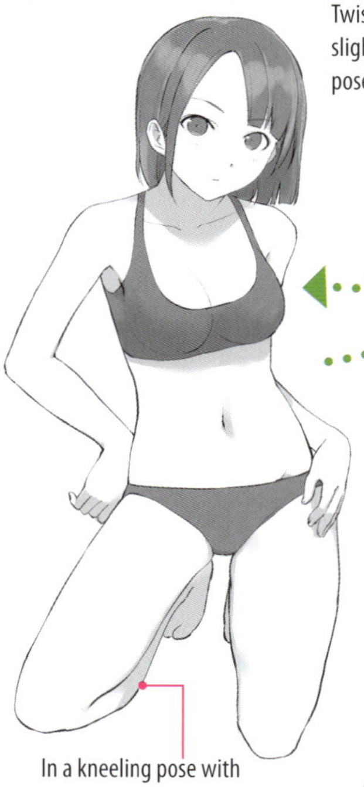

Twisting the waist slightly can make the pose more dynamic.

In a kneeling pose with toes pointed, the shins are lifted off the ground.

SHOWING THE UPPER BODY

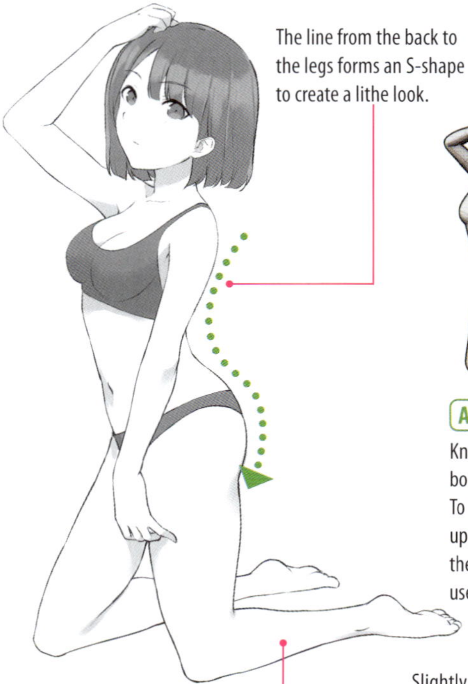

The line from the back to the legs forms an S-shape to create a lithe look.

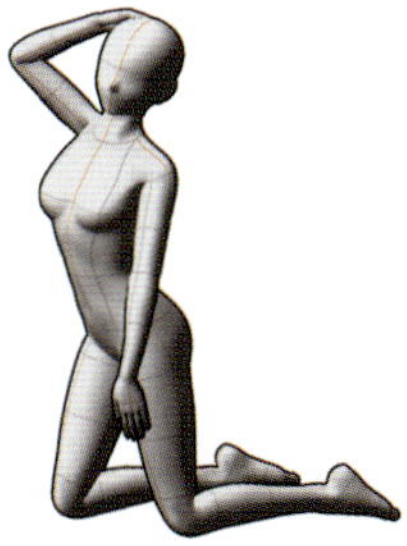

ANGLES

Kneeling emphasizes the upper body more than the lower body. To highlight the beauty of the upper body, such as the line from the shoulders to the abdomen, use a diagonal angle.

Slightly spreading the legs apart adds depth and movement, making the composition more cohesive.

SEEN FROM ABOVE

Lower the height of the waist and tilt the chin up, looking upward.

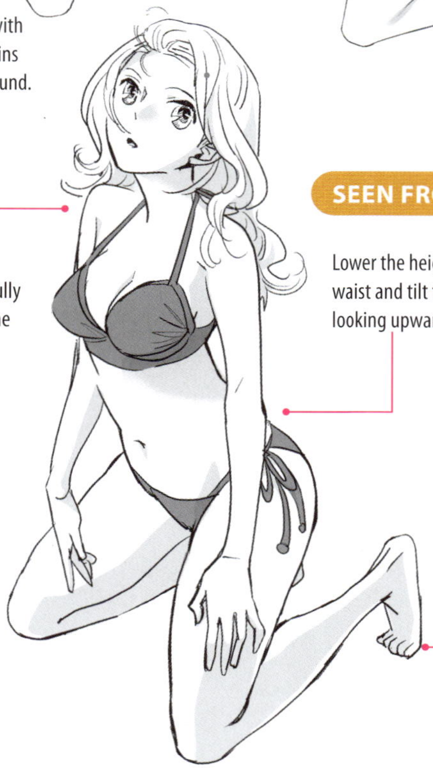

A high-angle shot beautifully showcases the line from the neck to the upper body.

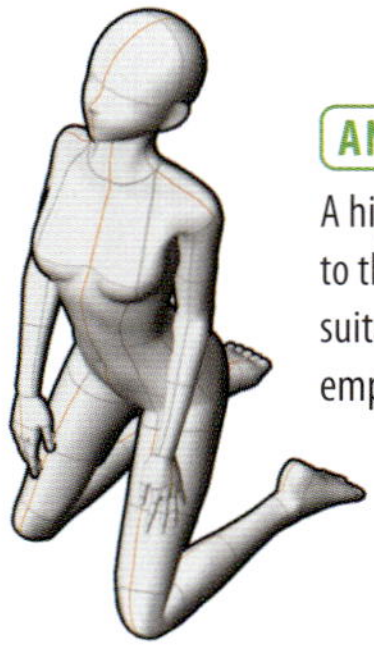

ANGLES

A high-angle shot draws attention to the face and chest, making it suitable for kneeling poses that emphasize the upper body.

Support the body with the knees and toes.

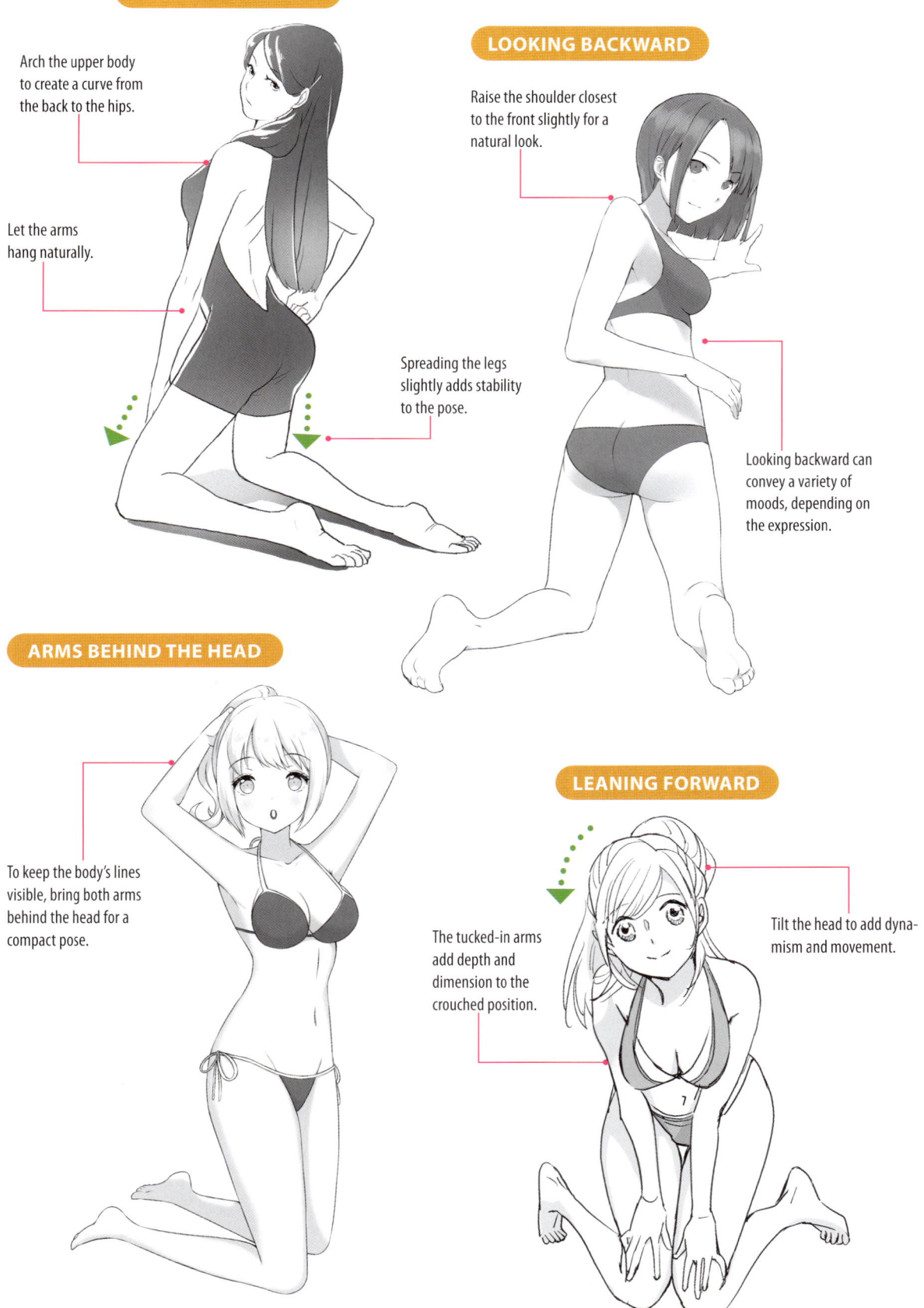

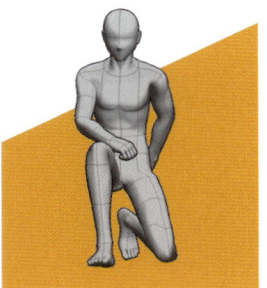

COMPLEX AND COMPACT
Down on One Knee

While resting or leaning on the knees and with lowered hips, this can be a challenging position to get right. It can convey a formal or submissive atmosphere and can also be used to highlight various proportions.

A PASSIVE POSE

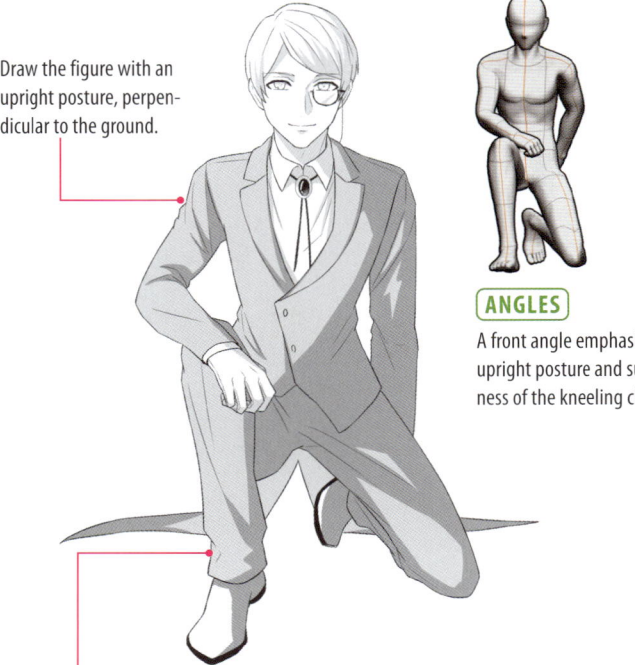

Draw the figure with an upright posture, perpendicular to the ground.

ANGLES
A front angle emphasizes the upright posture and submissiveness of the kneeling character.

The leg brought forward will be prominent.

EMPHASIZING PROPORTION

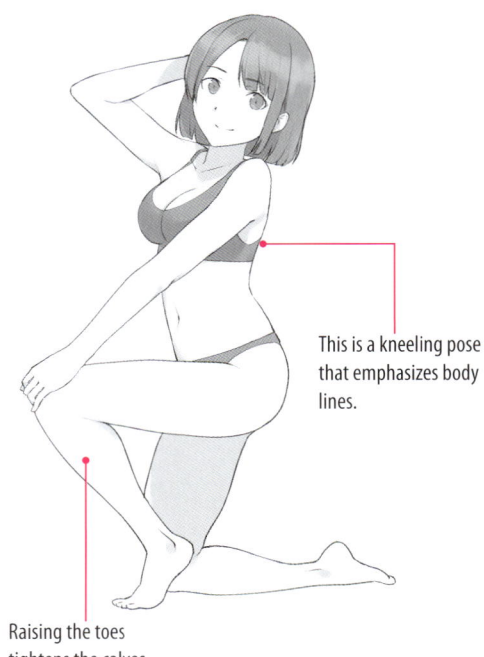

This is a kneeling pose that emphasizes body lines.

Raising the toes tightens the calves.

UPPER BODY LEANING FORWARD

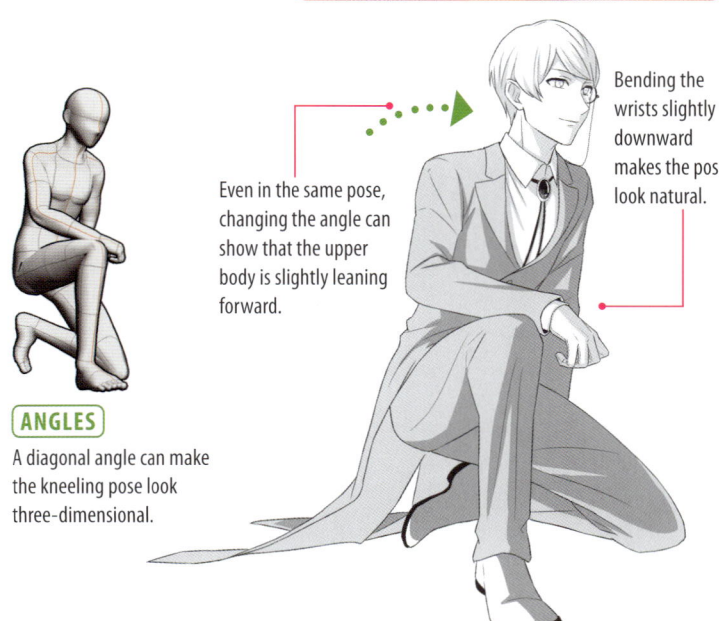

Even in the same pose, changing the angle can show that the upper body is slightly leaning forward.

Bending the wrists slightly downward makes the pose look natural.

ANGLES
A diagonal angle can make the kneeling pose look three-dimensional.

CROPPING — Showing the Toes

For kneeling poses, it is best to avoid cropping the legs, as it can make it difficult to convey the characteristics of the pose. Try to include the entire body in the frame.

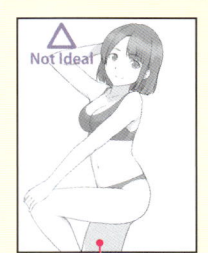
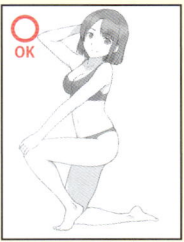

If the thighs are only partially visible, it becomes unclear what is happening below, making the image less effective.

DYNAMIC POSES
Crouching

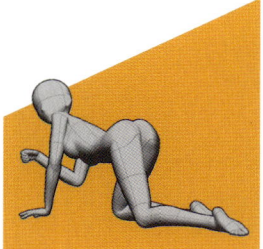

With this pose, both hands and knees are on the ground supporting the body weight. The abdomen is hidden, and the focus is on the back. It can add a sense of playfulness, as when a character is mimicking an animal.

EMPHASIZING THE BUTTOCKS

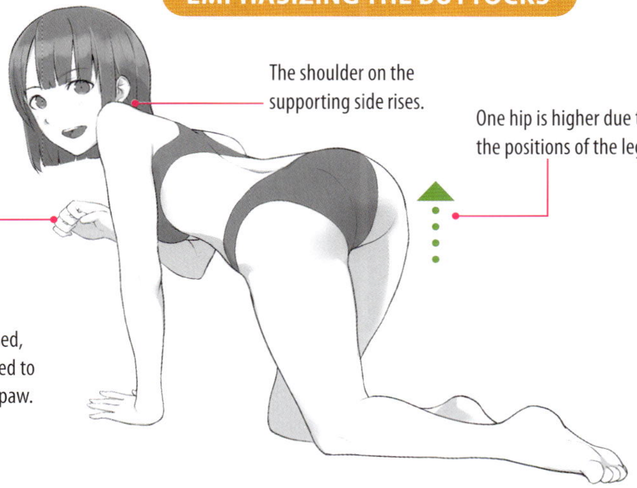

- The shoulder on the supporting side rises.
- One hip is higher due to the positions of the legs.
- The hand is raised, the fingers curled to suggest a cat's paw.

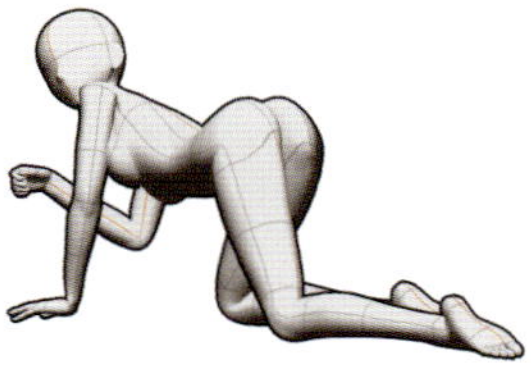

ANGLES
The rear angle can make the legs appear longer. It's also an angle that easily shows the soles of the feet.

CHEST ON THE GROUND

- Placing the chest on the ground creates a posture where the buttocks are raised higher.

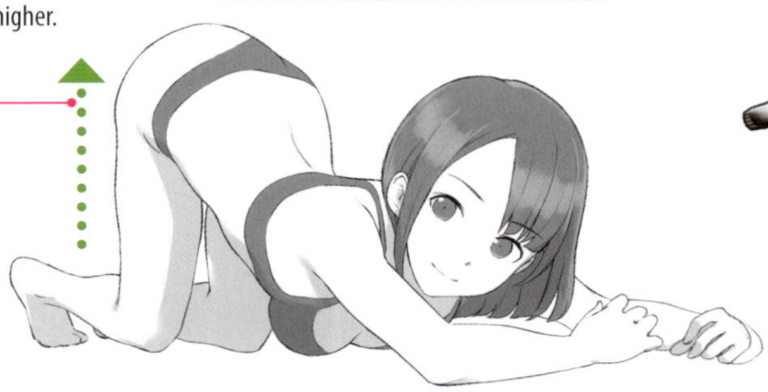

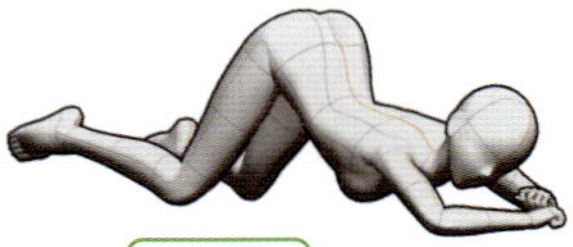

ANGLES
For this pose, keep the perspective low, in line with the character's gaze. Use a diagonal angle to emphasize the lines of the body.

FRONTAL VIEW

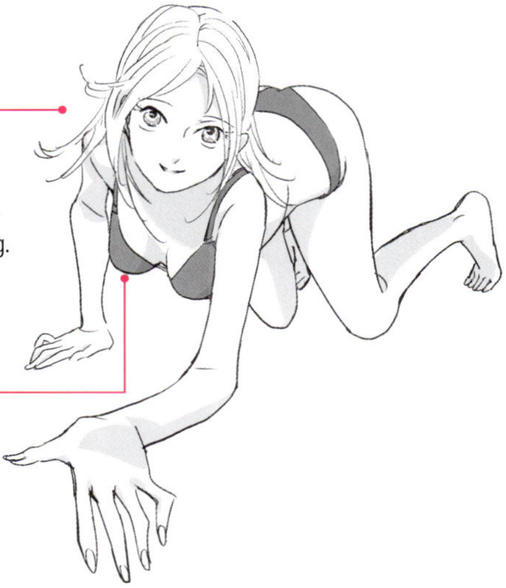

- This pose is like a carnivore stalking its prey, with a gaze directed forward as if approaching.
- Remember to leave space between the chest and the ground.

Tips — Ground Perspective
When assuming this position, incorrectly placing the hands, elbows and knees on the ground can look unnatural. Be aware of the ground perspective to ensure for proper positioning.

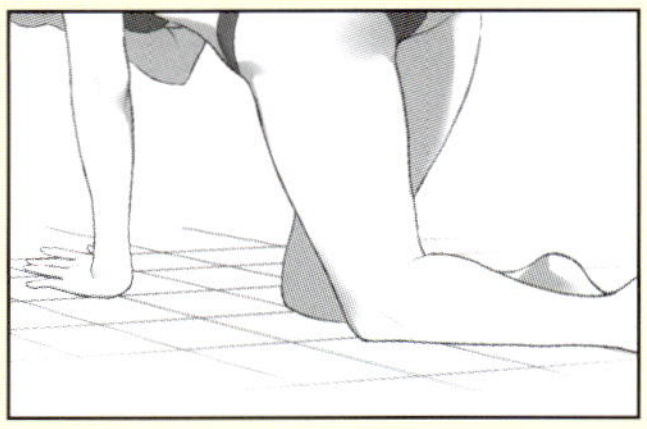

81

SLEEPING POSTURES
Lying on the Back

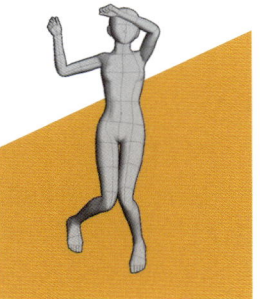

Lying on the back is a pose that shows the front of the body while conveying a sense of relaxation. When you want to create movement, you can add variations such as bending the arms and legs or arching the back.

VIEW FROM ABOVE

Arms and legs should not be aligned symmetrically to appear more relaxed.

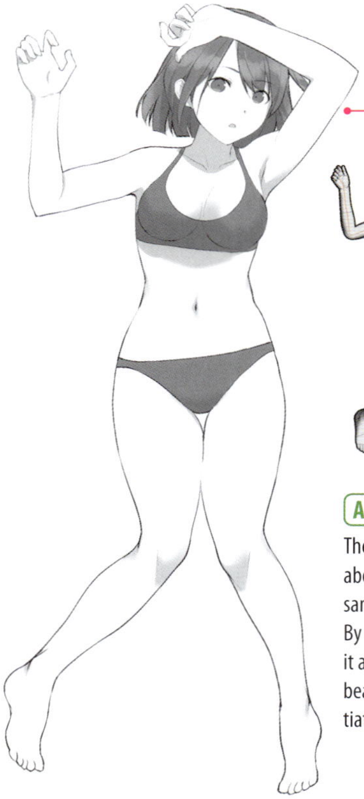

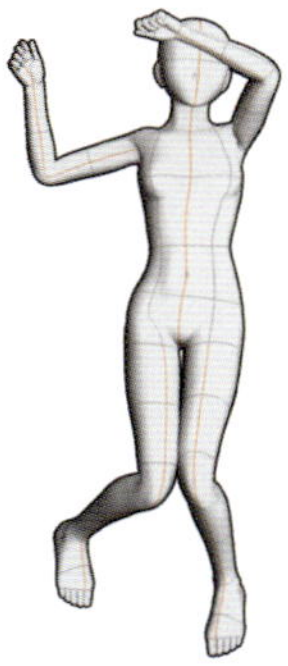

LEGS INWARD

Bringing the legs inward conveys a relaxed atmosphere. Slightly tilting to the side gives a natural movement.

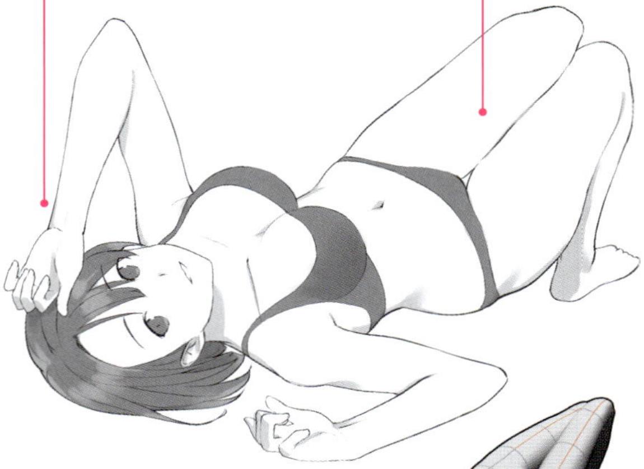

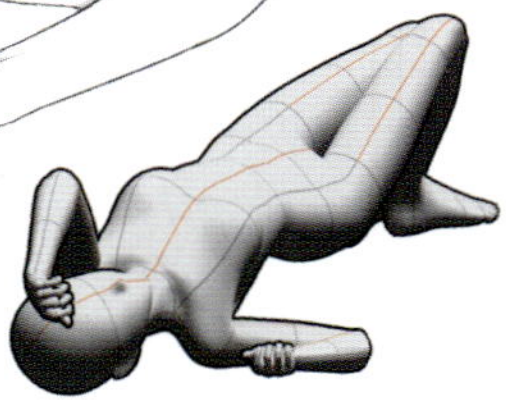

Placing a hand near the forehead as if dazzled can create a just-awakened effect.

ANGLES
The angle viewed directly from above can be drawn with the same sense as a standing figure. By stretching the toes and making it appear that the feet are not bearing weight, you can differentiate it from a standing figure.

ANGLES
Drawing from an angle that observes the sleeping person up close gives an impression of intimacy.

ARCHING THE BACK

Shift the legs asymmetrically and bend them to create a dynamic effect.

Keep in mind how body lines differ here from a standing posture.

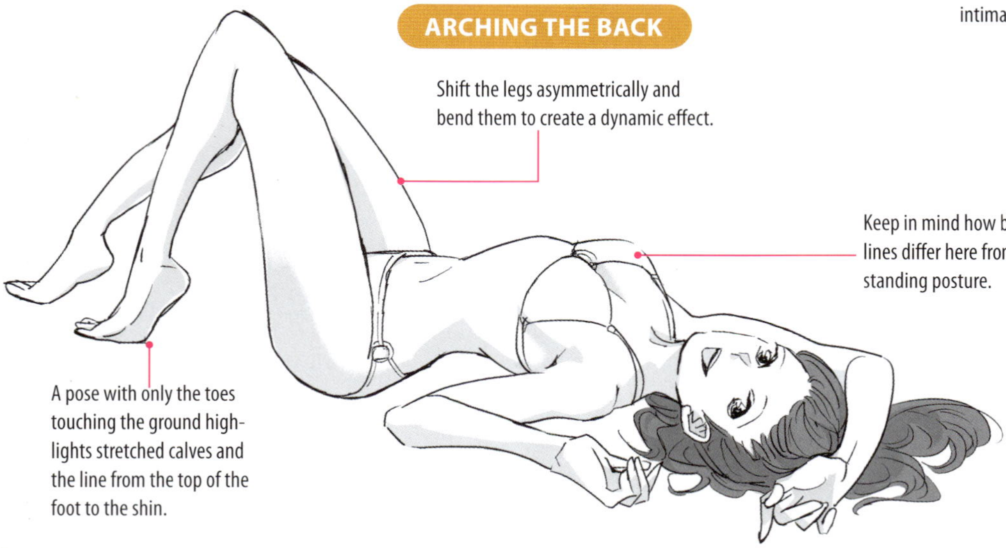

A pose with only the toes touching the ground highlights stretched calves and the line from the top of the foot to the shin.

82

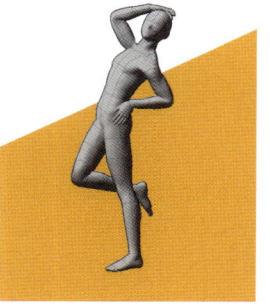

DRAMATICALLY ARCHING THE BODY
Arching Back

The reclining posture, only adopted by the highly flexibly, easily created an extraordinary impossible-to-look-away impression. It's used for scenes of wild self-abandon or to express a character's unconventional personality.

TWISTING THE WAIST

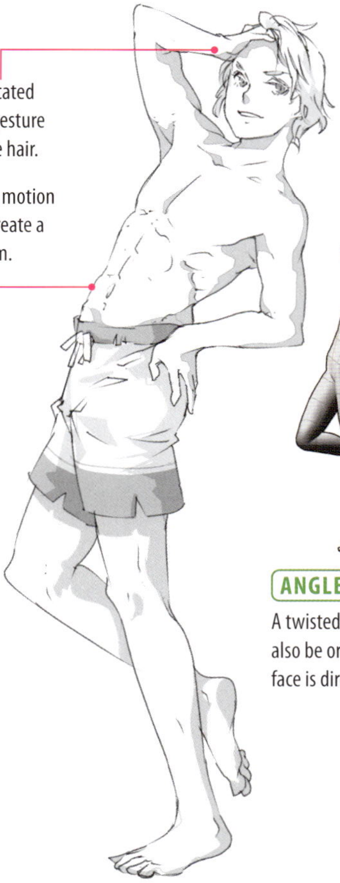

Portray a sophisticated character with a gesture of brushing up the hair.

Adding a twisting motion to the waist can create a sense of dynamism.

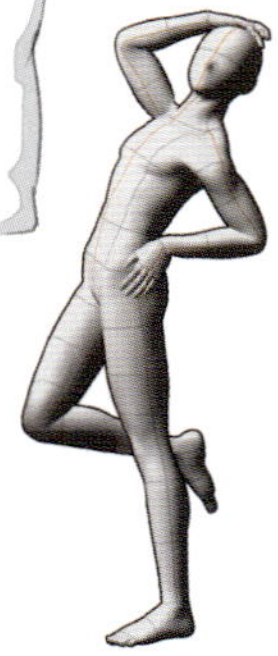

ARCHING THE UPPER BODY

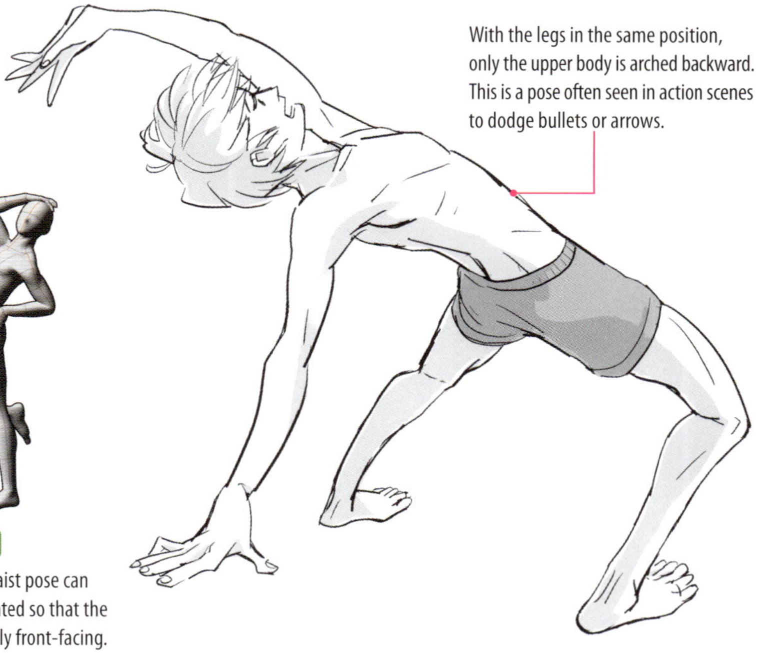

With the legs in the same position, only the upper body is arched backward. This is a pose often seen in action scenes to dodge bullets or arrows.

ANGLES
A twisted waist pose can also be oriented so that the face is directly front-facing.

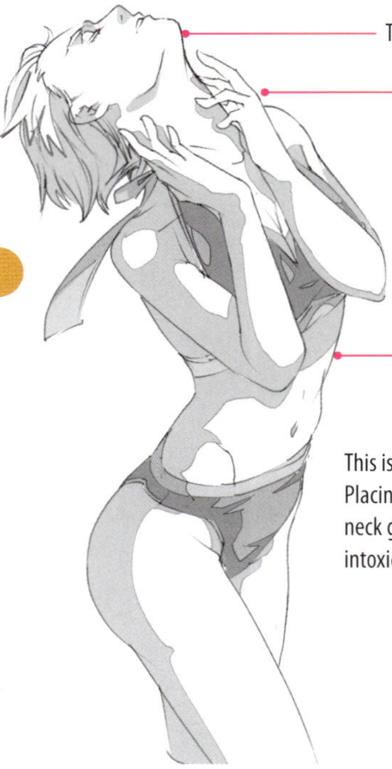

The face is turned directly upward.

Ensuring even the fingertips are energized adds a theatrical atmosphere.

DRAMATICALLY LOOKING UPWARD

This is a pose seen in stage dances. Placing both hands around the neck gives the impression of being intoxicated with oneself.

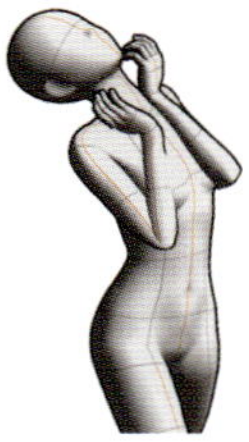

ANGLES
A slightly overhead angle allows emphasizing the upward-facing face and arms.

LOUNGING POSE
Lying on the Stomach

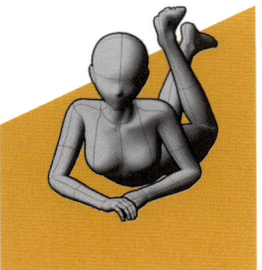

This pose shows the character lying with the stomach touching the floor, the back exposed. Drawing the legs fluttering alternately left and right makes it a compelling, dynamic pose.

SHOWING THE FULL BODY LINE

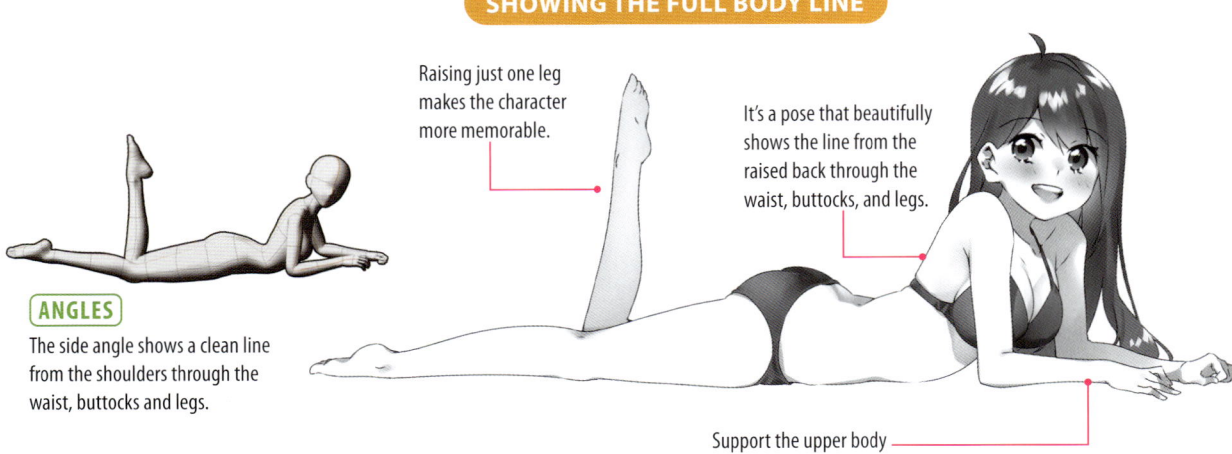

ANGLES
The side angle shows a clean line from the shoulders through the waist, buttocks and legs.

Raising just one leg makes the character more memorable.

It's a pose that beautifully shows the line from the raised back through the waist, buttocks, and legs.

Support the upper body with both arms.

EMPHASIZING THE FACE AND CHEST

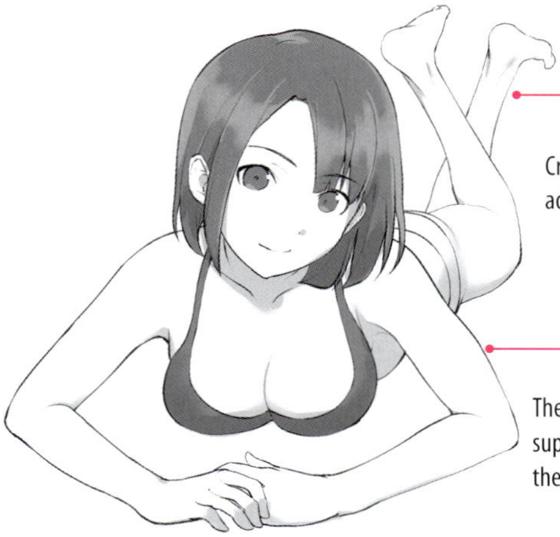

Crossing the legs casually adds movement.

The arms are extended forward, supporting the upper body on the elbows.

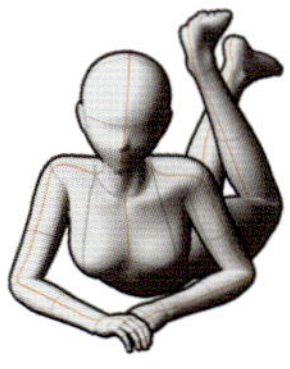

ANGLES
The front-forward angle emphasizes the face.

RELAXING

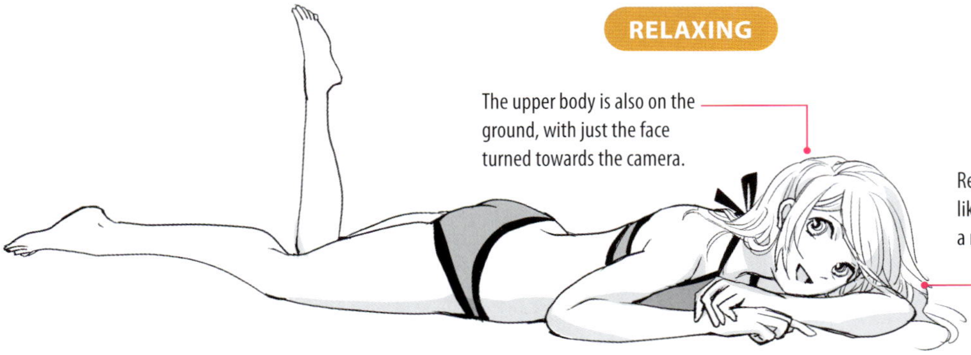

The upper body is also on the ground, with just the face turned towards the camera.

Resting the head on the arm like using it as a pillow gives a more relaxed impression.

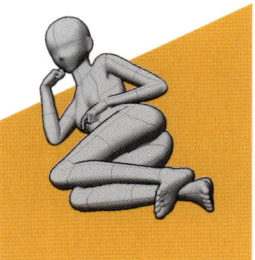

CASUAL POSES
Lying on the Side

Lying on the side is a comfortable posture suitable for everyday scenes, but it can also be used to highlight and emphasize the lines and contours of the body.

EMPHASIZING THE LEGS

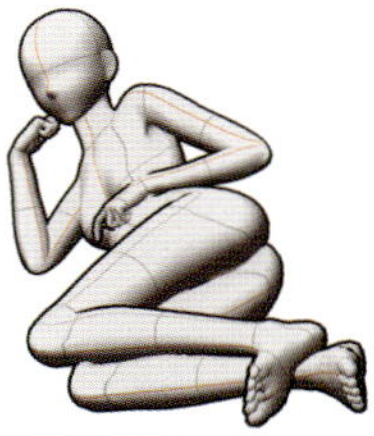

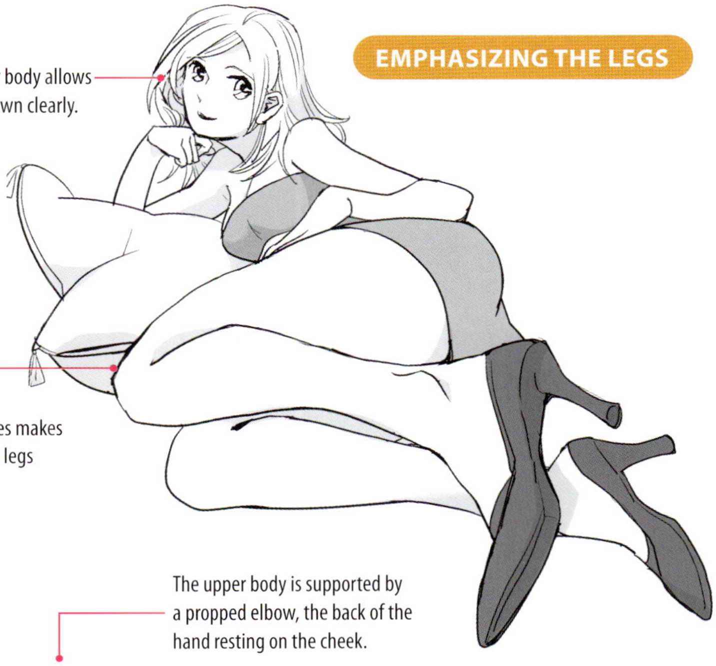

Raising the upper body allows the face to be shown clearly.

Bending the knees makes it easier to fit the legs into the frame.

ANGLES

From an angle taken from the direction of the feet, the legs are especially prominent.

RELAXING

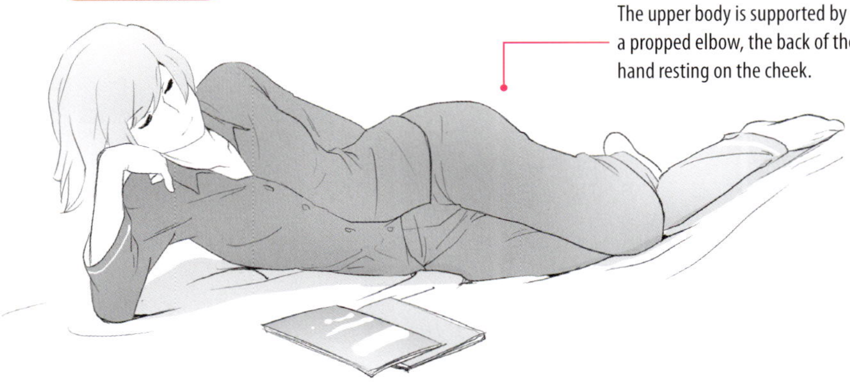

The upper body is supported by a propped elbow, the back of the hand resting on the cheek.

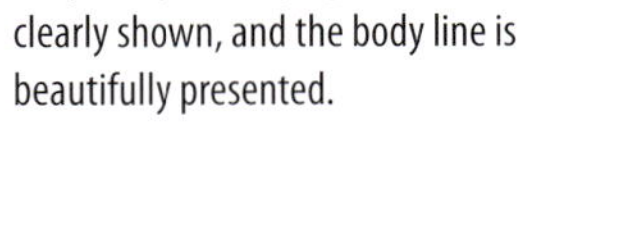

ANGLES

By taking a slightly overhead angle and focusing on the front of the body, the pose of lying down is clearly shown, and the body line is beautifully presented.

LEANING ON AN ELBOW

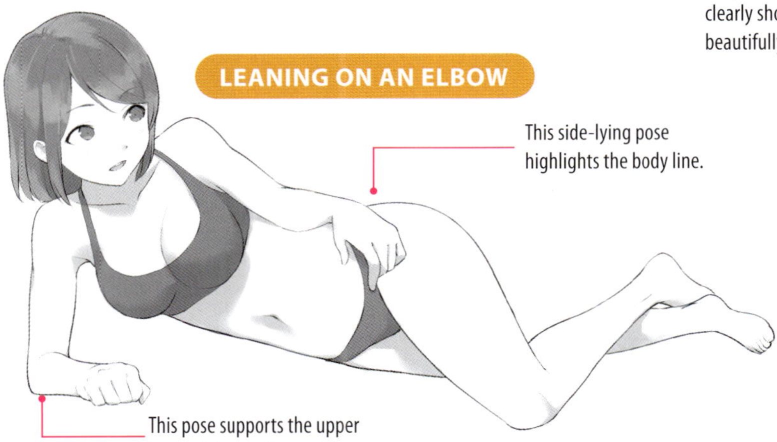

This side-lying pose highlights the body line.

This pose supports the upper body with one elbow.

85

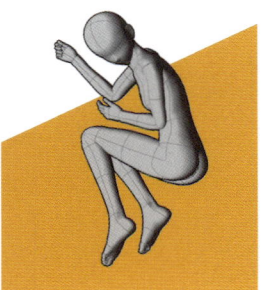

SLEEPING POSTURE
Fetal Position

Bending both legs together and bringing them closer to the upper body, this pose resembles a fetus in the mother's womb. It expresses an endearing need to be protected, evoked by the curled-up sleeping figure.

LOOSELY CURLING THE BODY

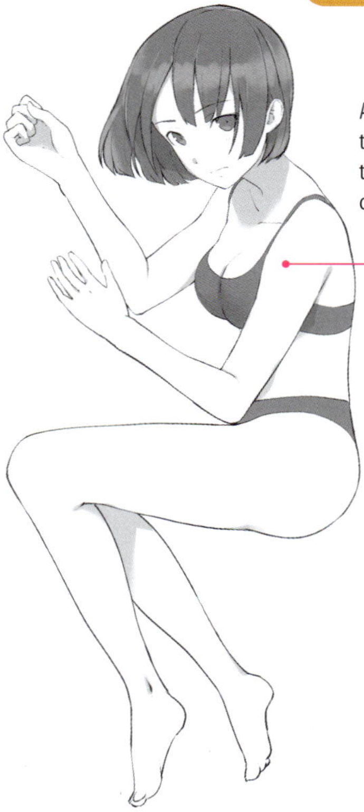

Arms and legs are bent, with elbows towards the lower body and knees towards the upper body. It's a relaxed, curled-up posture.

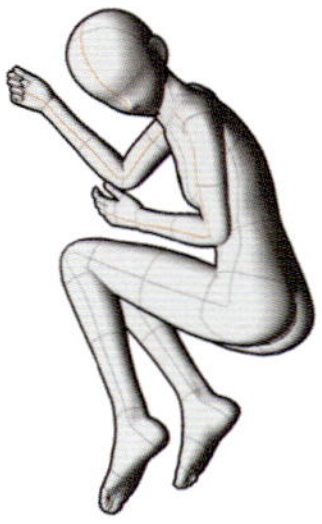

EMBRACING

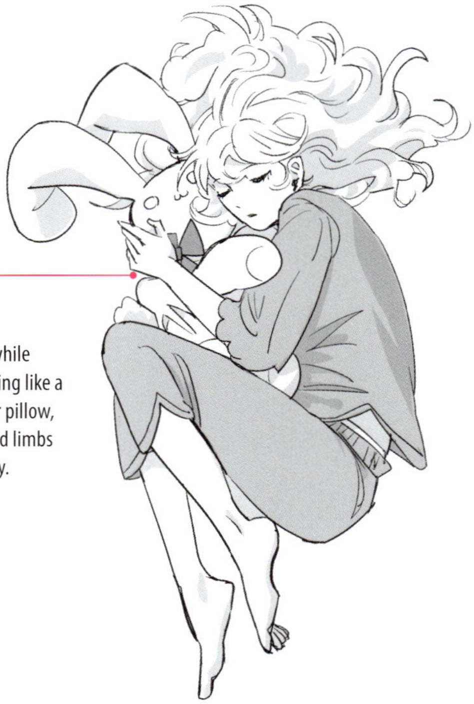

When sleeping while hugging something like a stuffed animal or pillow, bring the face and limbs closer to the body.

ANGLES
From a directly overhead angle, you can depict a fetal-like silhouette.

SIDE VIEW SLEEPING POSTURE

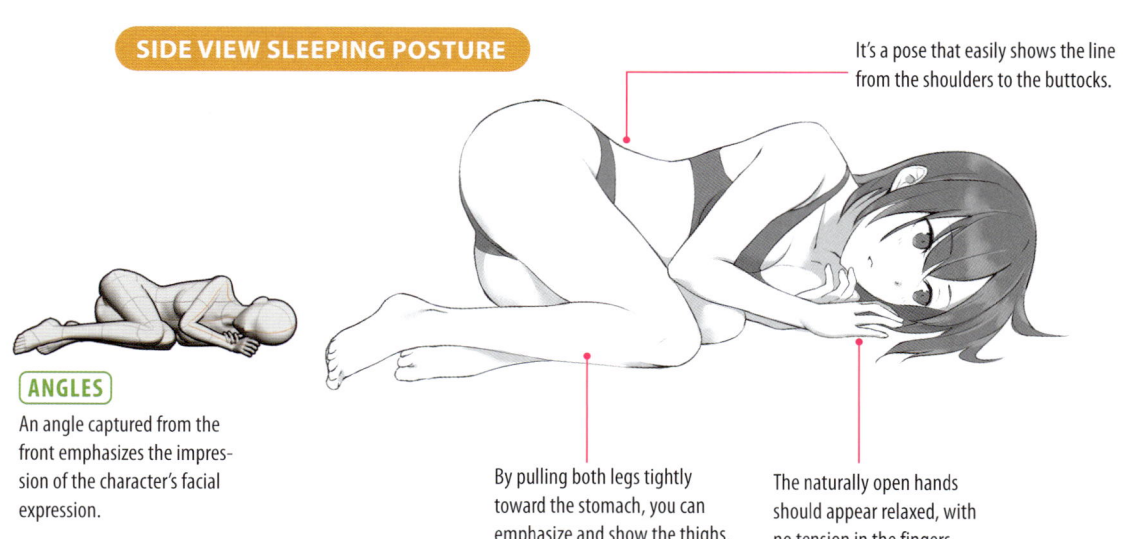

It's a pose that easily shows the line from the shoulders to the buttocks.

ANGLES
An angle captured from the front emphasizes the impression of the character's facial expression.

By pulling both legs tightly toward the stomach, you can emphasize and show the thighs.

The naturally open hands should appear relaxed, with no tension in the fingers.

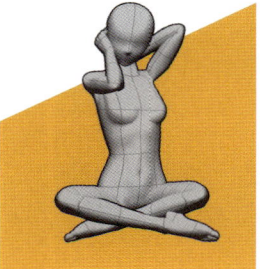

RELAXED SITTING POSTURE
Sitting Crosslegged

Sitting cross-legged creates a bold impression. Adding everyday gestures and actions yields a more naturalistic, realistic atmosphere. These poses work best for depicting characters resting confidently or showing their natural demeanor.

STRETCHING THE UPPER BODY

Tilting the head slightly gives an impression of a natural gesture.

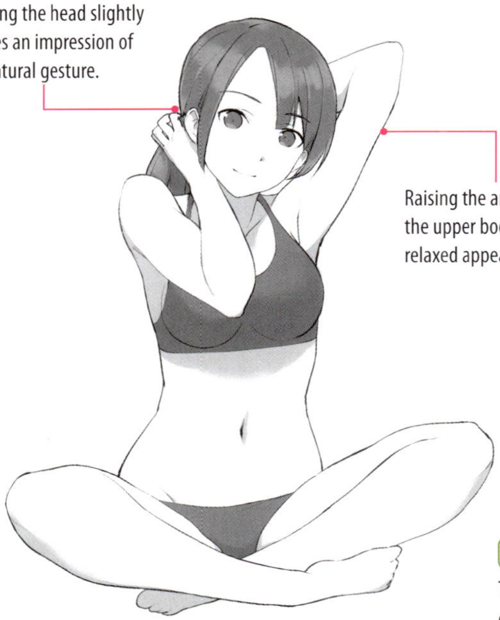

Raising the arms and stretching the upper body conveys a relaxed appearance.

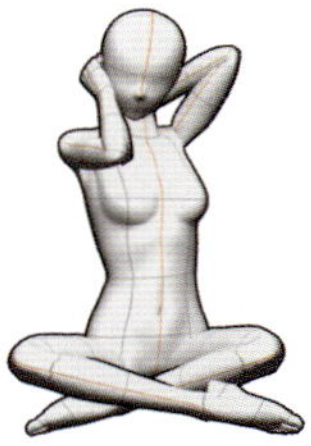

ANGLES
The front angle shows the legs' cross-legged pose clearly.

CROSS-LEGGED WITH A DRINK

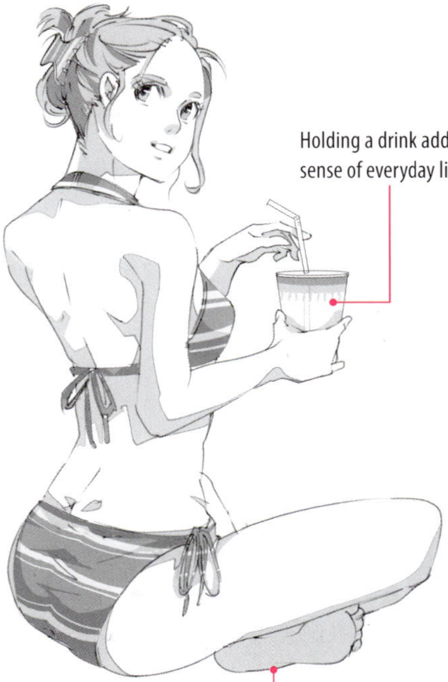

Holding a drink adds a sense of everyday life.

The back view is an angle where the cross-legged pose is less visible, but drawing the soles of the feet tucked under the thighs makes it clearly cross-legged.

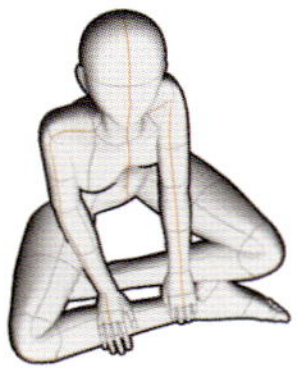

ANGLES
An upward-looking angle as if looking up at someone standing creates such a composition.

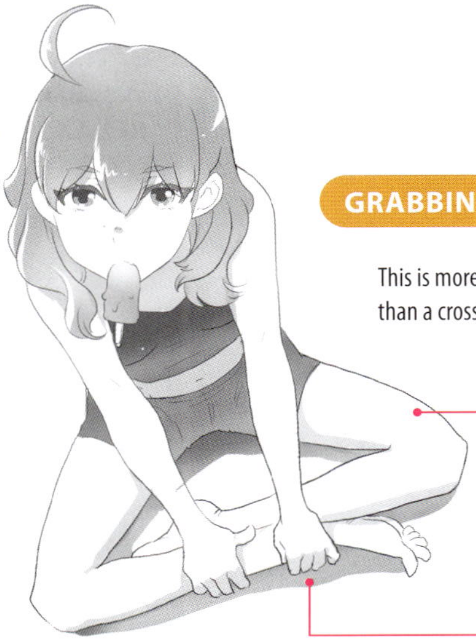

GRABBING THE LEGS

This is more of a close-legged than a crossed-legged sitting.

Holding the legs with both hands in a hunched posture gives a laid-back impression, suitable for a bored character.

87

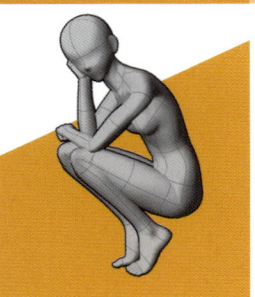

CLASSIC LOW-POSTURE POSE
Squatting

This compact pose can create either a bold or cute impression depending on how the hips are spread and how the posture is depicted. The body is compartmentalized, making it easier to fit the entire character into the frame.

SLIGHTLY ROUNDED BACK

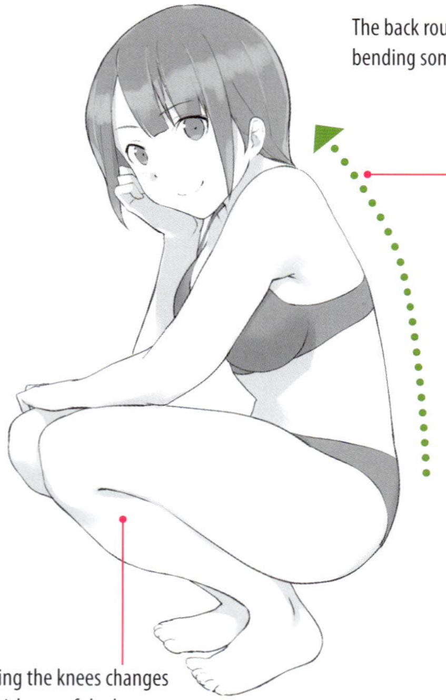

The back rounds slightly, bending somewhat forward.

Bending the knees changes the thickness of the legs from the usual, with the thighs and calves touching and muscles bulging.

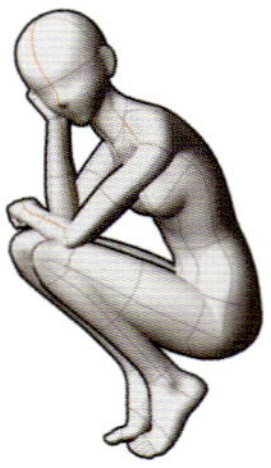

ANGLES
The side angle clearly shows the bent legs supporting the body weight.

CREATING BOLDNESS

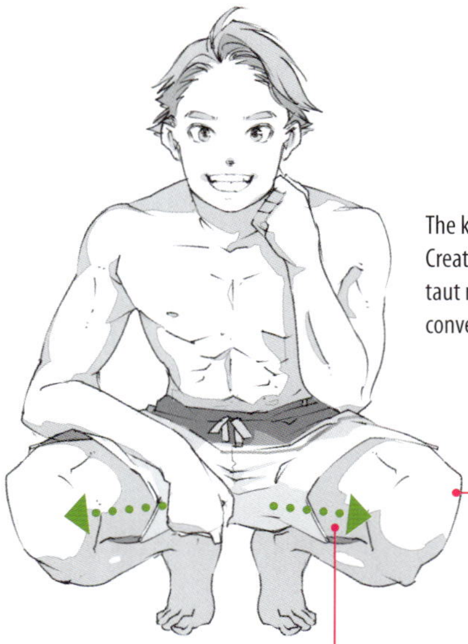

The knees protrude. Creating a sense of taut muscles can convey robustness.

Spreading the legs wide can create a bold impression.

RELAX THE ARMS

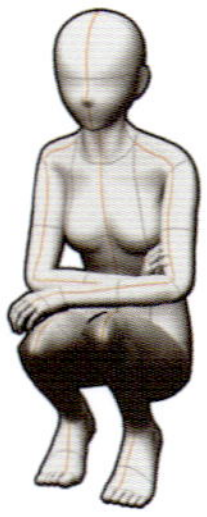

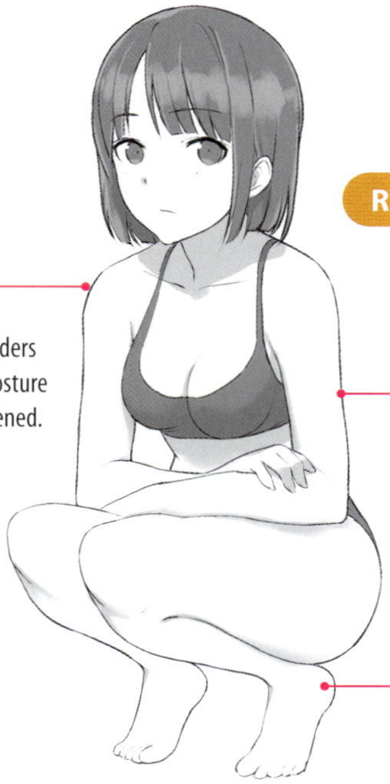

Lowering the shoulders creates a relaxed posture with the arms loosened.

Closing the armpits gives a casual impression.

Sit on the heels and support the body weight with the feet.

ANGLES
A diagonal angle clearly shows the degree of leg bending, making it easier to convey the posture of the squatting pose.

88

RAISING ONE LEG

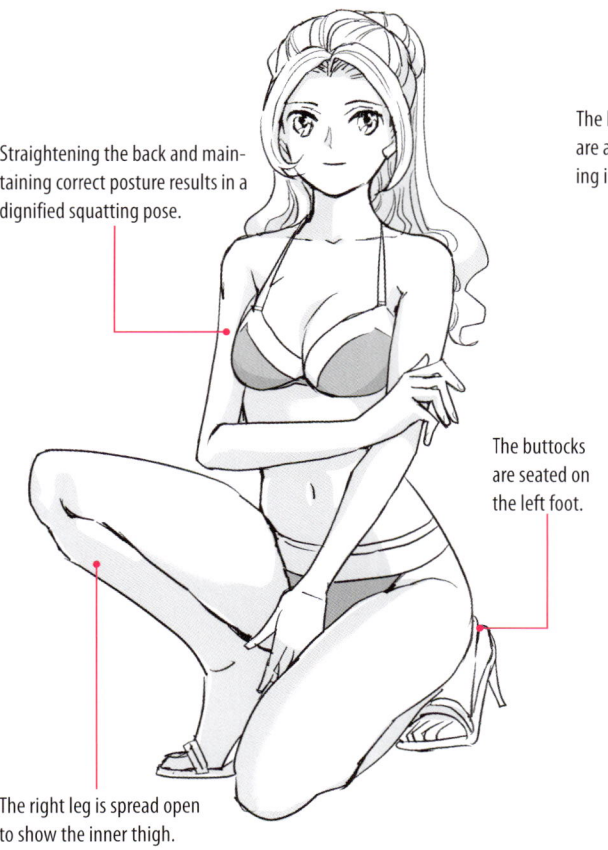

Straightening the back and maintaining correct posture results in a dignified squatting pose.

The buttocks are seated on the left foot.

The right leg is spread open to show the inner thigh.

ALIGNING BOTH FEET

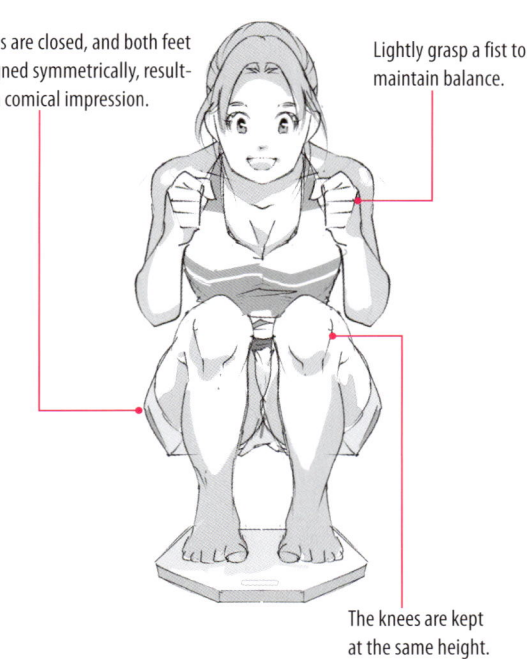

The legs are closed, and both feet are aligned symmetrically, resulting in a comical impression.

Lightly grasp a fist to maintain balance.

The knees are kept at the same height.

YANKEE SITTING

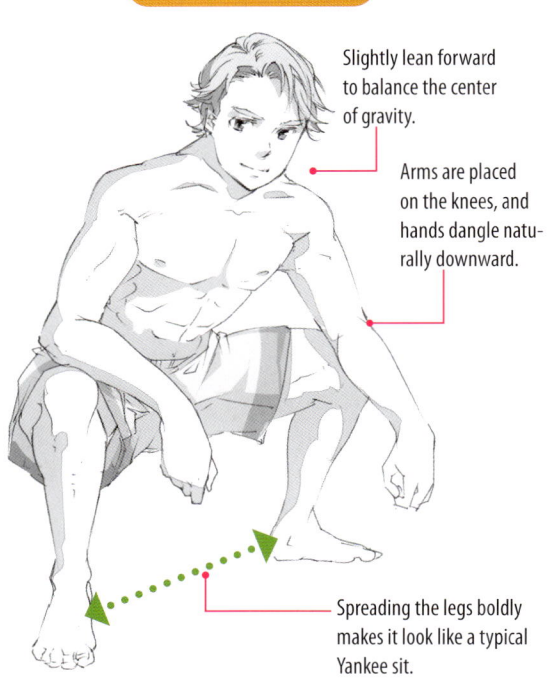

Slightly lean forward to balance the center of gravity.

Arms are placed on the knees, and hands dangle naturally downward.

Spreading the legs boldly makes it look like a typical Yankee sit.

SUFFERING

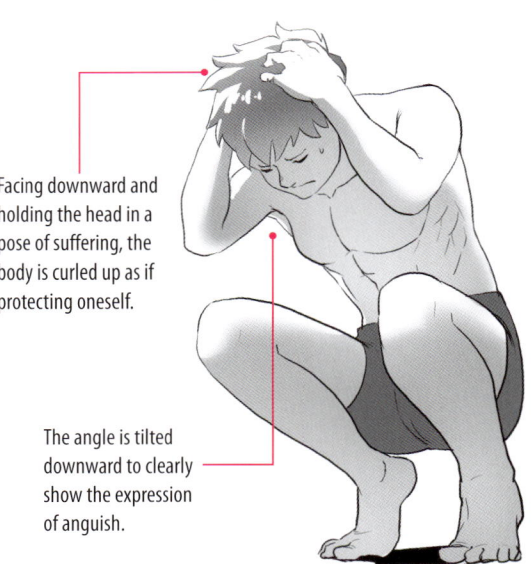

Facing downward and holding the head in a pose of suffering, the body is curled up as if protecting oneself.

The angle is tilted downward to clearly show the expression of anguish.

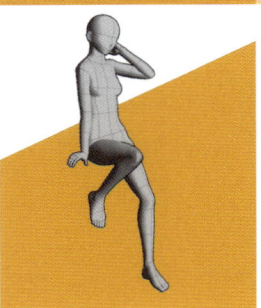

RELAXED MOMENTS
Sitting Down

Naturally, you'll need to show your characters in a relaxed and comfortable state. Here, the weight is placed mostly on the buttocks, so the legs don't need to exert as much force as in standing poses.

LIGHTLY SITTING

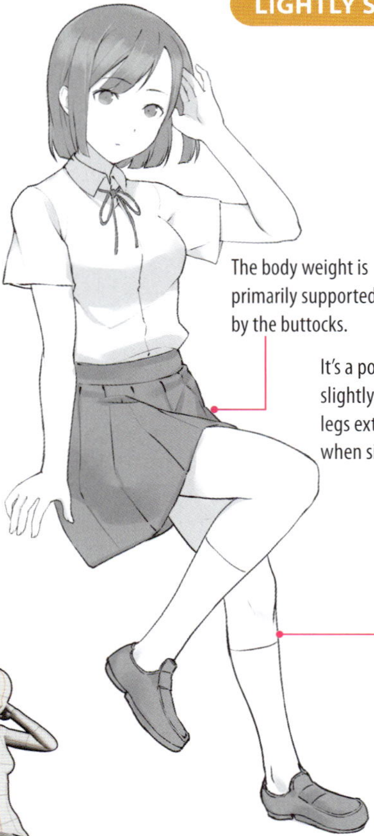

The body weight is primarily supported by the buttocks.

It's a pose of sitting slightly higher up. The legs extend more than when sitting on a chair.

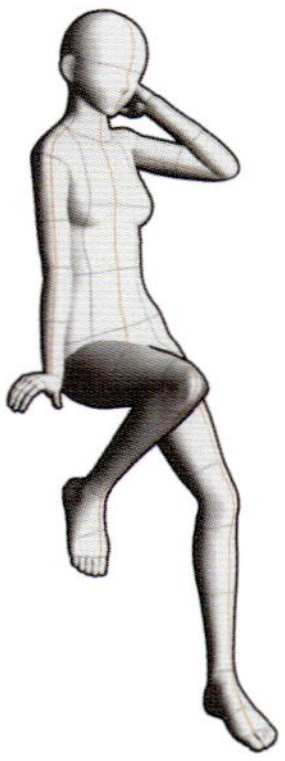

EMPHASIZING THE GAZE

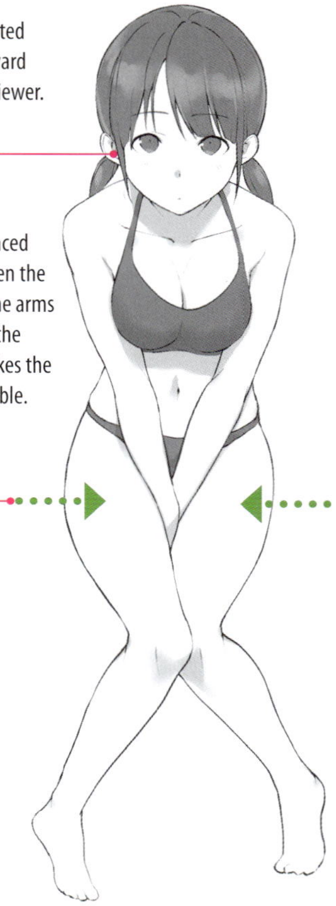

This is a pose where the seated character looks up. The upward gaze directly engages the viewer.

Both hands are placed in the gaps between the thighs. Bringing the arms and legs closer to the body's interior makes the character memorable.

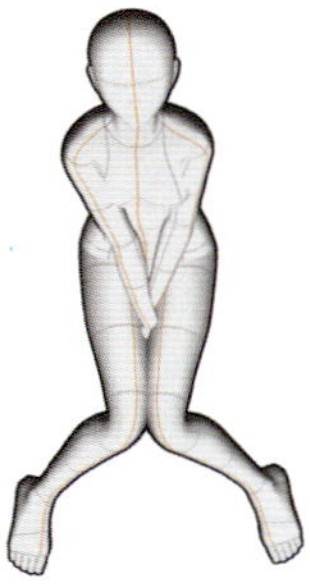

ANGLES

For a looking-up angle, adjusting it to a low angle to match the character's gaze makes it seem like they are looking at you.

ANGLES

A diagonal 45-degree angle can balance and show the full body of the character sitting down.

SHOWING THE BACK

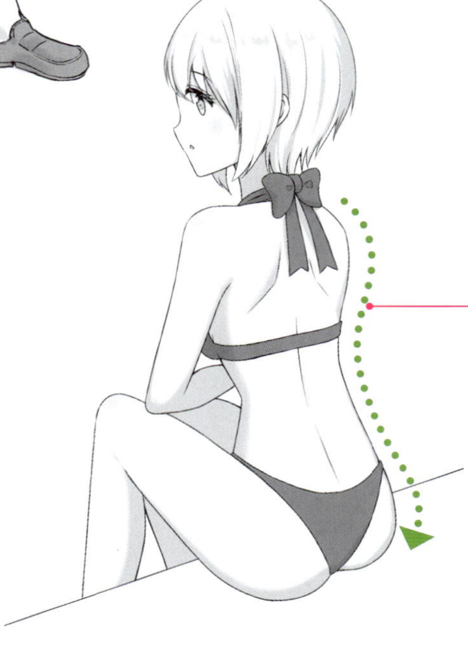

Sitting on a backless chair, platform, or stairs emphasizes the line from the shoulders through the waist to the buttocks.

SITTING ON STAIRS

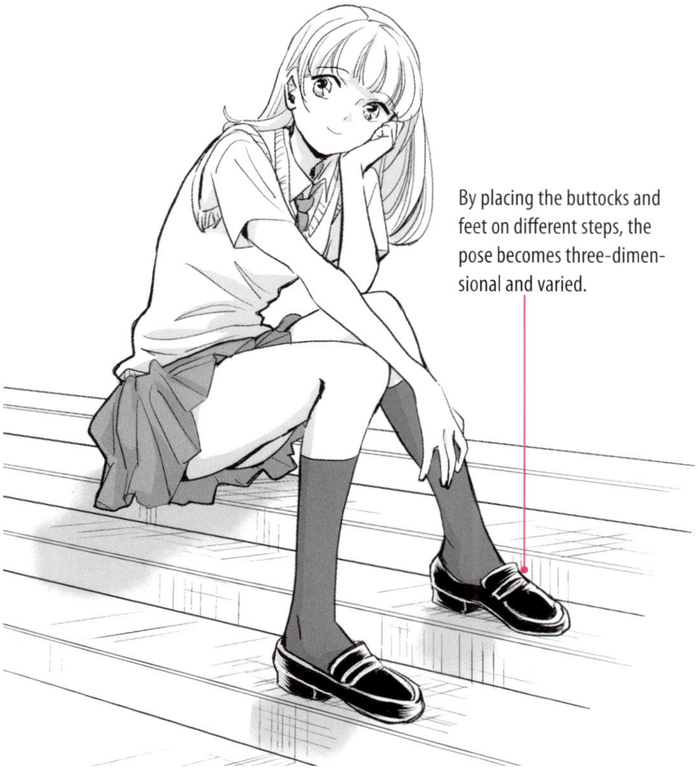

By placing the buttocks and feet on different steps, the pose becomes three-dimensional and varied.

SPREADING THE LEGS

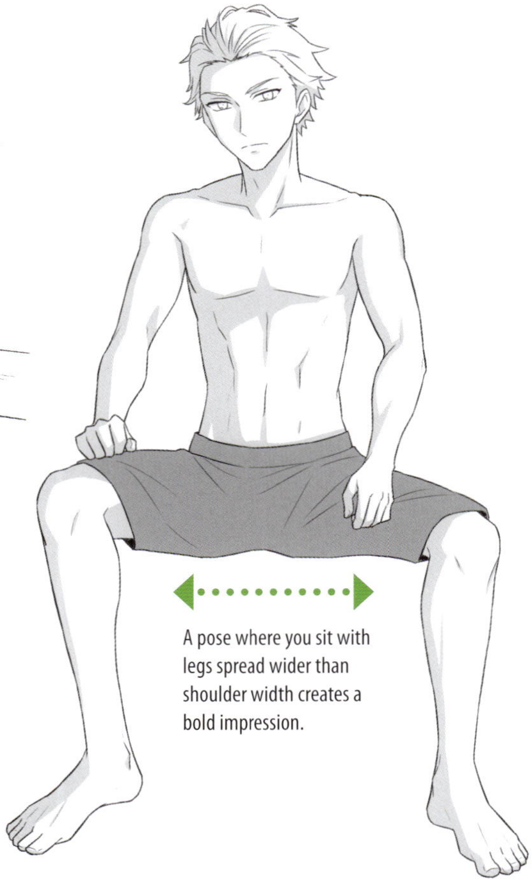

A pose where you sit with legs spread wider than shoulder width creates a bold impression.

SITTING WITH A HUNCHED BACK

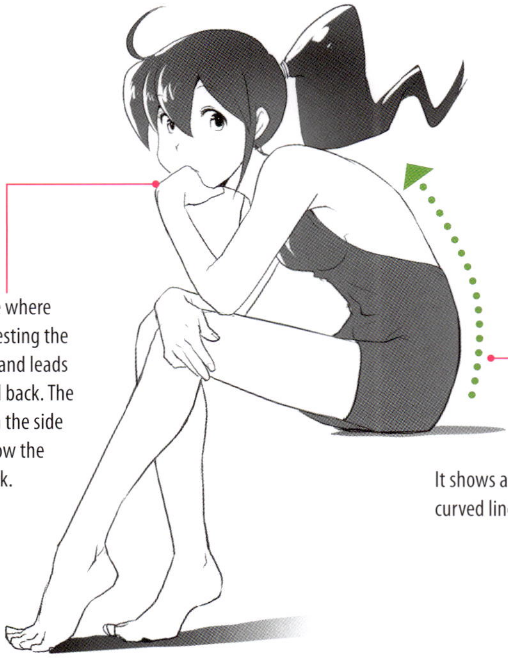

This is a pose where sitting and resting the cheek on a hand leads to a hunched back. The angle is from the side to clearly show the hunched back.

It shows a loosely curved line of the back.

CROPPING — Keep the Hips

When cropping a sitting pose, it is better not to crop around the buttocks which primarily support the center of gravity. Even if the legs are cropped, the pose of sitting can be conveyed as long as the hips are sufficiently visible in the frame.

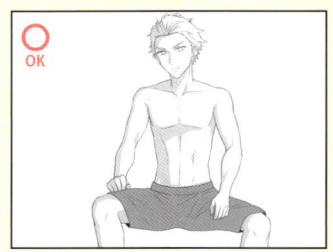

OK

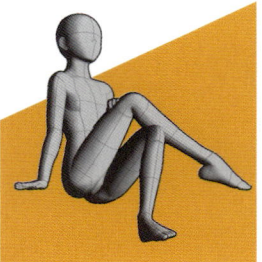

SITTING WITH CONFIDENCE
Crossing Legs

If you want to show your character seated in casual ease or with haughty confidence, this adaptable pose clearly showcases the lines of the legs. Placing the hands on the knees or beside the hips makes it appear more natural.

DEEPLY CROSSING LEGS

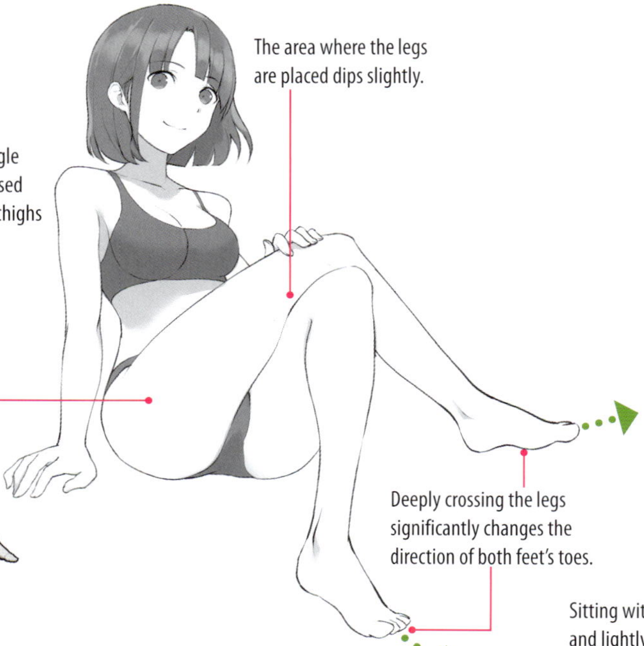

An upward tilted angle emphasizes the crossed legs and makes the thighs stand out.

The area where the legs are placed dips slightly.

Deeply crossing the legs significantly changes the direction of both feet's toes.

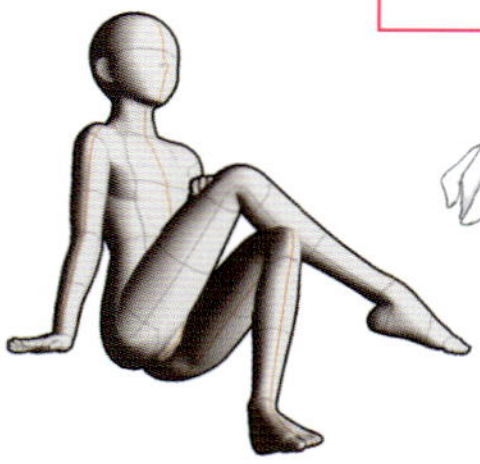

ANGLES
An upward tilted angle emphasizes the confident impression of the character with crossed legs.

LIGHTLY CROSSING LEGS

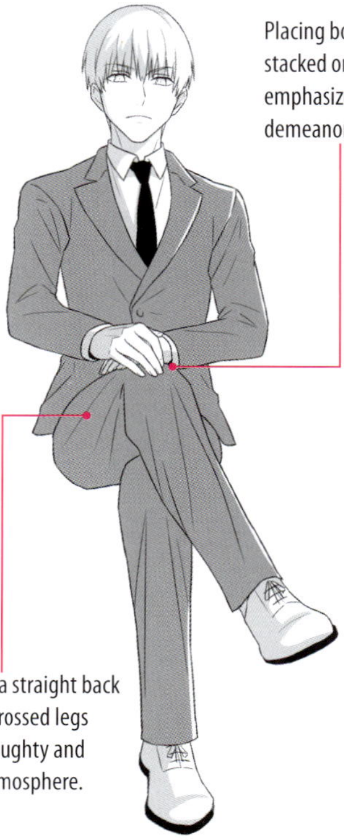

Placing both hands stacked on the legs emphasizes a polite demeanor.

Sitting with a straight back and lightly crossed legs conveys a haughty and confident atmosphere.

SITTING ON THE FLOOR

ANGLES
A slightly overhead diagonal angle does not overly emphasize the crossed legs, evenly showcasing the entire body.

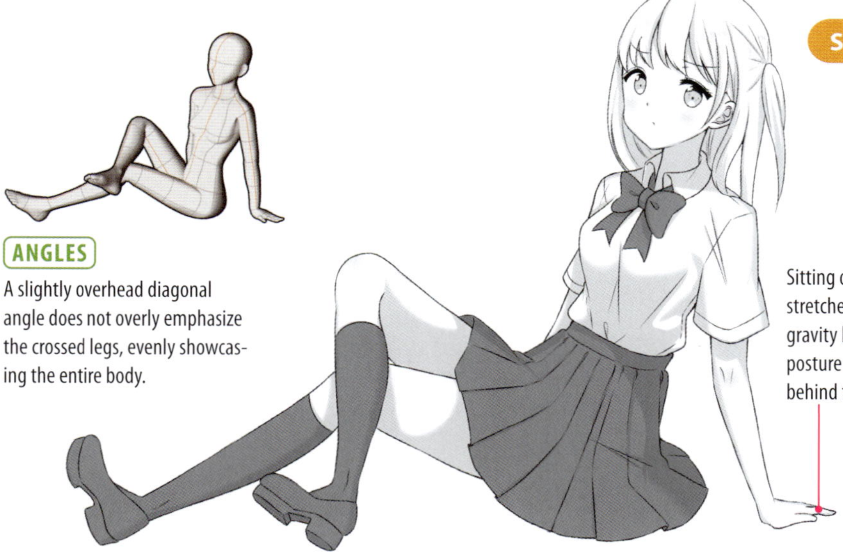

Sitting on the floor with legs stretched out shifts the center of gravity backward, resulting in a posture where the hands are placed behind to support the body.

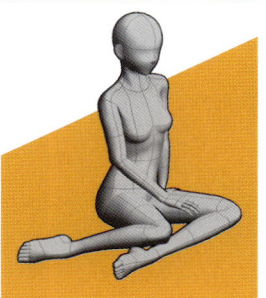

RELAXED POSTURES
Sitting to the Side

Curved and angular, this pose still creates an impression of comfort and relaxation. The center of gravity shifts to the side opposite the curved legs, so tilting the upper body is essential.

RELAXING

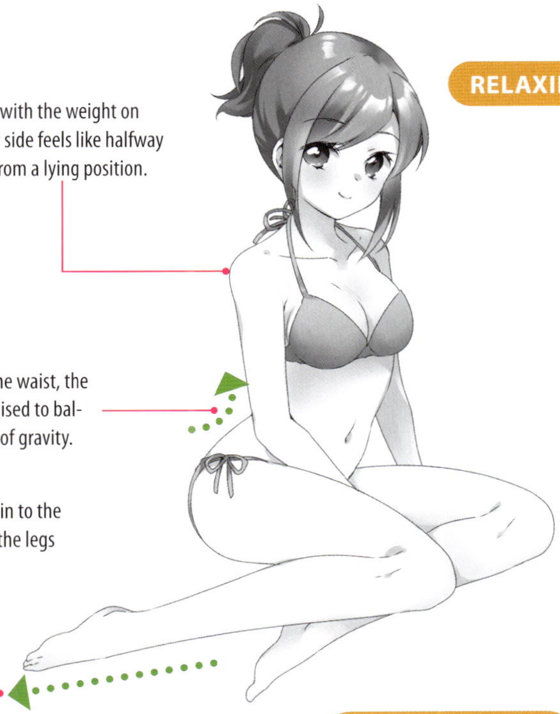

A pose with the weight on the left side feels like halfway rising from a lying position.

Bending from the waist, the upper body is raised to balance the center of gravity.

Drawing from the shin to the toes straight makes the legs appear lithe.

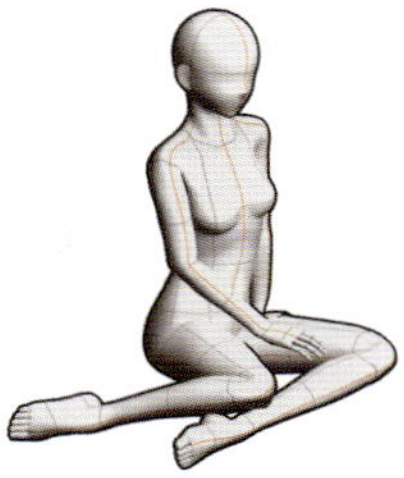

ANGLES

A diagonal and slightly overhead angle makes the collapsed leg's condition more understandable.

FRONTAL VIEW

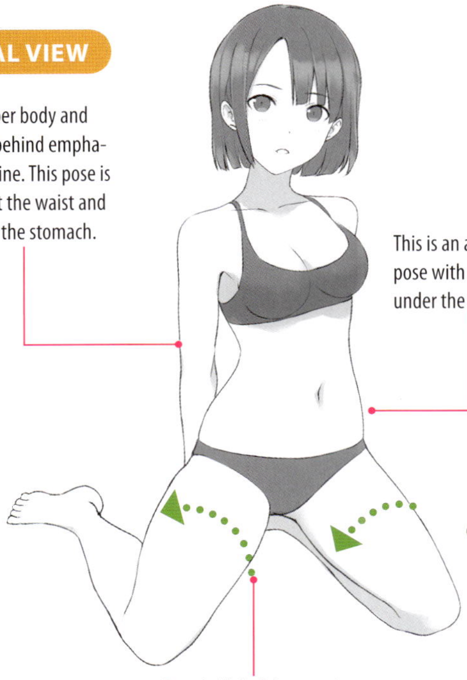

Raising the upper body and placing hands behind emphasizes the body line. This pose is drawn to depict the waist and the contours of the stomach.

EMPHASIZING THE LOWER BODY

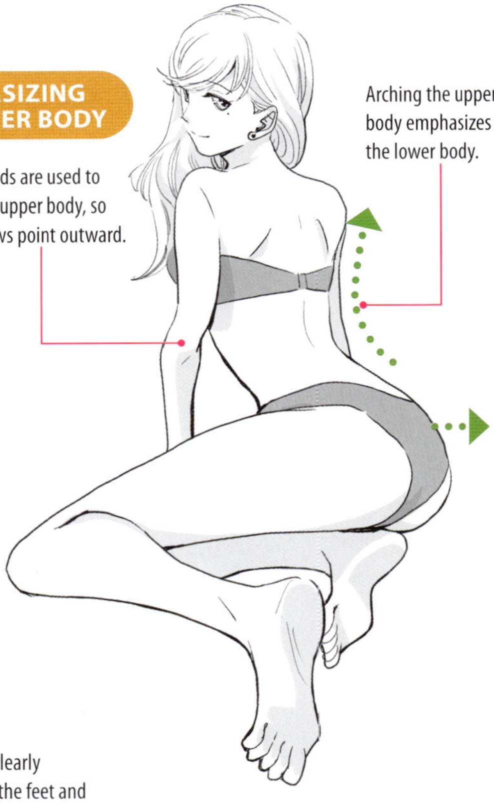

Both hands are used to raise the upper body, so the elbows point outward.

This is an arranged sitting pose with one leg placed under the buttocks.

Arching the upper body emphasizes the lower body.

Be mindful of the roundness of the thighs.

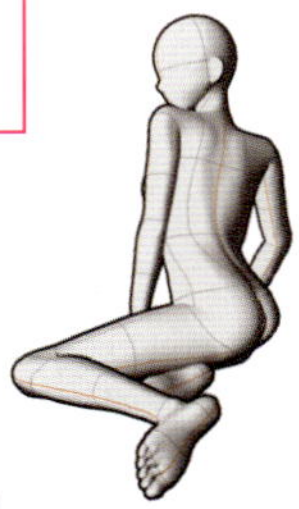

ANGLES

Use an angle that clearly shows the soles of the feet and emphasizes the lower body.

COMFORTABLE POSES
Kneeling, Viewed from Above

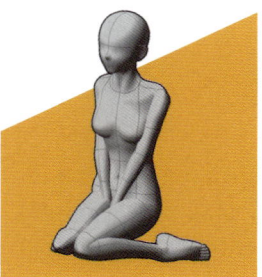

With the legs bent and pressed closely to the ground, the kneeling character is either on display or poised for action. Placing both hands between the legs helps maintain the overall balance.

BASIC FLAT SITTING

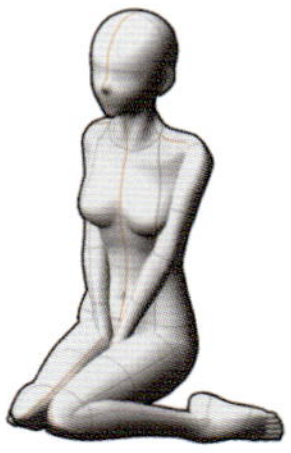

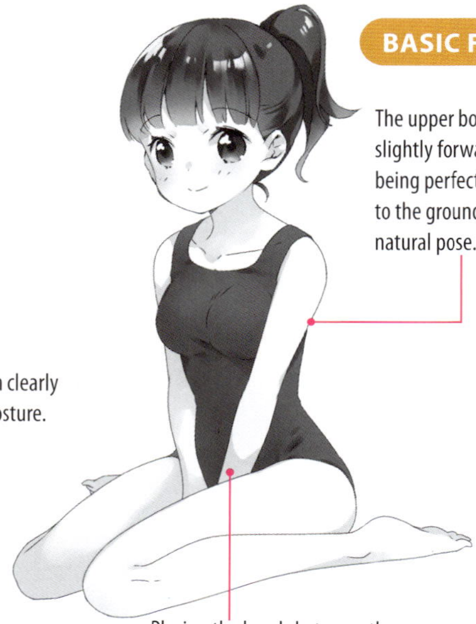

The upper body should lean slightly forward rather than being perfectly vertical to the ground for a more natural pose.

ANGLES

A diagonal angle can clearly convey the sitting posture.

Placing the hands between the thighs helps balance the look.

LEANING FORWARD

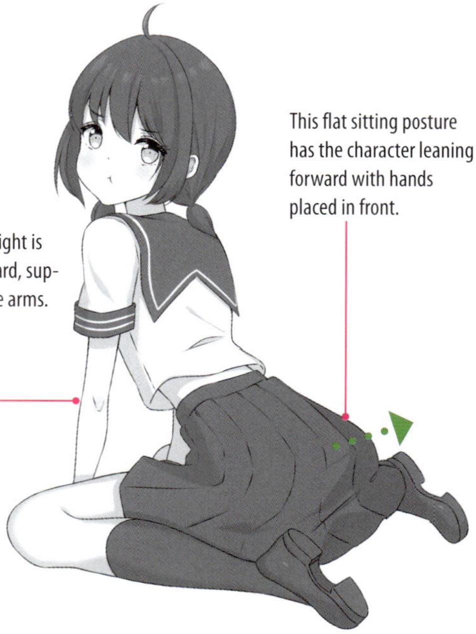

This flat sitting posture has the character leaning forward with hands placed in front.

The body weight is shifted forward, supported by the arms.

LOOKING UP

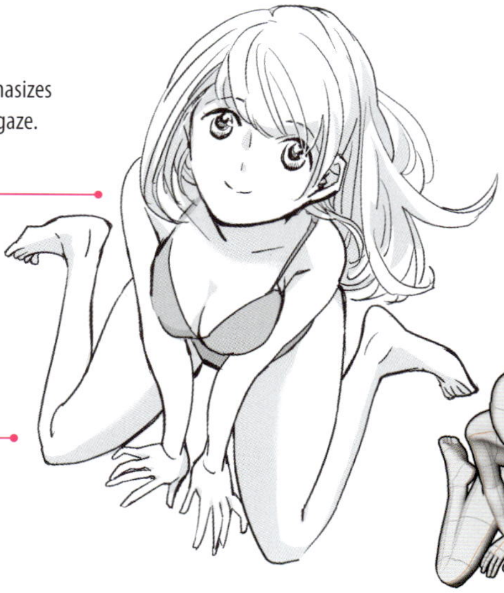

The angle emphasizes the character's gaze.

From a low angle, the knees are slightly pointed outward.

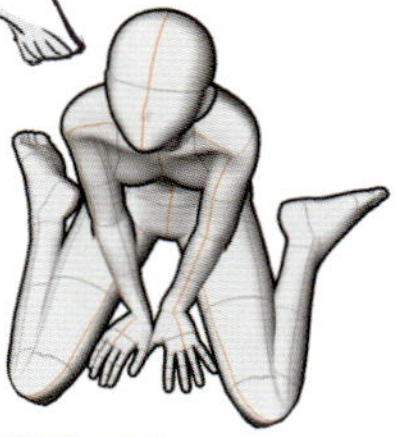

ANGLES

An angle from directly above allows focusing on the face while also showing the open-legged posture.

CROPPING — Don't Crop the Lower Body

While cropping the tips of the knees slightly in a flat sitting pose is acceptable, it's better not to crop the lower body much since the posture of the legs is a characteristic feature.

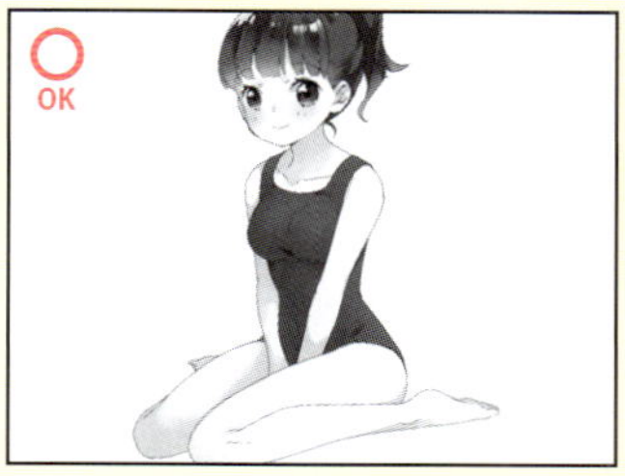

OK

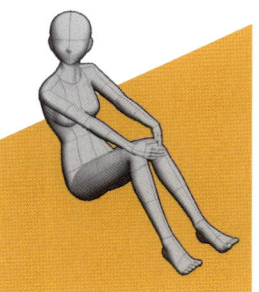

SITTING BY FOLDING LEGS
Holding the Legs

Here, the bent legs form a triangle. The basic form involves bringing the knees close to the chest and embracing them with both hands. This posture, where the body seems folded, can make the character appear smaller and more compact.

STRETCHING BACK AND LEGS

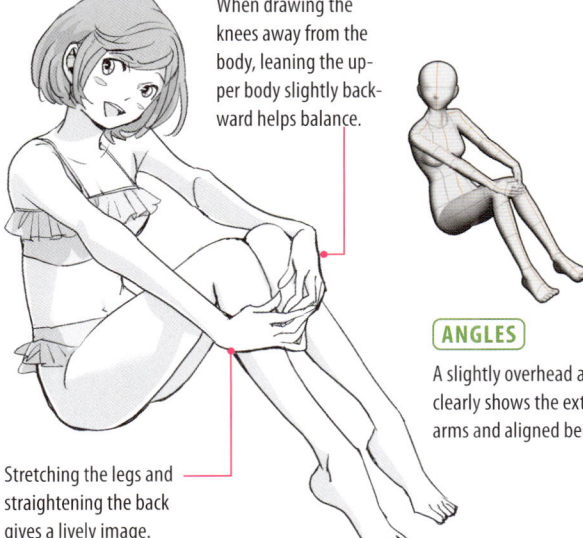

When drawing the knees away from the body, leaning the upper body slightly backward helps balance.

Stretching the legs and straightening the back gives a lively image.

ANGLES

A slightly overhead angle clearly shows the extended arms and aligned bent legs.

SITTING SMALL

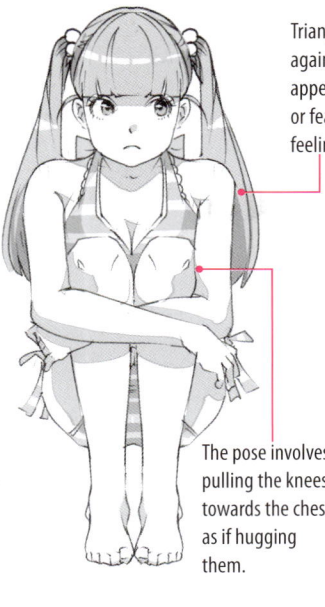

Triangle sitting with the knees pressed against the chest creates a pose that appears tightly curled due to tension or fear. It can express the character feeling small or intimidated.

The pose involves pulling the knees towards the chest as if hugging them.

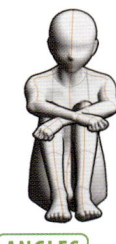

ANGLES

From a front angle, the body lines become less prominent, focusing attention on the facial expressions, making the pose more sympathetic to the character's emotions.

HANDS UNDER THE LEGS

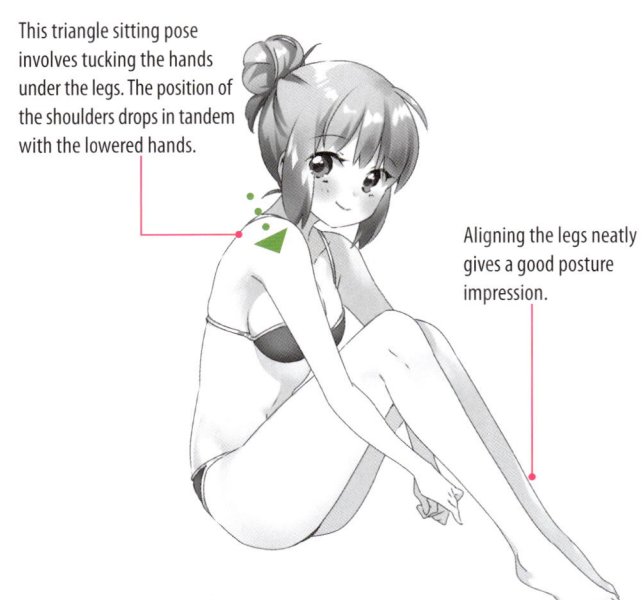

This triangle sitting pose involves tucking the hands under the legs. The position of the shoulders drops in tandem with the lowered hands.

Aligning the legs neatly gives a good posture impression.

> **Tips Triangular Seating**
>
> Drawing a large triangle formed by the ground, back and shins as a right triangle, and the triangle formed by the thighs, ground and calves as an isosceles triangle, results in a beautifully balanced pose.
>
>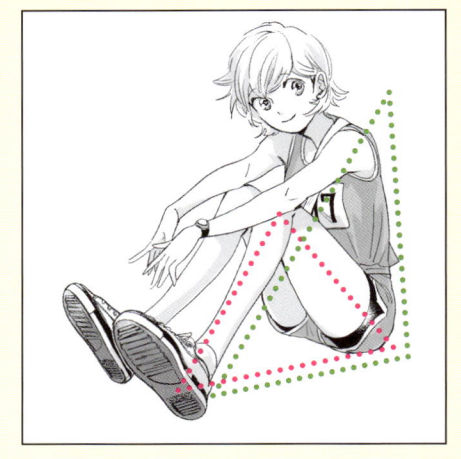

95

MAKING LEGS LOOK DYNAMIC
Extending the Legs

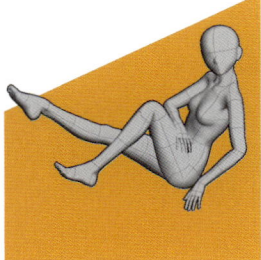

Lifting, stretching or extending the legs is a pose that really allows a character to stand out. These various stances focus on the lines of the legs, highlighting their musculature.

STRETCHING THE LEGS

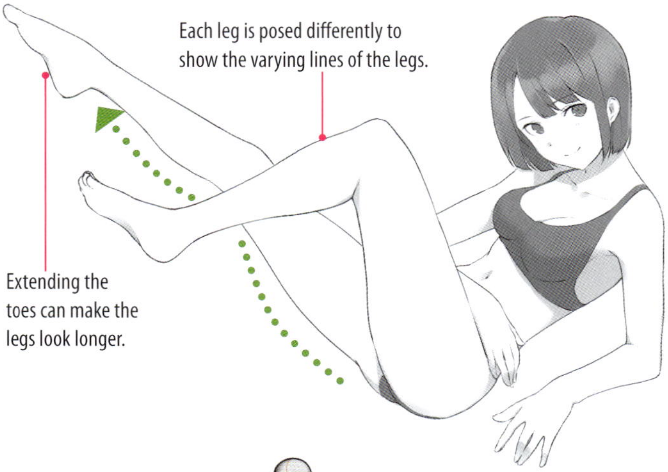

Each leg is posed differently to show the varying lines of the legs.

Extending the toes can make the legs look longer.

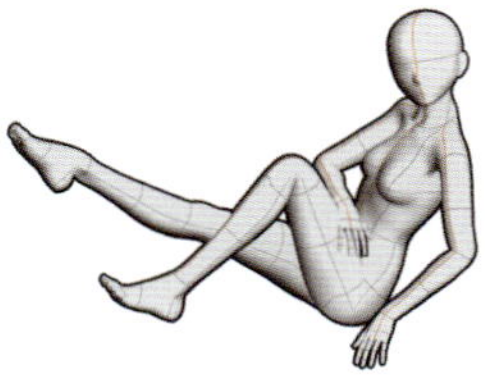

ANGLES
A slightly overhead side angle can display the line of the legs.

WITH KNEES CLOSED

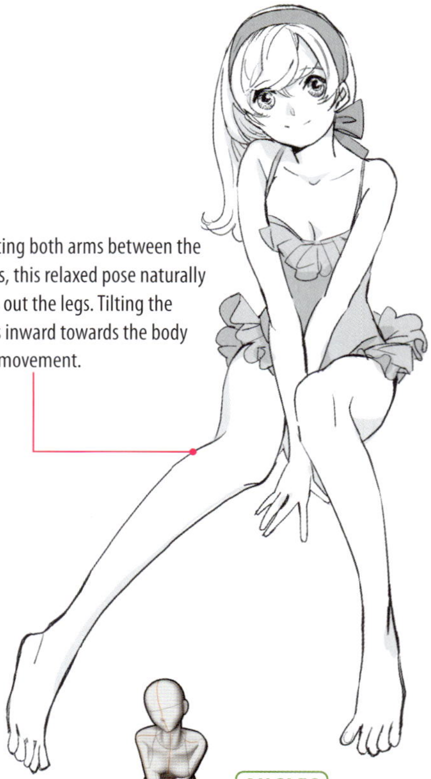

Inserting both arms between the thighs, this relaxed pose naturally flings out the legs. Tilting the knees inward towards the body adds movement.

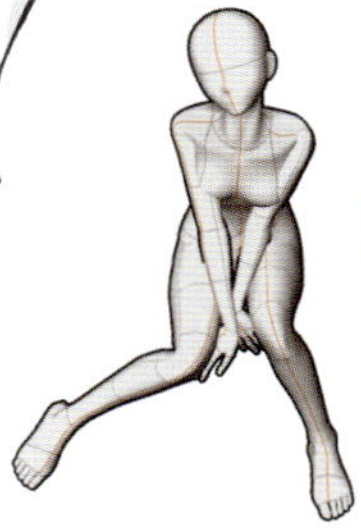

ANGLES
An overhead angle makes it easier to see the angle of the knock-kneed legs.

RAISING ONE LEG HIGH

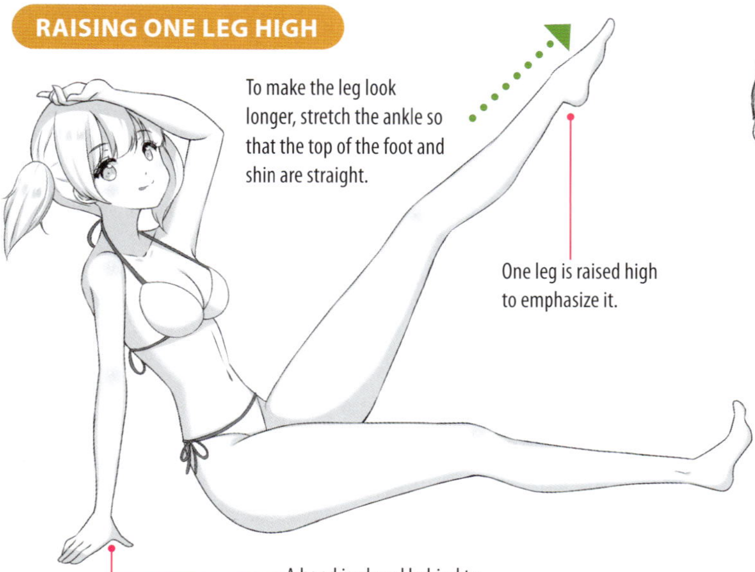

To make the leg look longer, stretch the ankle so that the top of the foot and shin are straight.

One leg is raised high to emphasize it.

A hand is placed behind to support the unstable posture.

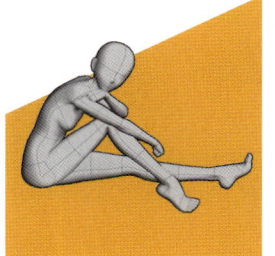

RESTING POSES

One Knee Raised

It's essential to know how to draw your characters in a simple, relaxed seating position. A classic posture is to rest the elbow on the raised knee. This creates a realistically appealing and natural pose.

RAISED LEG FORMS A TRIANGLE

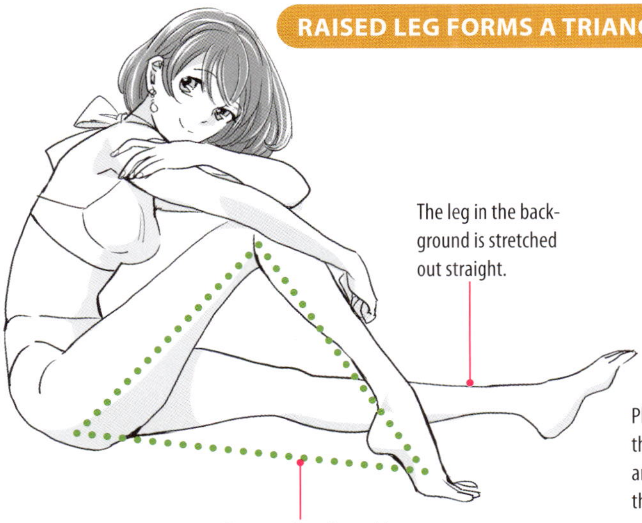

The leg in the background is stretched out straight.

The triangle is formed by the knee of the leg in the foreground when raised.

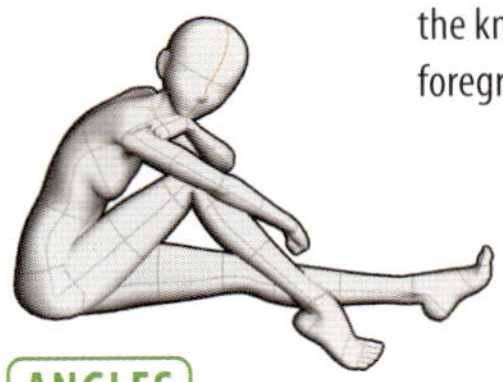

ANGLES
From a side angle, the knee raised into a triangle shape is clearly visible.

CROSSING LEGS IN AN X

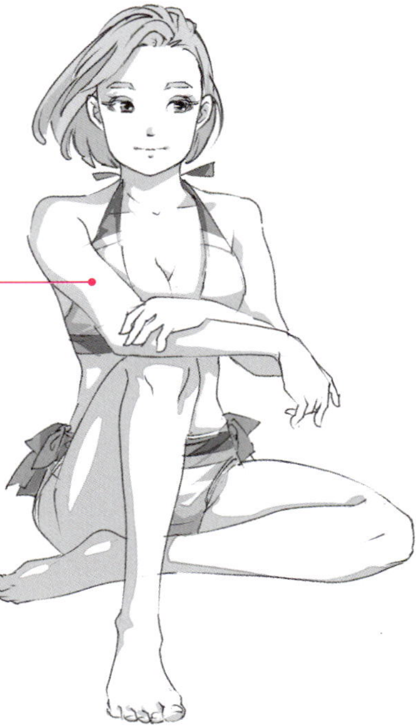

Rest the arms on the raised knee, letting the hands hang loosely and naturally.

Place the raised leg in front of the leg that is down, creating an X shape. From the front, the legs look neatly arranged.

CONFIDENT POSTURE

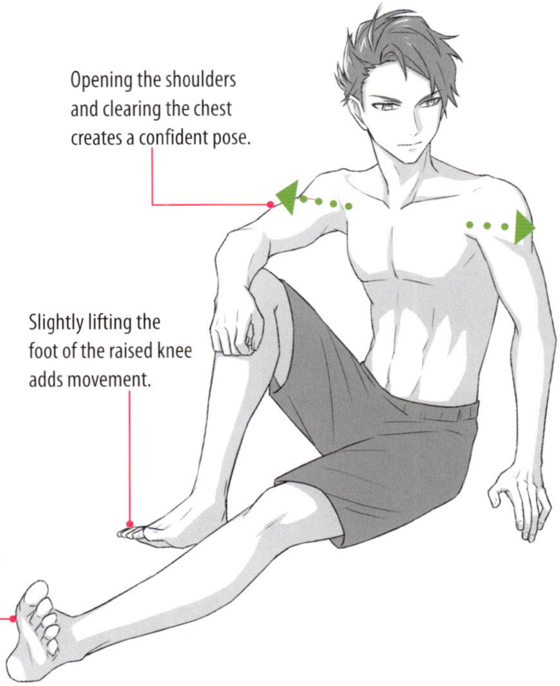

Opening the shoulders and clearing the chest creates a confident pose.

Slightly lifting the foot of the raised knee adds movement.

The toes point slightly outward.

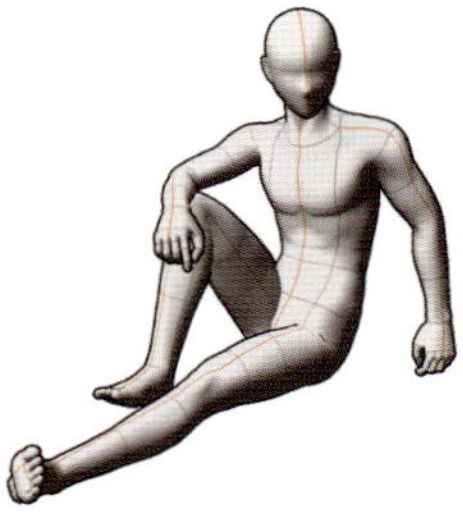

ANGLES
A low angle tends to give a static impression, so for a relaxed pose like one with a raised knee, it emphasizes a relaxed feel.

BASIC MOVEMENT POSES
Walking

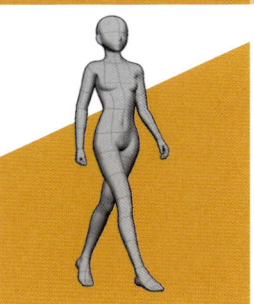

A large stride is perfect for giving off an energetic or confident impression, while a smaller stride suits more casual scenes. Either way, the right pose introduces a powerful sense of motion and dynamism to your illustration.

WALKING CONFIDENTLY

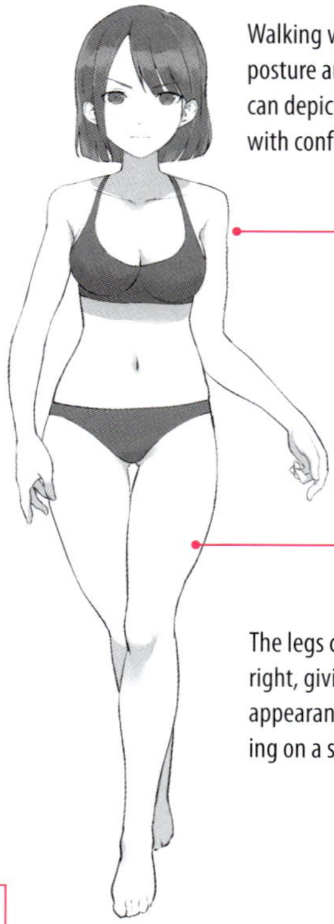

Walking with a straight posture and chest puffed out can depict a character filled with confidence.

The legs cross left and right, giving a neat appearance as if walking on a single line.

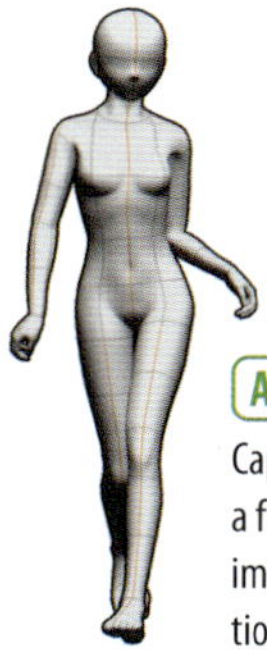

ANGLES
Capturing the walking pose from a front angle conveys an active impression, suggesting "motivation" and "intention to act."

WALKING WITH A STRUT

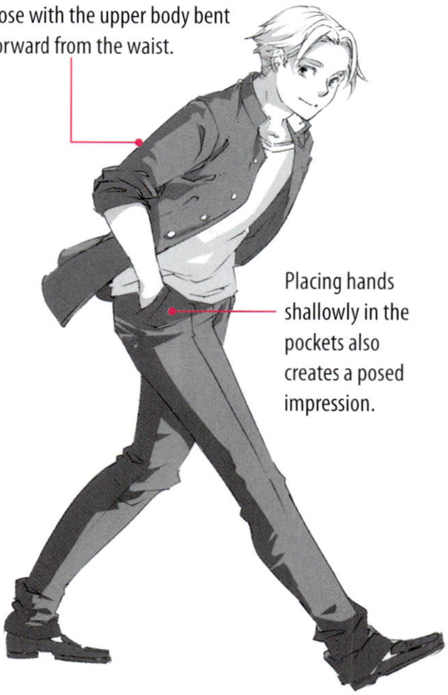

This is a strut-like walking pose with the upper body bent forward from the waist.

Placing hands shallowly in the pockets also creates a posed impression.

MODEL WALK

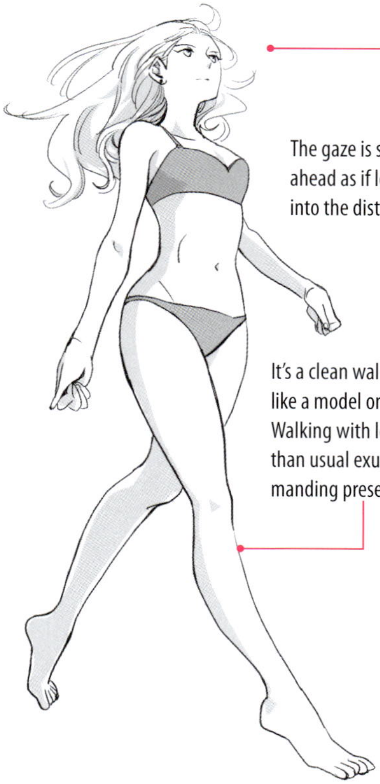

The gaze is straight ahead as if looking into the distance.

It's a clean walking pose like a model on a runway. Walking with longer strides than usual exudes a commanding presence.

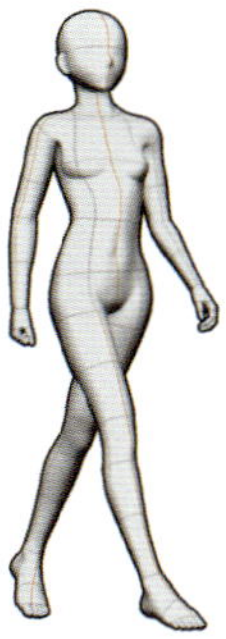

ANGLES
A low angle emphasizes the walking legs, enhancing the impact of the pose.

> **Tips — Matching Hand Swing with Stride**
>
> The movement of the legs and the swing of the hands are coordinated to create the pose. When walking with long strides, swing the arms broadly; with smaller strides, the arms move less.

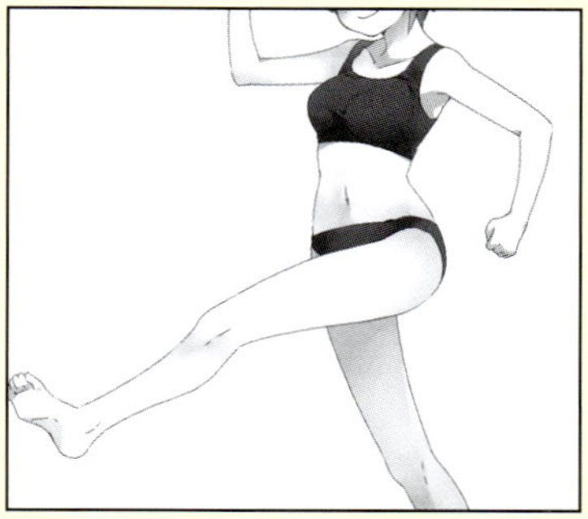

WALKING WHILE LOOKING BACK

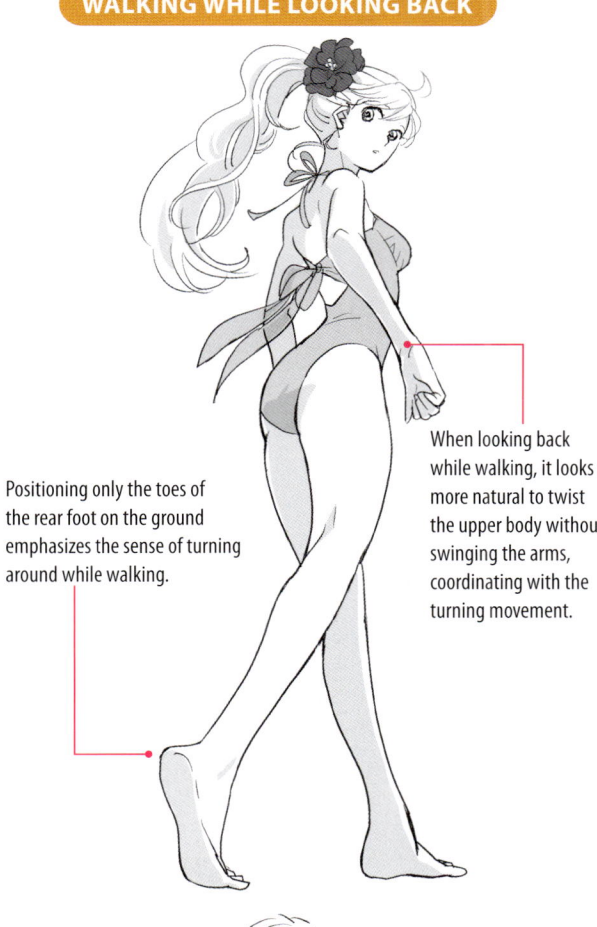

Positioning only the toes of the rear foot on the ground emphasizes the sense of turning around while walking.

When looking back while walking, it looks more natural to twist the upper body without swinging the arms, coordinating with the turning movement.

WALKING WHILE DEEP IN THOUGHT

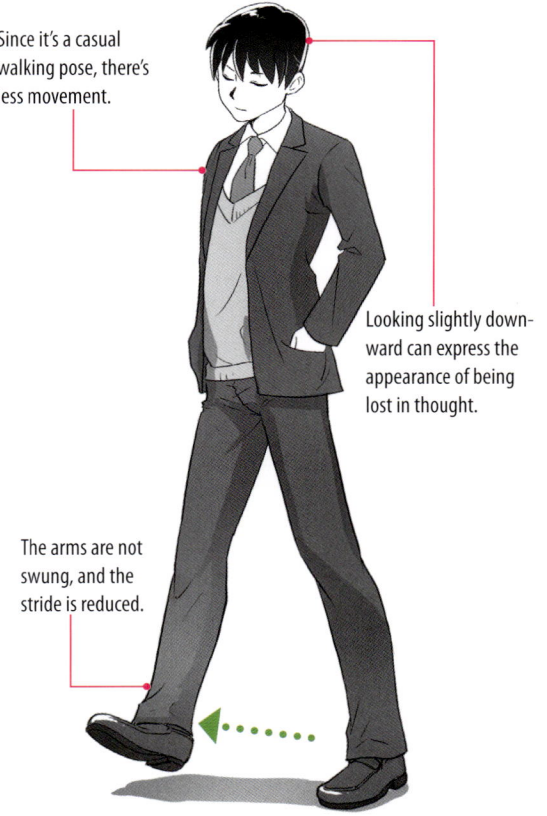

Since it's a casual walking pose, there's less movement.

Looking slightly downward can express the appearance of being lost in thought.

The arms are not swung, and the stride is reduced.

CITY WALKING

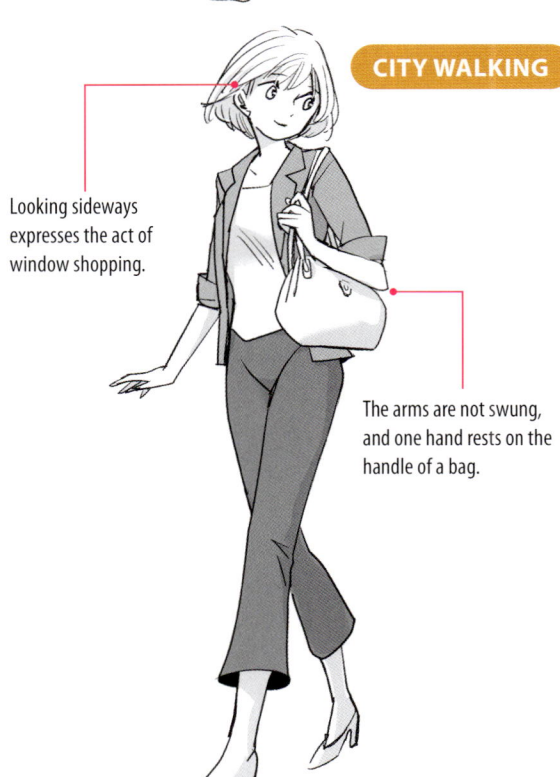

Looking sideways expresses the act of window shopping.

The arms are not swung, and one hand rests on the handle of a bag.

MARCHING WITH LONG STRIDES

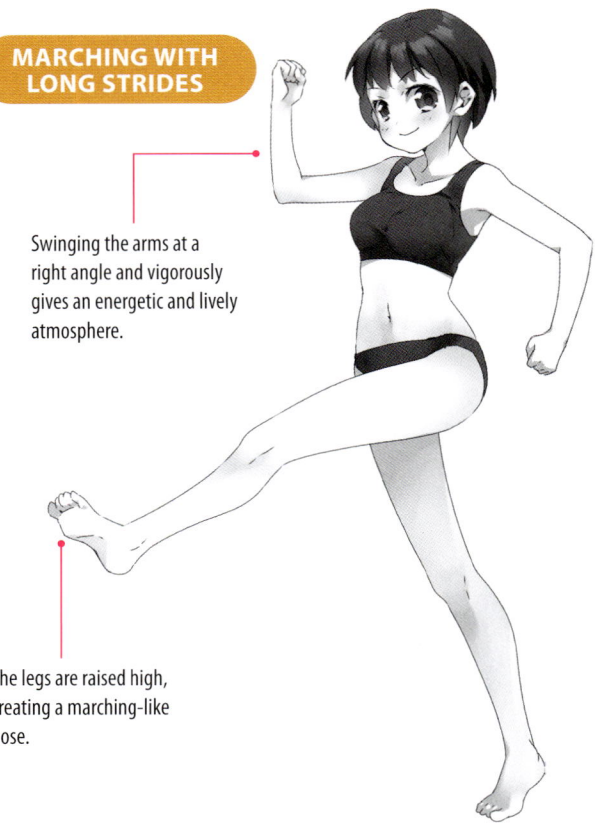

Swinging the arms at a right angle and vigorously gives an energetic and lively atmosphere.

The legs are raised high, creating a marching-like pose.

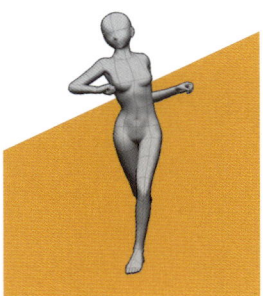

ENERGETIC, ATHLETIC POSES
Running

Your character is running at full speed, surging with power and energy. The dynamic movement of the dashing form can suggest a character charging toward a goal or triumphing over adversity.

LARGE ARM SWINGS

Drawing the arms swinging broadly enhances the sense of dynamism.

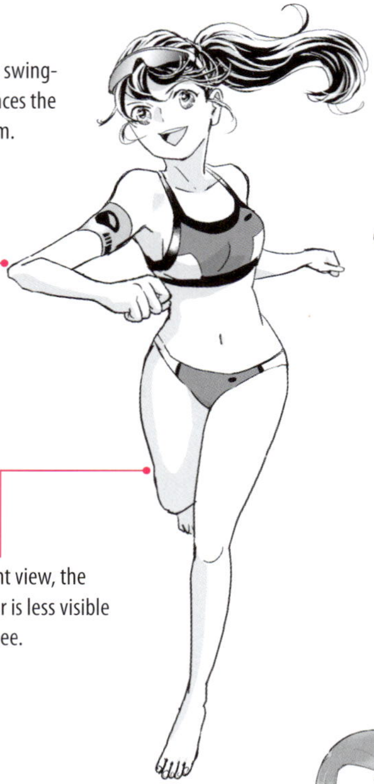

From the front view, the leg in the rear is less visible below the knee.

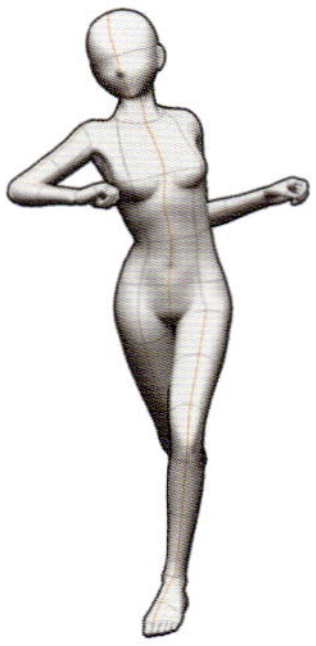

ANGLES
This angle looks at the running action from the same eye level as the character.

FIERCE DASH

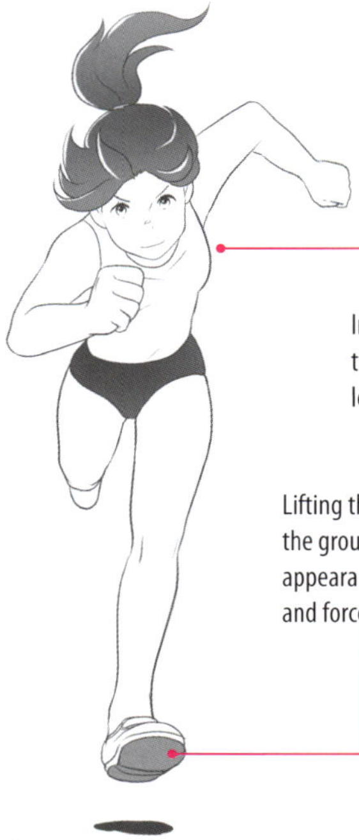

In a fierce dash, the upper body leans forward.

Lifting the forward foot off the ground emphasizes the appearance of running fast and forcefully.

BOUNDING RUN

Drawing the limbs aiming upward expresses a bounding movement.

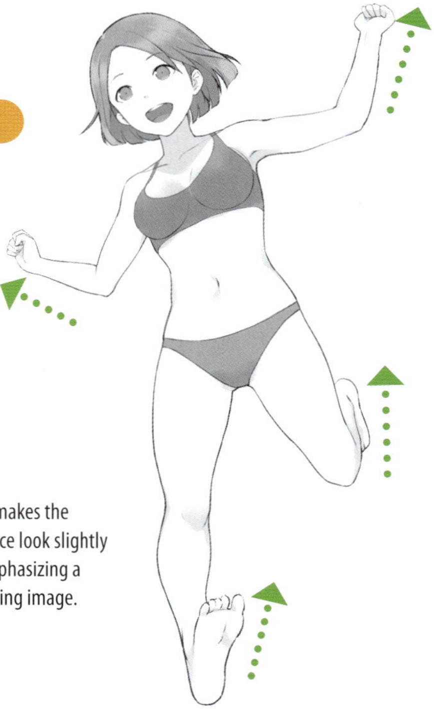

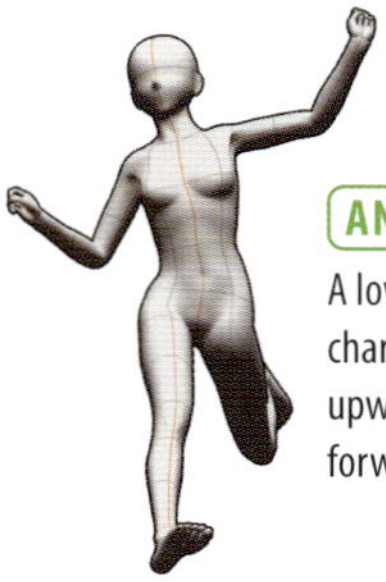

ANGLES
A low angle makes the character's face look slightly upwards, emphasizing a forward-looking image.

Tips Expressing Speed of Running

In running poses, the more the body leans forward, the faster the run appears.

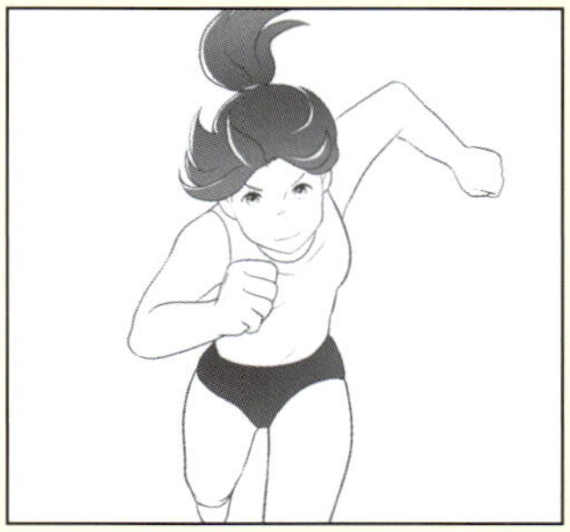

100

ADDING HUMOR TO MOVEMENT
Slipping

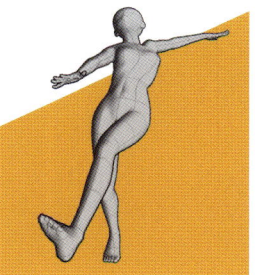

Is your character a klutz? This motion involves dynamically moving the arms while struggling to regain balance. The hand extended in the direction of the fall and the stumbling legs create a humorous and lively sense of action.

FALLING FORWARD

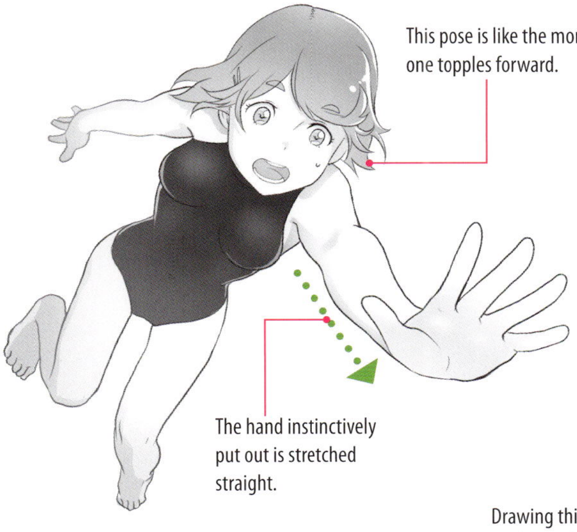

This pose is like the moment one topples forward.

The hand instinctively put out is stretched straight.

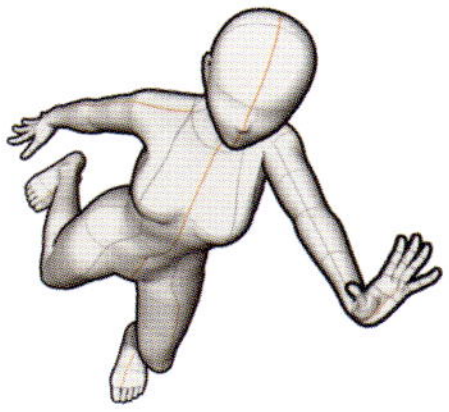

ANGLES
An angle set around the height of the character's eyes showcases the face and the hands pushed out prominently.

FALLING BACKWARD

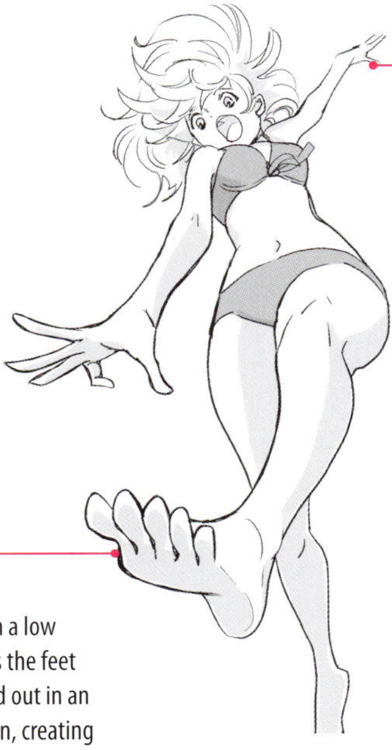

This is a pose of moving the hands dramatically as if trying to balance.

Drawing this from a low angle emphasizes the feet and hands pushed out in an attempt to hold on, creating a dynamic composition.

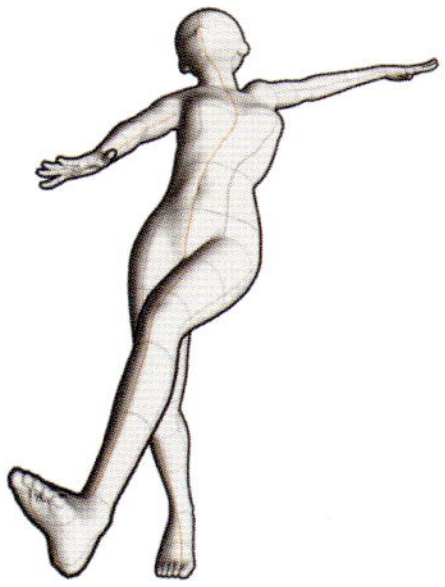

ANGLES
A low camera angle emphasizes the movement of the legs.

SLIPPING AND FALLING

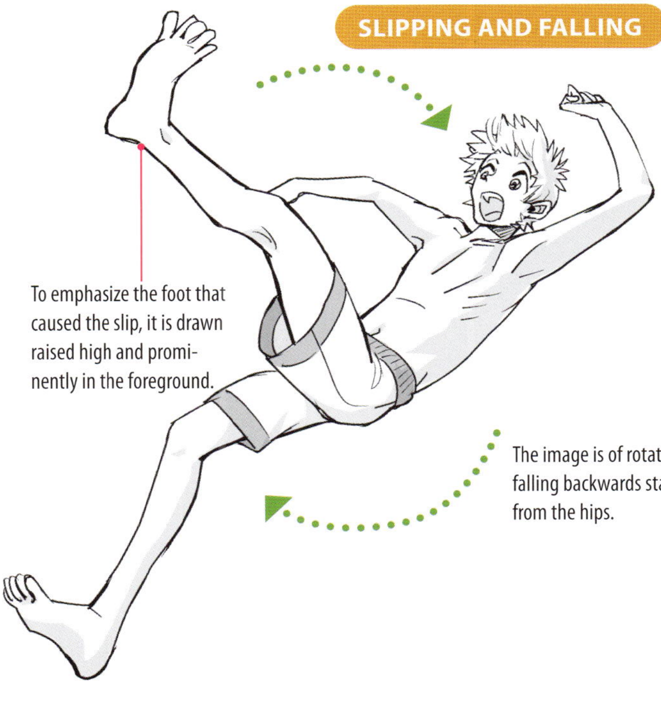

To emphasize the foot that caused the slip, it is drawn raised high and prominently in the foreground.

The image is of rotating and falling backwards starting from the hips.

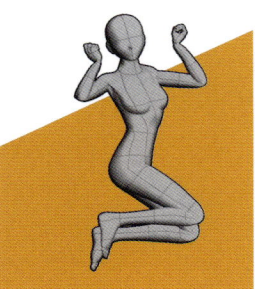

OVERFLOWING ENERGY BURSTING FORTH

Jumping

Defying gravity with bent legs lifted high captures a moment of youthful energy. The coiled energy of the body and the taut, contoured muscles create a memorable pose for your actively inclined characters.

LITTLE LEAP

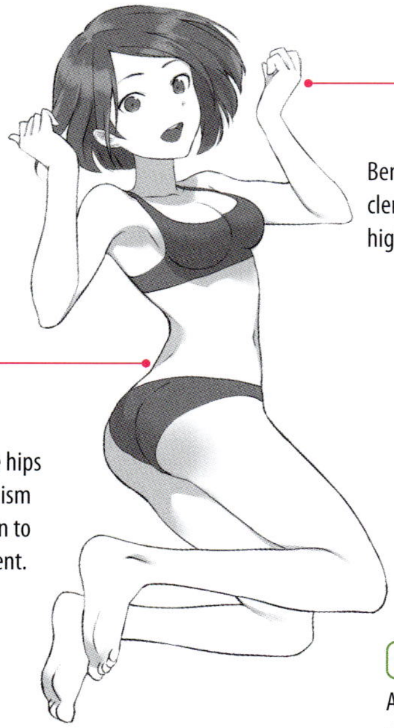

Bending the arms and placing clenched hands near the face highlights the expression.

Twisting the hips adds dynamism and variation to the movement.

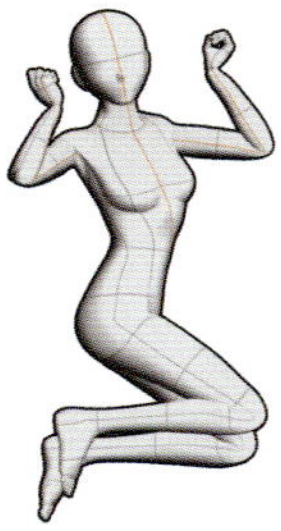

ANGLES
A diagonal angle allows for a clear view of the body lines, showcasing the proportions.

QUIET LEAP

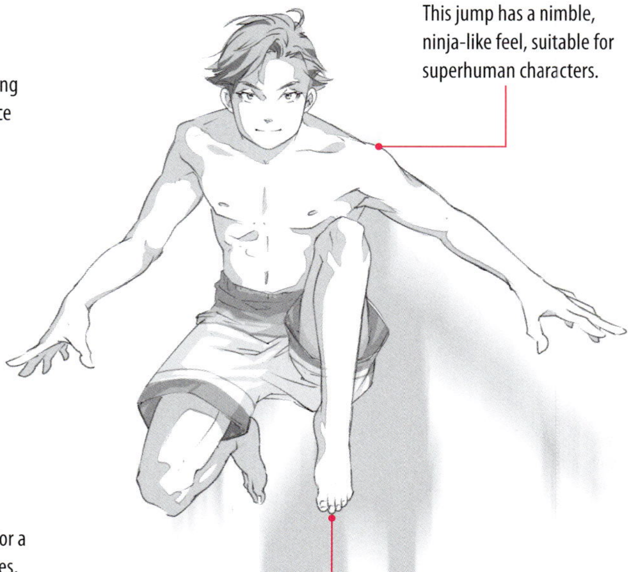

This jump has a nimble, ninja-like feel, suitable for superhuman characters.

The toes point downward to represent the moment in mid-air.

ENERGETICALLY AND VIGOROUSLY

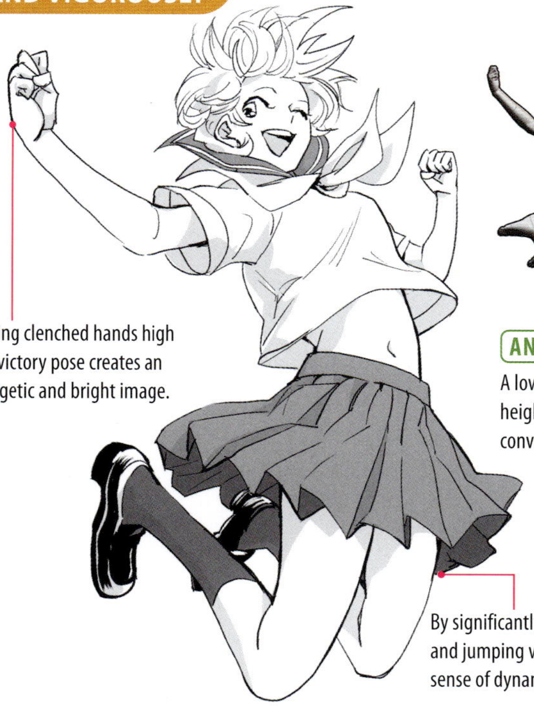

Raising clenched hands high in a victory pose creates an energetic and bright image.

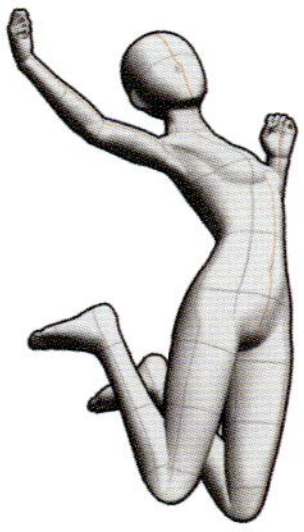

ANGLES
A low angle emphasizes the height of the subject, effectively conveying the force of the jump.

By significantly bending the knees and jumping with all might, the sense of dynamism is enhanced.

Tips: Jumping High with Bent Knees

The more the knees are bent, the higher the jump feels.

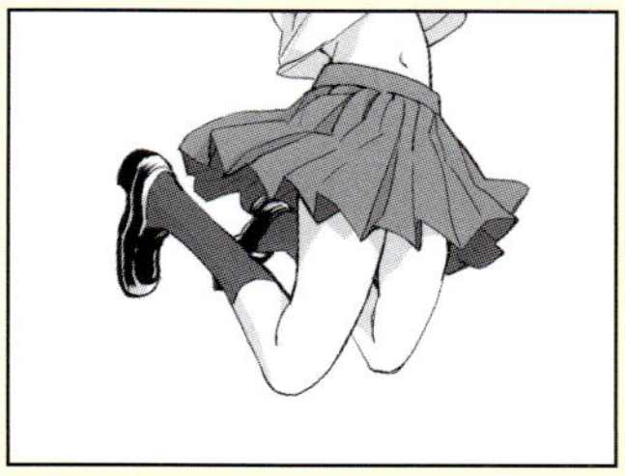

JUMPING WITH KNOCKED KNEES

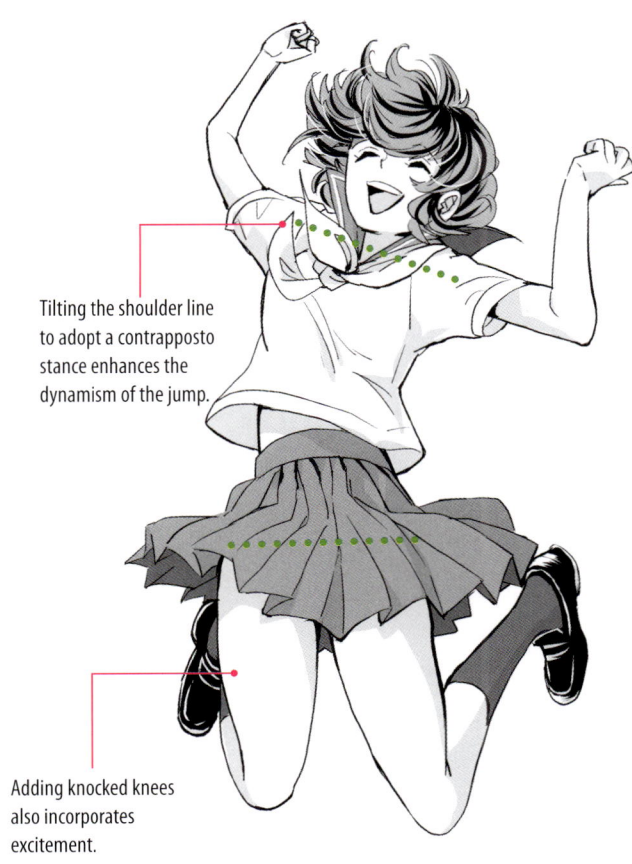

Tilting the shoulder line to adopt a contrapposto stance enhances the dynamism of the jump.

Adding knocked knees also incorporates excitement.

JUMPING OVER A FENCE

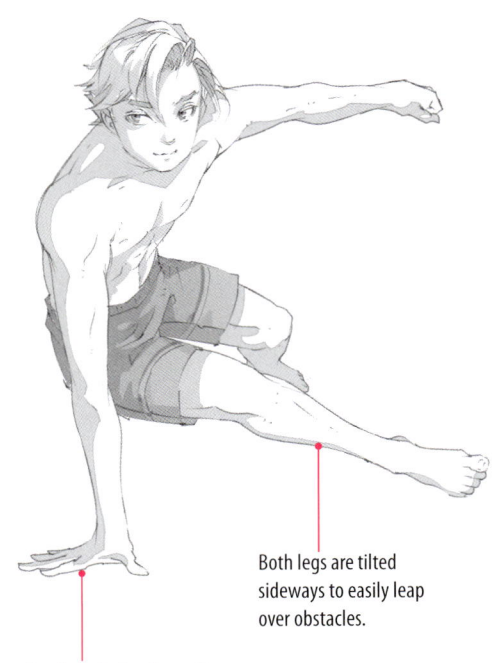

Both legs are tilted sideways to easily leap over obstacles.

This pose involves placing the entire body weight on one hand to jump over obstacles like a fence.

SPREADING BOTH LEGS

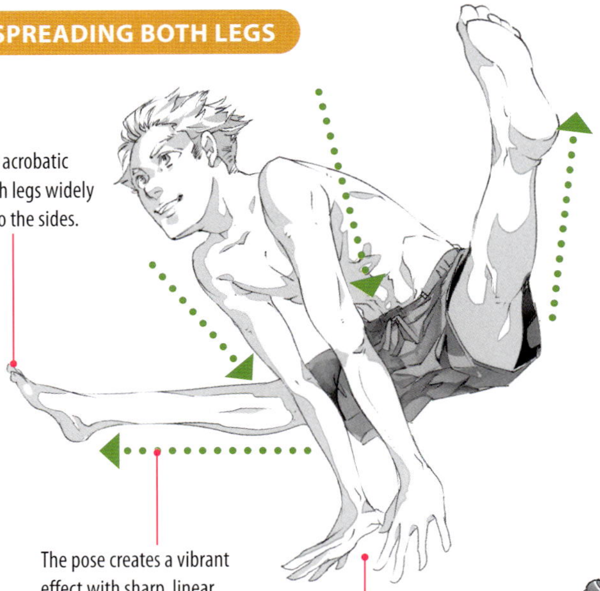

This is an acrobatic jump with legs widely opened to the sides.

The pose creates a vibrant effect with sharp, linear movements.

Aligning both arms as if jumping over a vault emphasizes the momentum of the jump.

JUMPING OVER A PUDDLE

A pose of leaping over a puddle with wide strides represents a lively and energetic character.

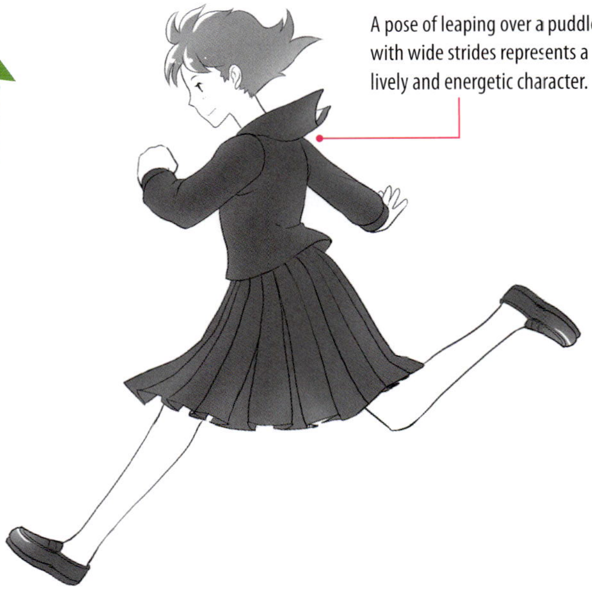

GRAVITY AND THE GROUND
Landing

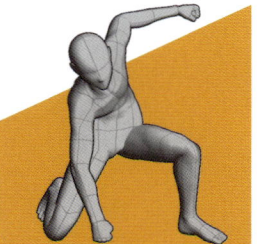

Various landings can be depicted through the positioning of the arms balancing the body and the movements of the legs upon touchdown. The post-landing pose, where both knees are deeply bent, indicates the significant impact and force of the landing.

CREATING A BOLD IMPRESSION

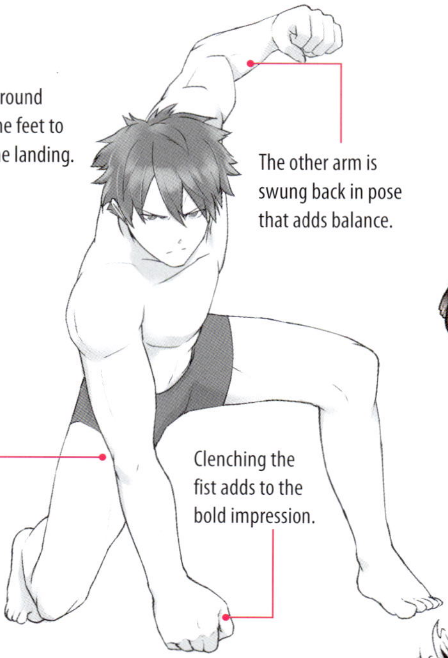

One arm touches the ground simultaneously with the feet to soften the impact of the landing.

The other arm is swung back in pose that adds balance.

Clenching the fist adds to the bold impression.

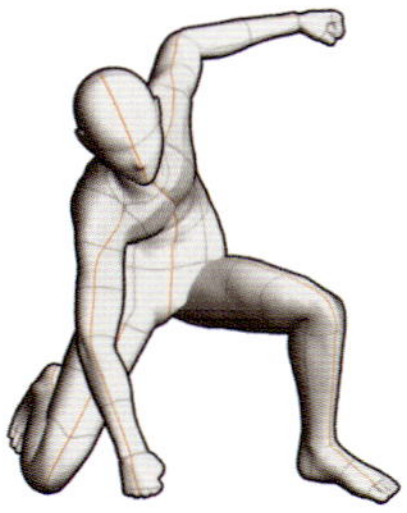

ANGLES

A frontal angle is suitable for conveying a commanding presence.

SOFTLY DESCENDING

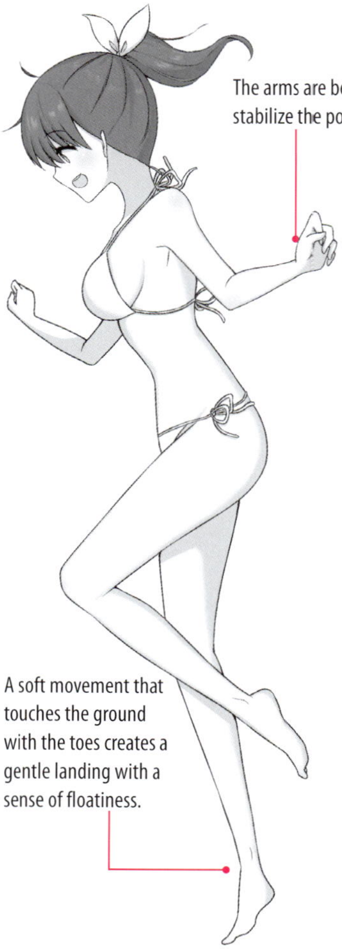

The arms are bent to stabilize the posture.

A soft movement that touches the ground with the toes creates a gentle landing with a sense of floatiness.

CONVEYING A SENSE OF SPEED

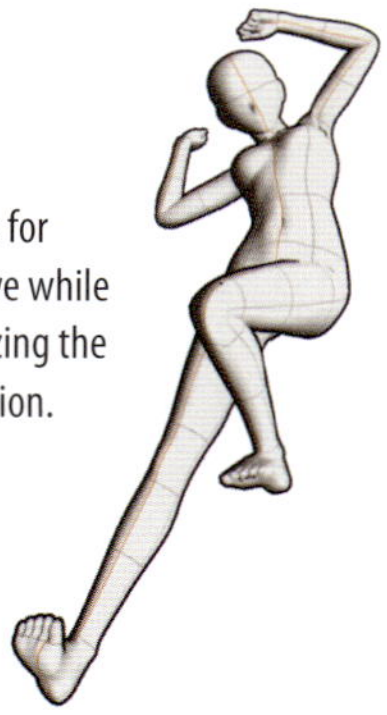

ANGLES

A low angle allows for creating perspective while drawing, emphasizing the intensity of the action.

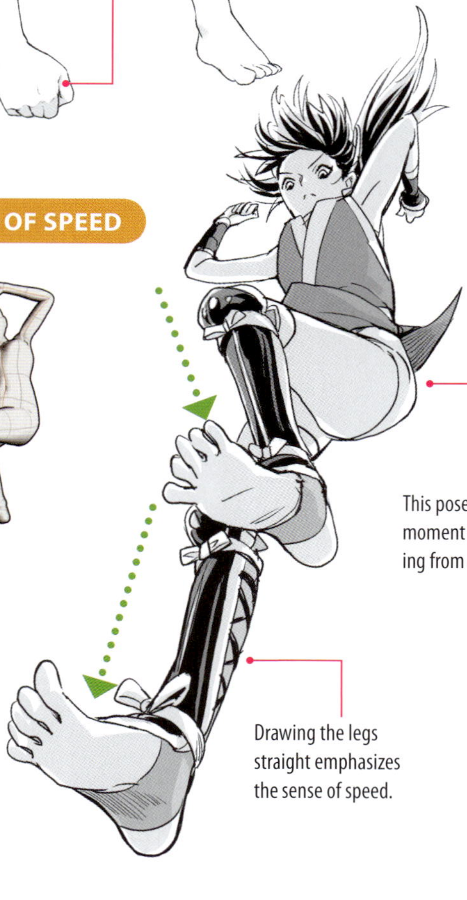

This pose captures the moment of forcefully landing from a high place.

Drawing the legs straight emphasizes the sense of speed.

SHOWING OFF THEIR MOVES
Dancing

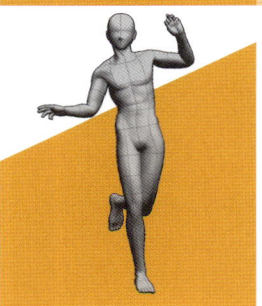

With dance moves, it's important to keep in mind the contrapposto elements that create a sense of dynamism. A toe tap, a slick slide or a graceful leap captures the joy, fun and intoxicating energy that surge from within when your characters bust a move.

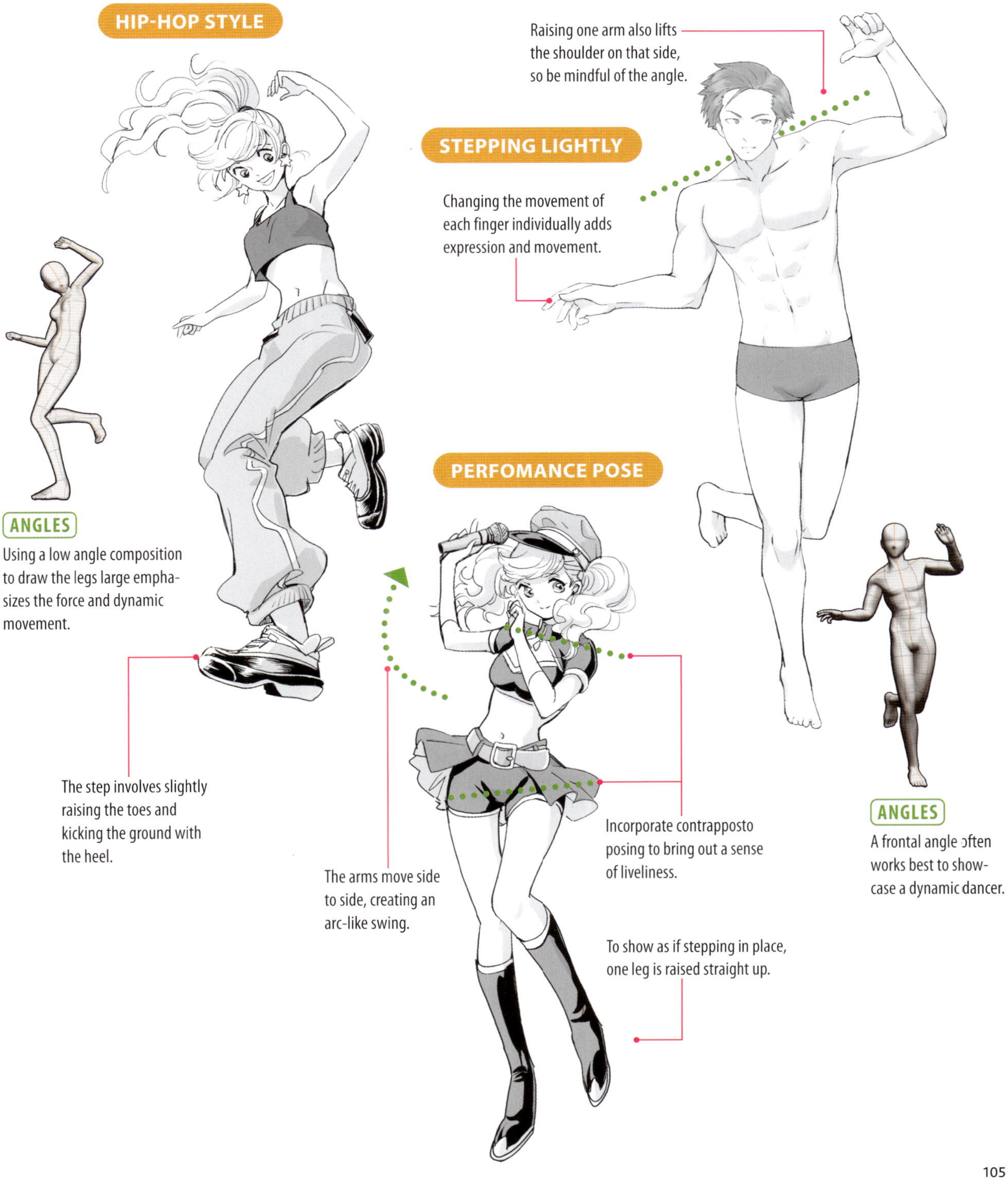

HIP-HOP STYLE

ANGLES
Using a low angle composition to draw the legs large emphasizes the force and dynamic movement.

The step involves slightly raising the toes and kicking the ground with the heel.

STEPPING LIGHTLY

Raising one arm also lifts the shoulder on that side, so be mindful of the angle.

Changing the movement of each finger individually adds expression and movement.

PERFOMANCE POSE

The arms move side to side, creating an arc-like swing.

Incorporate contrapposto posing to bring out a sense of liveliness.

To show as if stepping in place, one leg is raised straight up.

ANGLES
A frontal angle often works best to showcase a dynamic dancer.

105

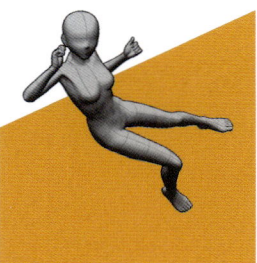

A SENSE OF WEIGHTLESSNESS
Suspended in Air

Sometimes you need poses that defy gravity. Soaring, suspended or flying through the air, it's important to tilt the body into an unstable position and extend the toes to clearly show that the character is floating and most definitely not on the ground.

CREATING A SENSE OF FLOATING

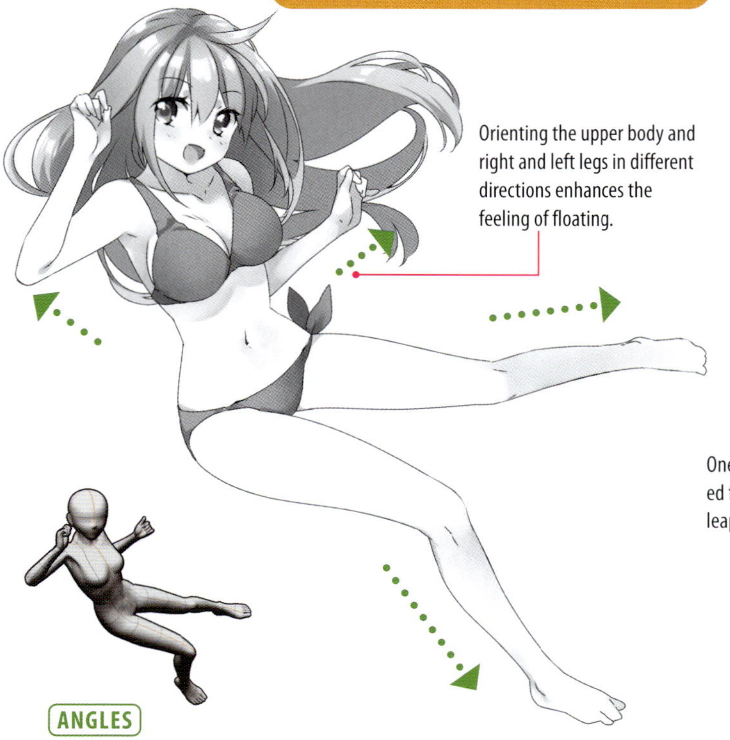

Orienting the upper body and right and left legs in different directions enhances the feeling of floating.

HERO'S FLIGHT

This is a classic pose seen when comic book heroes fly through the air. Clenched fists convey the heroic boldness.

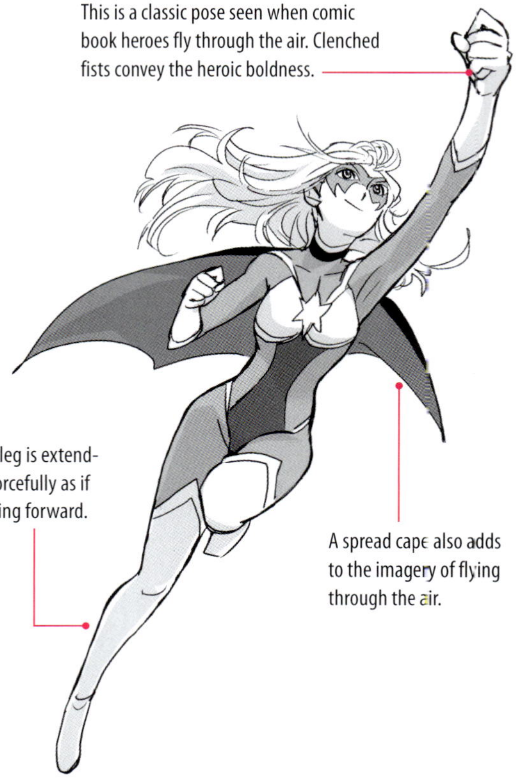

One leg is extended forcefully as if leaping forward.

A spread cape also adds to the imagery of flying through the air.

ANGLES

An oblique angle set at the eye level of the floating character allows a clear view of the body's proportions and facial expressions.

ARCHING THE BODY

To make it appear as if gently floating, lightly arch the body to create a smooth impression.

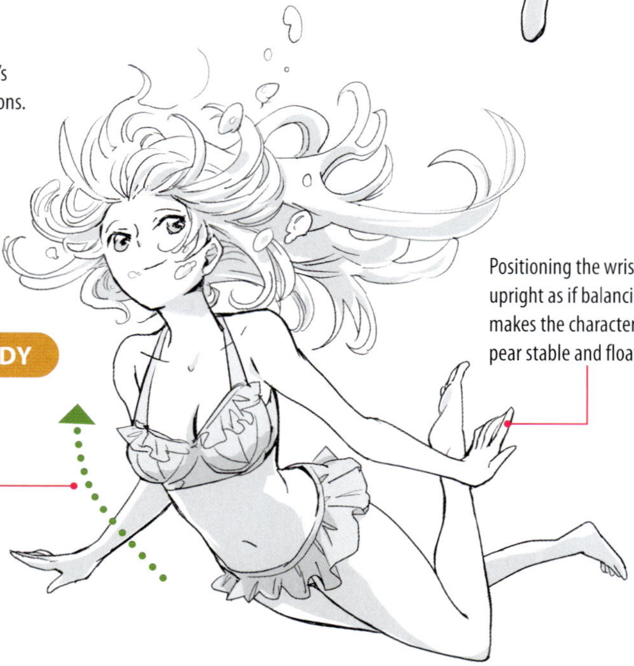

Positioning the wrists upright as if balancing makes the character appear stable and floating.

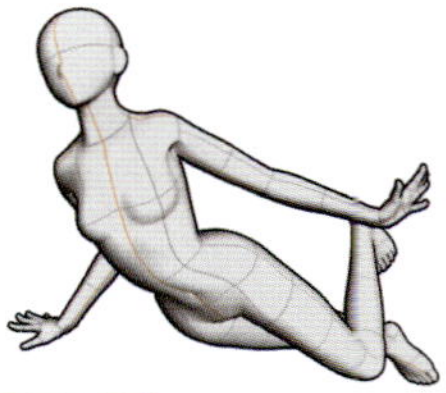

ANGLES

An angle viewed from below enhances the sensation of floating.

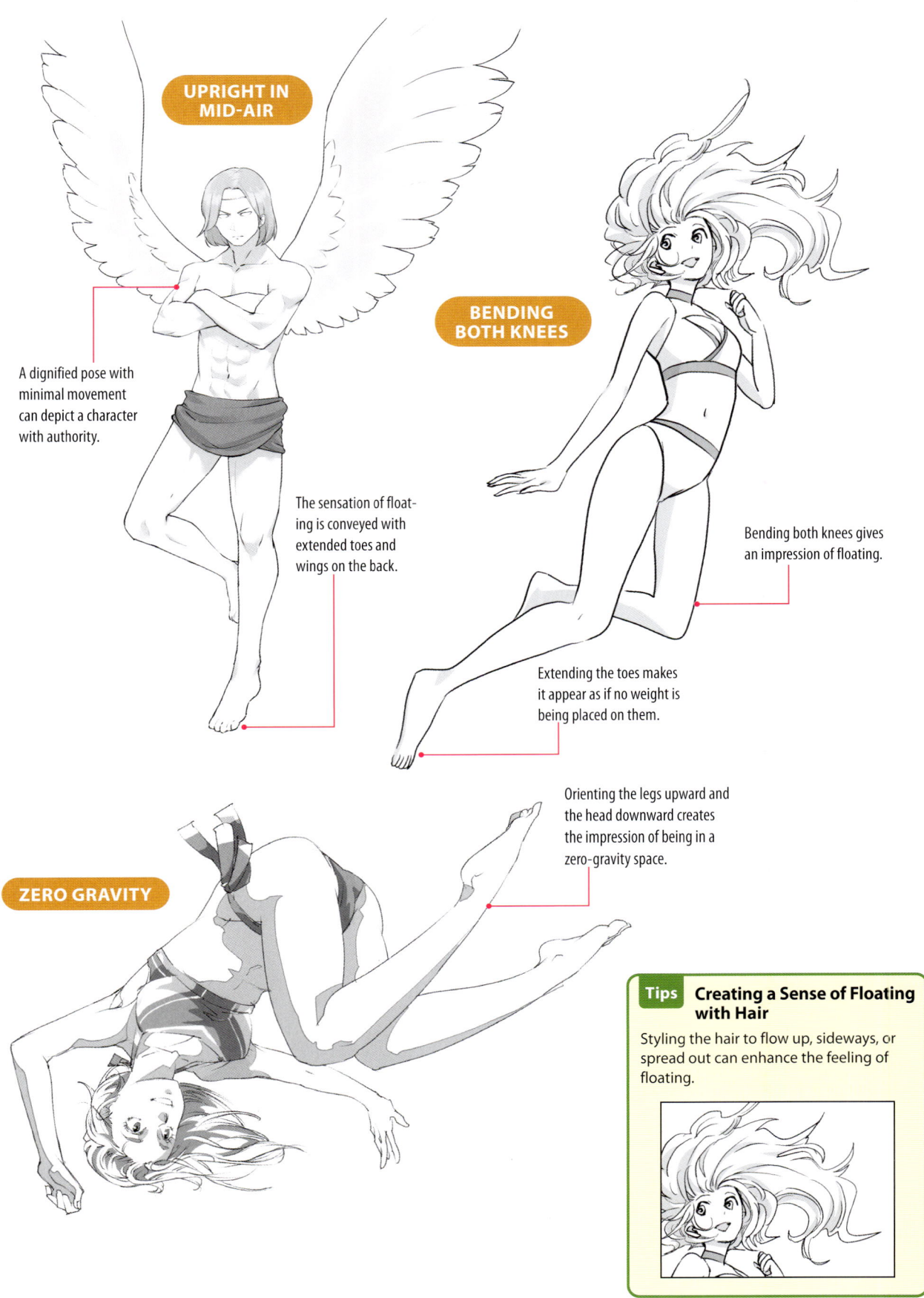

UPRIGHT IN MID-AIR

A dignified pose with minimal movement can depict a character with authority.

The sensation of floating is conveyed with extended toes and wings on the back.

BENDING BOTH KNEES

Bending both knees gives an impression of floating.

Extending the toes makes it appear as if no weight is being placed on them.

Orienting the legs upward and the head downward creates the impression of being in a zero-gravity space.

ZERO GRAVITY

Tips — Creating a Sense of Floating with Hair

Styling the hair to flow up, sideways, or spread out can enhance the feeling of floating.

POWERFUL COMBAT POSES
Sparring

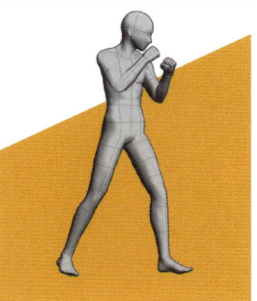

A good fighting pose is about being ready to switch to attack mode at any moment. The arms are extended in attack or defense. The lower body is poised like a coiled spring, with the knees slightly bent, ready for immediate movement.

EXPRESSING THE WILL TO FIGHT

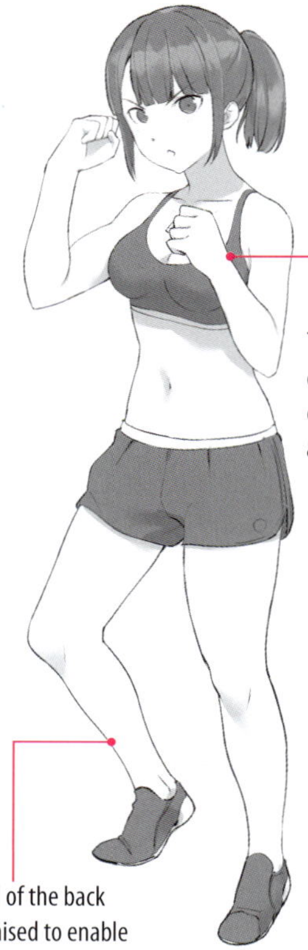

This is a brave pose with clenched fists. Raising the clenched fists symbolizes a readiness to fight.

The heel of the back foot is raised to enable quick movement.

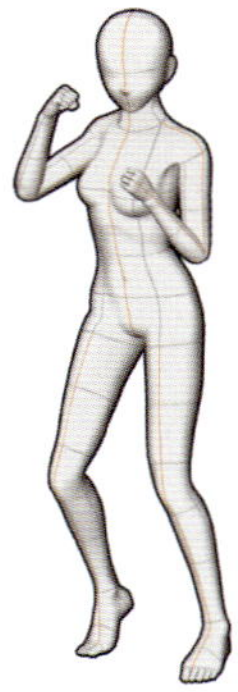

ANGLES
From a diagonal angle, the position of the arms and legs can be conveyed in three dimensions.

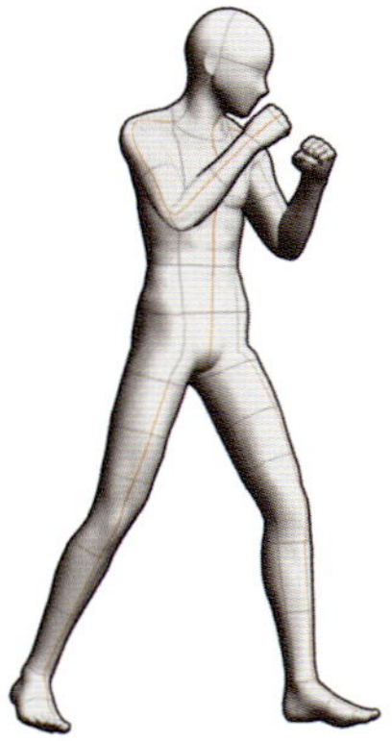

KARATE STANCE

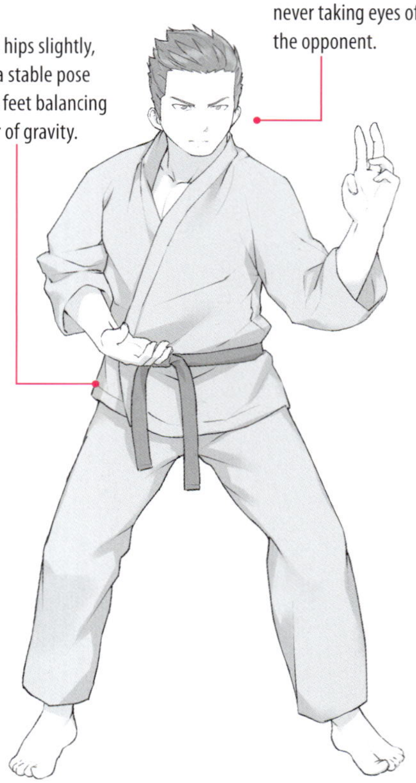

Maintain a stern gaze, never taking eyes off the opponent.

Lower the hips slightly, and hold a stable pose with both feet balancing the center of gravity.

SIDEWAYS STANCE

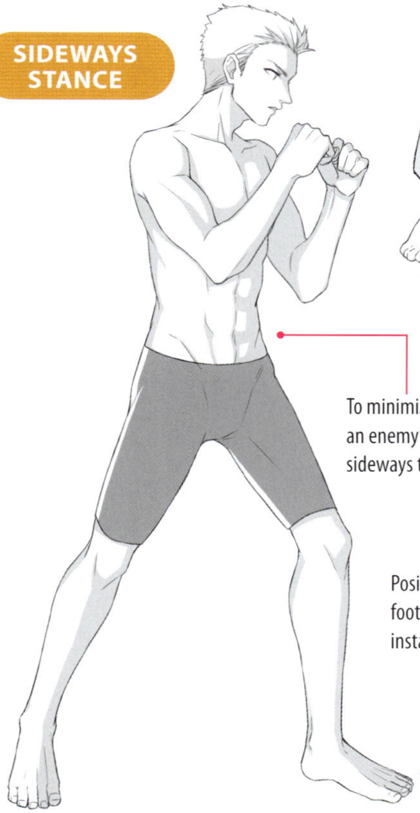

To minimize the area hit by an enemy's attack, stand sideways to the opponent.

Position the leading foot forward to respond instantly to attacks.

ANGLES
From a side angle, the positions of the arms and the spread of the legs are more visible, giving an explanatory impression.

108

POWERFUL STANCE

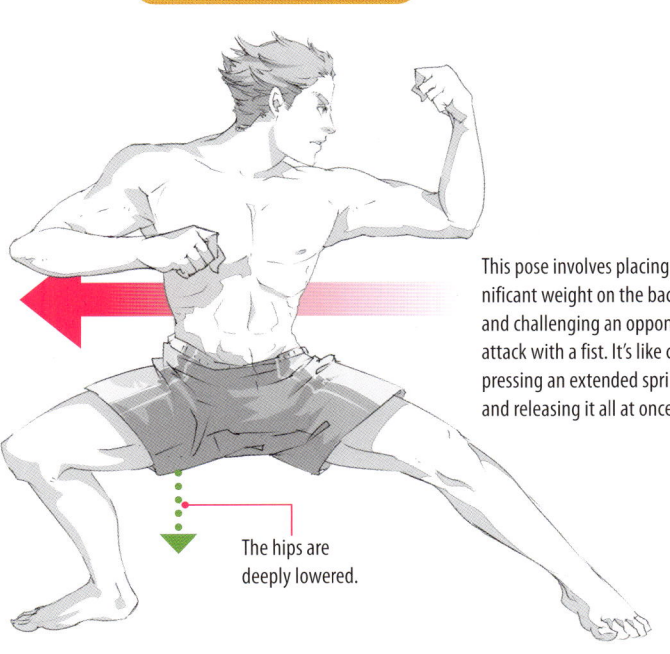

This pose involves placing significant weight on the back foot and challenging an opponent's attack with a fist. It's like compressing an extended spring and releasing it all at once.

The hips are deeply lowered.

LOWERING THE CENTER OF GRAVITY

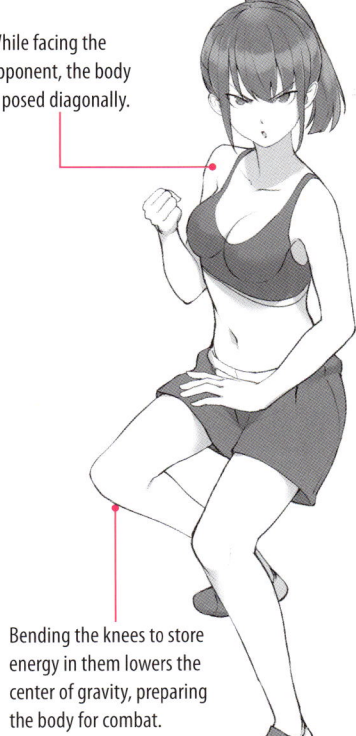

While facing the opponent, the body is posed diagonally.

Bending the knees to store energy in them lowers the center of gravity, preparing the body for combat.

SINGLE-LEG STANCE

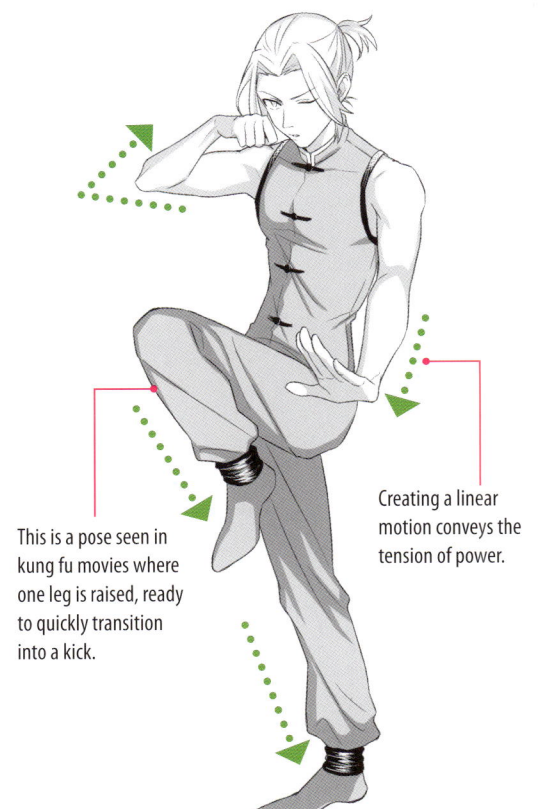

Creating a linear motion conveys the tension of power.

This is a pose seen in kung fu movies where one leg is raised, ready to quickly transition into a kick.

STANCE FOR A THROW

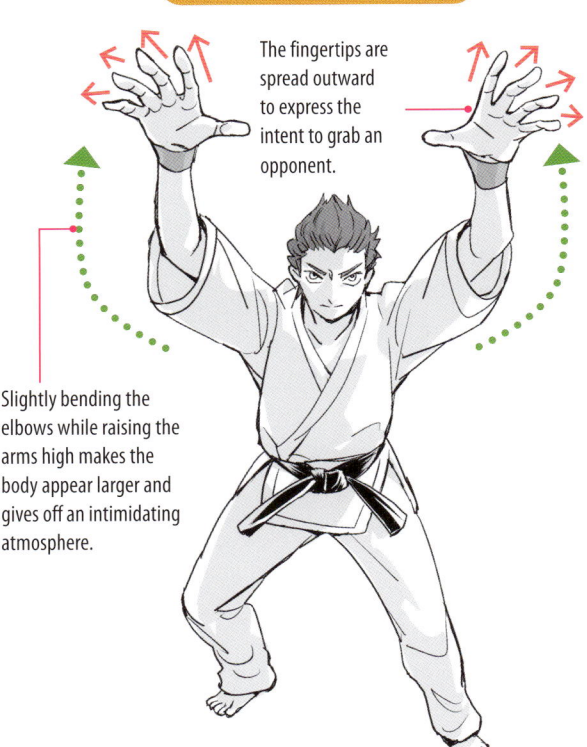

The fingertips are spread outward to express the intent to grab an opponent.

Slightly bending the elbows while raising the arms high makes the body appear larger and gives off an intimidating atmosphere.

LANDING A PUNCH
Boxing

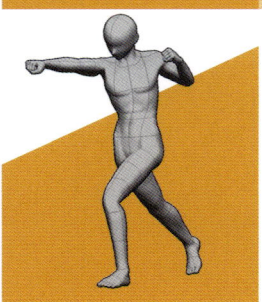

To effectively transfer power to a punch, a full-body movement is essential. Twisting the hips and stepping forward with the legs to shift the center of gravity forward help sell the pose and introduce a compelling sense of dynamism.

BASIC PUNCH

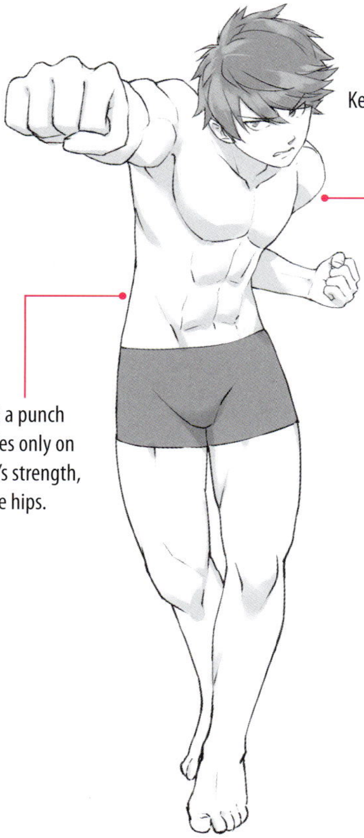

Keep the armpits tight.

To avoid a punch that relies only on the arm's strength, twist the hips.

STRIKING WITH FULL FORCE

A forceful punch is delivered by pulling back the chin and driving the punch forward.

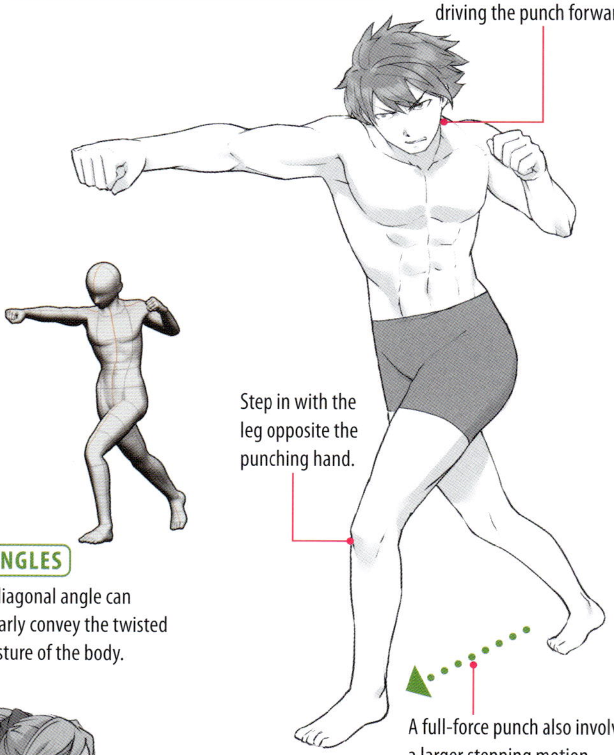

Step in with the leg opposite the punching hand.

ANGLES
A diagonal angle can clearly convey the twisted posture of the body.

A full-force punch also involves a larger stepping motion.

STRAIGHT PUNCH

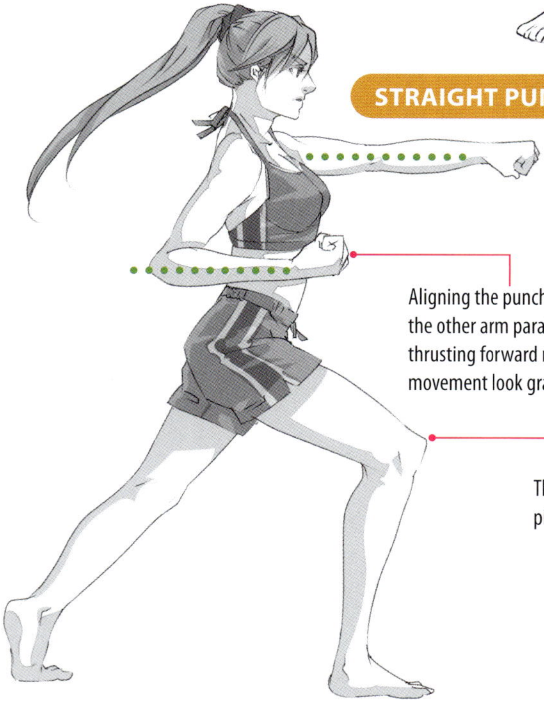

Aligning the punching arm and the other arm parallel when thrusting forward makes the movement look graceful.

The knee of the stepping leg protrudes.

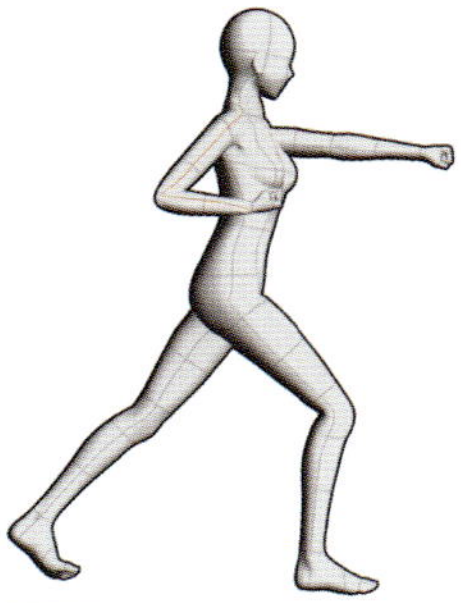

ANGLES
A side angle clearly shows the posture of the thrusting arm and stepping leg.

STABILIZING THE LOWER BODY

Extend the index finger slightly more than the other fingers.

Lowering the hips to stabilize the lower body makes the punch appear more powerful.

DELIVERING A HOOK

A hook punch, which follows a curved trajectory, is executed by bending the elbow and positioning the fist to come from the side, creating a pose that suggests centrifugal force.

To generate a dynamic stepping motion, extend the left leg.

LEAPING FORWARD

The punch is being delivered by the right hand in the back. Clenching the fingers tightly shows that power is being gathered.

Creating depth with the right and left hands while adding perspective to the entire body expresses the momentum of leaping at the opponent.

UPPERCUT

This pose involves swinging the fist powerfully from low to high. Draw the line from the armpit to the abdomen gracefully.

The expression is exaggerated, as if punching while jumping. The entire body is driven upward by strong energy.

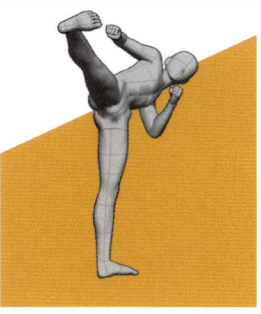

MARTIAL ARTS MOVEMENTS
Kicking

With the leg extended forward, this is definitely an in-your-face pose. Depending on the angle and perspective used, it can give the impression of delivering a powerful blow. Remember to use the arms to create a sense of balance.

EMPHASIZING THE KICKING LEG

Drawing the kicking leg prominently in the foreground increases its impact.

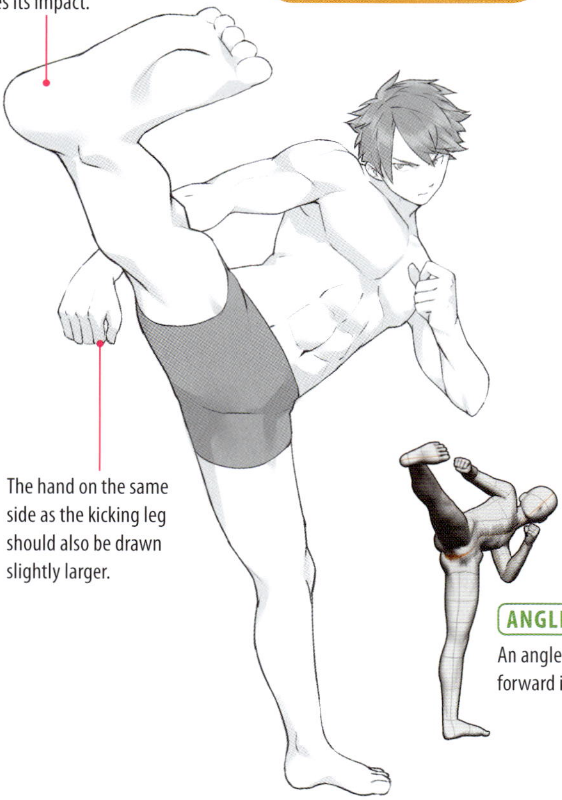

The hand on the same side as the kicking leg should also be drawn slightly larger.

PREPARING TO KICK

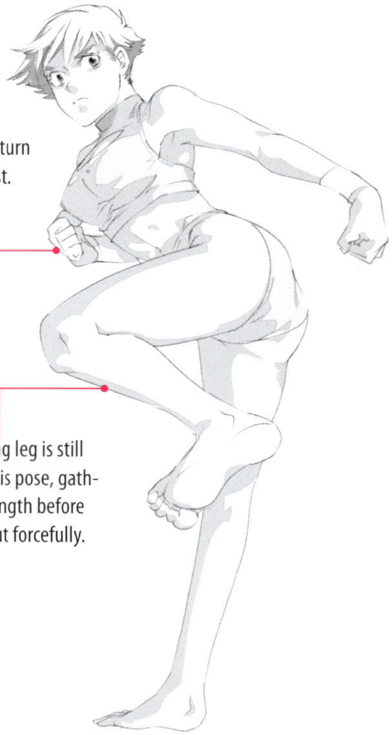

Twist the hips and turn the upper body first.

The kicking leg is still bent in this pose, gathering strength before kicking out forcefully.

ANGLES

An angle with the kicking leg thrust forward intensifies the pose.

SIDE VIEW KICK

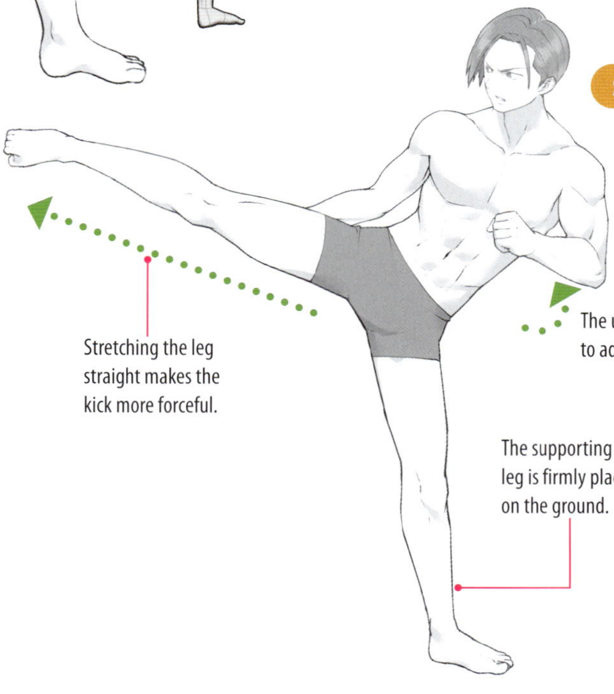

Stretching the leg straight makes the kick more forceful.

The upper body is raised to adjust the posture.

The supporting leg is firmly placed on the ground.

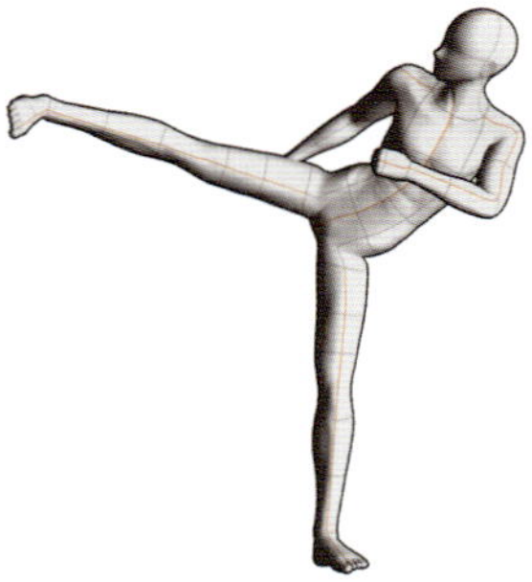

ANGLES

A side angle clearly shows the length and extension of the leg.

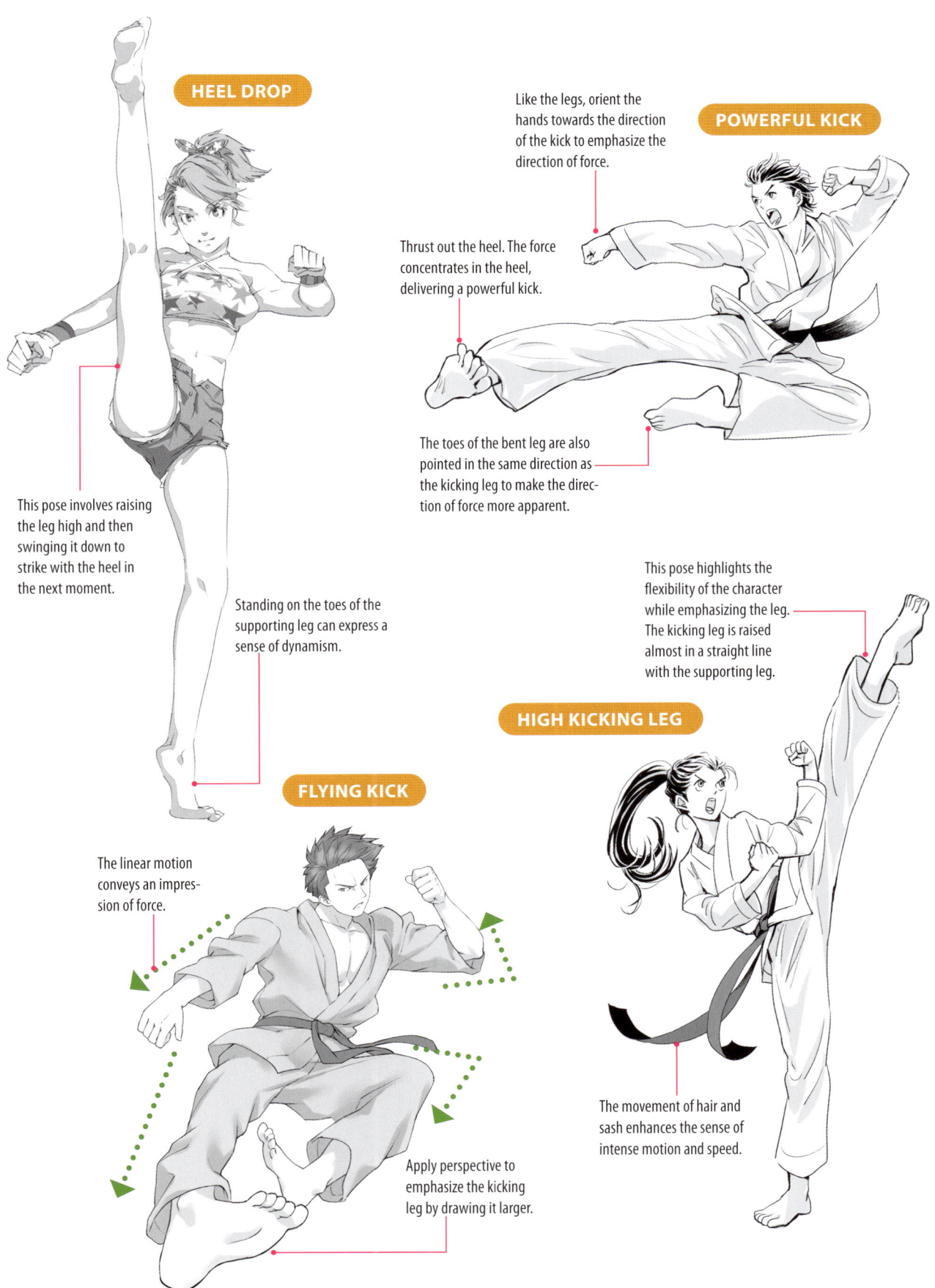

STANDING POSE VARIETIES

Leaning Against a Wall

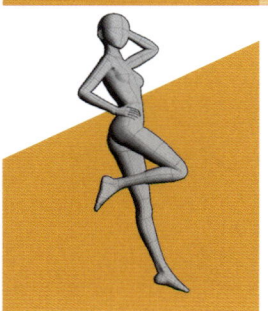

The impression of the pose changes depending on which part of the body—such as the back or hand—is leaning against the wall. The body's weight distributes differently, so be sure to create a sense of balance in your chosen pose.

LEANING WITH ONE ARM

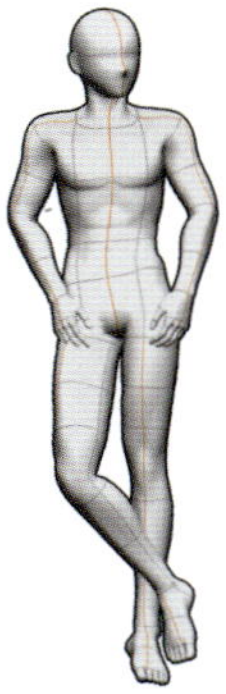

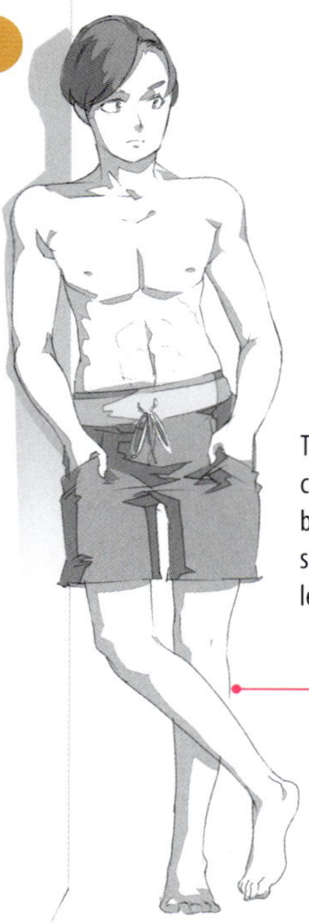

Leaning against the wall with one arm, the body is slightly tilted to show a relaxed posture.

The legs are crossed, and the body weight is supported by one leg and the wall.

ANGLES
From a frontal angle, the tilt of the leaning body is clearly visible.

SUPPORTING WITH ONE LEG AND BACK

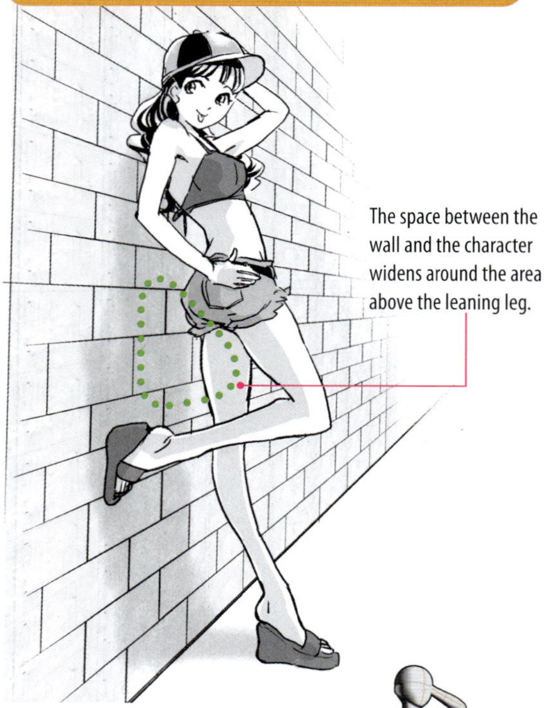

The space between the wall and the character widens around the area above the leaning leg.

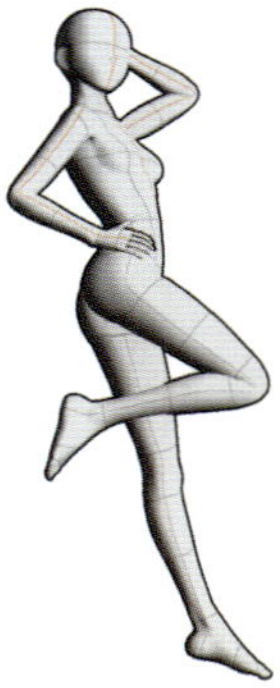

FRONTAL VIEW

From a frontal angle, the knee of the foot placed against the wall is forward.

ANGLES
A side angle on a pose with the sole against the wall makes it easier to understand the relationship between the leg and the wall.

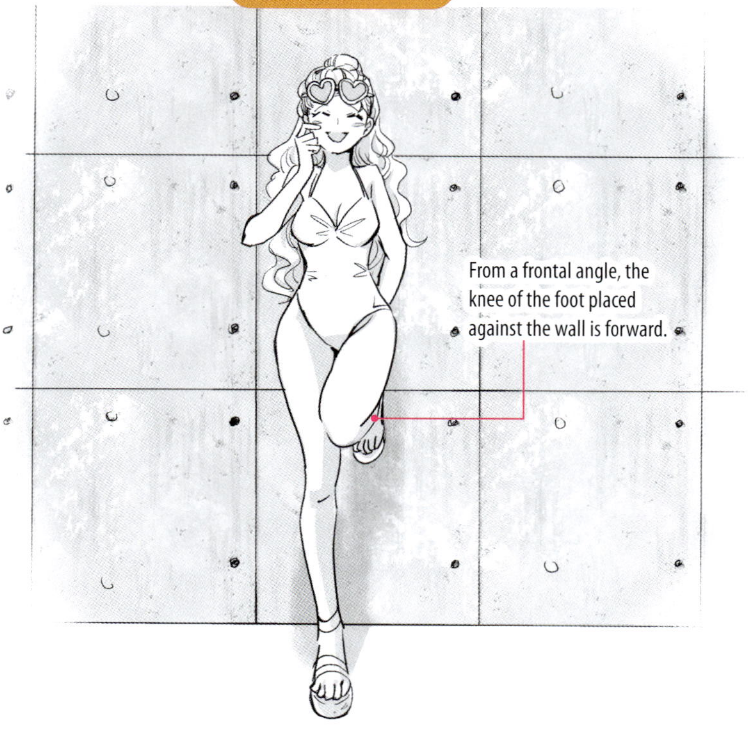

114

LEANING WITH ONE HAND

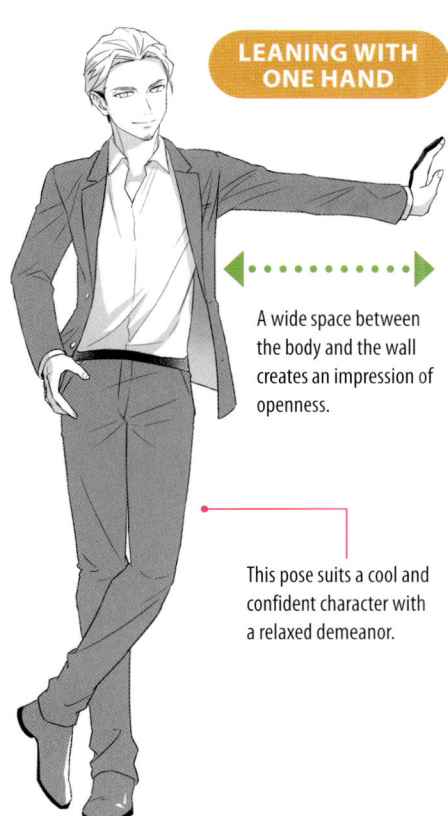

A wide space between the body and the wall creates an impression of openness.

This pose suits a cool and confident character with a relaxed demeanor.

LEANING FACE AGAINST THE WALL

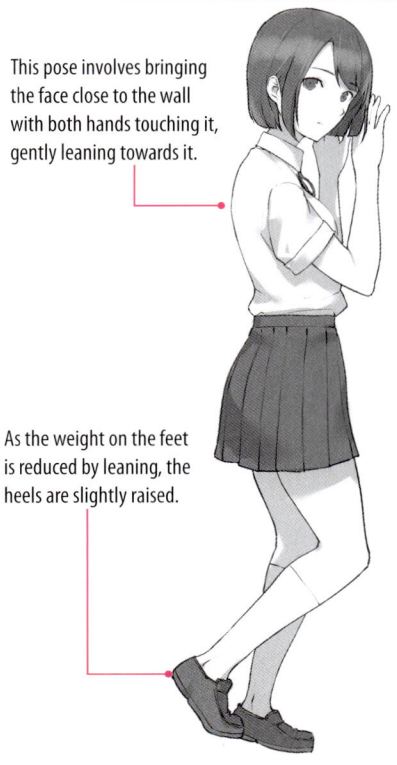

This pose involves bringing the face close to the wall with both hands touching it, gently leaning towards it.

As the weight on the feet is reduced by leaning, the heels are slightly raised.

LEANING ON THE ELBOW

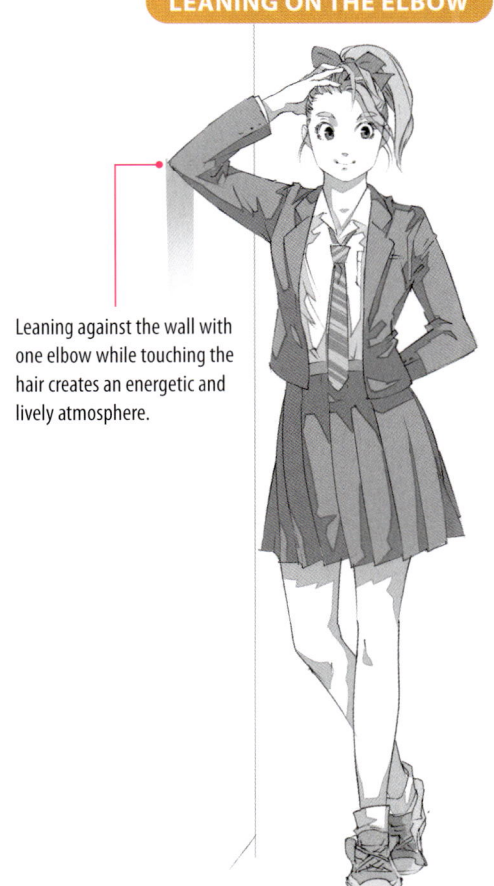

Leaning against the wall with one elbow while touching the hair creates an energetic and lively atmosphere.

LEANING ON THE SHOULDER

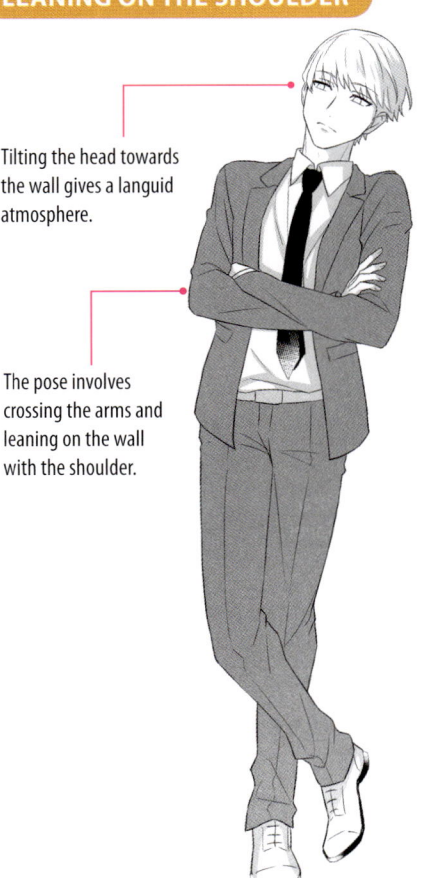

Tilting the head towards the wall gives a languid atmosphere.

The pose involves crossing the arms and leaning on the wall with the shoulder.

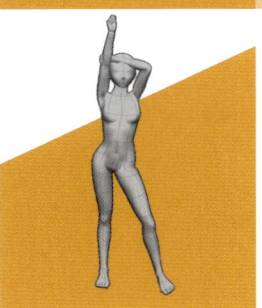

HIGHLIGHTING THE BODY'S LINES
Stretching

Incorporating a stretching pose can intensify the stance and add complexity to the scene. The subtle extension of the muscles and pressure exerted in the limbs yields a delicate and effective illustration.

STRETCHING THE ARMS

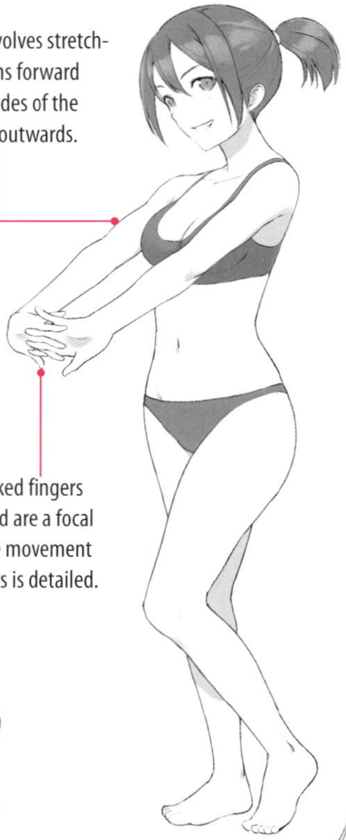

This pose involves stretching both arms forward with the insides of the arms facing outwards.

The interlocked fingers on each hand are a focal point, so the movement of the fingers is detailed.

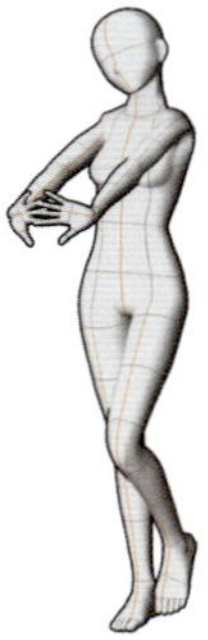

ANGLES
A diagonal angle allows for a clear view of the forward-stretched arms and the line of the shoulders.

SHOULDER STRETCH

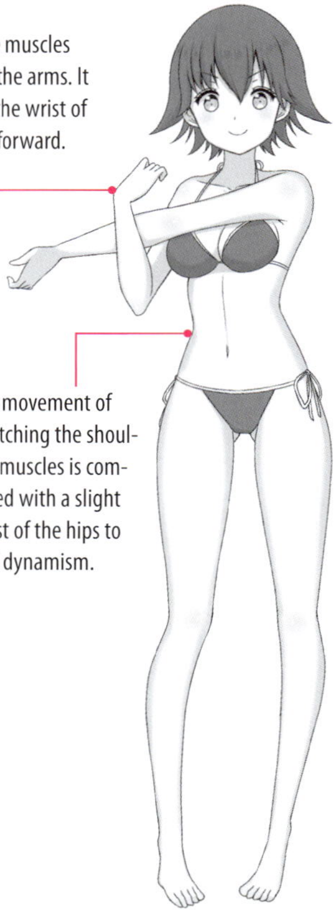

This pose stretches the muscles from the shoulders to the arms. It looks natural to bend the wrist of the arm that is pulled forward.

The movement of stretching the shoulder muscles is combined with a slight twist of the hips to add dynamism.

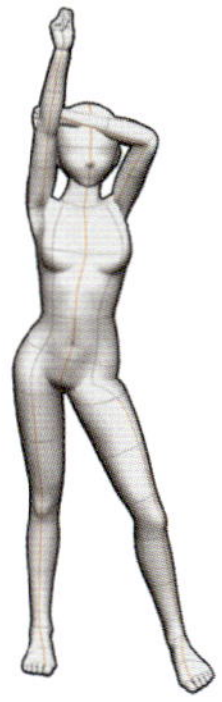

STRETCHING THE BACK

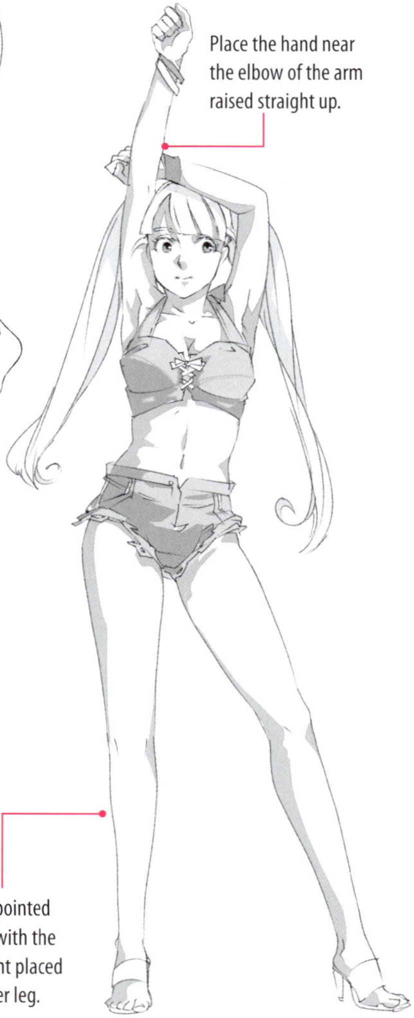

Place the hand near the elbow of the arm raised straight up.

One leg is pointed sideways, with the body weight placed on the other leg.

ANGLES
For a pose where the stretched arm, hips and leg align in a straight line, a frontal angle clearly conveys the appeal of the pose.

BODIES IN MOTION
Working Out

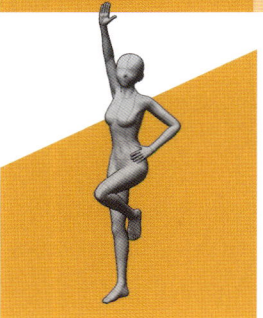

Does your character like to hit the gym? Workout poses feature dynamic movements such as twisting the hips and lifting the legs. When considering such actively aerobic poses, don't forget about the appropriate facial expression.

TWISTING THE HIPS

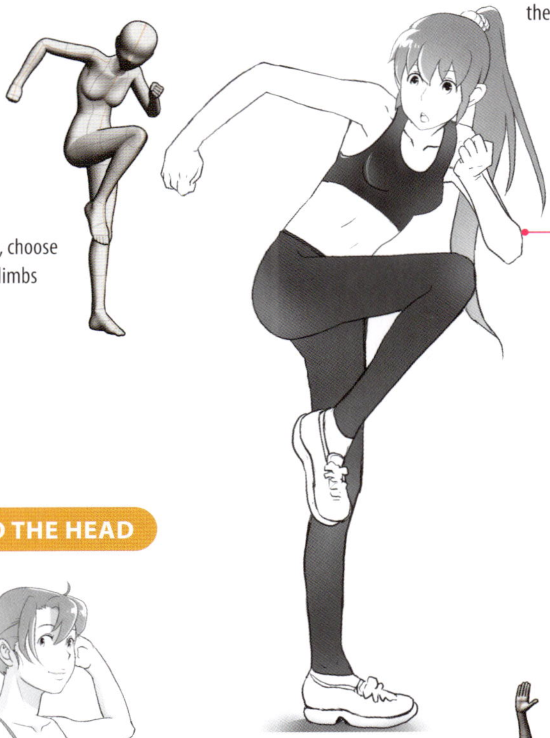

A pose where you twist the hips while leaning forward can create the sensation of bursting into a run.

ENERGETICALLY RAISING THE ARMS

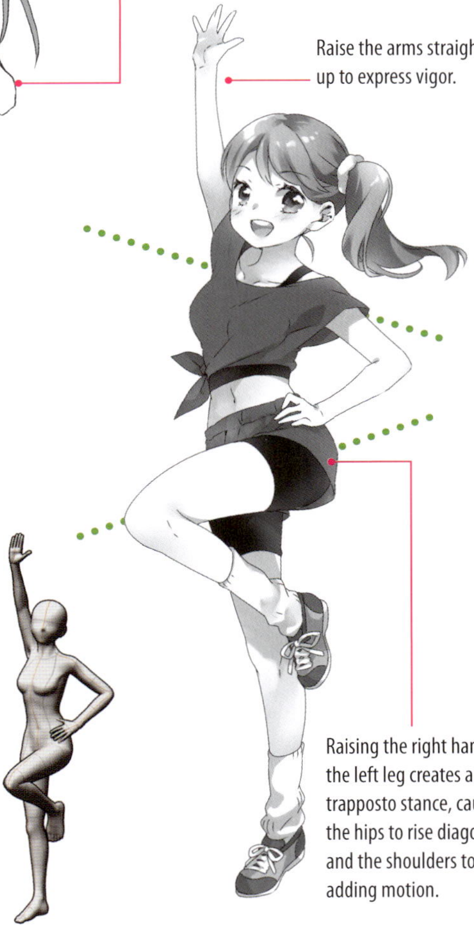

Raise the arms straight up to express vigor.

ANGLES

For poses with large swings, choose an angle where the moved limbs are visible.

HANDS BEHIND THE HEAD

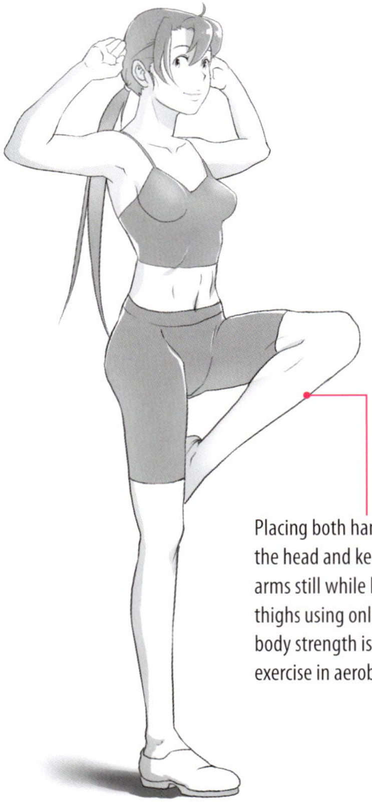

Placing both hands behind the head and keeping the arms still while lifting the thighs using only the lower body strength is a common exercise in aerobics.

Raising the right hand and the left leg creates a contrapposto stance, causing the hips to rise diagonally and the shoulders to drop, adding motion.

ANGLES

For poses like in aerobics, where the limbs move vigorously, a diagonal angle helps clearly convey the complex movements.

117

GREETING THE DAY
Waking Up

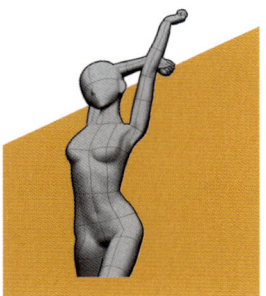

Scenes from daily life can express the softer side of a character. Incorporating gestures and details that indicate the character has just awakened, such as rubbing eyes or yawning, adds a greater sense of realism.

RUBBING EYES

The gesture of vaguely rubbing the eyes easily suggests that the character has just woken up.

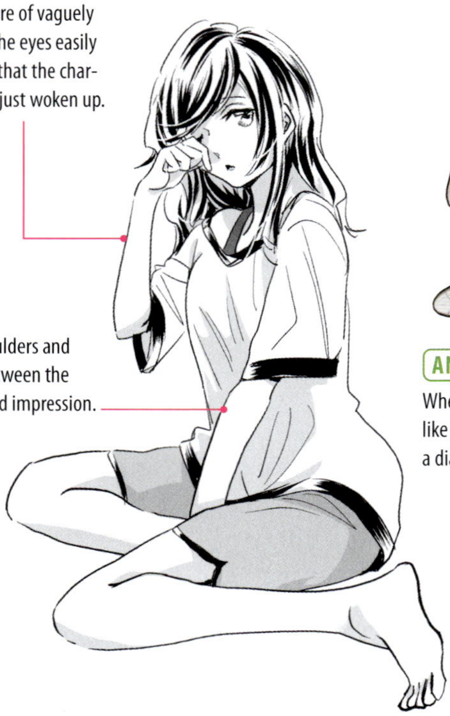

Hunching the shoulders and placing a hand between the legs gives a languid impression.

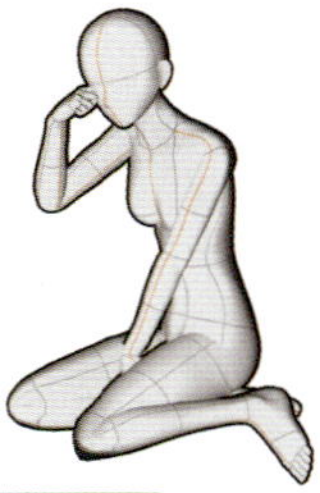

ANGLES
When depicting a routine gesture like rubbing eyes upon waking, a diagonal angle is safe.

STRETCHING

Yawning with tears welling up can also depict the state of just waking up, similar to rubbing eyes.

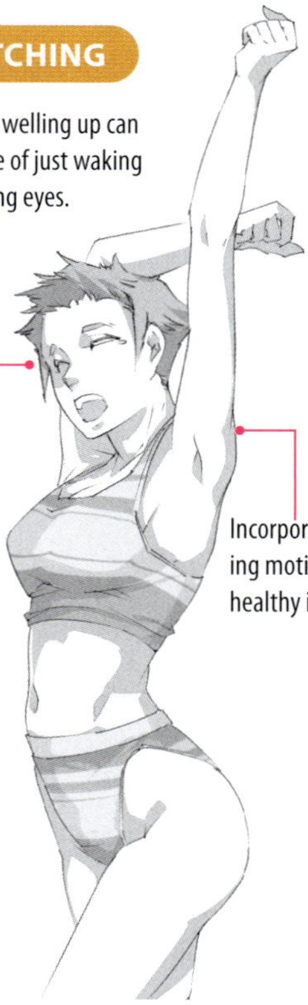

Incorporating a stretching motion conveys a healthy image.

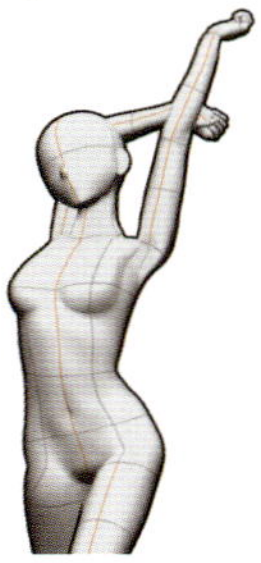

ANGLES
Adopt an angle that highlights the body lines when stretching.

SCRATCHING THE HEAD

Disheveling the hair languidly expresses a relaxed state.

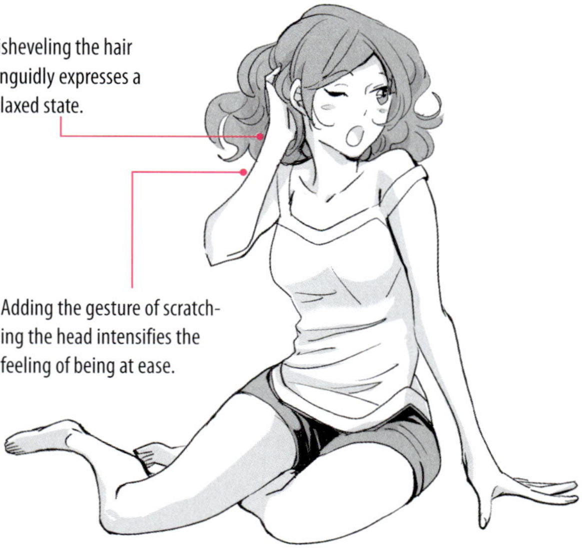

Adding the gesture of scratching the head intensifies the feeling of being at ease.

> **Tips** — **Expression of Yawning**
>
> A yawning expression involves closing the eyes and opening the mouth wide. Adding a few tears makes it more distinctly yawn-like.

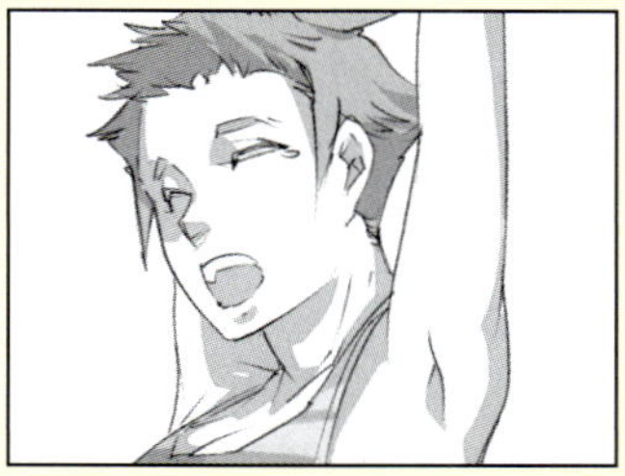

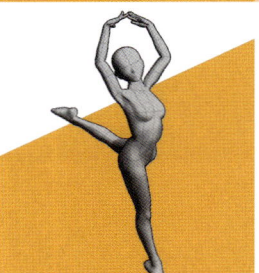

ENCHANTING WITH GRACEFUL MOVEMENTS

Doing Ballet

Ballet poses involve moving the body broadly and fluidly, showcasing the beauty of the physique. The lines of the legs rising from the toes and the elegant movements of the arms are crucial, making this style especially suited to characters with long limbs.

STANDING ON THE TOES OF ONE FOOT

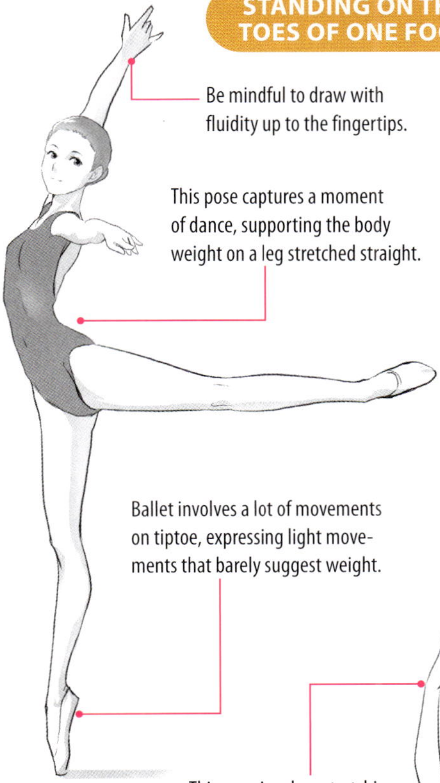

Be mindful to draw with fluidity up to the fingertips.

This pose captures a moment of dance, supporting the body weight on a leg stretched straight.

Ballet involves a lot of movements on tiptoe, expressing light movements that barely suggest weight.

LONG LIMBS SHINE

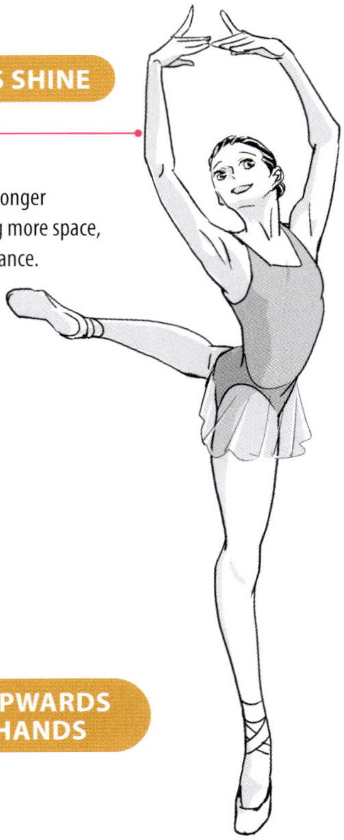

Drawing the limbs longer allows for capturing more space, enhancing the elegance.

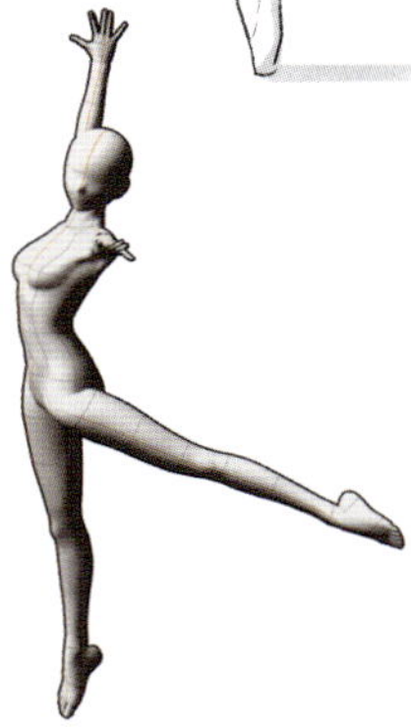

REACHING UPWARDS WITH THE HANDS

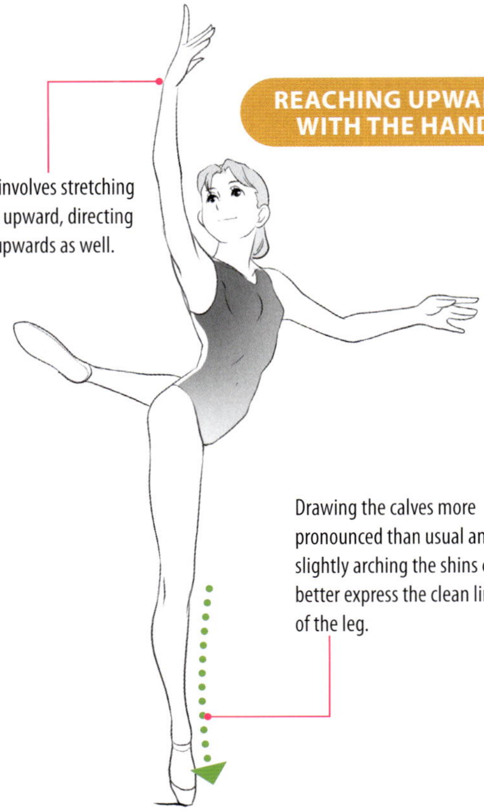

This pose involves stretching the hands upward, directing the gaze upwards as well.

Drawing the calves more pronounced than usual and slightly arching the shins can better express the clean line of the leg.

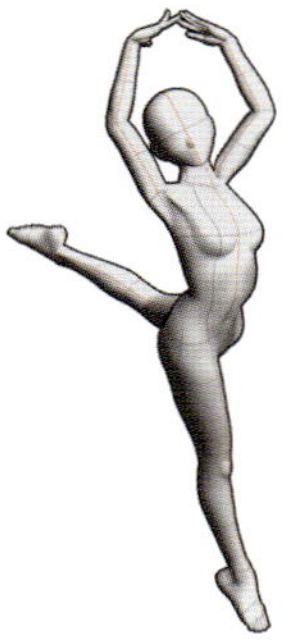

(ANGLES)

Choose an angle that showcases the fluidity of ballet movements, making the extended arms and legs appear graceful.

(ANGLES)

This pose is also common in ballet, but an angle that clearly shows the distinctive shape of the arms is desirable.

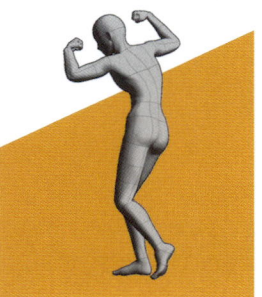

SHOWCASING A ROBUST PHYSIQUE
Bodybuilder's Pose

This pose highlights the well-defined muscles, movements and contoured lines of a muscular character. The bent arms and legs and the taut, flexed muscles give you a chance to show off your evolving abilities at drawing the human form.

HIGHLIGHTING THE PECTORAL MUSCLES

HIGHLIGHTING THE BACK MUSCLES

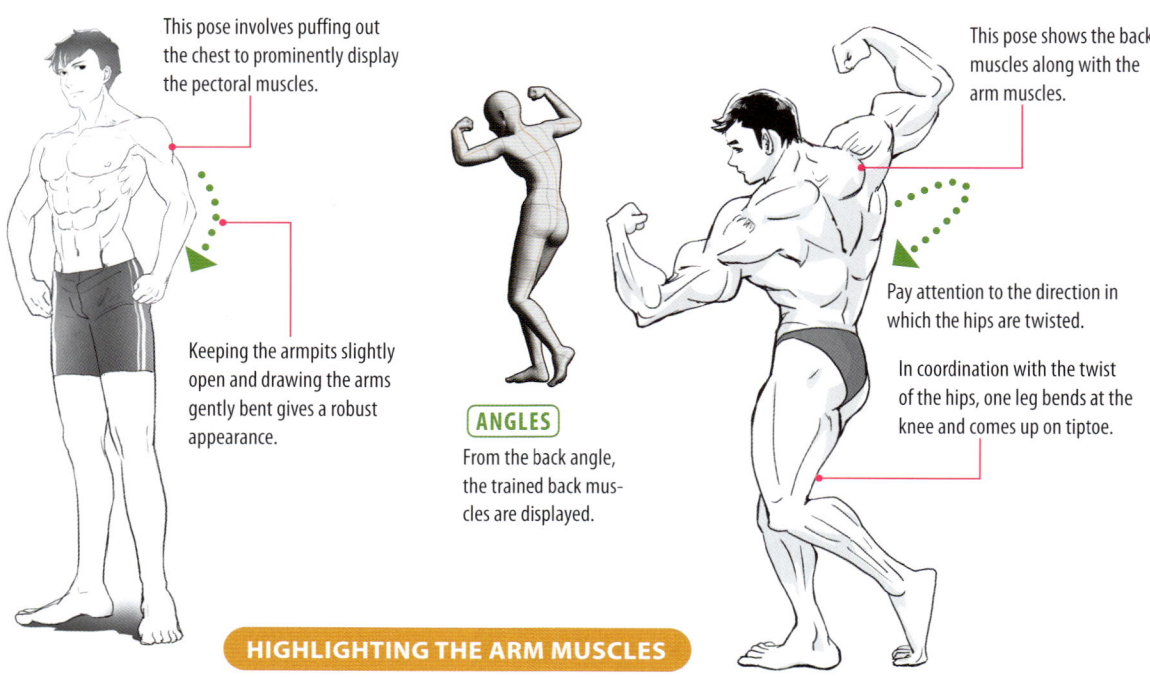

This pose involves puffing out the chest to prominently display the pectoral muscles.

Keeping the armpits slightly open and drawing the arms gently bent gives a robust appearance.

ANGLES
From the back angle, the trained back muscles are displayed.

This pose shows the back muscles along with the arm muscles.

Pay attention to the direction in which the hips are twisted.

In coordination with the twist of the hips, one leg bends at the knee and comes up on tiptoe.

HIGHLIGHTING THE ARM MUSCLES

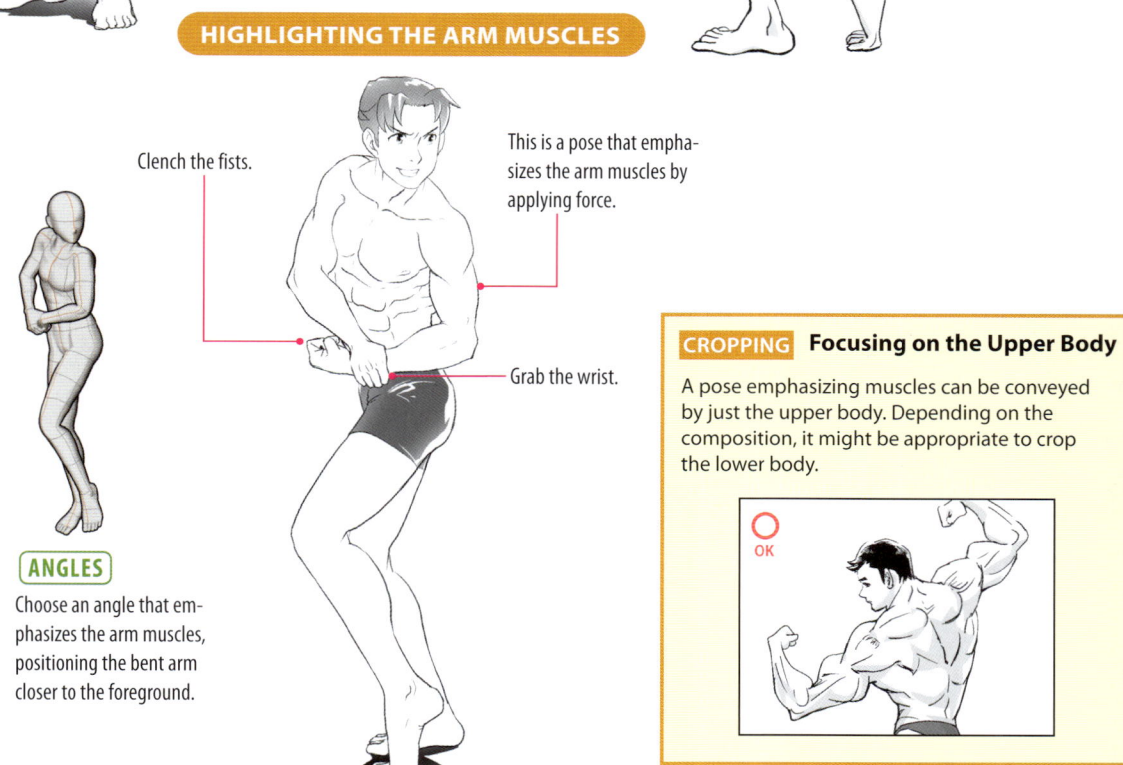

Clench the fists.

This is a pose that emphasizes the arm muscles by applying force.

Grab the wrist.

ANGLES
Choose an angle that emphasizes the arm muscles, positioning the bent arm closer to the foreground.

CROPPING Focusing on the Upper Body

A pose emphasizing muscles can be conveyed by just the upper body. Depending on the composition, it might be appropriate to crop the lower body.

OK

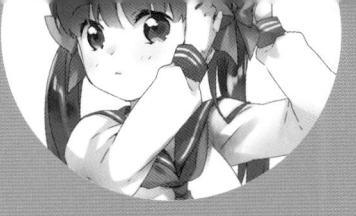
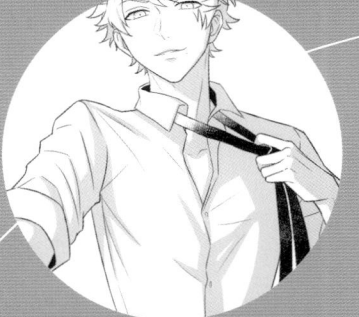
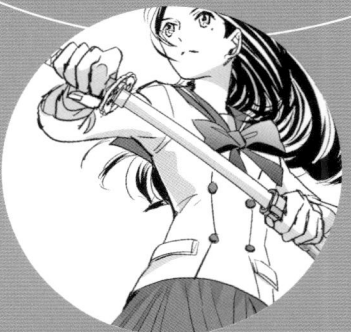
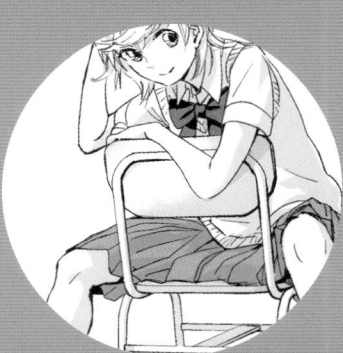
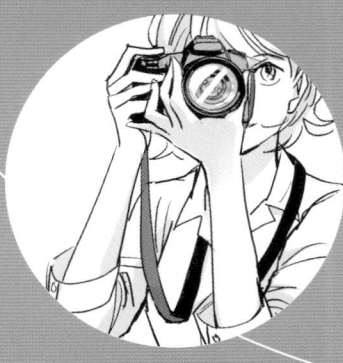

PART 4

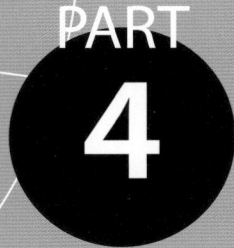

Using Objects and Accessories

This section explains poses involving various items like accessories and costumes.

Pushing Up Glasses
Putting on a Tie
Pulling Down a Hat
Putting on a Jacket
Fixing a Skirt
Tightening a Hairbow
Pulling off Gloves
Adjusting a Shoe
Fixing the Fit
Putting on Lipstick
Wearing Aprons
Serious and Studious
Holding a Bouquet
Holding a Phone
Taking a Picture
Holding a Bag
Holding an Umbrella
Leaning on a Desk
Sitting with Legs Crossed

Wielding a Sword
Drawing a Katana
Holding a Gun
Using a Bow
Holding a Curved Blade
Casting a Spell
Using a Whip
Eating
Drinking
Smoking
Wearing Handcuffs
Using a Mask
Holding a Megaphone
Conducting
Listening to Music
Holding a Guitar
Singing

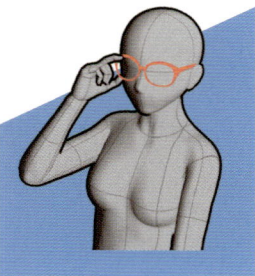

SUITABLE FOR INTELLECTUAL CHARACTERS

Pushing Up Glasses

Glasses naturally suit characters with a serious or intellectual image. Add movement to the illustration by having them touch the glasses or grasp the frame. When grabbing glasses, it's basic to use the thumb and index finger.

ADJUSTING WITH THUMB AND INDEX FINGER

Have the character lift and adjust the position of the glasses using the thumb and index finger.

Intellectual characters maintain good posture.

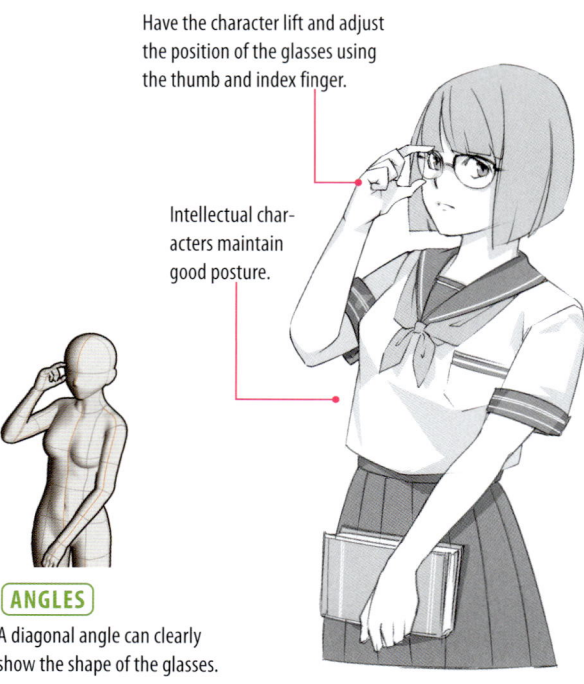

ANGLES
A diagonal angle can clearly show the shape of the glasses.

PUTTING ON GLASSES

This is the moment when the glasses are put on.

Raising the elbow can make the action of putting on glasses appear more significant. In this case, it looks natural to have the palm facing upward when holding the glasses.

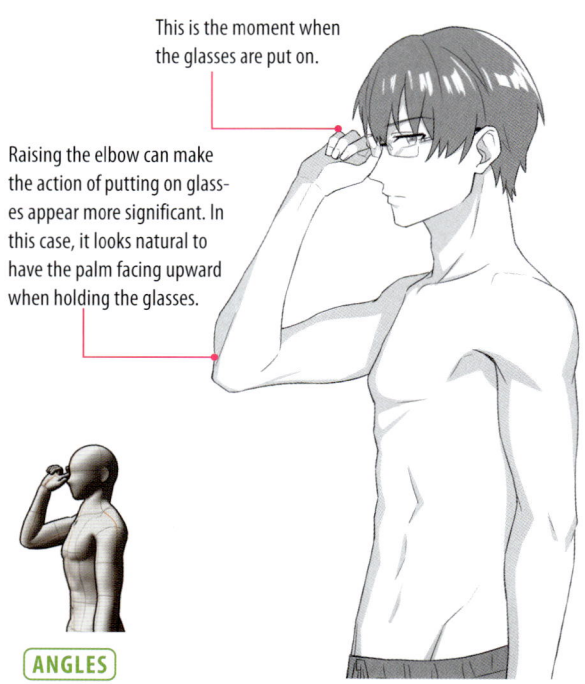

ANGLES
From the side angle, the lens on the far side becomes less visible.

Here the character takes off the glasses and lightly bites the tip. It's often used when pondering or plotting something.

BITING GLASSES

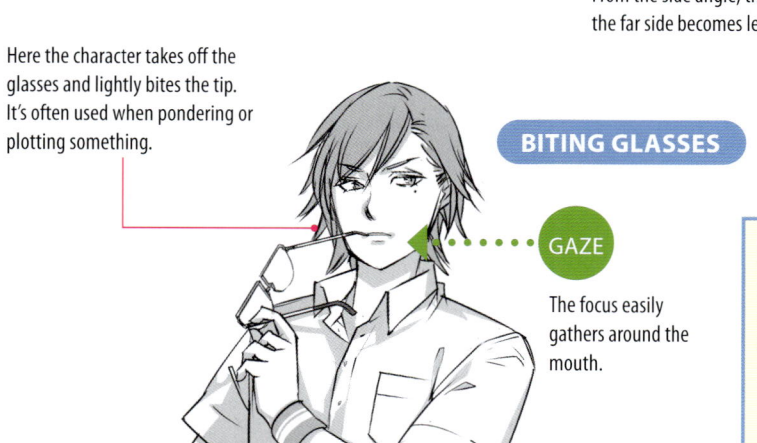

GAZE
The focus easily gathers around the mouth.

CROPPING Showing Hand Poses

Since the pose of the hand touching the glasses is crucial, crop the image to clearly show the movement of the hands and arms.

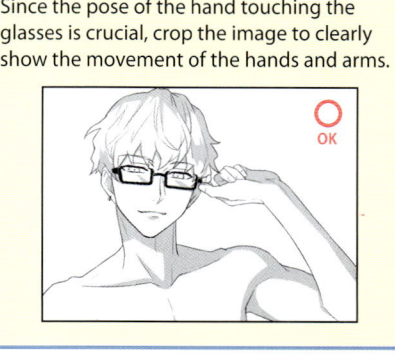
OK

PUSHING UP THE BRIDGE

Pushing up the bridge of the glasses with the index finger is a pose used to adjust the position of the glasses. It's a classic pose for characters with a sharp mind.

This pose is used when someone comes up with an idea or is deducing something.

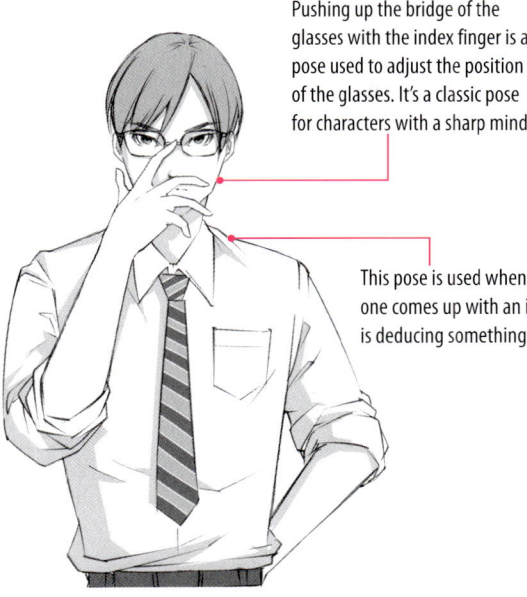

STRAIGHTENING GLASSES

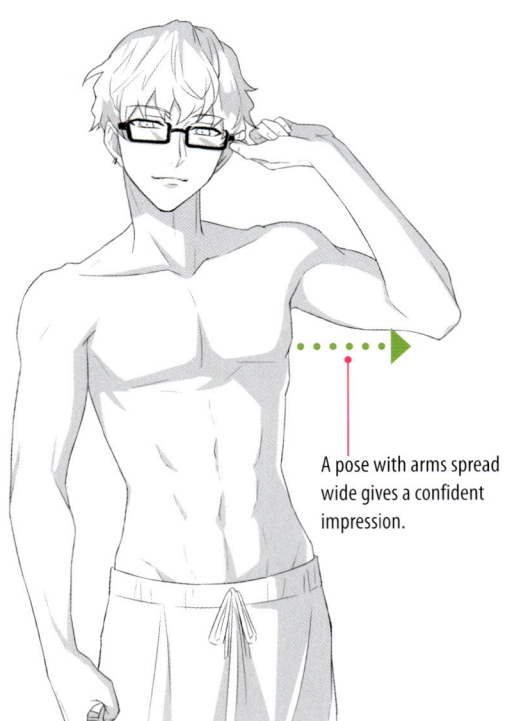

A pose with arms spread wide gives a confident impression.

REMOVING GLASSES

Handling the glasses carefully with both hands gives a refined image to the character.

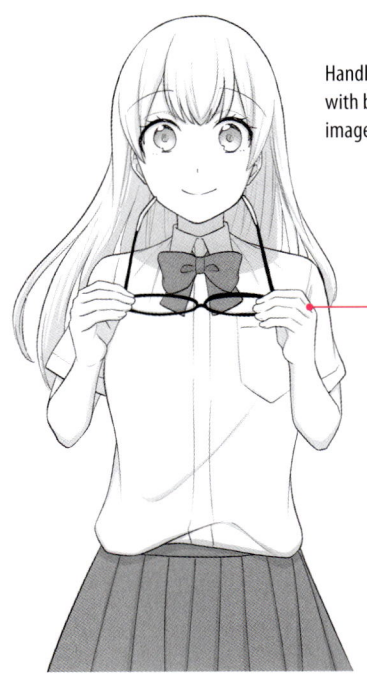

PUTTING ON GLASSES WITH BOTH HANDS

Creating symmetrical movements with both hands produces a more balanced pose.

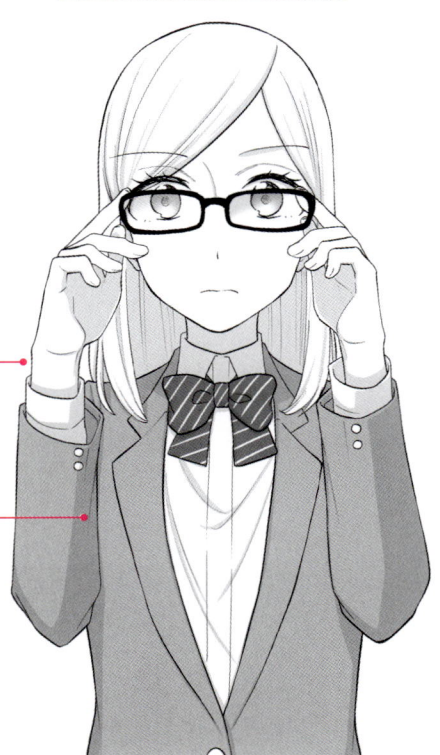

Putting on glasses with the arms close to the body can suggest a reserved character.

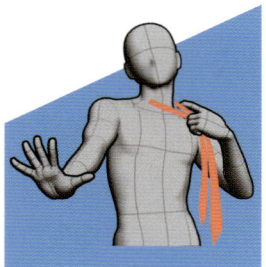

BUSINESS ATTIRE
Putting on a Tie

A classic item for formal attire, your character can tug at, manipulate or adjust a necktie, presenting a range of possibilities and motions.

TIGHTENING THE TIE

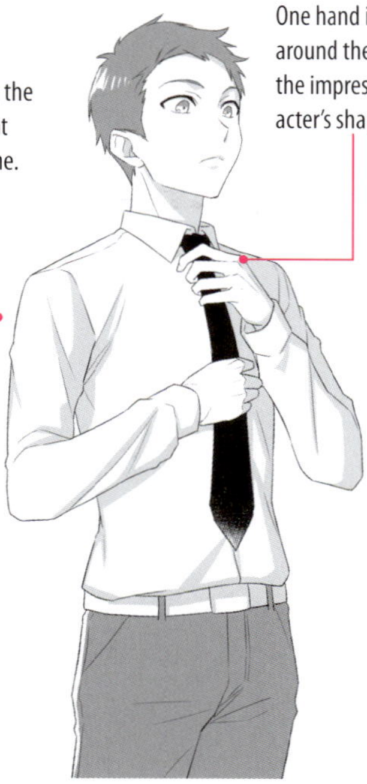

When tightening the tie, it's a pose that stretches the spine.

One hand is placed around the knot, giving the impression the character's shaping it.

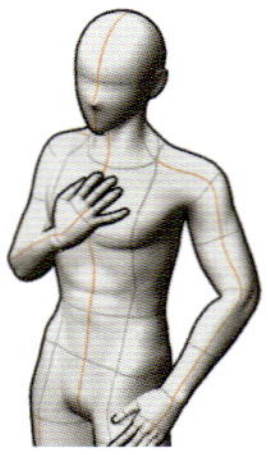

ANGLES
A diagonal and slightly overhead angle emphasizes the shape of the tie.

ADJUSTING THE TIE

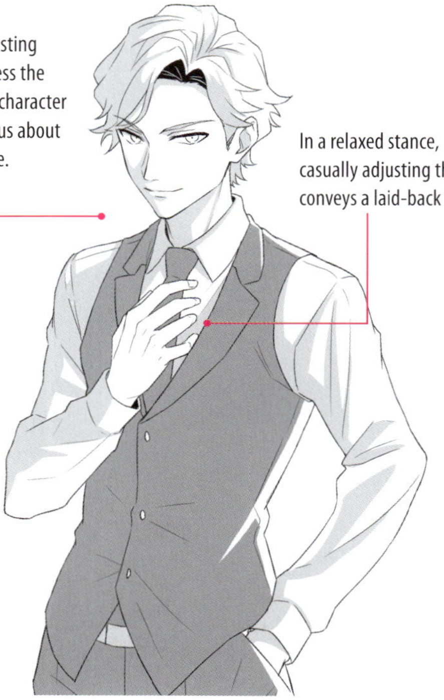

The pose of adjusting the tie can express the personality of a character who is meticulous about their appearance.

In a relaxed stance, casually adjusting the tie conveys a laid-back feel.

LOOSENING THE TIE

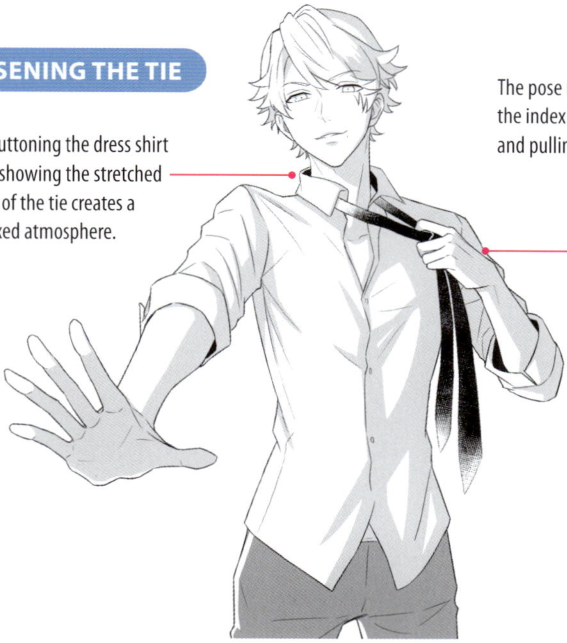

Unbuttoning the dress shirt and showing the stretched part of the tie creates a relaxed atmosphere.

The pose involves placing the index finger at the knot and pulling the tie.

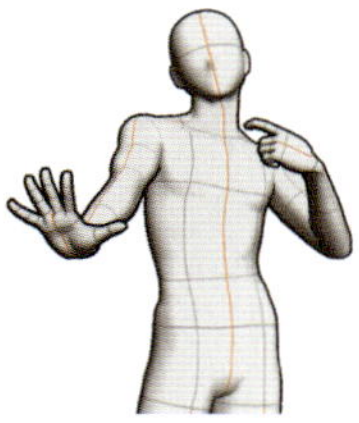

ANGLES
With a front-facing angle, slightly looking up makes the stretched and pulled part clearly visible.

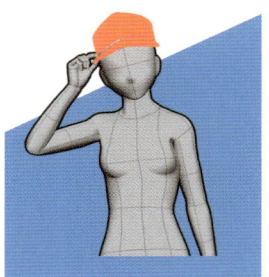

UPGRADE YOUR STYLE
Pulling Down a Hat

Hats are accessories that naturally draw attention to the face. Is your character holding the brim during a gust of wind, tipping a hat in greeting or striking a distinctive photographic pose? Either way, a hat makes the perfect addition to your illustration.

GRABBING THE BRIM OF THE HAT

HOLDING THE HAT WITH BOTH HANDS

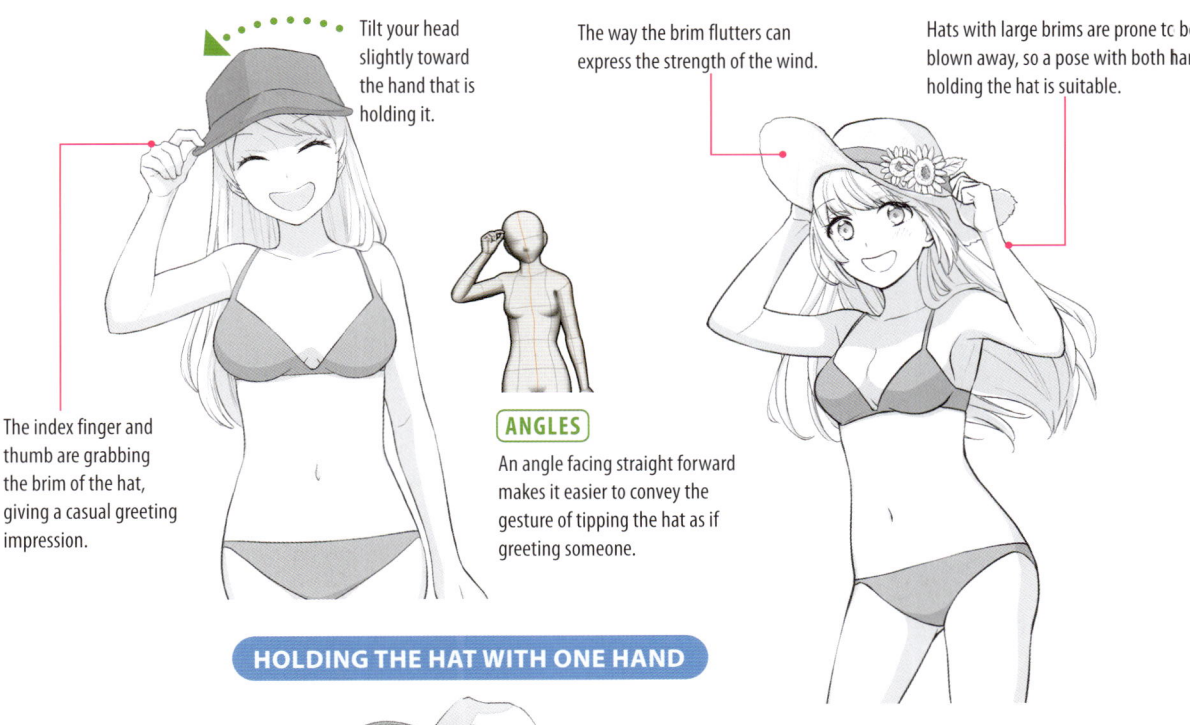

Tilt your head slightly toward the hand that is holding it.

The index finger and thumb are grabbing the brim of the hat, giving a casual greeting impression.

ANGLES
An angle facing straight forward makes it easier to convey the gesture of tipping the hat as if greeting someone.

The way the brim flutters can express the strength of the wind.

Hats with large brims are prone to being blown away, so a pose with both hands holding the hat is suitable.

HOLDING THE HAT WITH ONE HAND

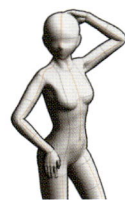

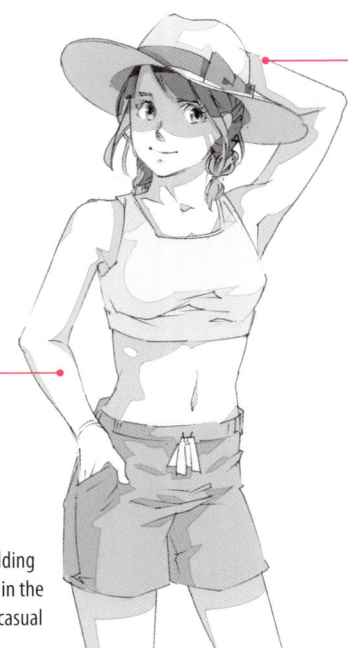

To avoid covering the face, the hand holding the hat is placed behind.

ANGLES
If you want to show the three-dimensionality of the hat, use a diagonal angle. The example makes the pose such that you can also see the ribbon of the hat by turning the face away.

The hand not holding the hat is placed in the pocket, giving a casual impression.

Tips — Orientation of the Hat and Face

Fashion models might pose in a way that shows off the hat nicely by turning their face away. In illustrations, it's good to pay attention to the direction of the face and the orientation of the hat.

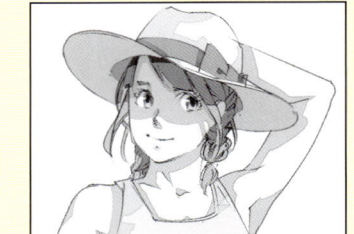

FORMAL ELEGANCE
Putting on a Jacket

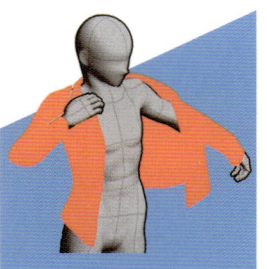

Jackets can give your character an elegant or casual impression. They add motion and depth in the way they're put on, taken off or dangled from a shoulder.

TAKING OFF THE JACKET

Arching the shoulders backward makes the chest protrude.

Like the phrase "rolling up one's sleeves," the gesture of taking off a jacket exudes an atmosphere of getting serious about the task at hand.

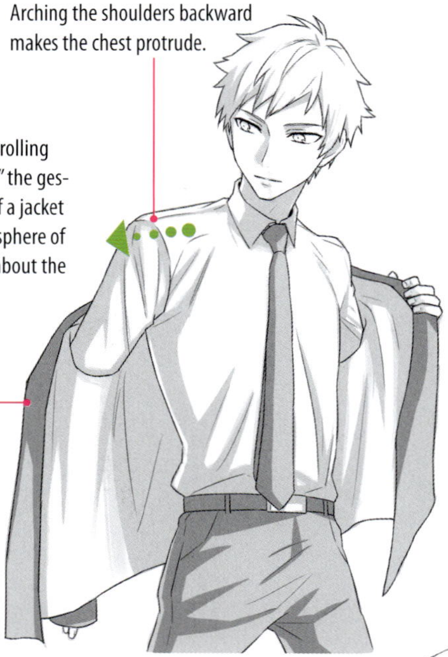

ADJUSTING THE COLLAR

The gesture of straightening the collar can represent characters who are confident in their appearance or who are stylish.

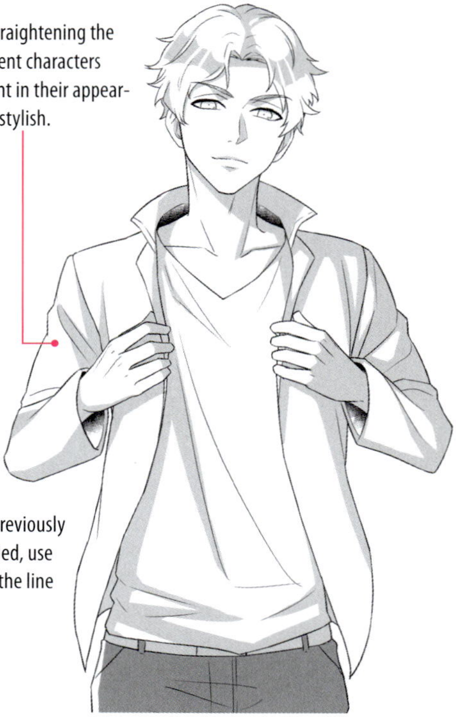

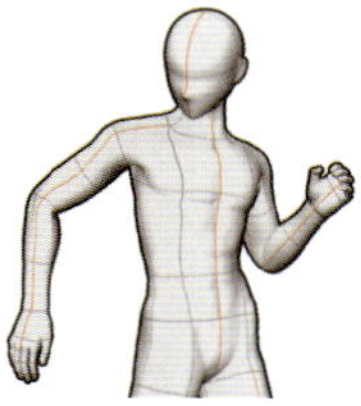

ANGLES

Since it's a pose where the previously covered shoulders are revealed, use an angle that clearly shows the line of both shoulders.

DONNING THE JACKET

The right shoulder, just having slipped through the sleeve, appears slightly lifted, depicting the act of donning the jacket.

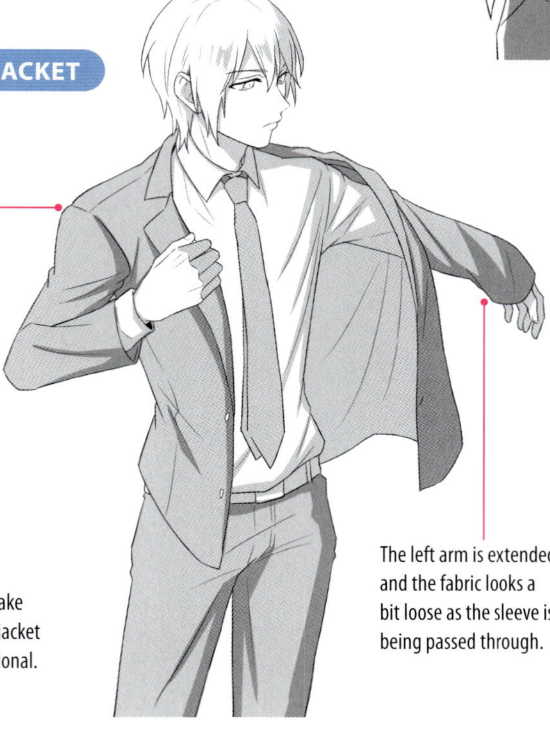

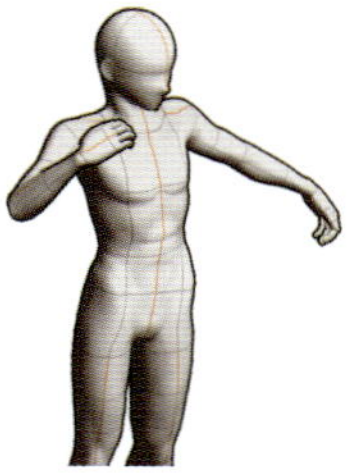

ANGLES

A slightly high angle can make the motion of donning the jacket appear more three-dimensional.

The left arm is extended, and the fabric looks a bit loose as the sleeve is being passed through.

CARRYING THE JACKET

Holding the jacket as if carrying it on the back can give off a rough vibe.

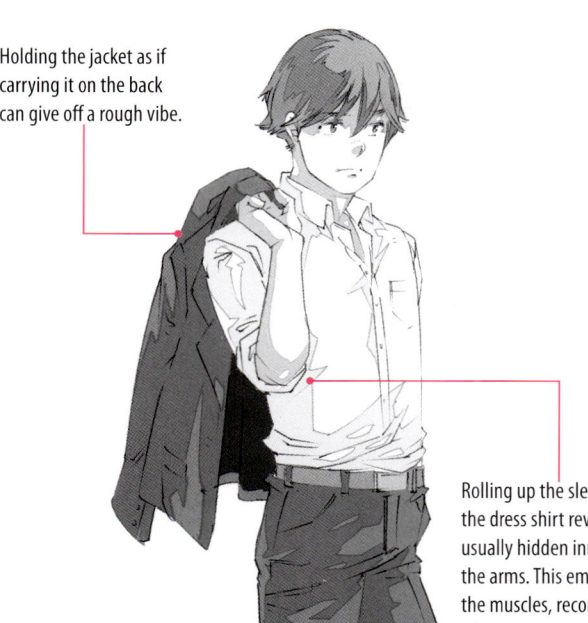

Rolling up the sleeves of the dress shirt reveals the usually hidden inner side of the arms. This emphasizes the muscles, recommended when you want to add a sense of strength.

HOLDING THE JACKET WITH ONE HAND

This pose involves hanging the jacket over one arm and putting the other hand in the pocket, which makes the elbows stick out, giving a confident impression.

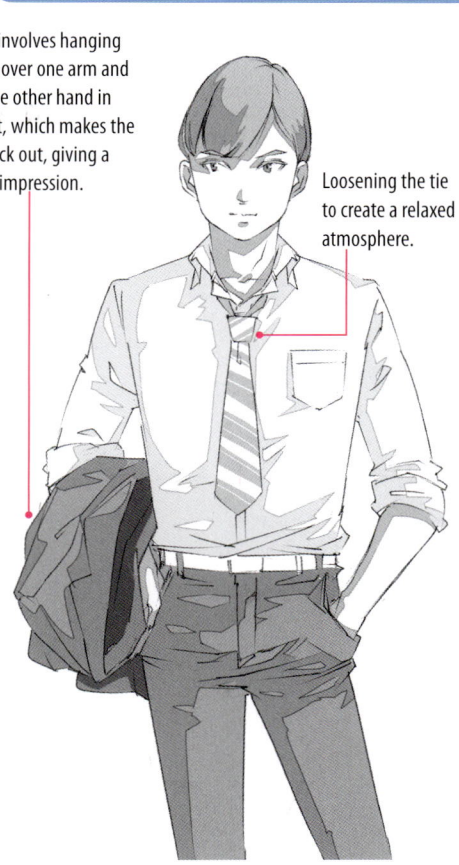

Loosening the tie to create a relaxed atmosphere.

ADJUSTING THE JACKET

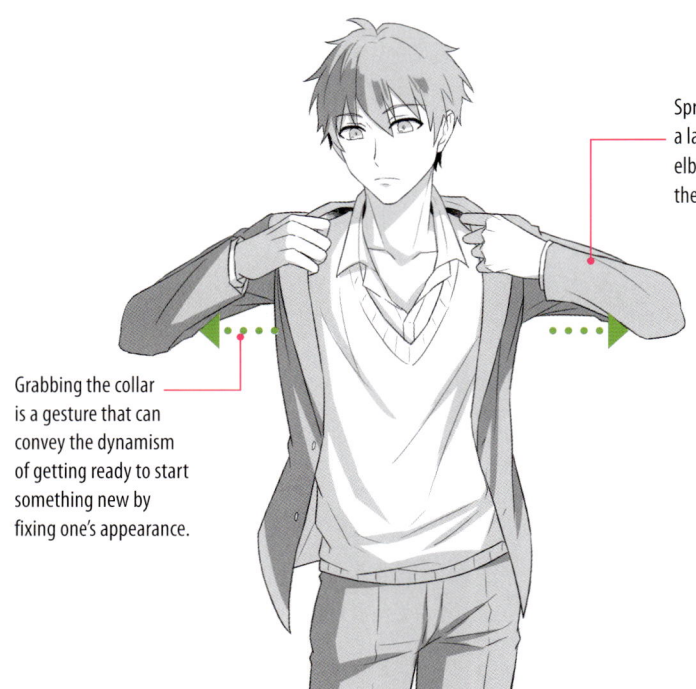

Spreading both sides and making a large movement with the elbows out to the sides enhances the sense of dynamism.

Grabbing the collar is a gesture that can convey the dynamism of getting ready to start something new by fixing one's appearance.

> **CROPPING** **Bust Shot to Adjust the Collar**
>
> Even if the jacket cannot be fully shown on screen, the pose of adjusting the jacket's collar can be depicted in a bust shot focused around the collar area.
>
>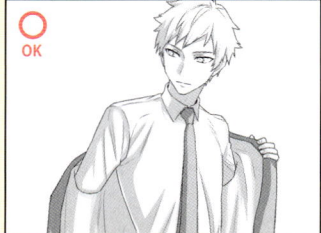
> OK

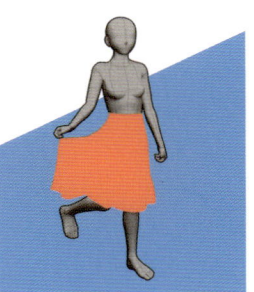

FASHION POSES
Fixing a Skirt

A skirt adds movement to a scene. When the skirt moves in sync with the character's motion, swaying in the wind or spreading out, it adds simple variation to the pose.

RUNNING

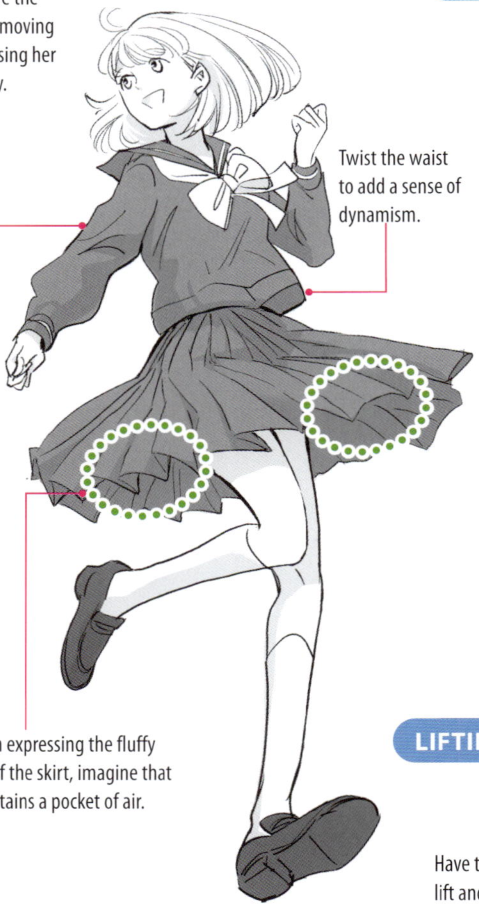

A pose where the character is moving around, causing her skirt to sway.

Twist the waist to add a sense of dynamism.

When expressing the fluffy feel of the skirt, imagine that it contains a pocket of air.

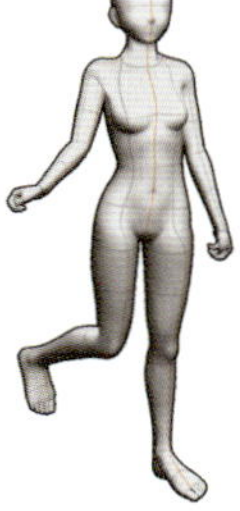

ANGLES
A diagonal angle from the side where the skirt is being lifted clearly shows the shape of the skirt being pulled up.

HOLDING DOWN THE SKIRT

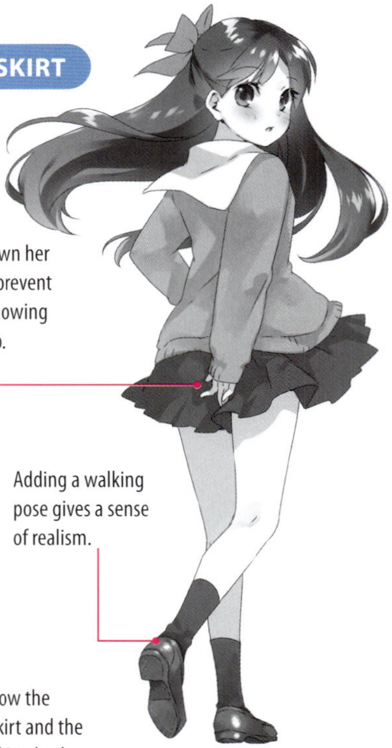

The character holds down her skirt with her hand to prevent her underwear from showing as the wind blows it up.

Adding a walking pose gives a sense of realism.

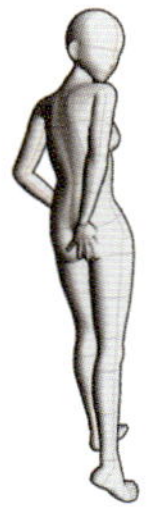

ANGLES
From an angle behind, show the hand holding down the skirt and the expression of her face looking back.

LIFTING WITH ONE HAND

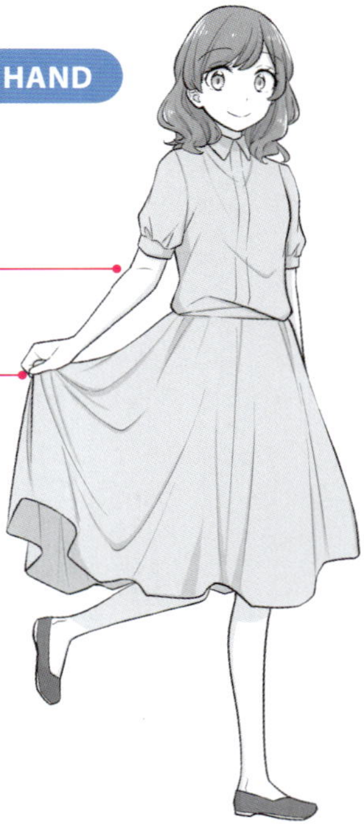

Have the character slightly lift and spread her skirt, emphasizing it.

The arm lifting the skirt should have a slightly bent elbow to convey a modest lifting gesture.

128

LIFTING WITH BOTH HANDS

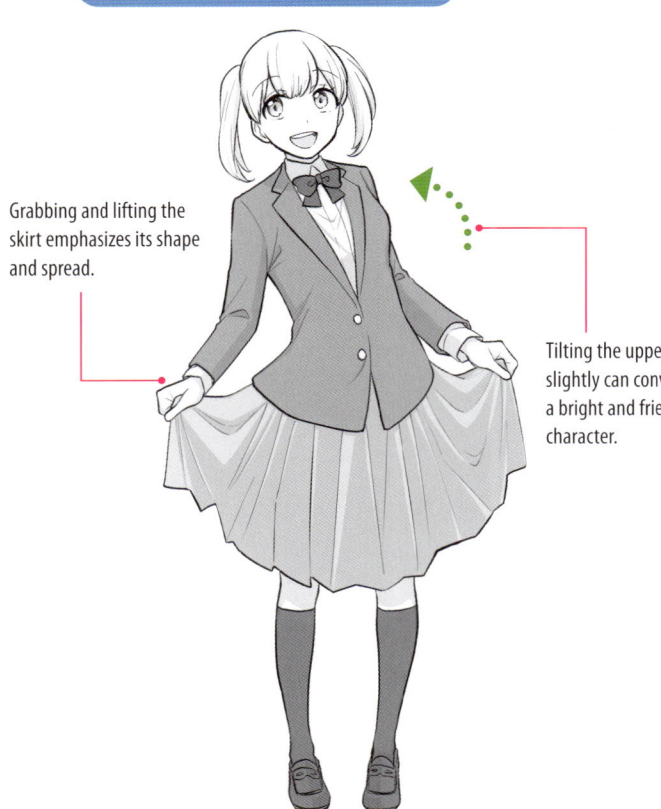

Grabbing and lifting the skirt emphasizes its shape and spread.

Tilting the upper body slightly can convey a bright and friendly character.

WRINGING A WET SKIRT

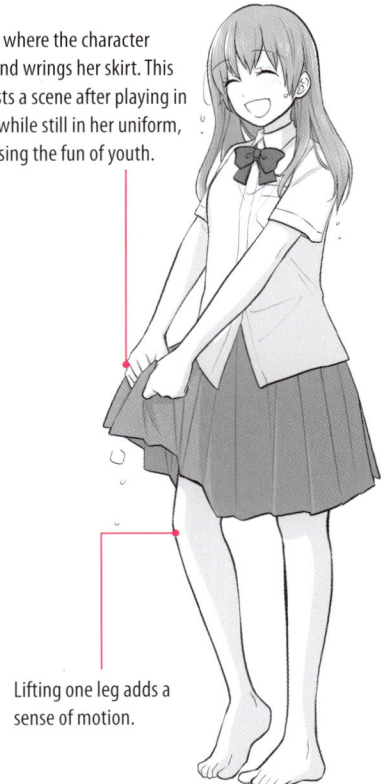

A pose where the character grips and wrings her skirt. This suggests a scene after playing in water while still in her uniform, expressing the fun of youth.

Lifting one leg adds a sense of motion.

HOLDING DOWN WITH BOTH HANDS

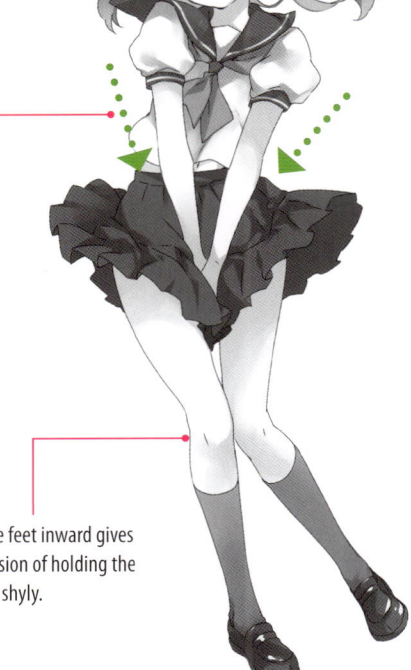

The skirt is held down by both hands to prevent it from lifting in a sudden gust of wind.

Turning the feet inward gives the impression of holding the skirt down shyly.

CROPPING: Showing a Bit of Leg

To emphasize the skirt, it is ideal to show as much of the legs emerging from it as possible. However, if cropping is necessary, cut just above the shin or the knee.

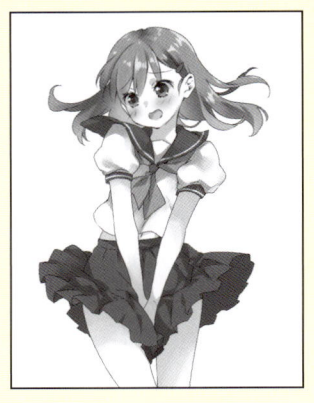

RIBBONS AS ACCESSORIES
Tightening a Hairbow

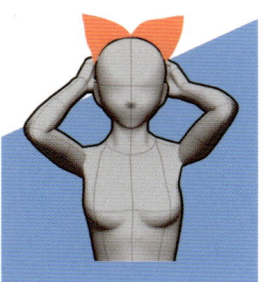

Ribbons are much more than mere hair embellishments. They can also be used to add movement to a pose and to suggest the qualities and traits of the characters wearing or adjusting them.

TYING A RIBBON IN HAIR

A pose where the character ties a ribbon to one of her twin tails. Choose an angle and posture that does not hide her face with her hand.

Raising her arm causes her uniform to stretch upward, revealing a bit of her stomach. This creates an image of her being focused on tying the ribbon.

ADJUSTING A RIBBON ON THE HEAD

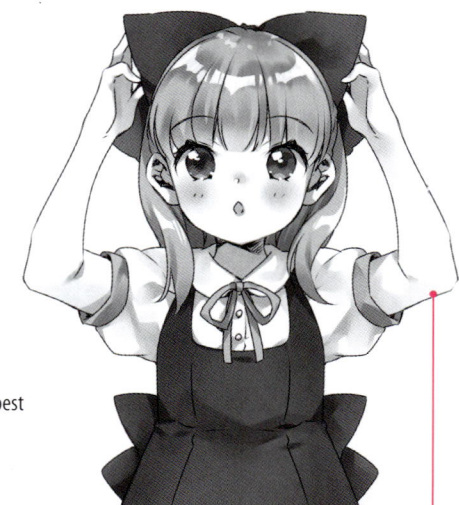

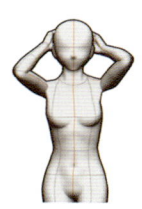

ANGLES
A front angle is best to highlight the symmetry.

The character raises both hands to adjust the balance of a large ribbon on her head. To match the ribbon, position the arms and elbows symmetrically for a more cohesive look.

TYING A RIBBON ON THE CHEST

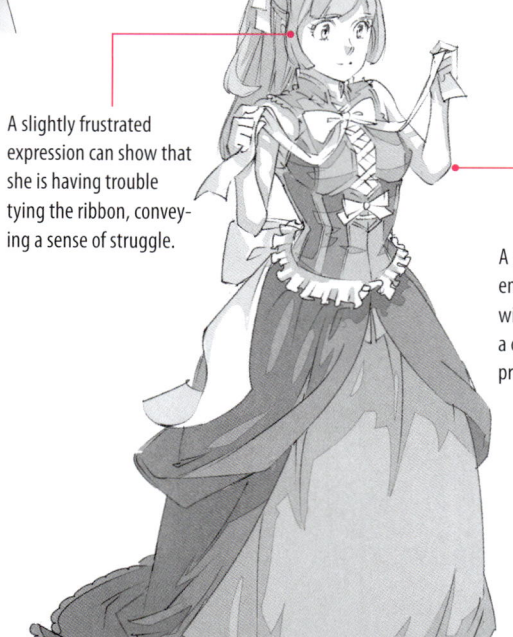

ANGLES
A diagonal angle is used so that both her expression and the act of tying the ribbon are clearly visible.

A slightly frustrated expression can show that she is having trouble tying the ribbon, conveying a sense of struggle.

A pose where she holds the ends of the ribbon on her chest with both hands. Ribbons are a classic feature on dresses of princess-like characters.

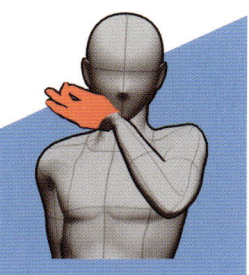

USING GLOVES TO EXPRESS PERSONALITY
Pulling Off Gloves

Putting on or removing gloves naturally draws attention to your character's hands. A character's personality traits can be highlighted or suggested by this very detailed, specific motion.

REMOVING FROM THE WRIST WITH THE MOUTH

The character bites the wrist part of the glove to remove it. Biting the wrist part rather than the fingertips gives a more hurried impression.

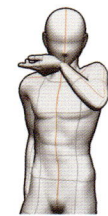

ANGLES
Choose an angle that clearly shows the mouth removing the glove.

PUTTING ON GLOVES

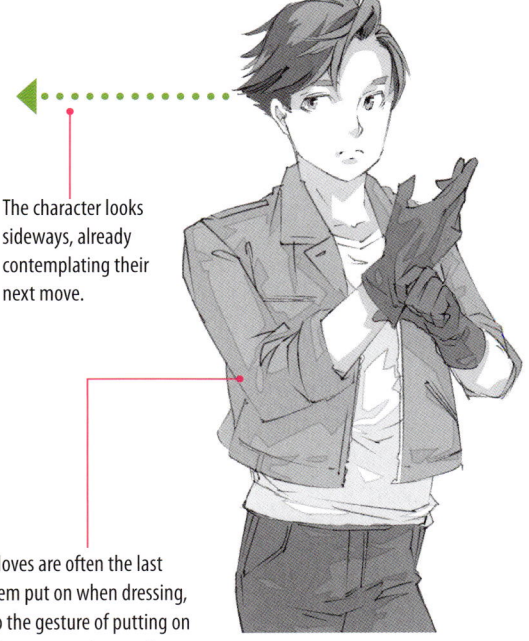

The character looks sideways, already contemplating their next move.

Gloves are often the last item put on when dressing, so the gesture of putting on gloves suggests a readiness to proceed to the next task.

REMOVING FROM THE FINGER TIPS WITH THE MOUTH

A pose where the character bites the fingertip part of the glove to remove it. Since the fingertips are narrow, the mouth should open slightly when biting them. This creates a somewhat elegant impression.

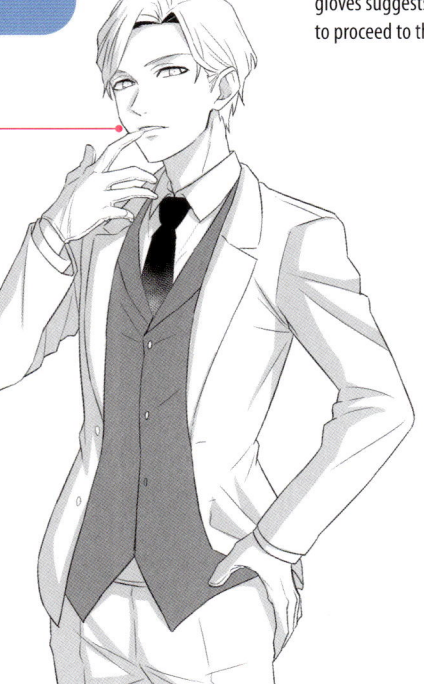

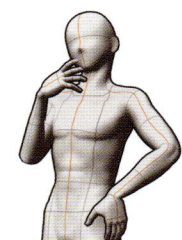

ANGLES
Use a diagonal angle with a slight tilt to create a cool atmosphere from the character's sideways glance.

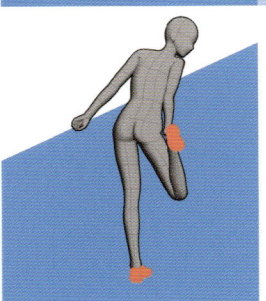

ITEMS TO ADORN THE FEET
Adjusting a Shoe

This is an everyday gesture with the advantage of involving the whole body, making it easy to create dynamic illustrations. Whether adjusting or tying the shoes, these poses highlight the angles and contours of the legs.

SLIPPING ON SHOES

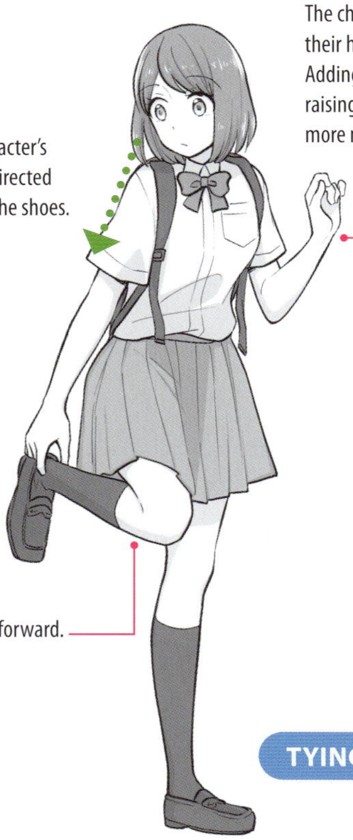

The character lightly raises their hand to maintain balance. Adding small details like slightly raising the pinky finger can add more movement.

The character's gaze is directed toward the shoes.

Bend the knee forward.

TILTING THE BODY FOR A NATURAL POSTURE

Tilt the body slightly to naturally reach the shoes.

Extend one arm to maintain balance.

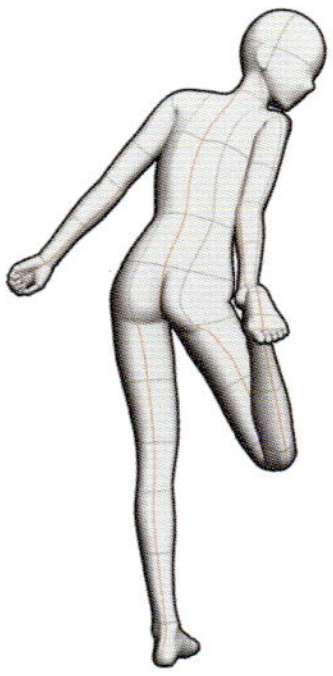

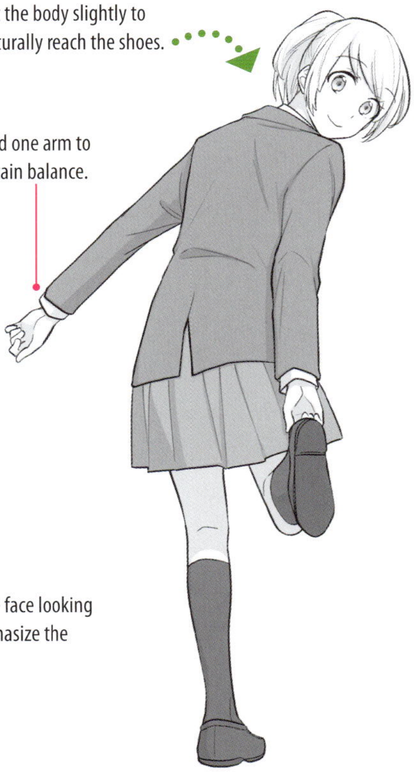

ANGLES
An angle that shows the face looking back allows you to emphasize the character's expression.

TYING THE LACES

The character bends down to make it easier to tie the laces. The shoulders should be slightly lowered, as if being pulled by the arms.

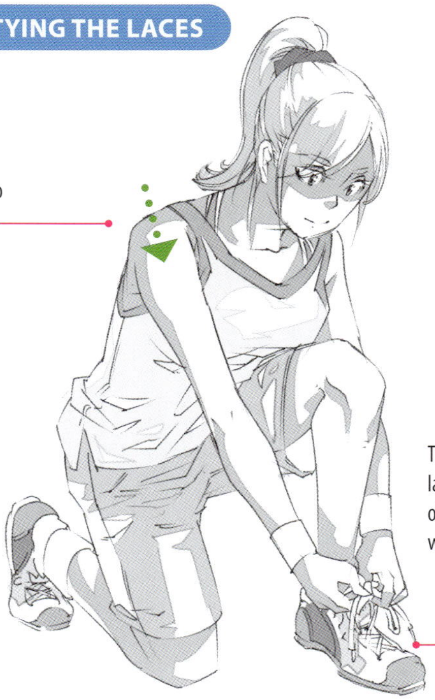

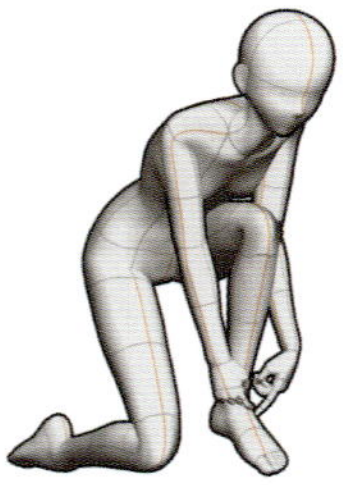

ANGLES
Using a low angle, as if the camera is placed low, allows you to clearly show the hands tying the laces.

The gaze is directed at the fingers tying the laces, which strengthens the impression of the shoes. This pose is useful when you want to emphasize the shoes.

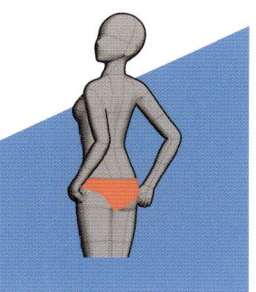

THE COMMON GESTURE OF ADJUSTING WITH FINGERS

Fixing the Fit

Putting on or adjusting swimwear or underwear is a common pose that gives your scene a sense of everyday realism. If you want to emphasize the shorts themselves, use a low angle to highlight the garment.

ADJUSTING WEDGIES

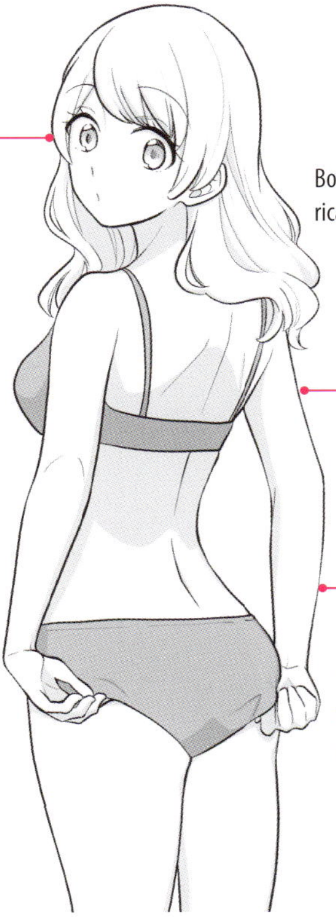

The character's gaze is directed toward their backside.

Both arms move symmetrically to adjust the shorts.

Using fingers to pinch the fabric, the character pulls to fix the wedgie.

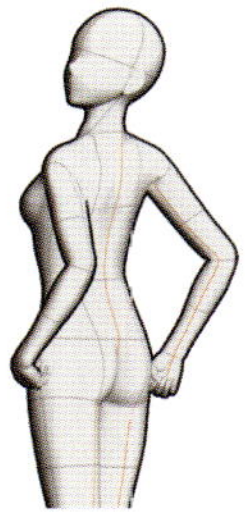

PUTTING ON SHORTS

A pose where the character pinches the edge of the shorts and pulls them up.

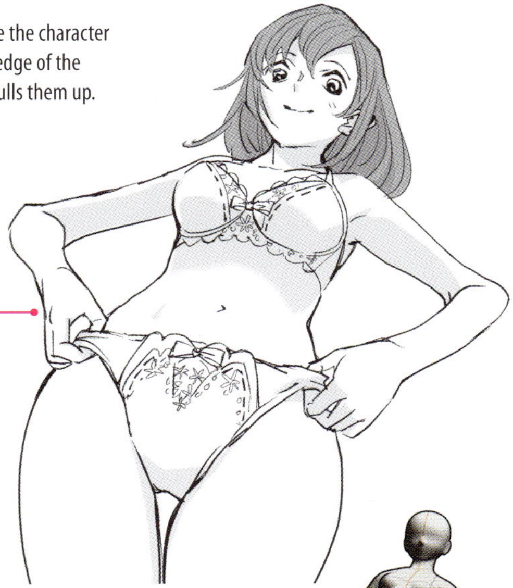

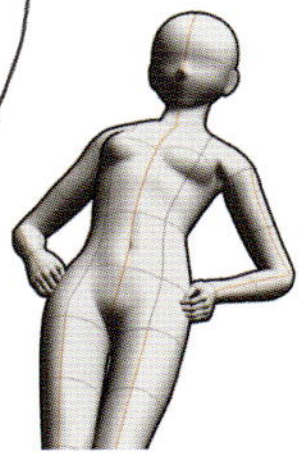

ANGLES
A low angle is used to emphasize the shorts.

ADJUSTING UNDERWEAR

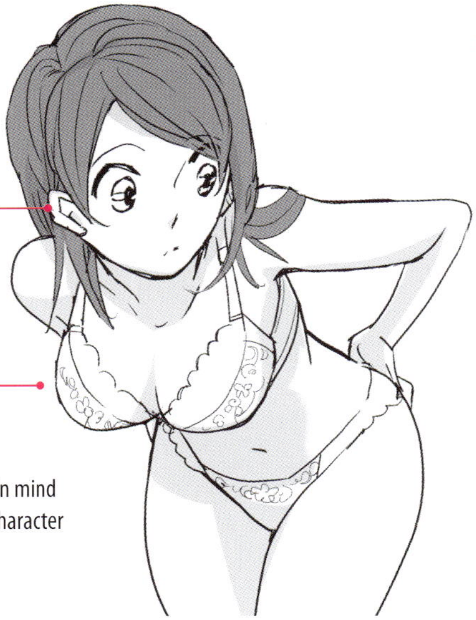

Positioning the head forward enhances the impression of the character's expression.

Keep perspective in mind when drawing a character bending forward.

ANGLES
Using a rear angle allows both hands, reaching behind to adjust the shorts, to be visible, clearly showing the adjustment gesture.

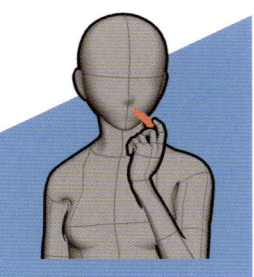

SUBTLE MOVEMENTS
Putting on Lipstick

Do you want to draw attention to a character's mouth? Lipstick does the trick! Consider the position of the lips and mouth and the variation of applying lipstick with a finger instead of a tube or brush.

APPLYING LIPSTICK GESTURE

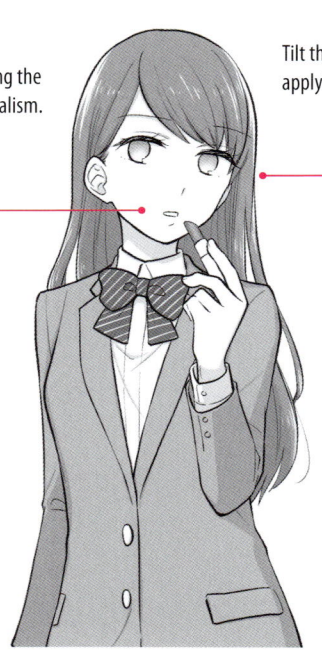

Slightly opening the mouth adds realism.

Tilt the face naturally to make applying the lipstick easier.

APPLYING WITH A FINGER

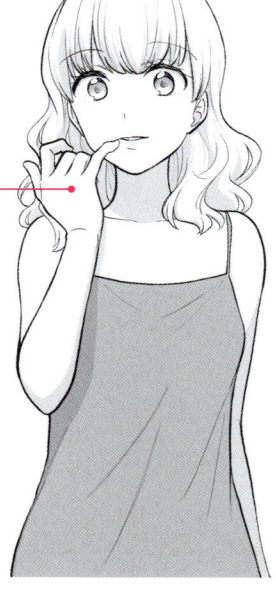

When adjusting or blending lipstick, using the finger, particularly the pinky, adds the final touch.

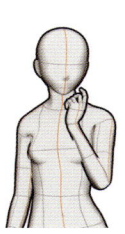

ANGLES
Choose an angle that clearly shows the lipstick, the lips, and the moving fingertips.

SHOWING THE SIDE PROFILE

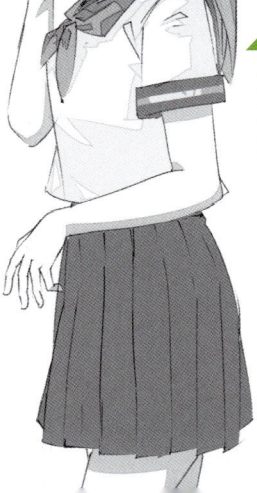

The gaze is directed at the mirror.

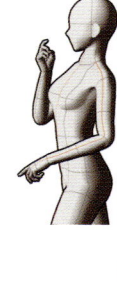

ANGLES
A side angle effectively shows the lipstick being applied to the lips.

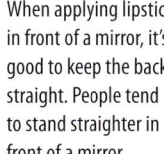

When applying lipstick in front of a mirror, it's good to keep the back straight. People tend to stand straighter in front of a mirror.

CROPPING Expressing with Just the Mouth

The pose of applying lipstick can convey the movement of the fingers, so a bold crop that focuses on the mouth can still effectively convey the pose's charm.

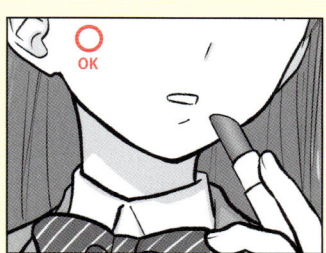

DOMESTIC SCENES
Wearing Aprons

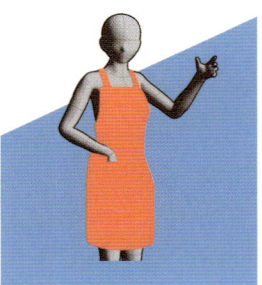

Dressing a character in an apron emphasizes friendliness and warmth or indicates a flavor-addicted foodie. Putting your character's hands in the pockets or tying the apron strings can make the item, and your character's contours, stand out more.

PUTTING HANDS IN POCKETS

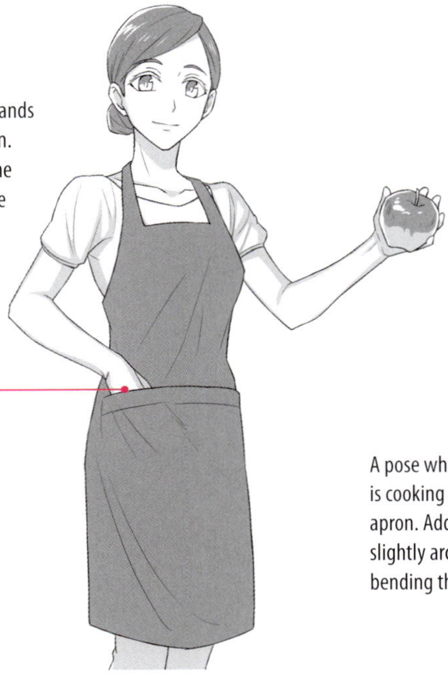

The character puts their hands in the pockets of the apron. Since the pockets are at the front, draw the back of the hands facing forward.

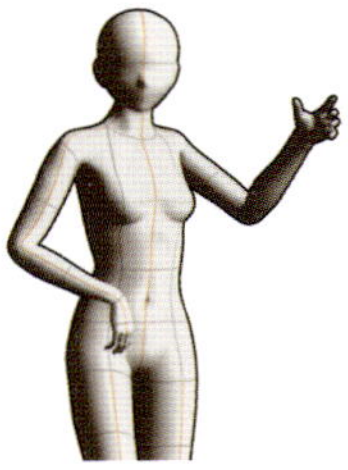

ANGLES
A diagonal angle can effectively show the body lines wrapped in the apron.

COOKING IN AN APRON

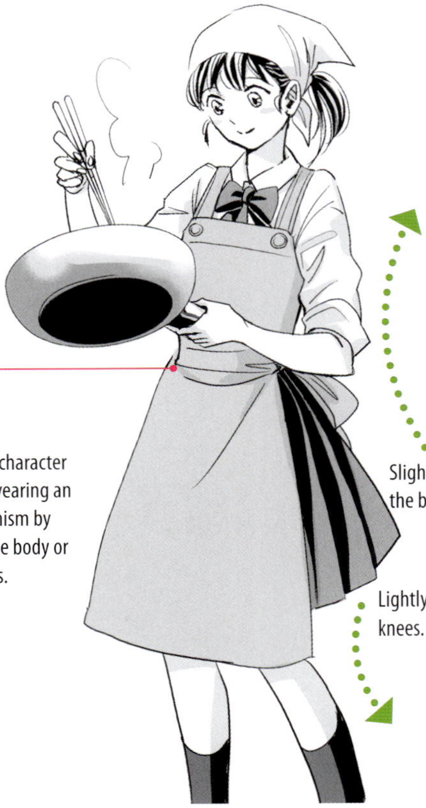

A pose where the character is cooking while wearing an apron. Add dynamism by slightly arching the body or bending the knees.

Slightly arch the body.

Lightly bend the knees.

TYING THE STRINGS

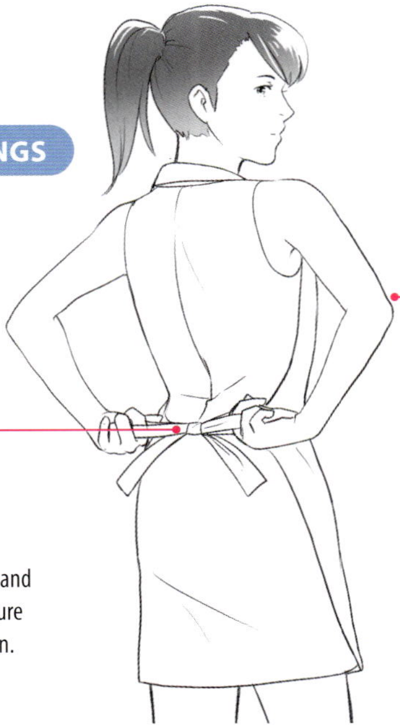

Raise the elbows to show the action of pulling the tied strings.

Straightening the back and maintaining good posture gives a sharp impression.

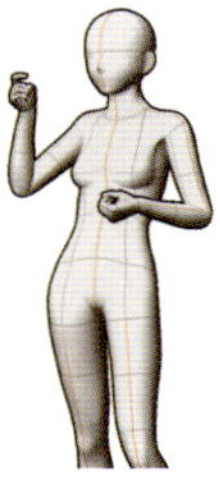

ANGLES
In an illustration of a cooking scene, a low angle emphasizes the frying pan, while a high angle emphasizes the food in the frying pan. Here, since we want to highlight the apron, the viewpoint is set at about the character's eye level.

CONVEYING A SERIOUS AND INTELLIGENT IMAGE

Serious and Studious

A book naturally emphasizes a character's seriousness and intelligence, making it a fitting item for a student or budding intellectual. Pay attention to the size variation depending on whether it's a hardcover, paperback or a comic book.

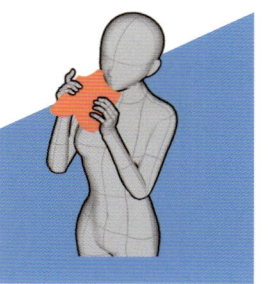

HOLDING A BOOK

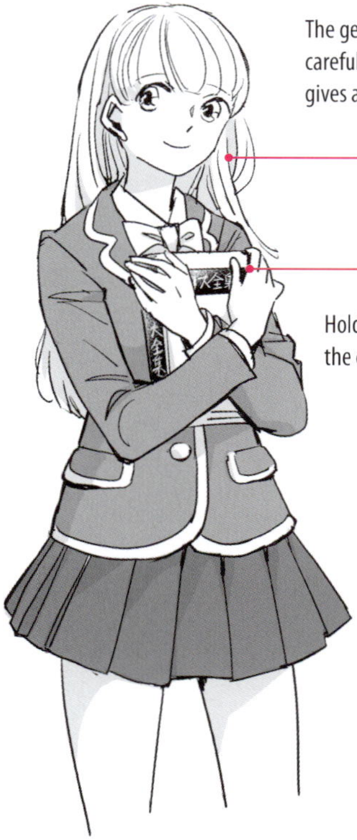

The gesture of holding a book carefully with both hands gives a serious impression.

Hold the book around the chest area.

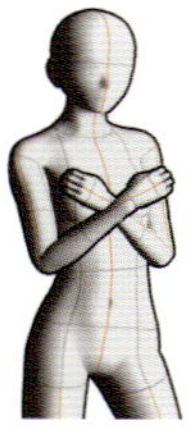

ANGLES

A diagonal angle effectively conveys the image of holding the book with both arms.

BRINGING THE BOOK CLOSE TO THE FACE

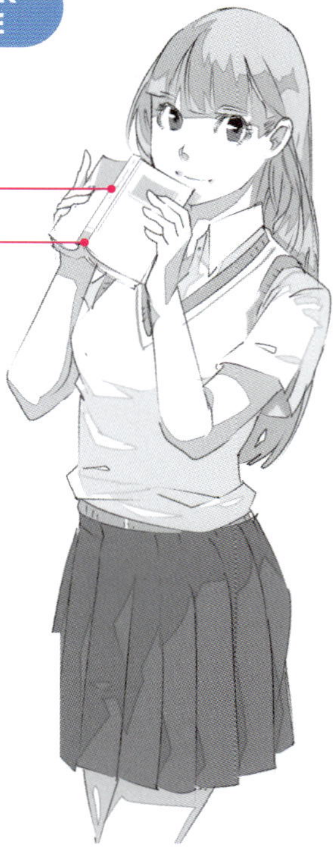

Holding the book close to the face creates a shy pose.

Using a small-sized book reduces the area of the character hidden by the book.

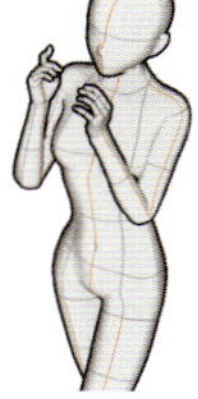

SITTING AND READING

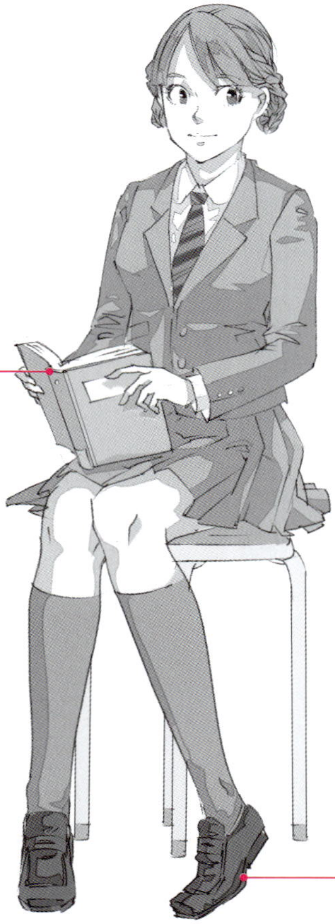

With a heavy hardcover book, the character reads it without lifting it, placing it on their lap.

ANGLES

A slightly high-angle viewpoint can make the character appear to be looking up.

One leg is positioned at a different angle to add dynamism to the illustration.

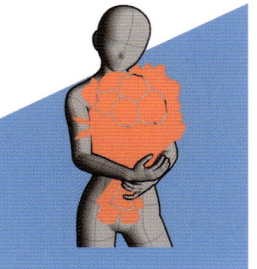

ADDING GLAMOUR TO THE SCENE
Holding a Bouquet

Having a character hold a bouquet can enhance and emphasize facial features. Just be sure the beatiful blooms don't distract from the true center of attention in your illustration: your character.

HOLDING NEAR THE FACE

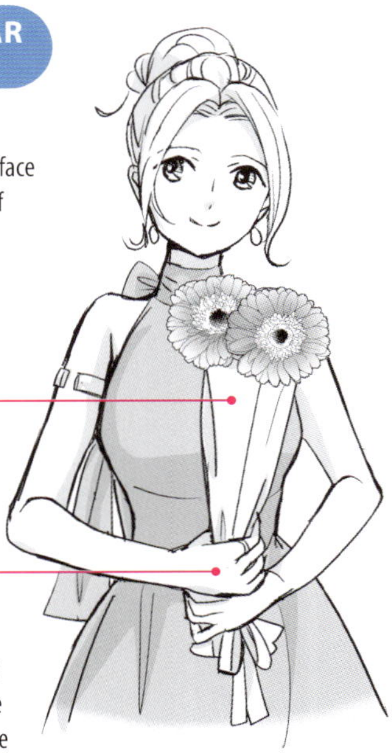

Placing flowers near the face highlights the delicacy of the expression.

The hand holding the small bouquet should not grip too tightly, giving the impression of handling the flowers with care.

HOLDING A LARGE BOUQUET

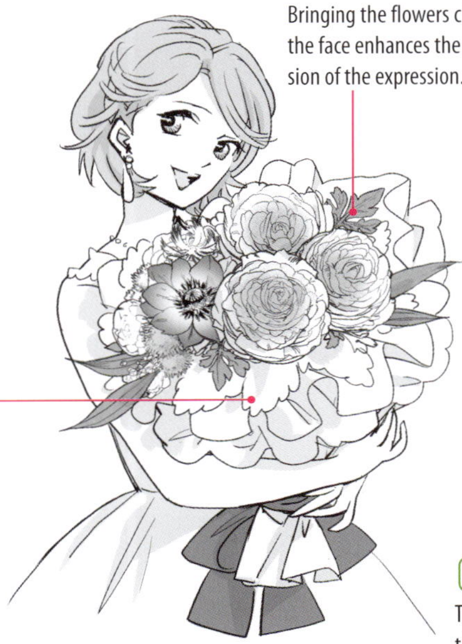

Bringing the flowers close to the face enhances the impression of the expression.

Holding a large bouquet in an embracing pose suggests a celebratory atmosphere.

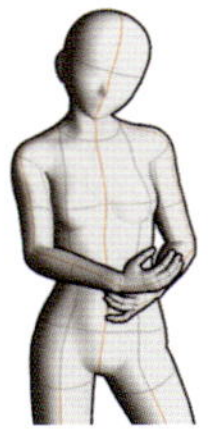

ANGLES
To make the flowers held by the character standing sideways prominent, position the flowers at a front-facing angle.

HIDDEN BEHIND

ANGLES
Use a slightly diagonal angle to show both the hidden flowers and the character's expression.

A pose showing the character bending down and sneaking up, suggesting a story of surprising someone with flowers.

The bouquet is held with the unseen hand and supported by the left hand. The left hand gently supports the bottom of the bouquet without touching the flowers.

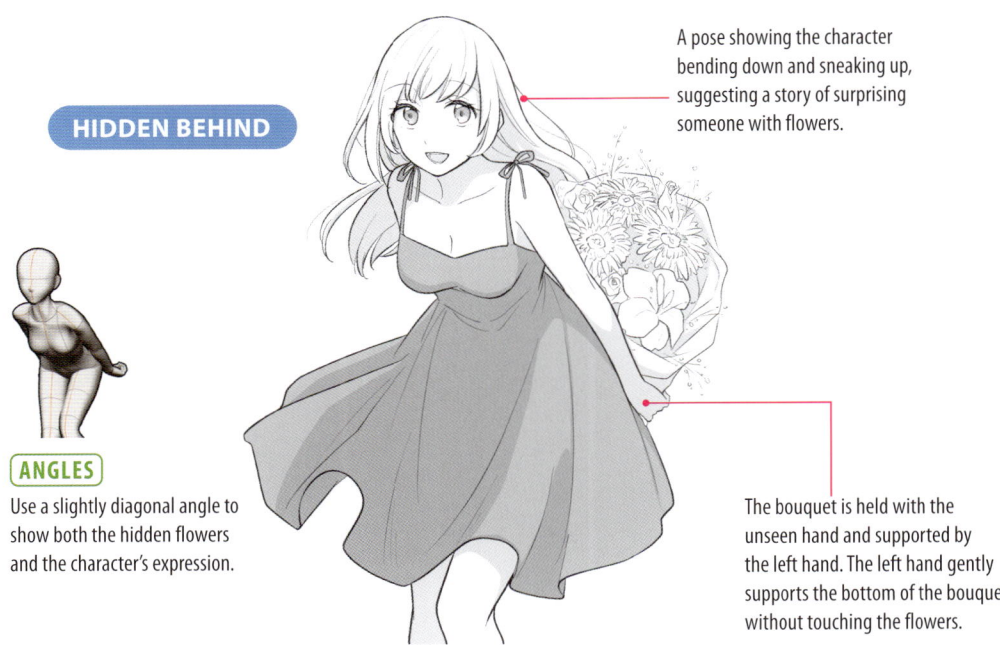

ESSENTIAL ITEMS
Holding a Phone

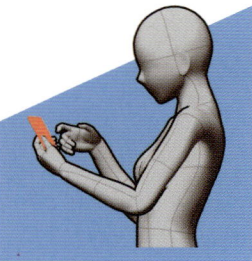

It wouldn't be surprising to see a phone in your character's hands. If the dominant hand is the right hand, the smartphone is usually held with the left hand for right-handed operation; but for selfie poses, it's held with the dominant hand.

OPERATING GESTURE

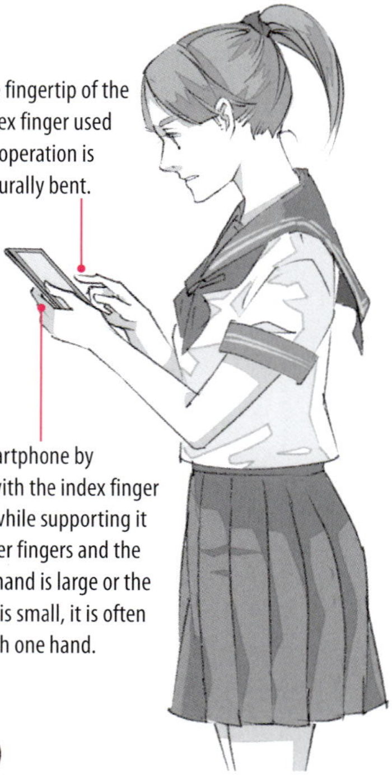

The fingertip of the index finger used for operation is naturally bent.

Hold the smartphone by pinching it with the index finger and thumb while supporting it with the other fingers and the palm. If the hand is large or the smartphone is small, it is often operated with one hand.

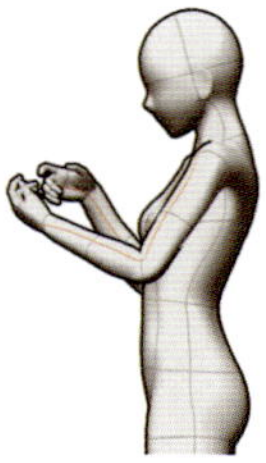

ANGLES

A side angle creates an explanatory impression, which fits the mood of someone looking something up.

LYING DOWN AND VIEWING

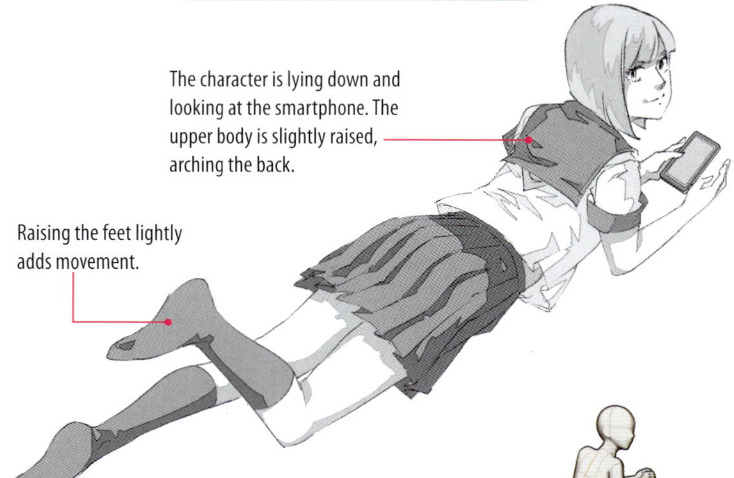

The character is lying down and looking at the smartphone. The upper body is slightly raised, arching the back.

Raising the feet lightly adds movement.

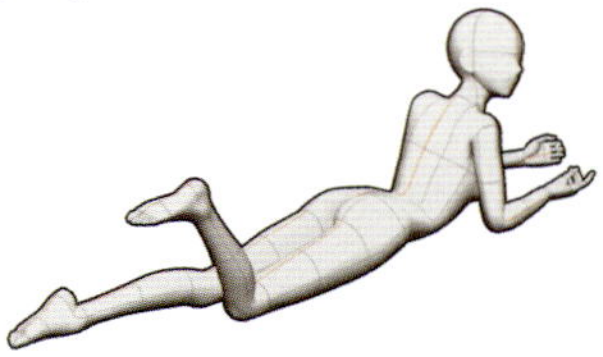

ANGLES

An angle from behind the character shows the smartphone screen, enhancing the impression of the smartphone.

SELFIE

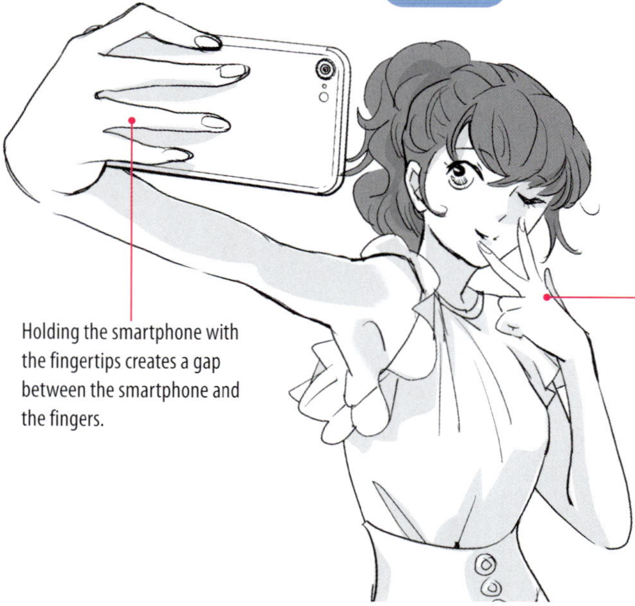

Holding the smartphone with the fingertips creates a gap between the smartphone and the fingers.

The other hand makes a fun pose for the selfie.

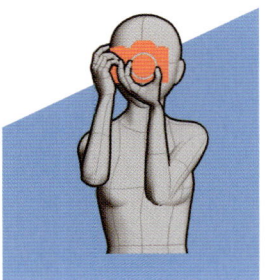

USING CAMERAS
Taking a Picture

Is your character a shutter bug? When using a tradition camera, they're held with both hands, so the line of the arms is accentuated. In shooting poses, the zoom lens is supported from below.

POSING WITH THE CAMERA

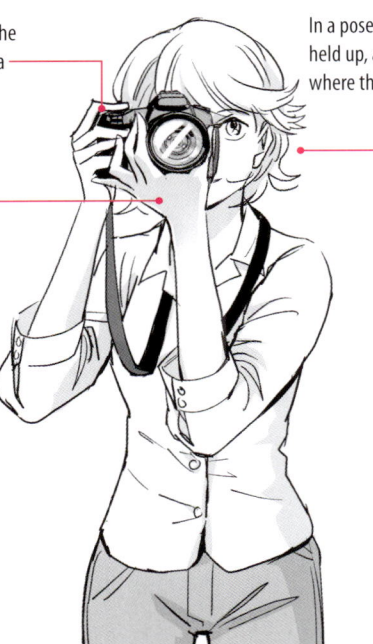

The index finger on the shutter button adds a sense of movement.

Pinch the zoom lens with the index finger and thumb, supporting it with the palm.

In a pose with the camera held up, attention is drawn to where the camera is pointing.

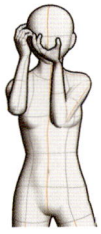

ANGLES
A front angle for a pose with the camera held up makes the camera lens more striking.

SEARCHING FOR A SUBJECT

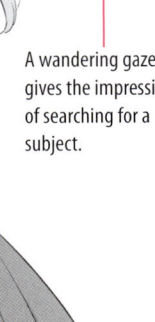

Holding an SLR camera with both hands is the basic stance.

A wandering gaze gives the impression of searching for a subject.

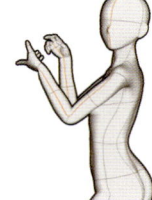

ANGLES
For poses like the example, a side angle makes it look like the camera and the character are side by side, drawing attention to both.

TURNING WITH THE CAMERA

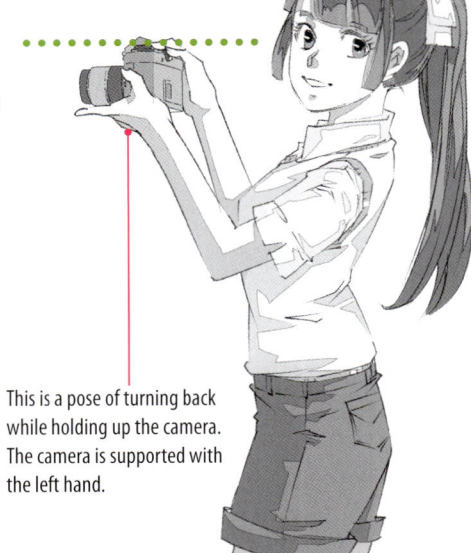

Raising the camera to face level creates the scene of looking back while taking a photo.

This is a pose of turning back while holding up the camera. The camera is supported with the left hand.

Tips — Adding Density to the Illustration

Cameras, with their many small parts, add density to an illustration even in close-up shots.

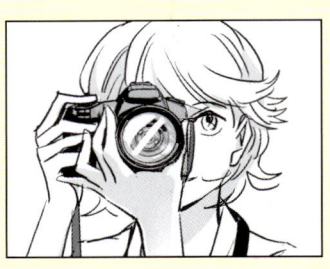

EVERYDAY ITEMS
Holding a Bag

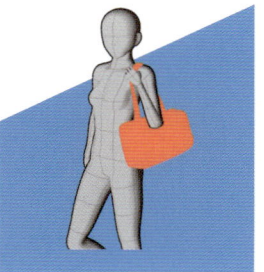

The type of bag used changes depending on the situation, such as going to school, traveling or walking around town. Additionally, the appropriate way to hold a bag differs depending on the type, so adjust your chosen pose accordingly.

SHOULDER CARRYING A SCHOOL BAG

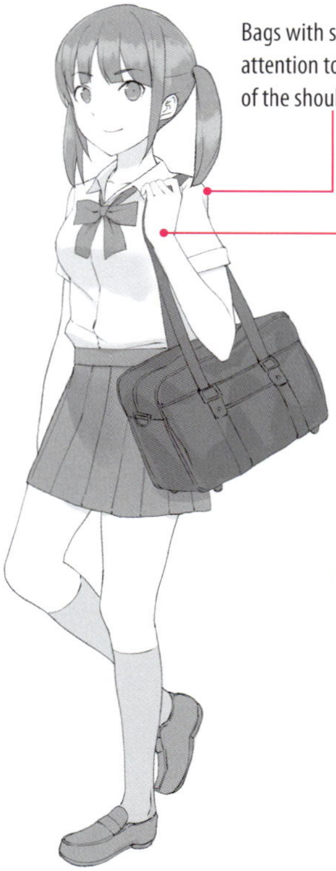

Bags with straps draw attention to the contours of the shoulder.

Raising the index finger above the other fingers adds expression to the hand's pose.

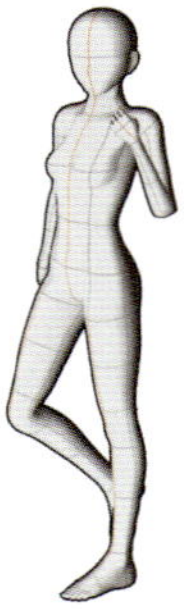

ANGLES

If you want to highlight the bag, position the viewpoint on the side holding the bag. A diagonal angle helps convey the shape of the bag and the hand holding it.

WEARING A BACKPACK

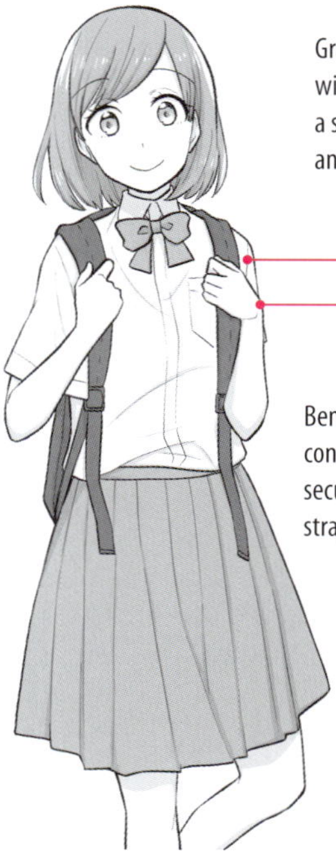

Grabbing each strap with both hands creates a sense of excitement and readiness.

Bending the wrists conveys a sense of securely holding the straps.

SITTING ON A SUITCASE

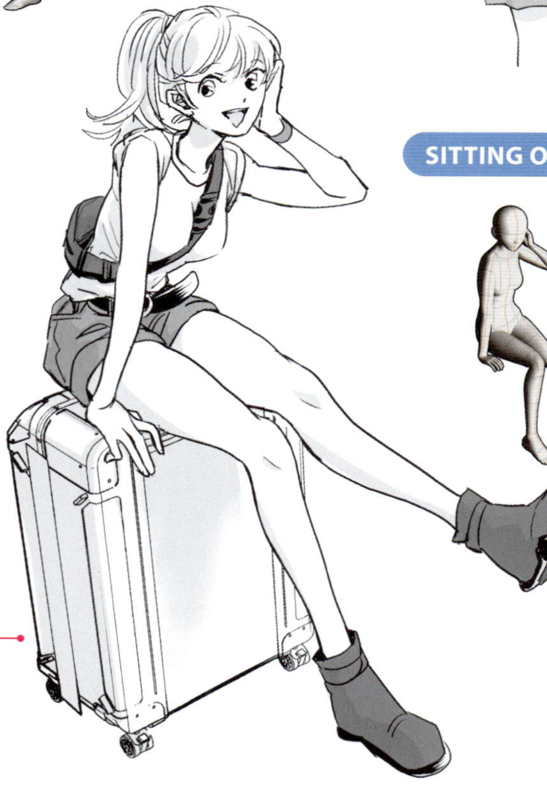

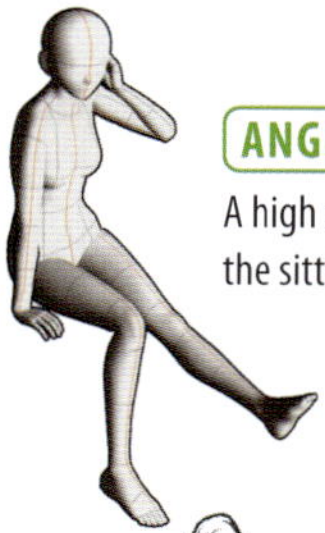

ANGLES

A high angle clearly shows the sitting posture.

A large suitcase can easily accommodate a person sitting on top. It can also convey a sense of travel.

CARRYING A SHOULDER BAG

CARRYING A SCHOOL BAG OVER THE SHOULDER

Carrying a school bag over the shoulder is also a classic pose.

The palm faces upward.

Relax the arm that isn't holding the bag to create a casual and relaxed impression.

A common way to carry a shoulder bag is to sling it over the shoulder and grab the lower part of the strap.

Leaving a slight gap under the arm helps create a natural pose.

HOLDING SHOPPING BAGS

Numerous shopping bags dangle from the arm. Since shopping bags are wider at the bottom, draw them fanning out toward the bottom.

The kicked-back leg adds to the fun and casual atmosphere.

HOLDING A TRUNK

When holding a heavy bag with both hands, draw the arms slightly extended.

141

SHELTER FROM THE RAIN
Holding an Umbrella

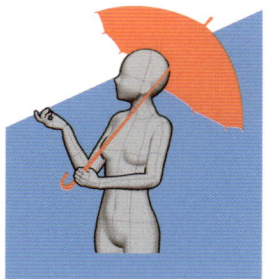

Rain in illustrations is often used to conjure a sad or somber mood, so a character holding an umbrella tends to evoke an emotional atmosphere. Alternately, an aura of romance or a contemplative moment can be suggested with this adaptable accessory.

CHECKING THE RAIN

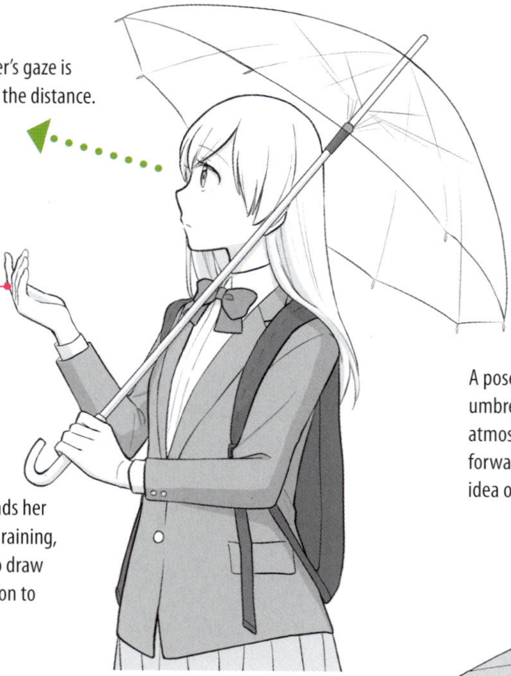

The character's gaze is looking into the distance.

The character extends her hand to check if it's raining, a pose that tends to draw the viewer's attention to the extended hand.

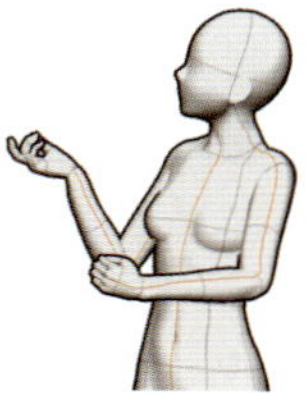

ANGLES
A diagonal angle is used to emphasize the hand checking the rain.

WALKING WITH A CLOSED UMBRELLA

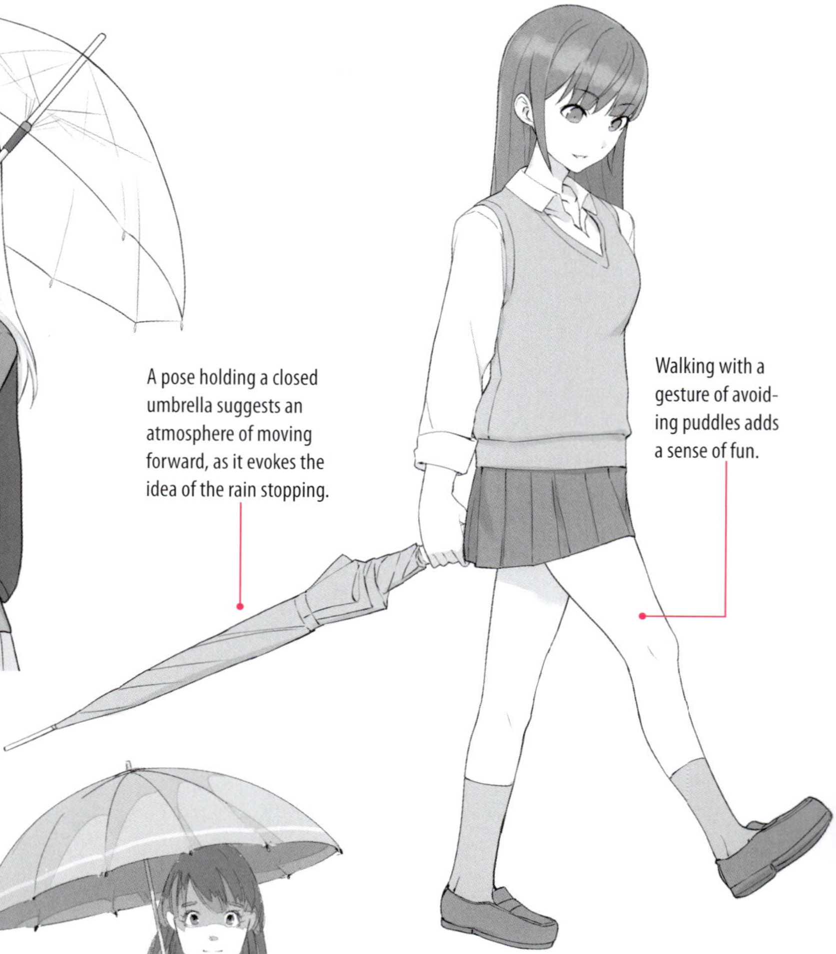

A pose holding a closed umbrella suggests an atmosphere of moving forward, as it evokes the idea of the rain stopping.

Walking with a gesture of avoiding puddles adds a sense of fun.

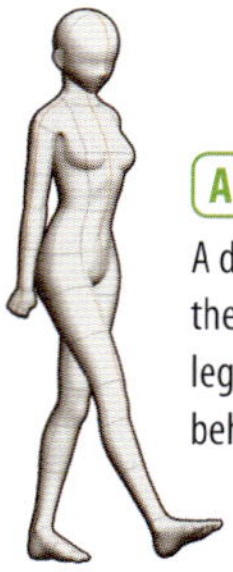

HOLDING WITH BOTH HANDS

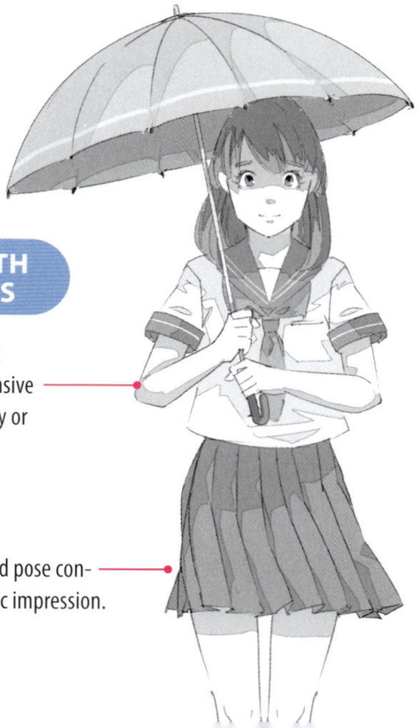

Holding the umbrella with both hands creates a defensive posture, expressing anxiety or loneliness.

A restrained pose conveys a static impression.

ANGLES
A diagonal angle shows the forward-extended leg and the umbrella held behind well.

142

TURNING BACK WITH AN UMBRELLA

SHOWING THE RIBS OF THE UMBRELLA

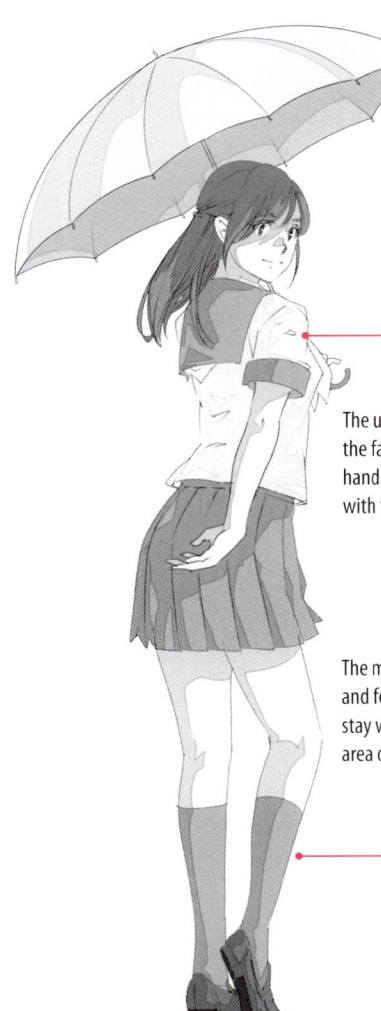

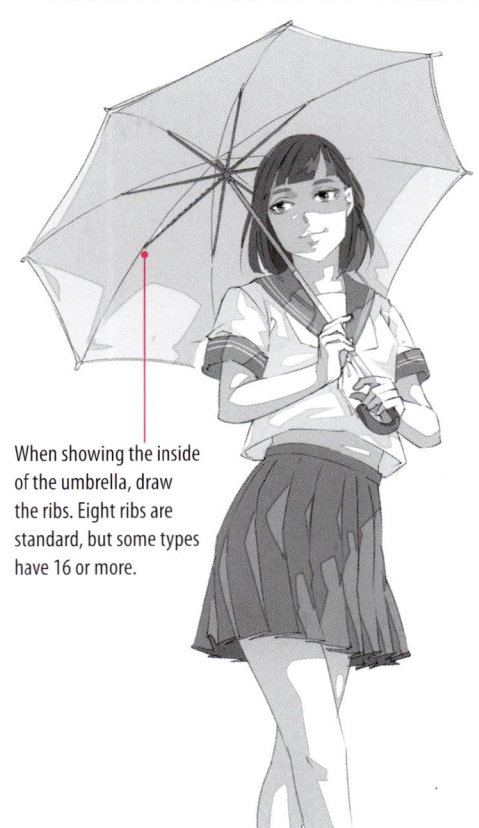

The umbrella is held with the far hand, keeping the handle from overlapping with the character.

When showing the inside of the umbrella, draw the ribs. Eight ribs are standard, but some types have 16 or more.

The movements of the hands and feet are kept small to stay within the sheltered area of the umbrella.

CROUCHING WITH AN UMBRELLA

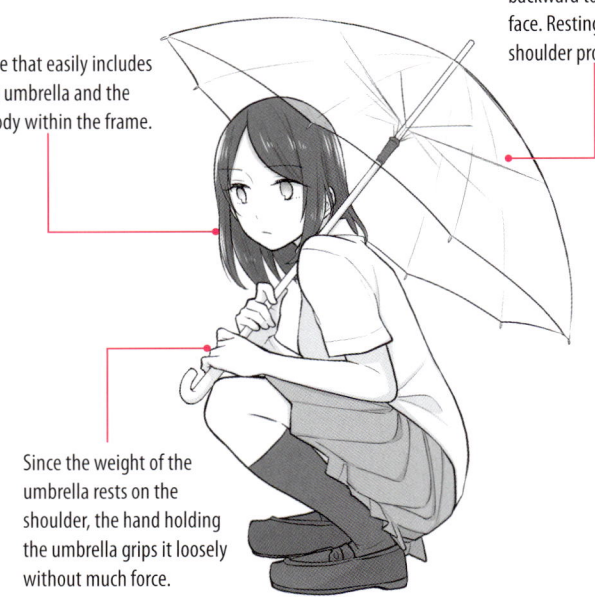

Tilt the umbrella slightly backward to avoid covering the face. Resting the handle on the shoulder provides stability.

It's a pose that easily includes both the umbrella and the entire body within the frame.

Since the weight of the umbrella rests on the shoulder, the hand holding the umbrella grips it loosely without much force.

Tips — Size of the Umbrella

It's important to establish the size of the umbrella and maintain proper proportion with the character. The width of an open umbrella ranges from 32 to 40 inches (80-100 cm).

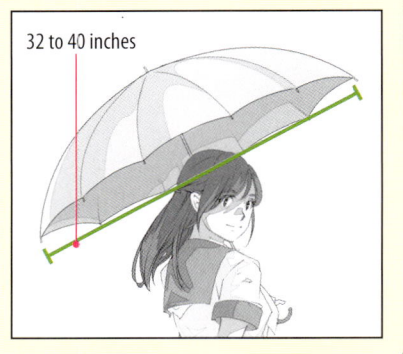

32 to 40 inches

SCHOOL SCENES
Leaning on a Desk

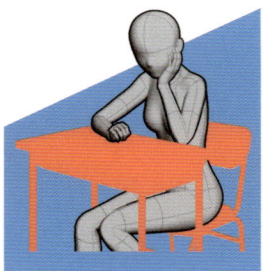

Everyday scenes from school life are commonly depicted in illustrations. There's no need to adhere strictly to proper sitting posture; instead, decide on poses based on the situation and the character's traits.

RESTING ELBOWS

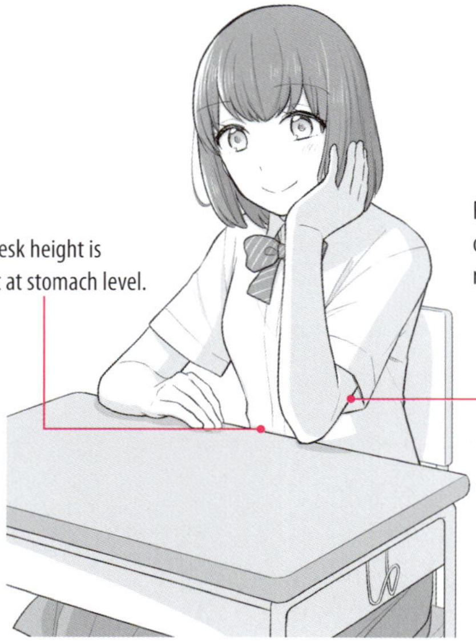

The desk height is about at stomach level.

Rest the elbows on the desk for a relaxed posture.

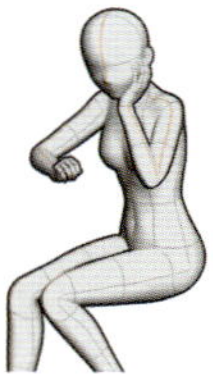

ANGLES
A slightly high angle shows the desk surface well.

SITTING SIDEWAYS

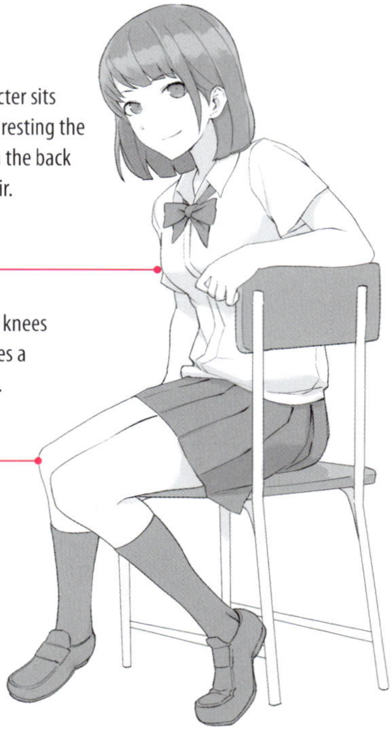

The character sits sideways, resting the elbows on the back of the chair.

Bringing the knees together gives a modest look.

LAYING FACE DOWN

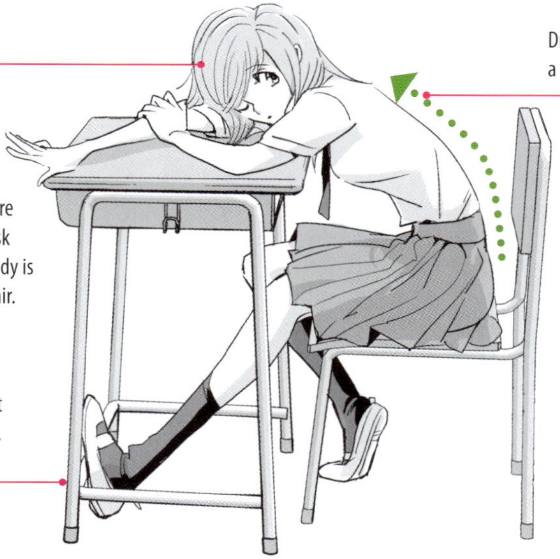

Draw the back with a gentle curve.

The head and arms are supported by the desk surface, while the body is supported by the chair.

The soles of the feet touch the desk legs.

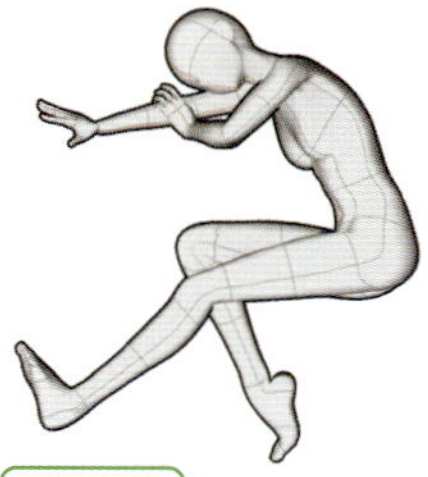

ANGLES
A side view angle clearly shows the relationship between the desk and the character.

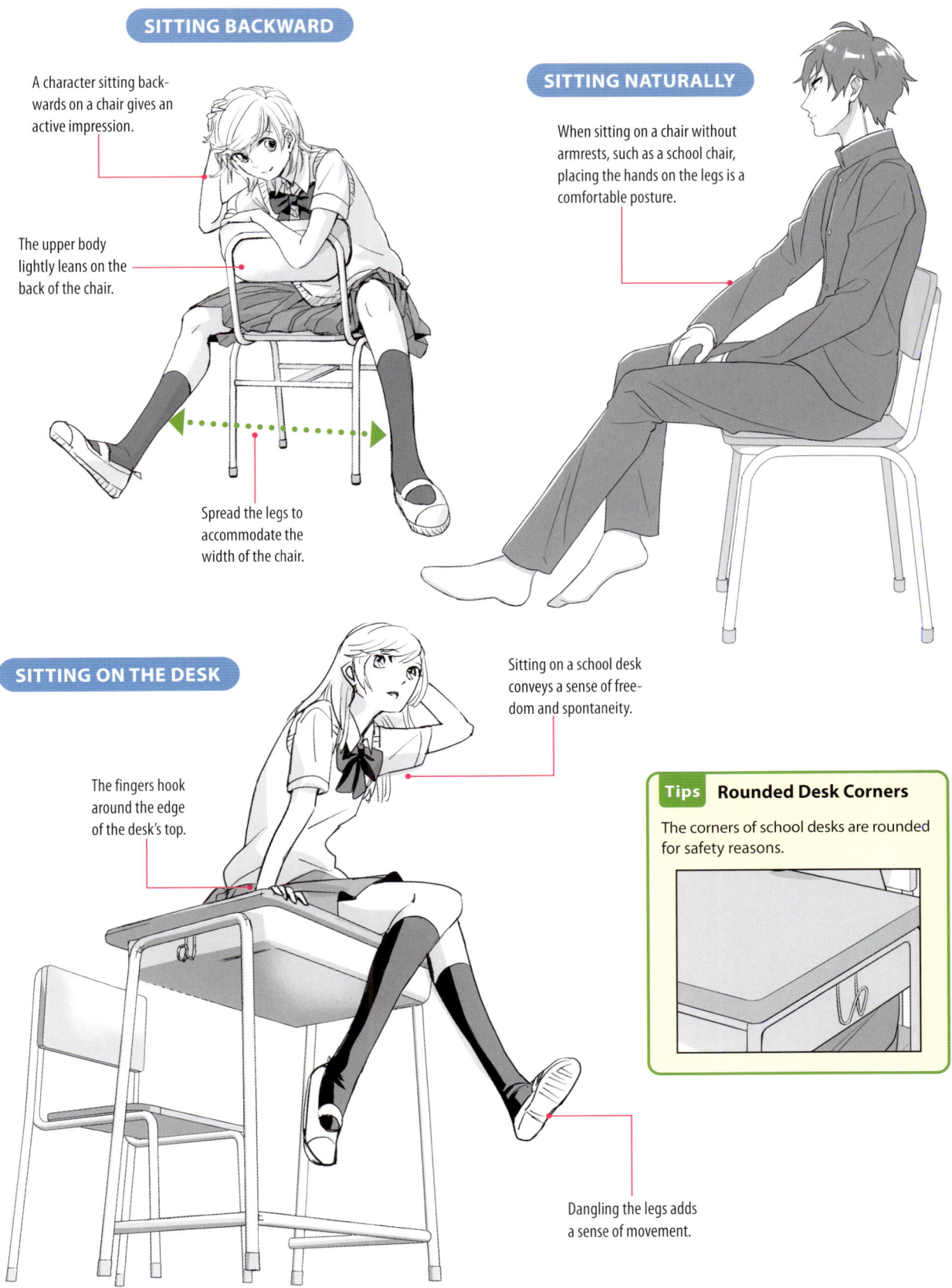

SITTING QUIETLY

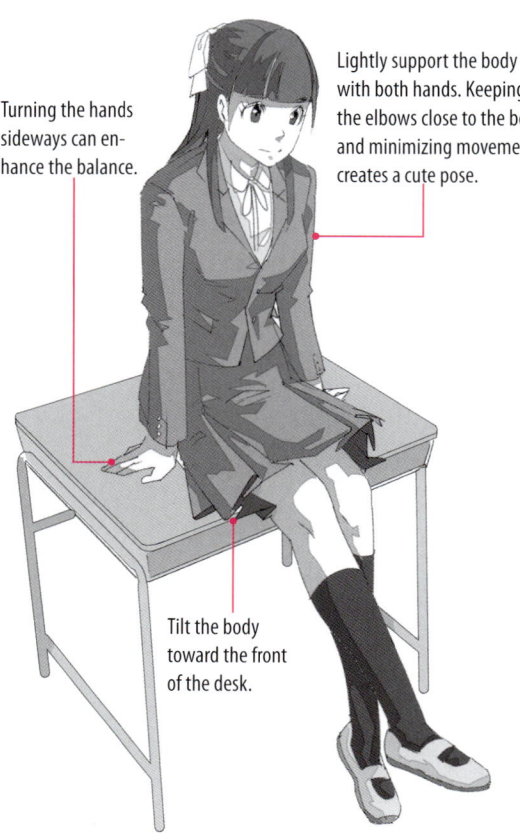

Turning the hands sideways can enhance the balance.

Lightly support the body with both hands. Keeping the elbows close to the body and minimizing movement creates a cute pose.

Tilt the body toward the front of the desk.

EATING LUNCH

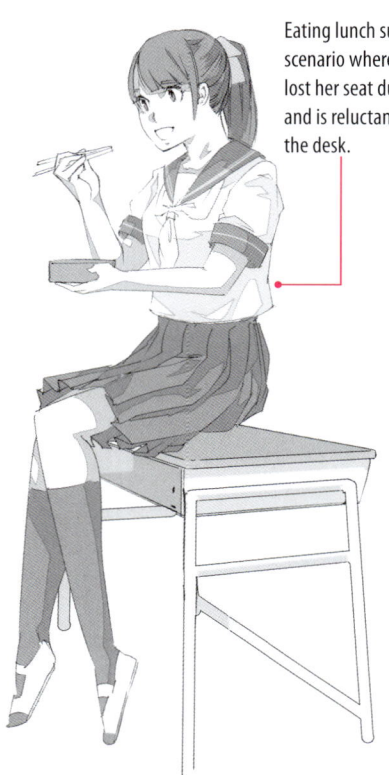

Eating lunch suggests a scenario where the character lost her seat during lunchtime and is reluctantly sitting on the desk.

Tips — Size of the Desk Top

Measure the size of the desk to ensure it looks natural when combined with the character. For school desks, the standard tabletop width is 26 inches (65 cm), and the depth is 18 inches (45 cm).

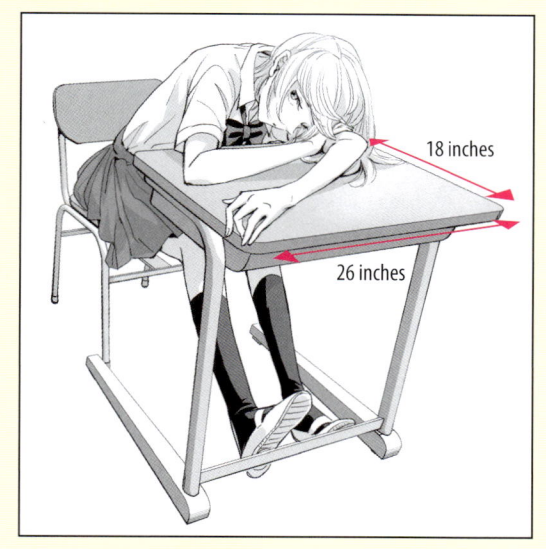

18 inches

26 inches

USING ARMS AS A PILLOW

The head is resting on the crossed arms used as a pillow.

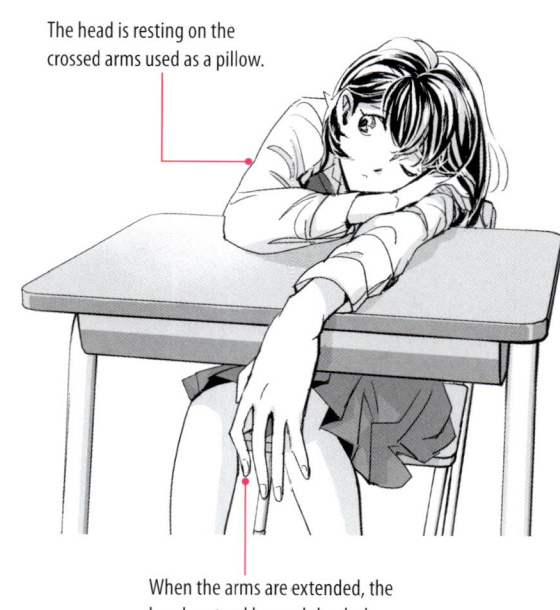

When the arms are extended, the hands extend beyond the desk.

FROM THRONES TO SOFAS
Sitting with Legs Crossed

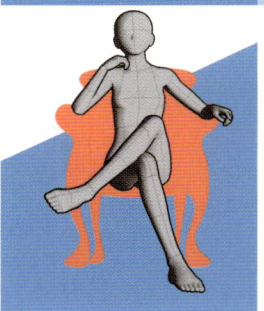

To emphasize a relaxed impression, adopt a straigh posture and place the elbows or hands on the armrests. The pose varies depending on the shape, width and design of the backrest and armrests of the chair.

SITTING AUTHORITATIVELY

Sitting with legs crossed on a grand chair, like a throne, conveys a sense of high status.

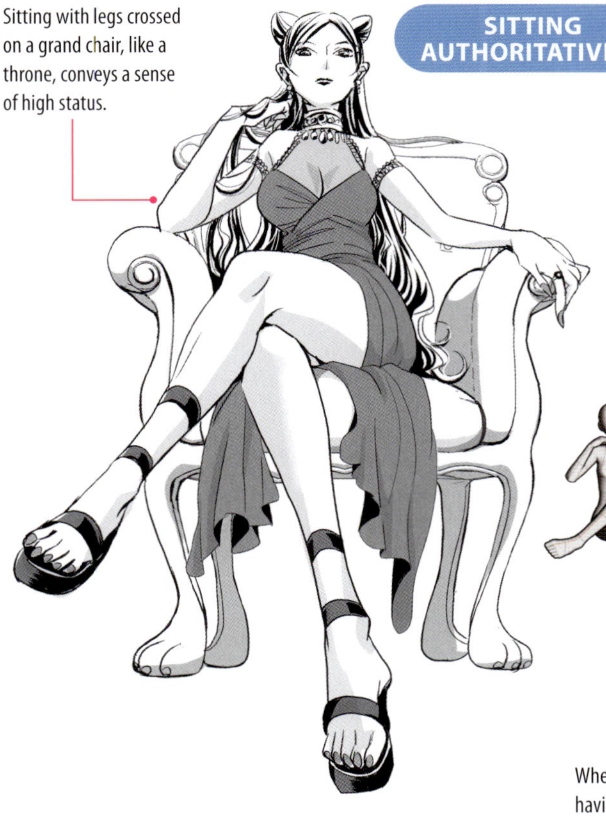

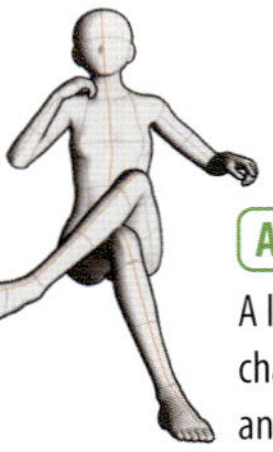

SITTING AND THINKING

When sitting deeply in a chair, rest the back against the backrest.

A pose of sitting with arms crossed can express a thoughtful state.

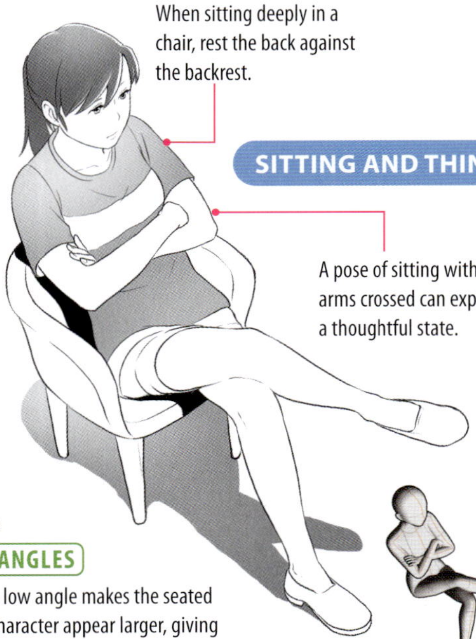

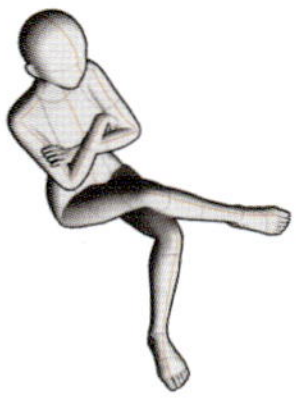

ANGLES

A low angle makes the seated character appear larger, giving an imposing impression.

ANGLES

A high angle doesn't convey the same intensity as a low angle, but it makes the overall pose clearer and often results in a cleaner composition.

LYING ON A SOFA

A sofa is the perfect set piece for a relaxed or casual scene.

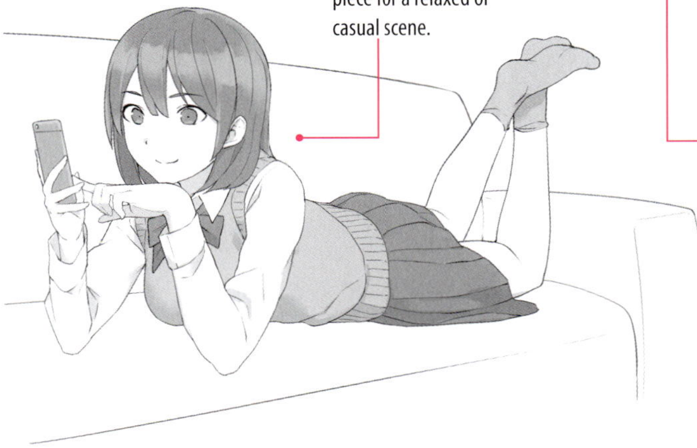

When using a sofa, having the character stretch her legs along the edge helps create a stable composition.

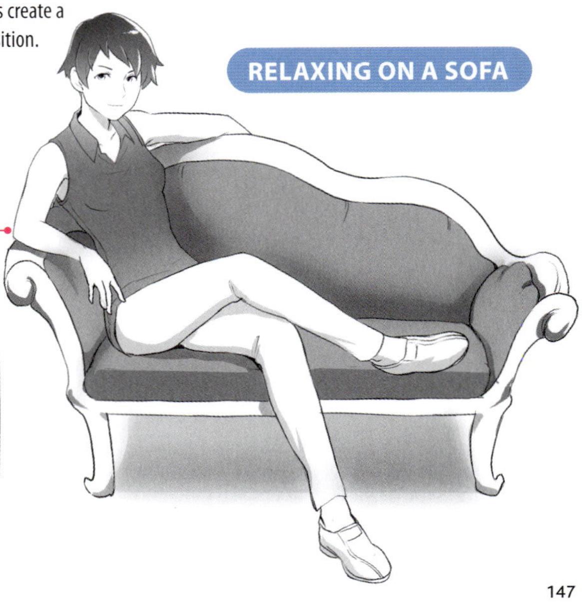

RELAXING ON A SOFA

HANDHELD WEAPONS
Wielding a Sword

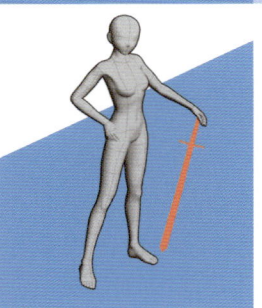

Sword-based poses are determined by the type of weapon being wielded but also the character in possession of it. A heavy sword is generally held with both hands, but a character with immense strength can easily hold it with one hand.

MIDDLE GUARD STANCE

Point the tip of the sword slightly upward, toward the opponent.

Keep the elbows close to the body and extend the arms.

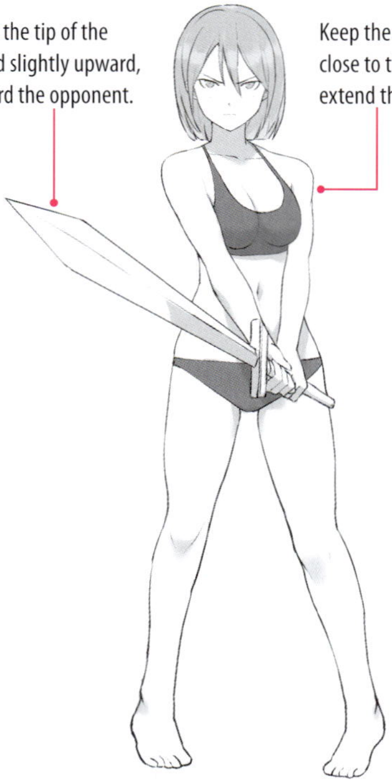

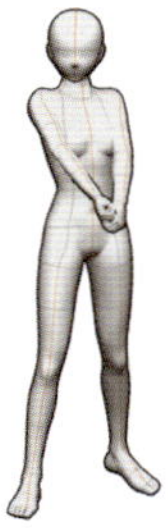

ANGLES

A front angle emphasizes the character's aggressive expression as they glare at the enemy, creating an intense impression.

POINTING THE SWORD UPWARD

The sword points toward the sky. The character's posture is upright, exuding a brisk and spirited atmosphere.

To make the sword and the character parallel, keep the back straight.

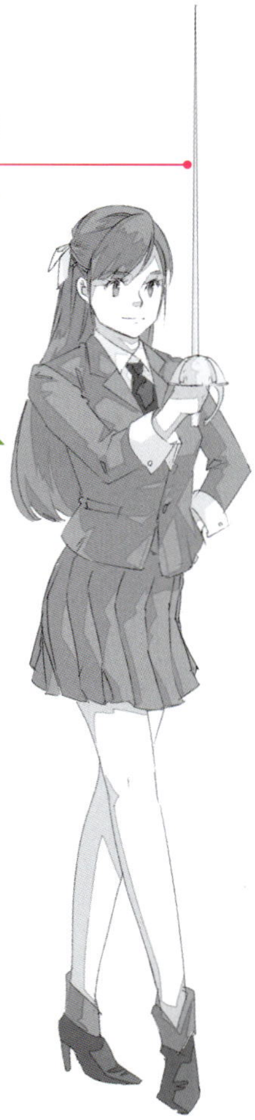

LEANING ON THE SWORD

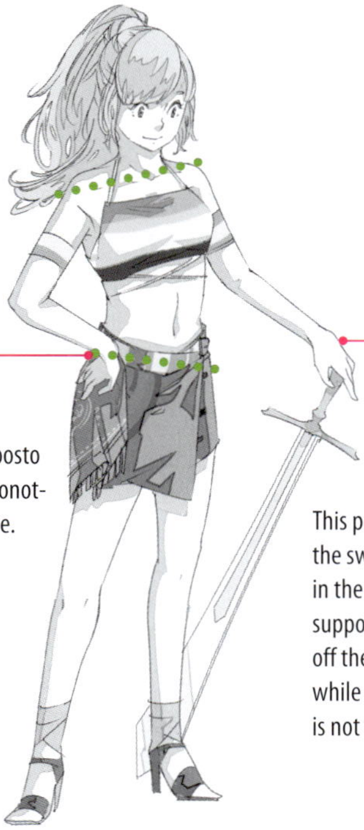

Consider a contrapposto stance to avoid a monotonous standing pose.

This pose involves holding the sword, which is planted in the ground, with one hand supporting the hilt. It shows off the shape of the sword while indicating the character is not currently in battle.

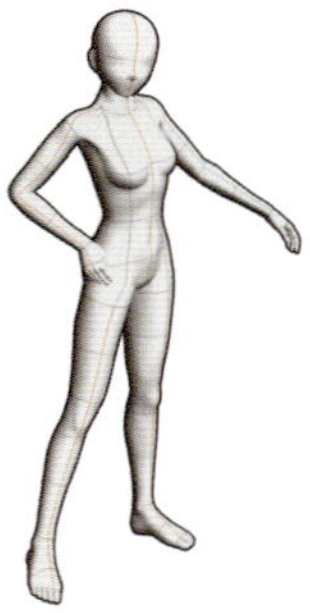

ANGLES

Use a slightly high and diagonal angle to clearly show the character's proportions, with the sword turned to display its blade prominently.

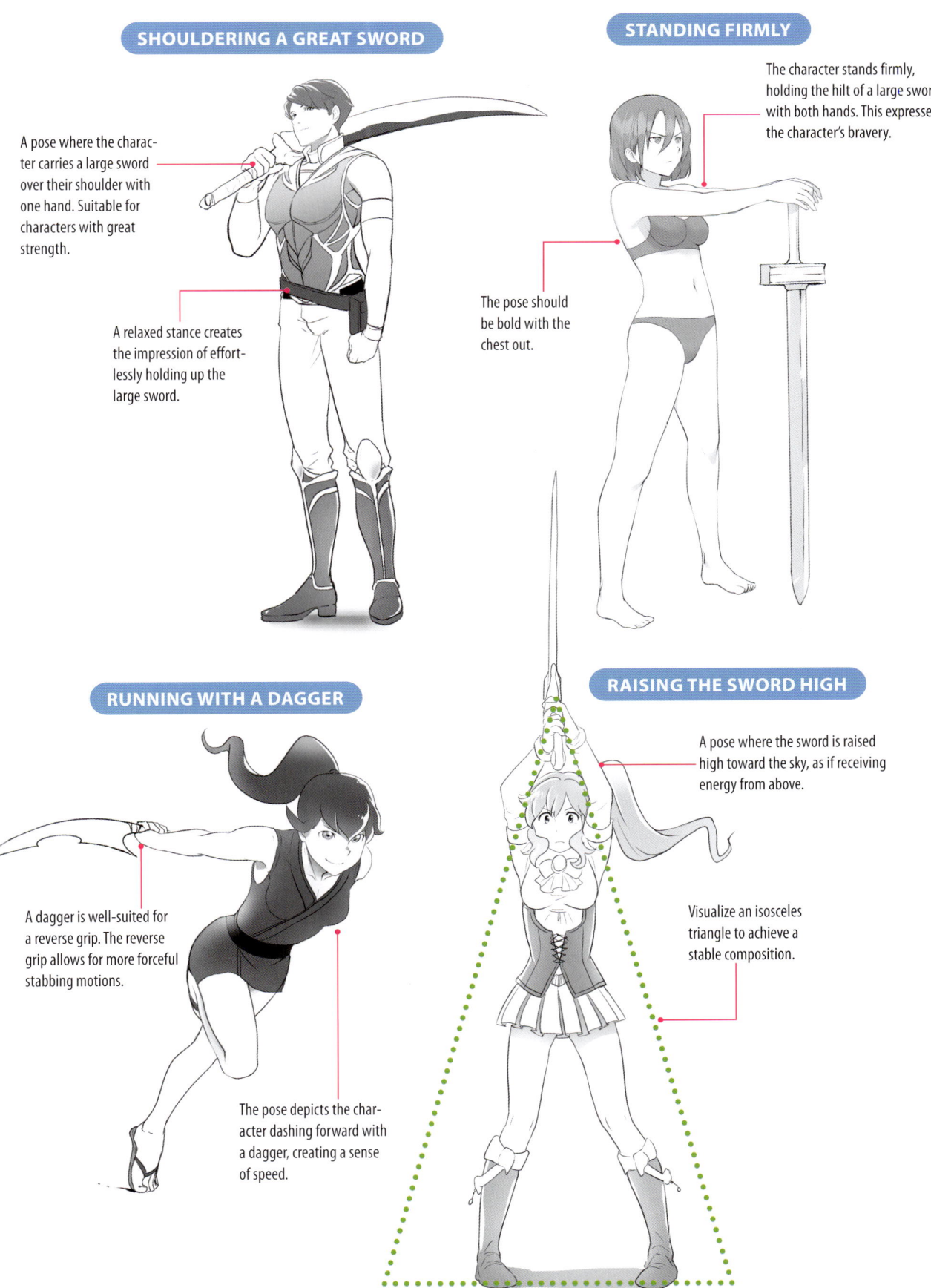

SHOULDERING A GREAT SWORD

A pose where the character carries a large sword over their shoulder with one hand. Suitable for characters with great strength.

A relaxed stance creates the impression of effortlessly holding up the large sword.

STANDING FIRMLY

The character stands firmly, holding the hilt of a large sword with both hands. This expresses the character's bravery.

The pose should be bold with the chest out.

RUNNING WITH A DAGGER

A dagger is well-suited for a reverse grip. The reverse grip allows for more forceful stabbing motions.

The pose depicts the character dashing forward with a dagger, creating a sense of speed.

RAISING THE SWORD HIGH

A pose where the sword is raised high toward the sky, as if receiving energy from above.

Visualize an isosceles triangle to achieve a stable composition.

A TRADITIONAL JAPANESE WEAPON
Drawing a Katana

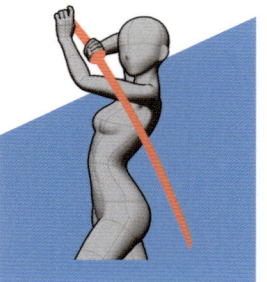

The blade of a katana has a curve, and the combination of this curve with the body lines determines the composition of the pose. By incorporating the sheath (saya), you can create impressive poses, such as dramatically drawing the sword.

LOOKING AT THE BLADE

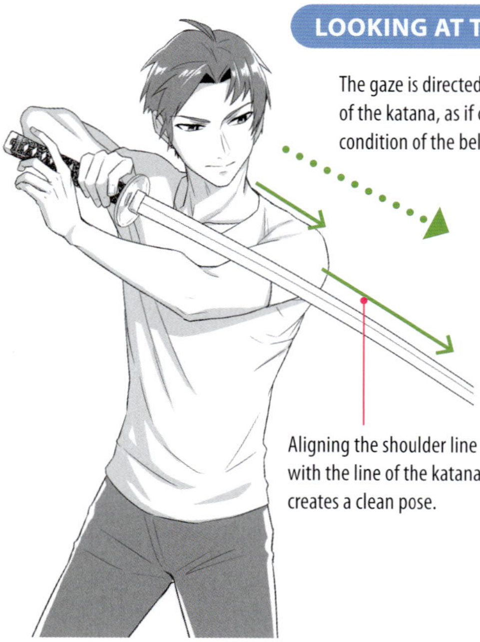

The gaze is directed toward the tip of the katana, as if checking the condition of the beloved sword.

Aligning the shoulder line with the line of the katana creates a clean pose.

JUST BEFORE DRAWING

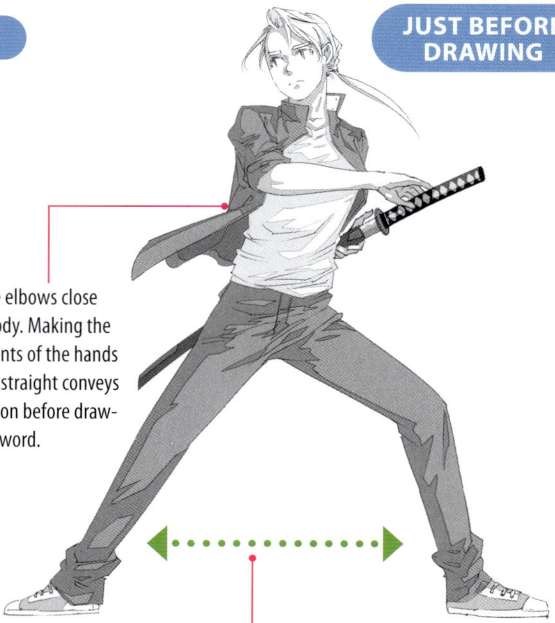

Keep the elbows close to the body. Making the movements of the hands and feet straight conveys the tension before drawing the sword.

The character glares at the opponent while gripping the hilt, just before drawing the sword. Spreading the legs wide creates a stable stance.

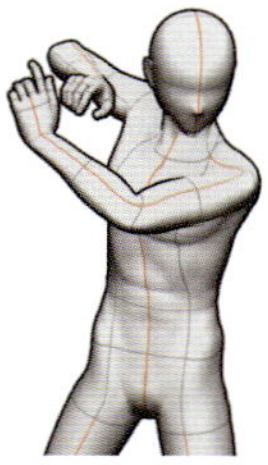

ANGLES

Choose an angle that shows the beautiful lines of the katana and the arm pose.

STANDING THE KATANA UPRIGHT

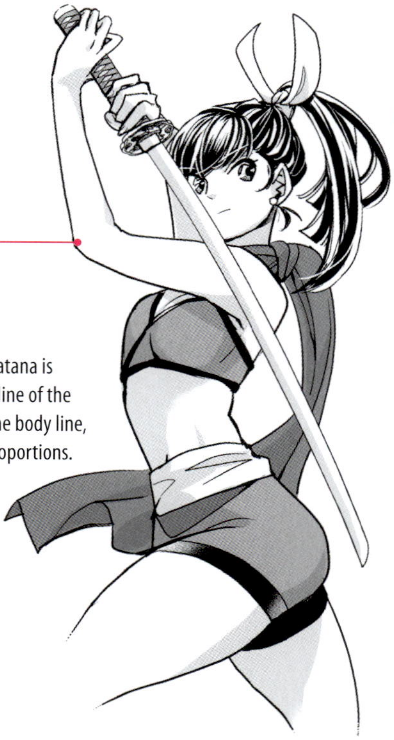

A pose where the katana is held vertically. The line of the blade aligns with the body line, emphasizing the proportions.

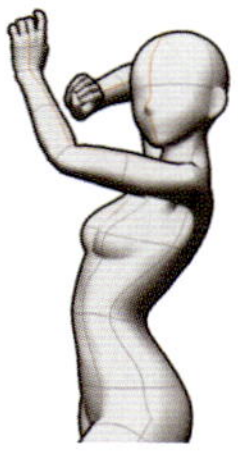

ANGLES

An angle that showcases the character's expression, the chest's posture, and the line of the hips, while also clearly displaying the katana.

150

TILTING THE BLADE

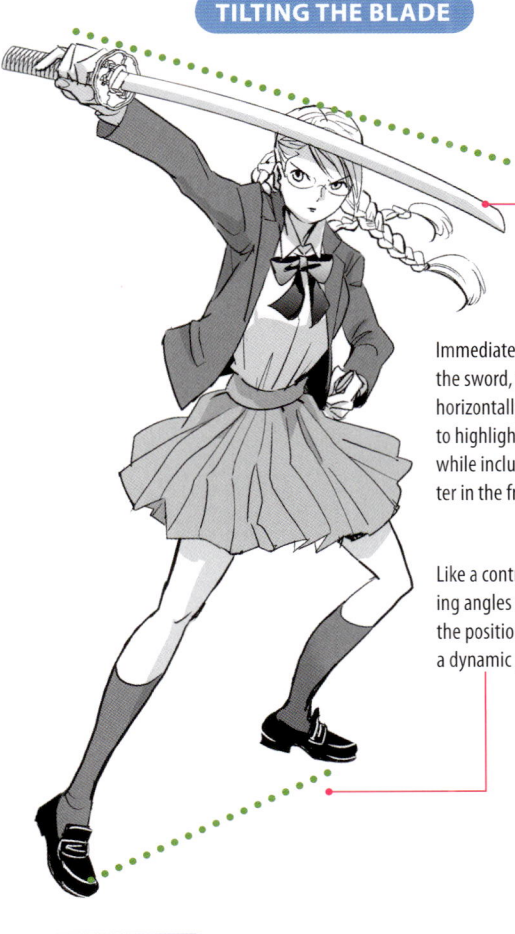

Immediately after drawing the sword, tilting the blade horizontally makes it easier to highlight the katana while including the character in the frame.

Like a contrapposto, the opposing angles of the katana and the positions of the legs create a dynamic pose.

PULLED FROM THE SHEATH

A pose at the moment of drawing the katana. Placing the slightly visible blade near the face keeps the viewer's gaze focused.

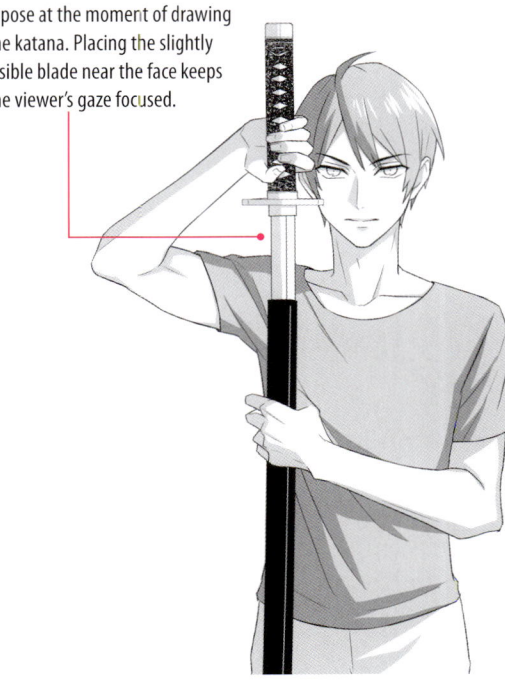

HIGH GUARD

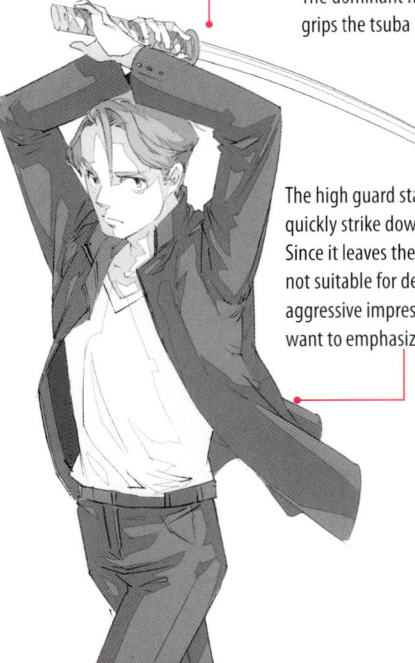

The dominant hand grips the tsuba (guard).

The high guard stance is ready to quickly strike down with the sword. Since it leaves the torso exposed and is not suitable for defense, it conveys an aggressive impression, ideal when you want to emphasize offense.

During the act of drawing the katana, creating consistent lines with the weapon, sheath, hair and skirt results in a dynamic pose.

DRAWING THE SWORD

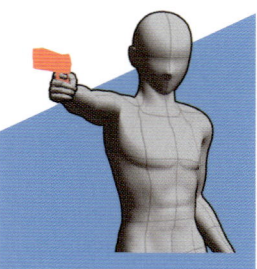

ESSENTIAL WEAPON FOR MODERN ACTION

Holding a Gun

Guns are a common sight in action movies and anime. They're primarily used to take down distant targets, so they're an effective addition when drawing your viewer's attention outside the frame of the illustration.

AIMING

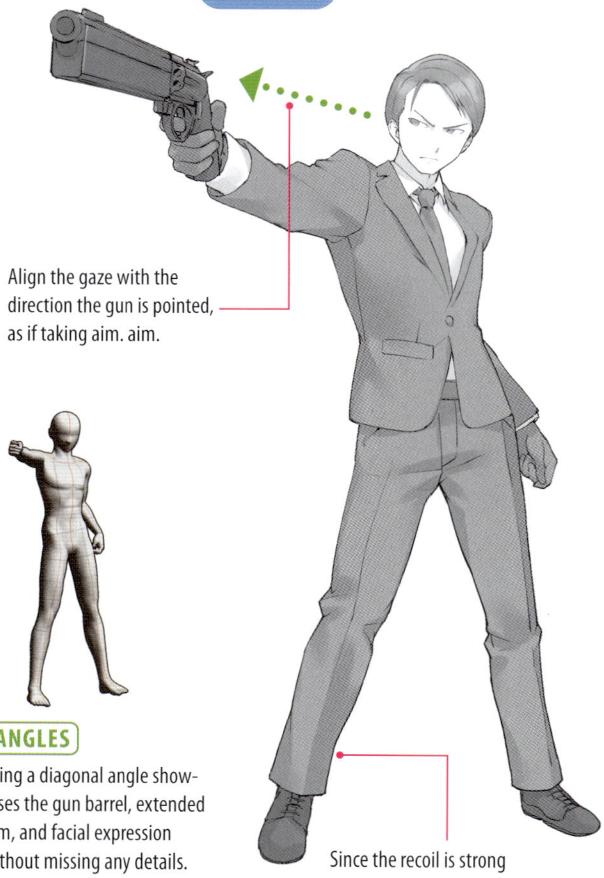

Align the gaze with the direction the gun is pointed, as if taking aim. aim.

ANGLES
Using a diagonal angle showcases the gun barrel, extended arm, and facial expression without missing any details.

Since the recoil is strong when firing, stand firmly on both legs to stabilize the posture.

POINTING THE GUN UPWARD

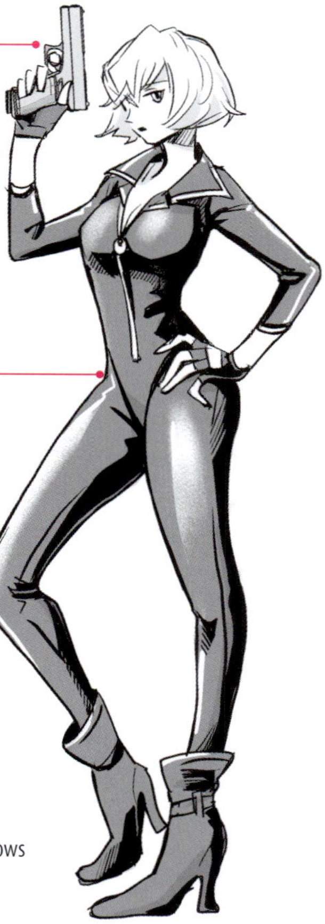

Pointing the gun barrel upward indicates a non-combat state.

Emphasize the proportions by creating a striking pose with the hips jutting out.

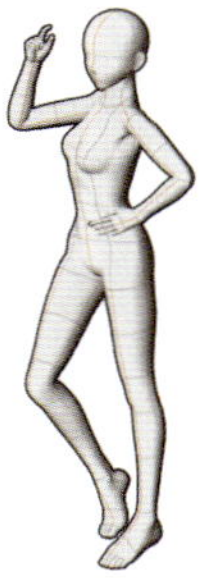

ANGLES
A side angle clearly shows the shape of the gun pointed upward.

SHOOTING WHILE LEAPING SIDEWAYS

While the body is tilted sideways, keep the head and gun perpendicular to the ground for accurate aiming.

This is an acrobatic action pose of shooting while leaping sideways.

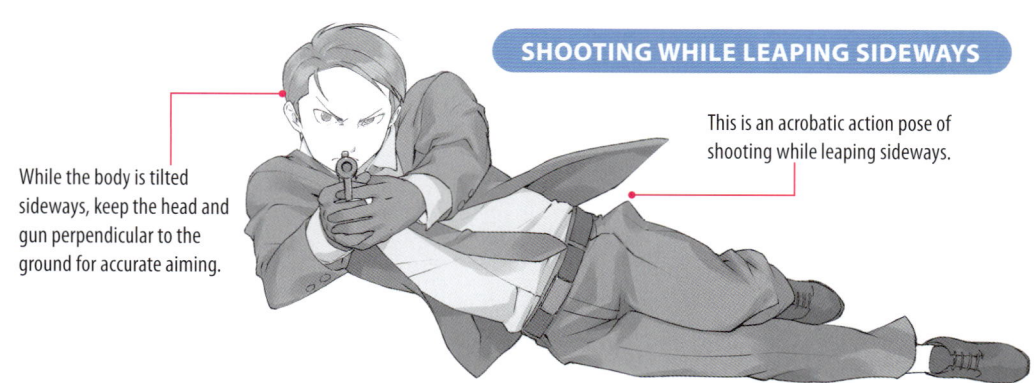

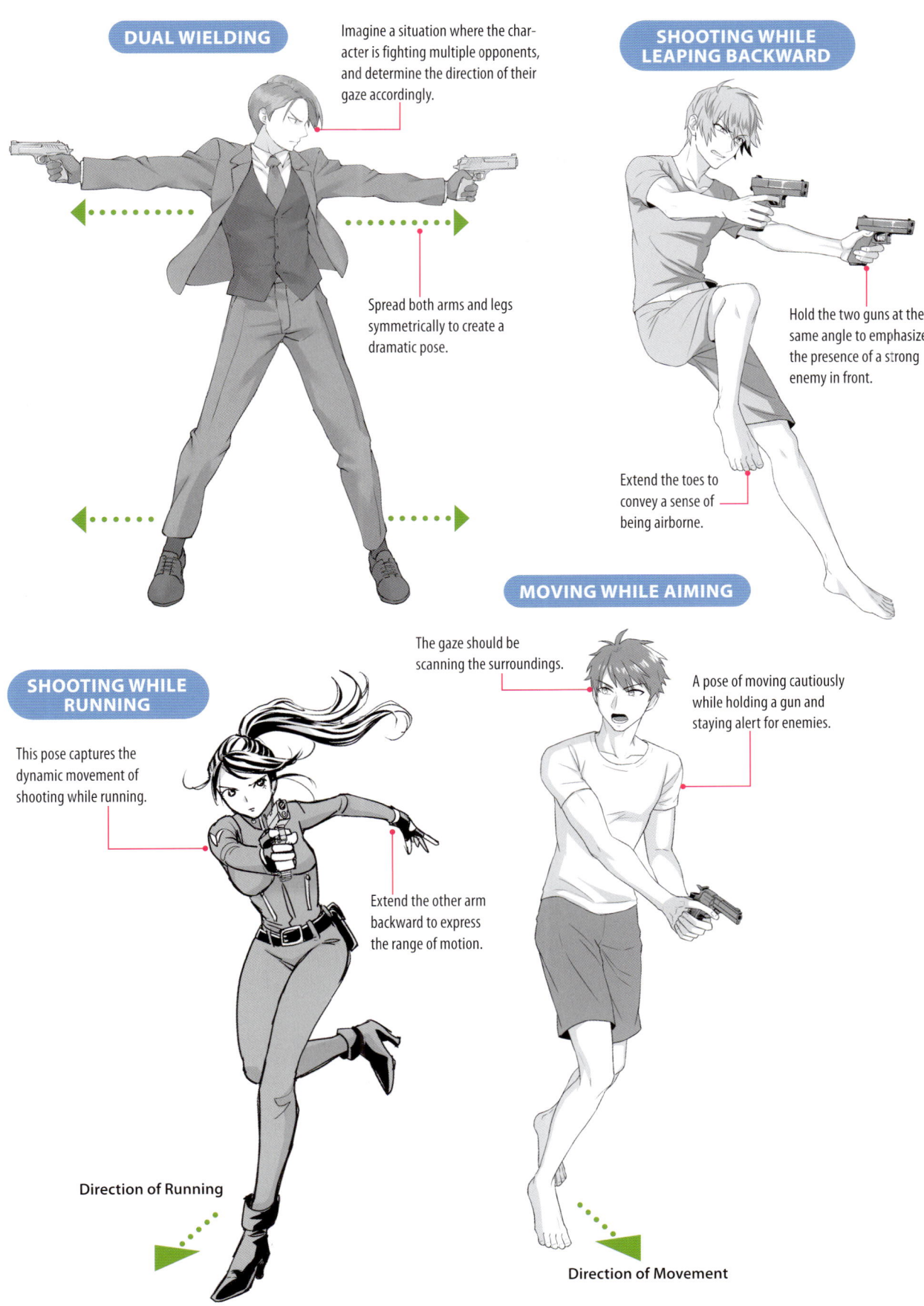

HOLDING THE GUN SIDEWAYS

Tilting the head slightly can portray a character with a defiant attitude.

Holding the gun sideways is a stylish pose that gives off a gangster-like vibe.

CRADLING A RIFLE

This pose involves cradling the rifle to cover the body, contrasting the character with the formidable weapon while emphasizing both.

HOLDING A RIFLE

The character supports the long, heavy barrel with both hands.

Pointing the muzzle downward indicates a non-hostile stance. When aiming at an enemy, the barrel should be horizontal.

Stand firmly on both feet to maintain a stable posture.

AIMING WHILE PRONE

This pose tends to obscure the face, so choose an angle that keeps the character's face visible.

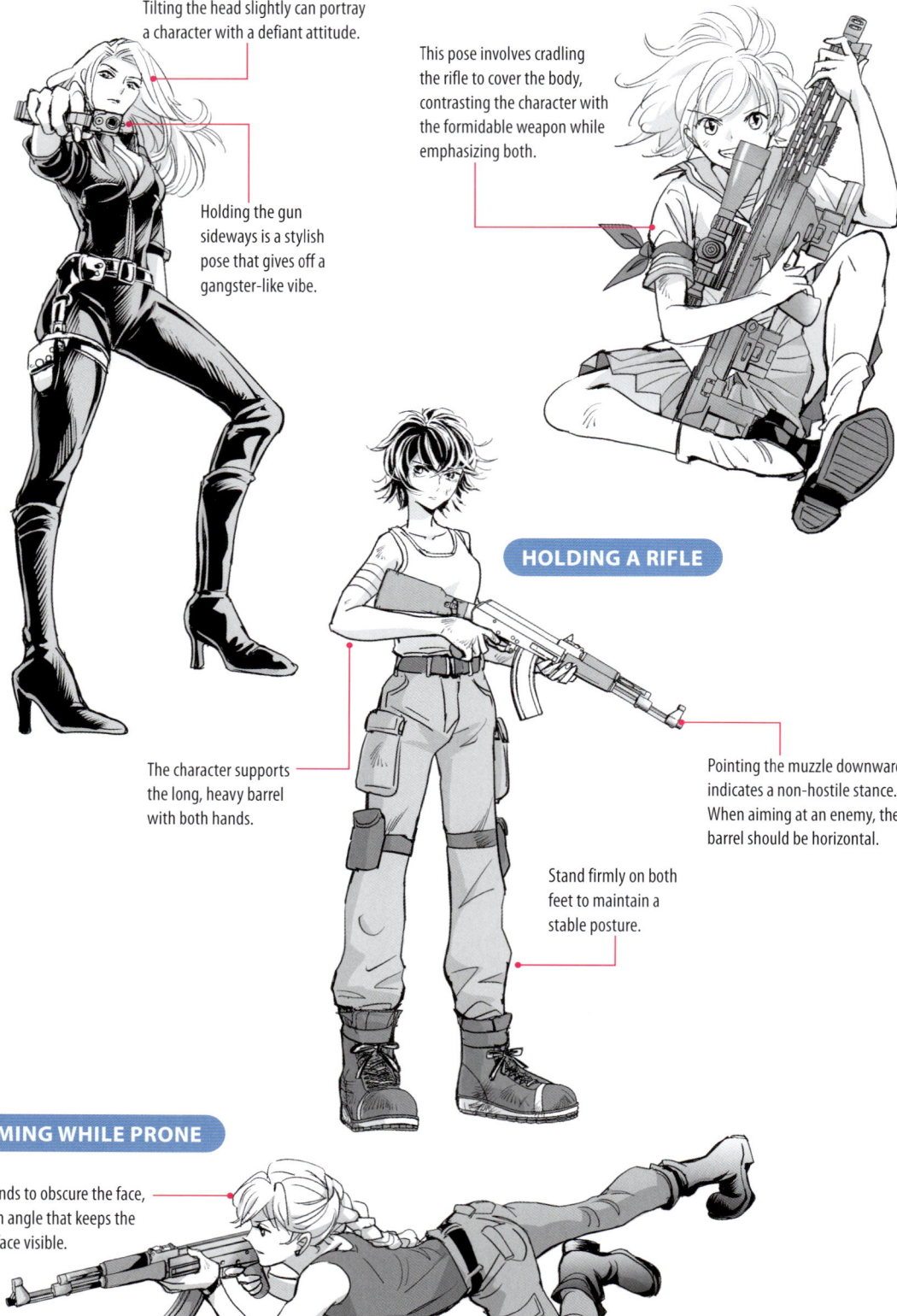

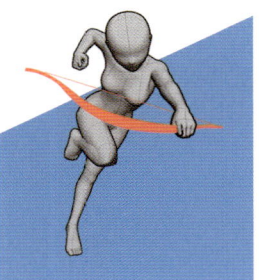

LARGE MOVEMENTS FOR LONG-RANGE ATTACKS

Using a Bow

Using a bow involves large movements, making it easy to create a sense of dynamism. The pose of drawing a bowstring exudes a tense, taut feeling, while the pose of releasing an arrow conveys a sense of release.

AIMING AT A DISTANCE

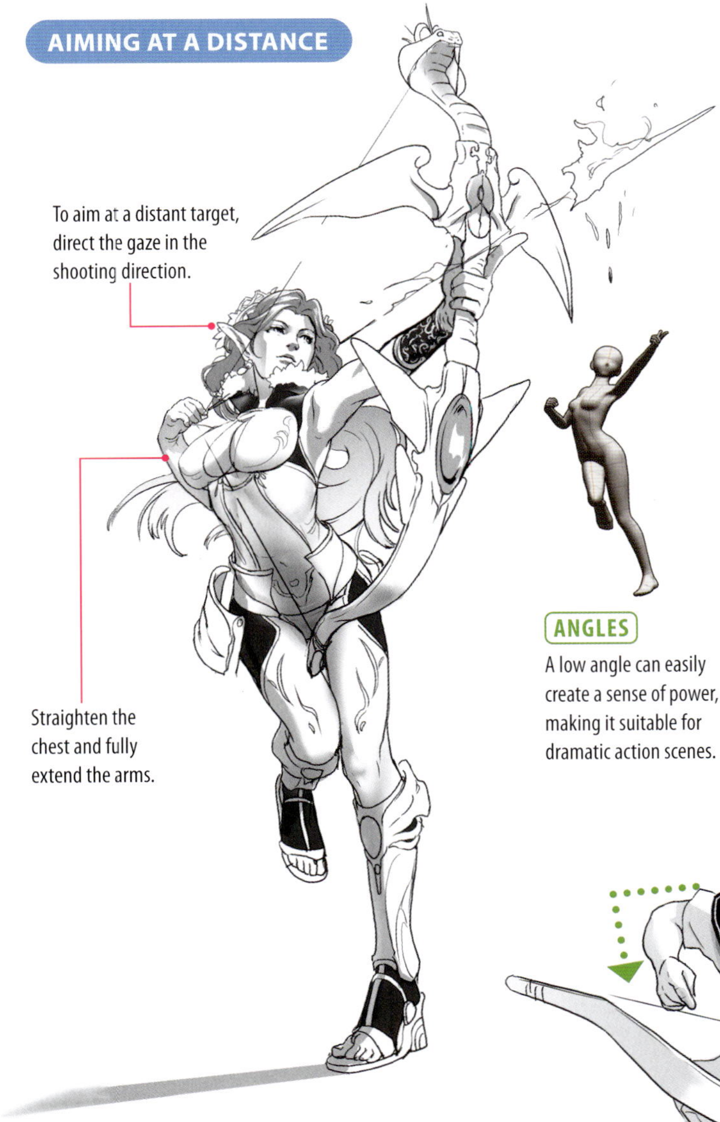

To aim at a distant target, direct the gaze in the shooting direction.

Straighten the chest and fully extend the arms.

ANGLES

A low angle can easily create a sense of power, making it suitable for dramatic action scenes.

LOWERING THE BOW

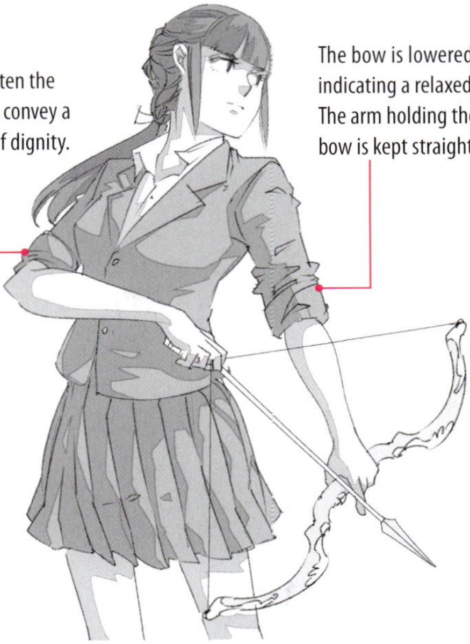

Straighten the back to convey a sense of dignity.

The bow is lowered, indicating a relaxed stance. The arm holding the bow is kept straight.

SHOOTING WHILE RUNNING

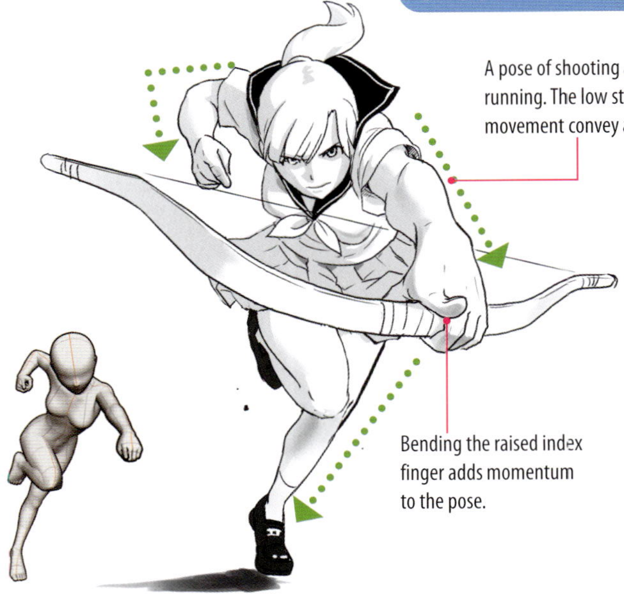

A pose of shooting an arrow while running. The low stance and linear movement convey a sense of speed.

Bending the raised index finger adds momentum to the pose.

ANGLES

Using a front angle that captures the bow emphasizes its size and enhances the dynamic impression as if the character is coming towards the viewer.

155

USING LONG-HANDLED WEAPONS
Holding a Curved Blade

Long-handled weapons like naginata and spears are difficult to fit into the frame. Angling them or thrusting them forward can help create a composition that fits while directly engaging the viewer.

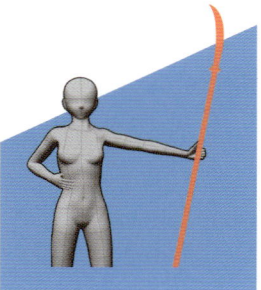

HOLDING A NAGINATA UPRIGHT

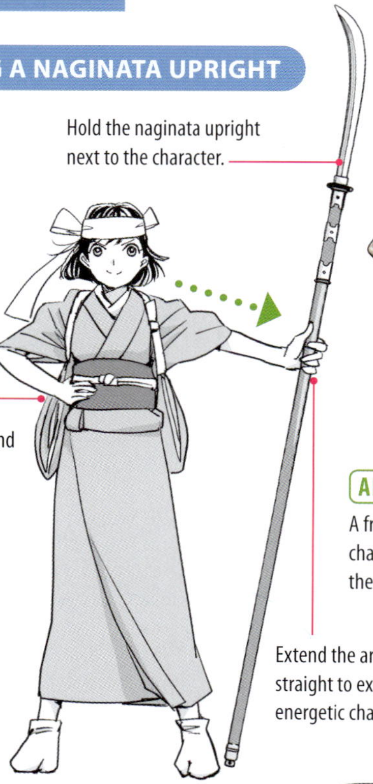

Hold the naginata upright next to the character.

Place one hand on the belt.

Extend the arms straight to express an energetic character.

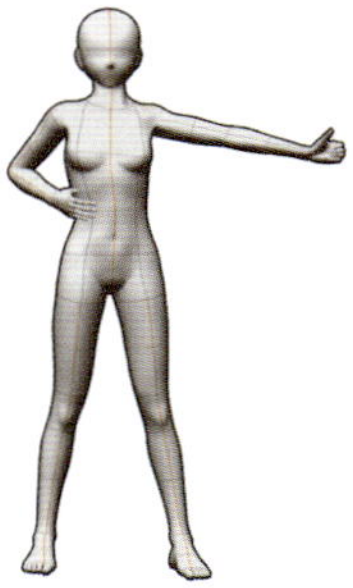

ANGLES
A front angle showcases both the character standing firmly and the upright naginata clearly.

SLASHING ACTION

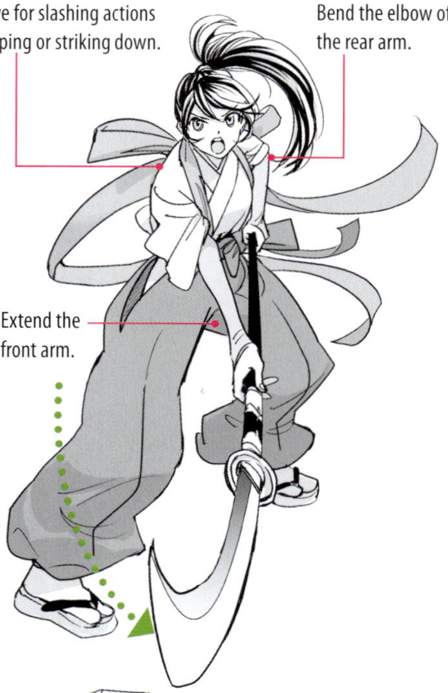

The naginata, with a long handle and a blade at the end, is effective for slashing actions like sweeping or striking down.

Bend the elbow of the rear arm.

Extend the front arm.

THRUSTING STANCE

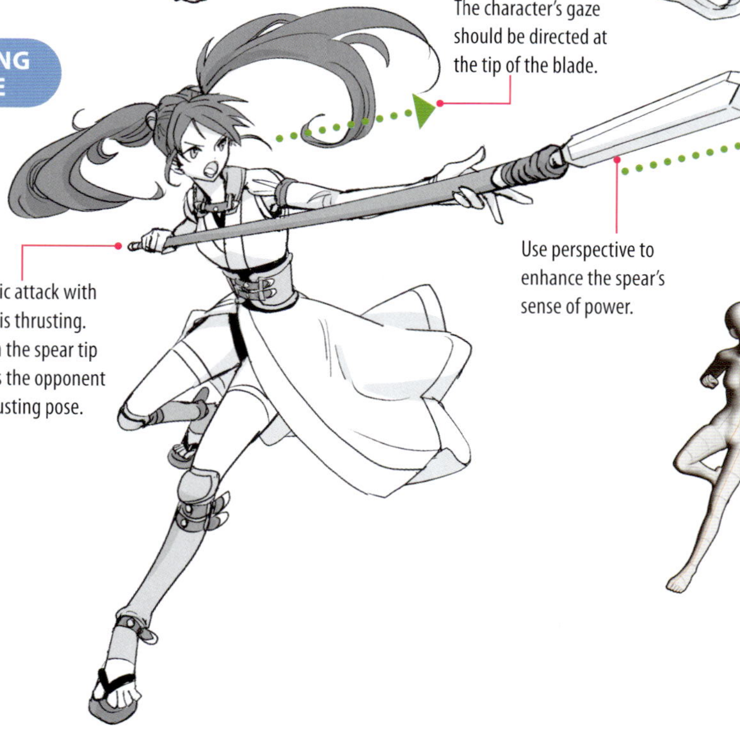

The character's gaze should be directed at the tip of the blade.

The basic attack with a spear is thrusting. Position the spear tip towards the opponent in a thrusting pose.

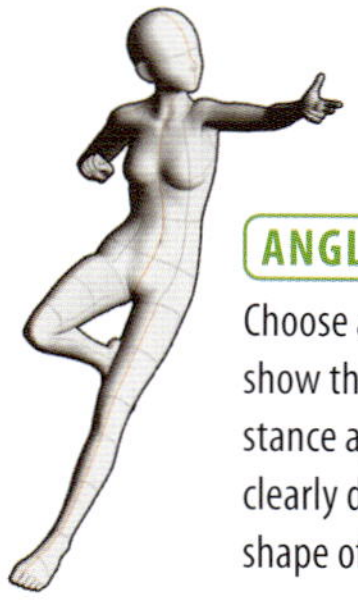

Use perspective to enhance the spear's sense of power.

ANGLES
Choose a slightly side angle to show the character in a half-body stance against the opponent, clearly displaying the pose and the shape of the spear.

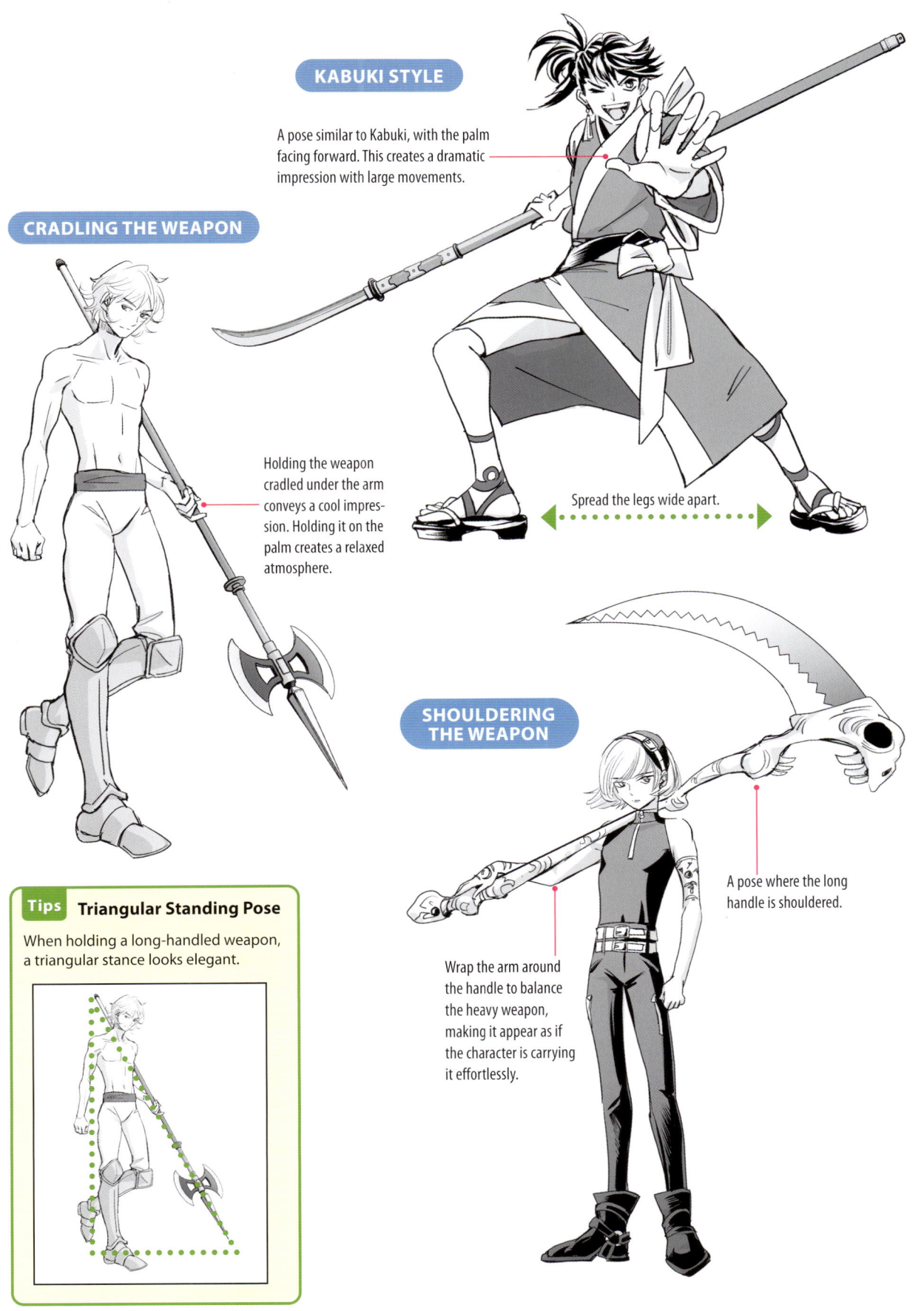

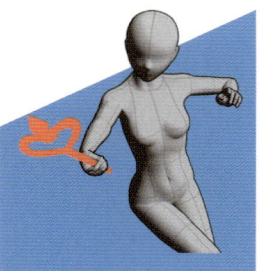

CASTING MAGIC WITH A SINGLE WAVE
Casting a Spell

Magic wands make frequent appearances in fantasy manga and anime. This ultimate accessory can serve as a dramatic extension of the arms. When posing, the focus is more on the character's traits, emphasizing glamour and drama, rather than realism.

EXTENDING TO THE SIDE

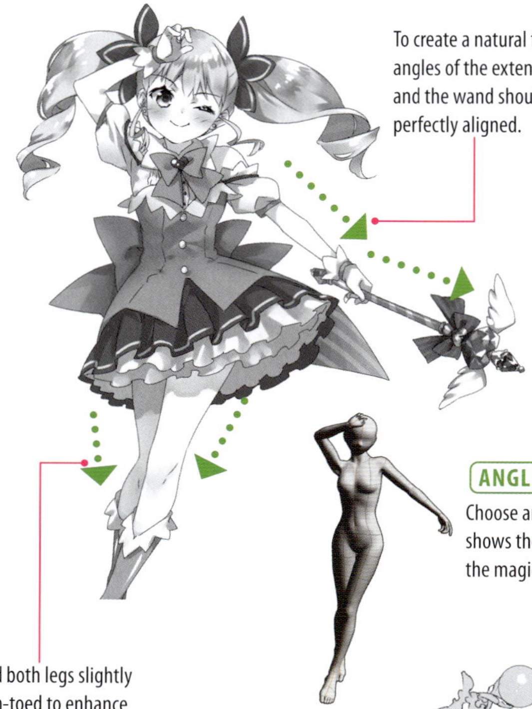

To create a natural feel, the angles of the extended arm and the wand should not be perfectly aligned.

ANGLES
Choose an angle that clearly shows the extended arm and the magic wand.

Extend both legs slightly pigeon-toed to enhance elegance.

THRUSTING FORWARD

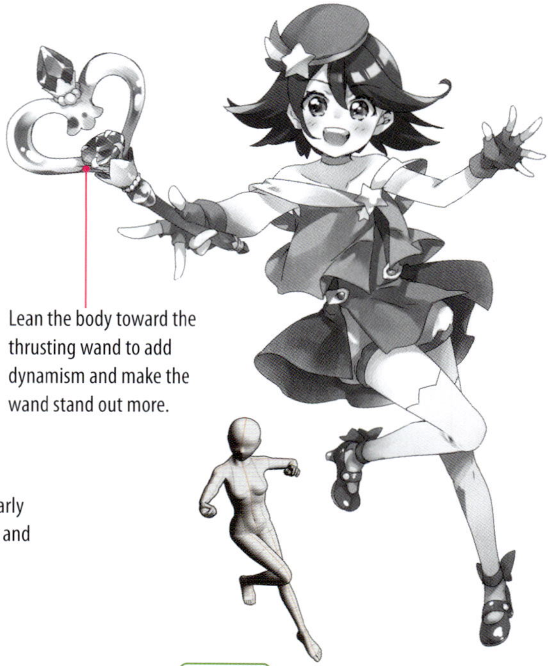

Lean the body toward the thrusting wand to add dynamism and make the wand stand out more.

ANGLES
A diagonal angle with a sense of depth emphasizes the thrusting motion of the magic wand.

RAISING UPWARD

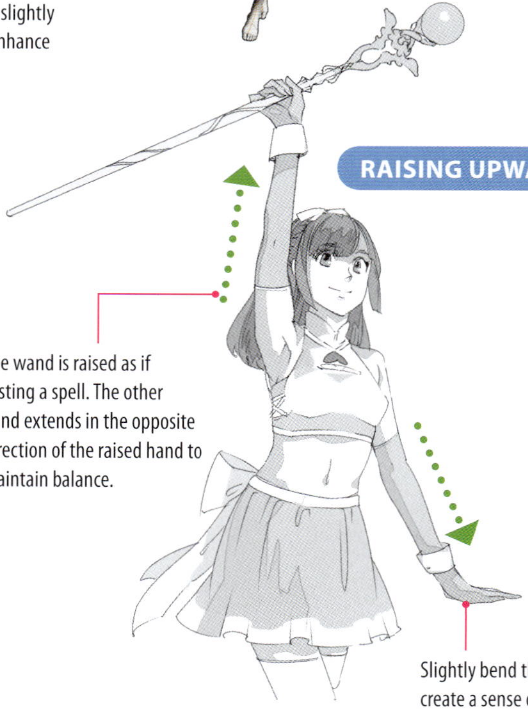

The wand is raised as if casting a spell. The other hand extends in the opposite direction of the raised hand to maintain balance.

Slightly bend the wrist to create a sense of balance.

Tips — Length of the Wand

A short wand tends to create a playful atmosphere, while a long wand gives a more mystical impression.

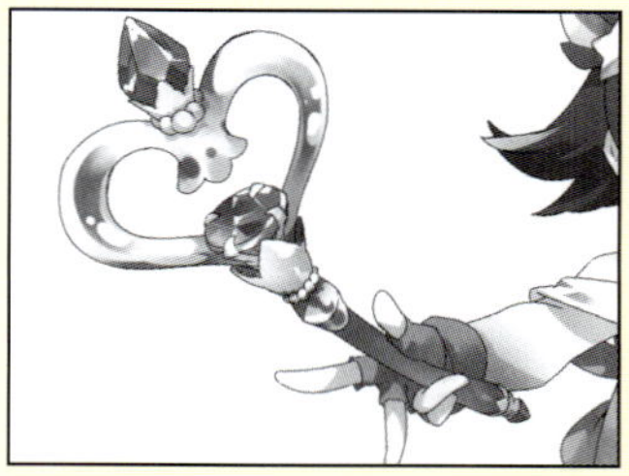

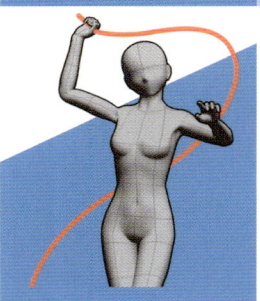

POWERFUL POSES

Using a Whip

The whip is a weapon with a strong association with punishment and torture, making it suitable for aggressive or dominant characters. Pay attention to the facial expression to finish off the intimidating pose.

SWINGING THE WHIP

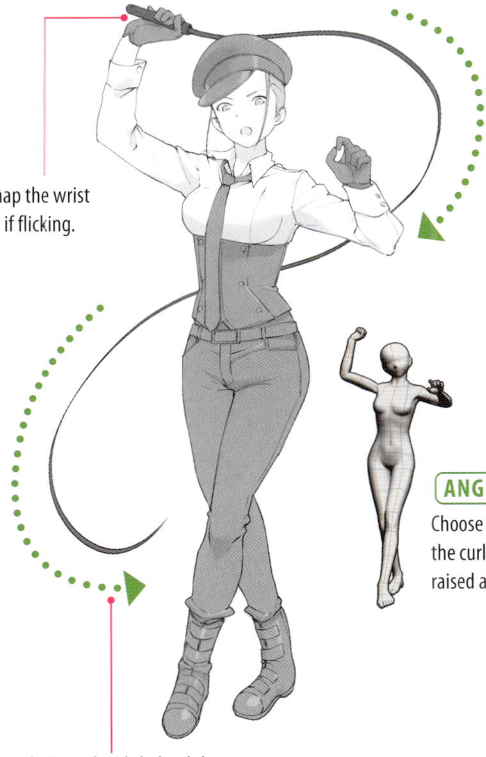

Snap the wrist as if flicking.

The whip's cord curls behind the body. Drawing it in an S-shape with large curves makes it look more natural.

ANGLES
Choose an angle that shows the curling whip and the raised arm.

PULLING THE WHIP

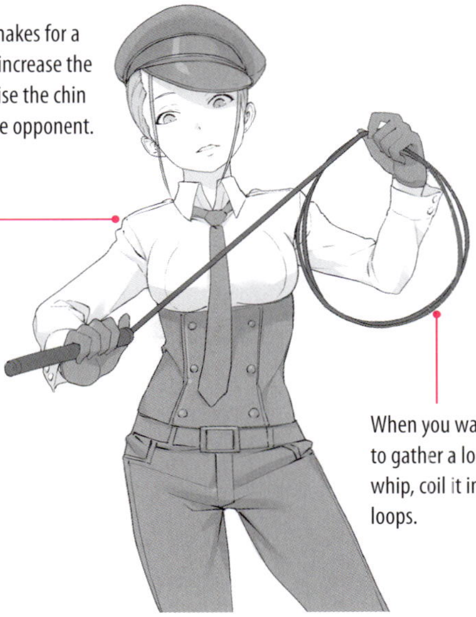

Pulling the whip makes for a powerful pose. To increase the impact, slightly raise the chin to look down at the opponent.

When you want to gather a long whip, coil it into loops.

SLAPPING THE PALM

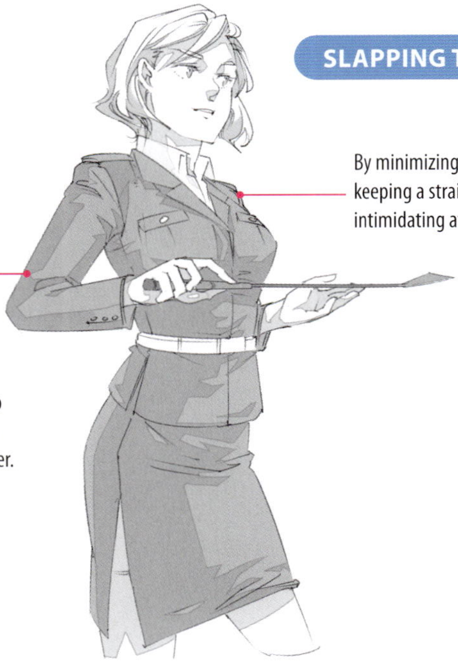

By minimizing movement and keeping a straight posture, a cool and intimidating atmosphere is created.

Slapping a riding crop against the palm can evoke a sense of power.

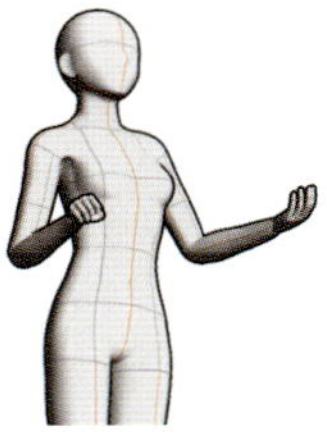

ANGLES
If you want to enhance the intimidating impression, use a low angle.

159

EVERYDAY ACTIONS
Eating

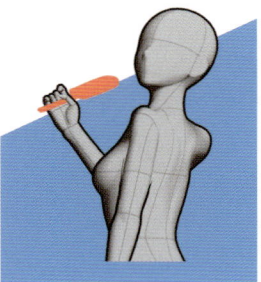

Using food is another effective way of highlighting a character's mouth and facial expression. The focus on the food or on the utensils being used adds everyday details and realism to your scene.

EATING ICE CREAM

Be aware of perspective and proportions.

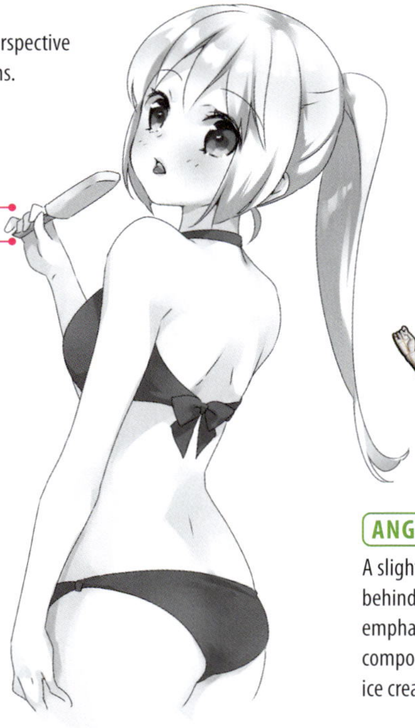

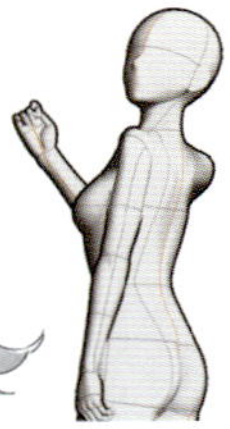

Bringing it close to the face enhances the features. It also ties easily into popular digital illustration themes like "summer" and "sunny weather."

ANGLES
A slightly angled pose from behind, turning to look back, emphasizes the face. The composition also makes the ice cream clearly visible.

EATING GRAPES

The character lifts their face and attempts to eat the grapes from below.

Raise the upper arm slightly above a parallel line to the ground.

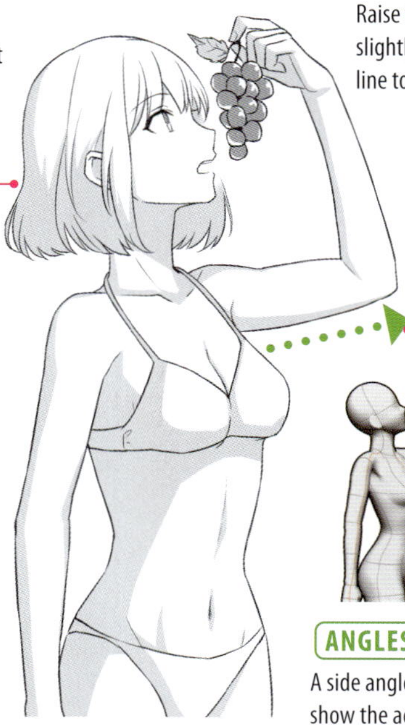

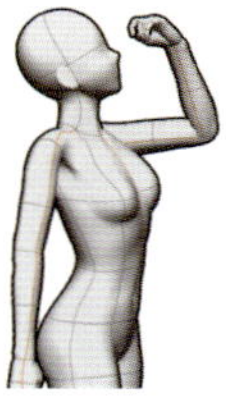

ANGLES
A side angle is ideal to clearly show the act of bringing the grapes to the mouth.

LICKING A LOLLIPOP

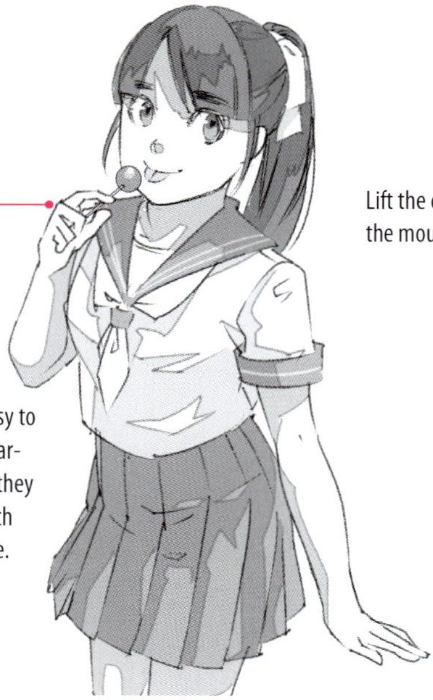

Lollipops with sticks are easy to draw and simple for the character to hold. Being small, they don't obstruct the face much even when positioned close.

TAKING A BIG BITE

Lift the chin and open the mouth wide.

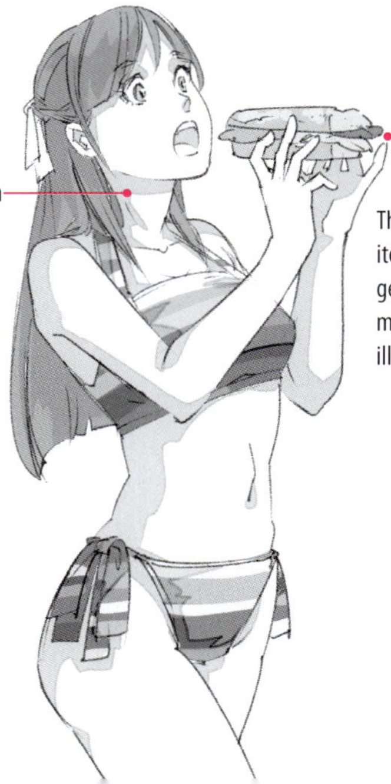

The larger the food item, the more exaggerated the character's movements, making the illustration more lively.

EATING ELEGANTLY

Eating with proper posture gives an elegant appearance. Using a hand to tack hair behind the ear adds to the impression.

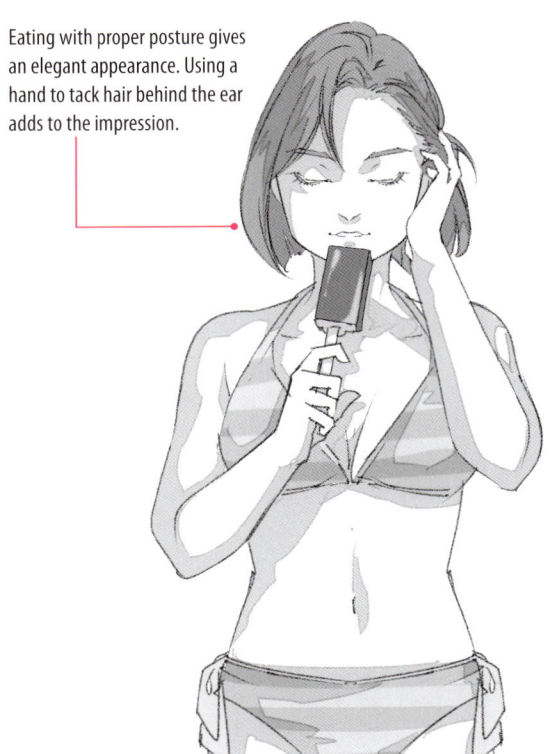

EMPHASIZING THE FOOD

To particularly highlight the food, place it separately from the character. Positioning it in front of the character can make it stand out more.

The character's gaze should be directed at the food.

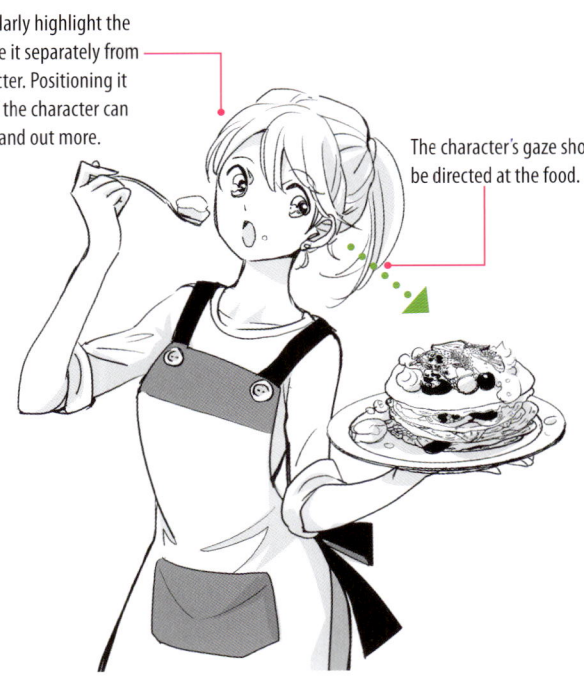

EATING WITH KNIFE AND FORK

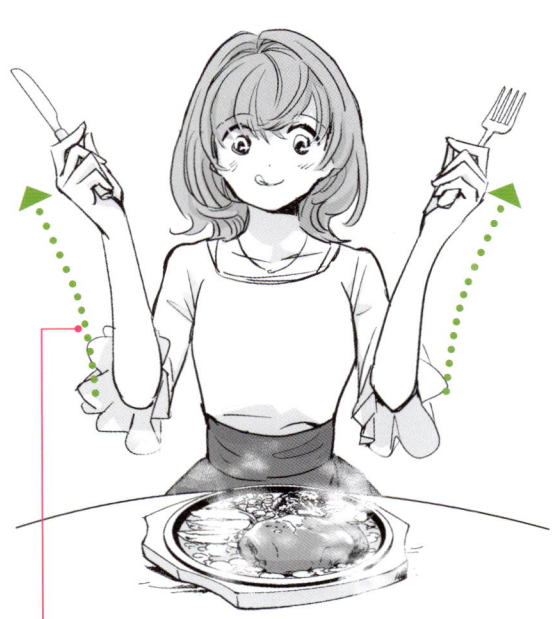

Placing the food in the center and arranging the pose symmetrically creates a stable composition.

HOLDING A PLATE WHILE EATING

Tilt the face toward the food.

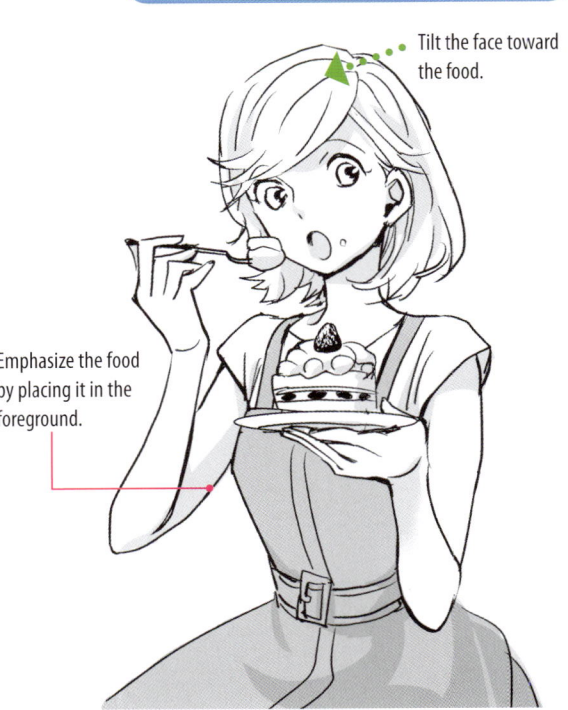

Emphasize the food by placing it in the foreground.

ANOTHER COMMON ACTION
Drinking

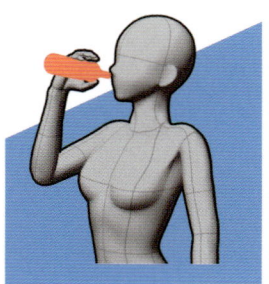

Is your character thirsty? When introducing beverages, it's more effective to focus on the container than the liquid itself. The way the container is held also changes depending on the drink, so consider your character's drinking habits when staging your scene.

BASICS OF DRINKING POSE

Pay attention to the tilt of the container. If it contains a lot of liquid, tilting it too much will look unnatural.

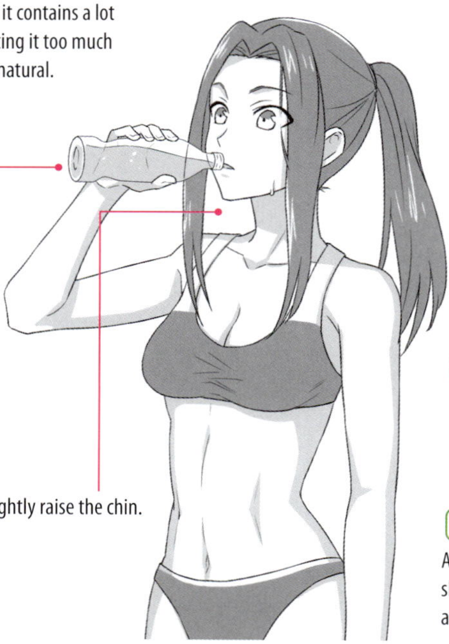

Slightly raise the chin.

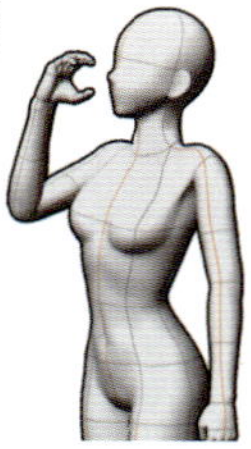

ANGLES
A 45° diagonal angle clearly shows the container's shape and the act of drinking.

HOLDING ELEGANTLY

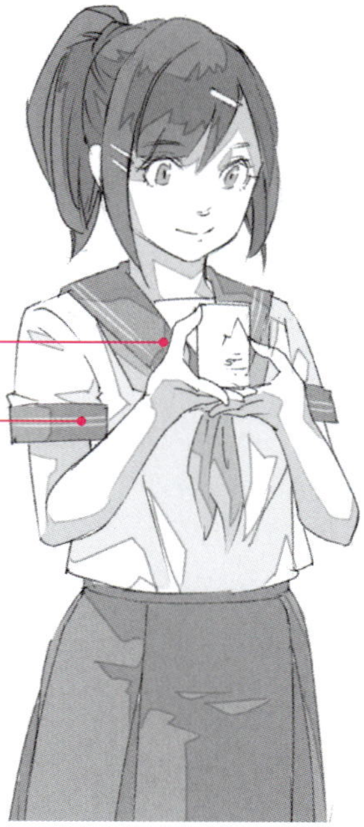

Hold with both hands elegantly.

Keep the elbows close to the body and straighten the back for a refined gesture.

TOUCHING THE FACE WITH THE CONTAINER

This gesture involves touching the container to the cheek. Touching an item to the cheek can create a charming pose.

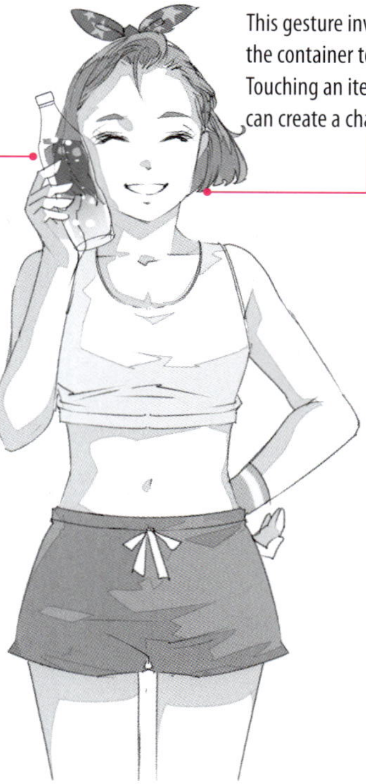

Tilt the container slightly to match the shape of the face.

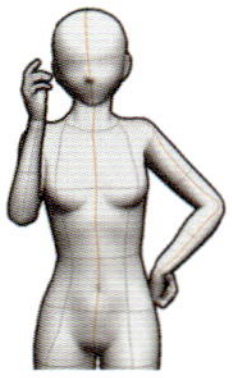

ANGLES
A front angle effectively conveys the facial expression.

CROPPING Showing the Mouth

Unless you want to highlight the design of the container, cropping most of the container while showing the mouth can still convey the act of drinking.

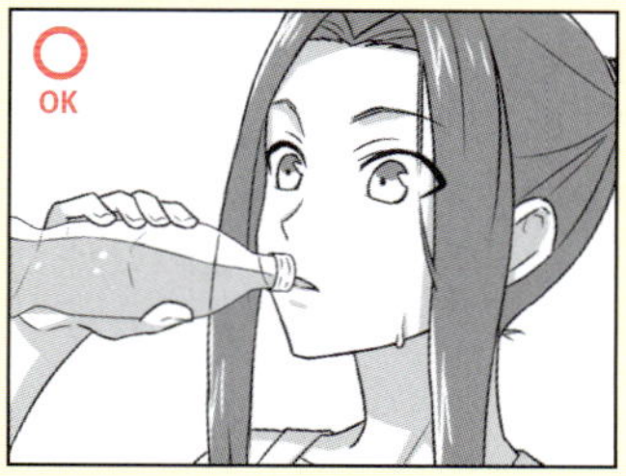

O OK

162

TEA TIME

A graceful pose of drinking with a teacup. Balance the placement of the face, teacup, and plate to attract the viewer's gaze.

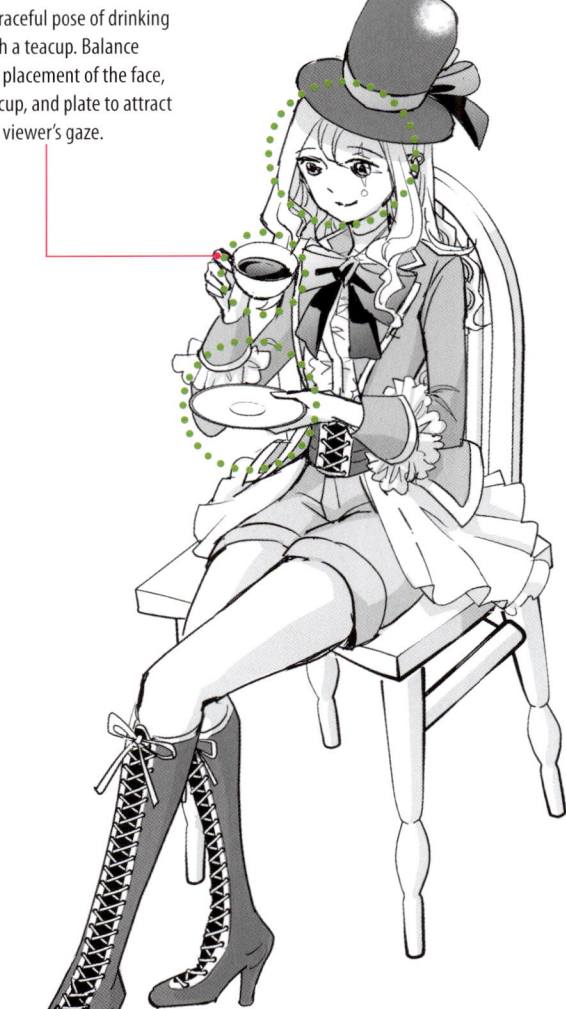

OFFERING A DRINK

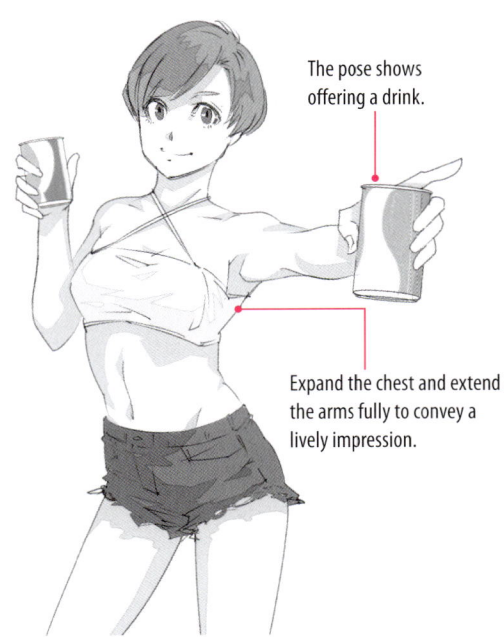

The pose shows offering a drink.

Expand the chest and extend the arms fully to convey a lively impression.

RAISING A GLASS

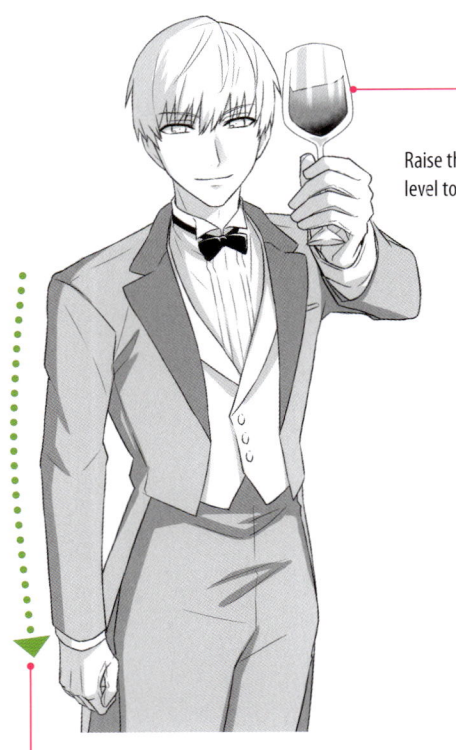

Raise the glass to face level to emphasize it.

Keep the arm line in a gentle curve to create a natural, relaxed look.

Tips — Emphasizing the Drink

To emphasize the drink, place it close to the character's face.

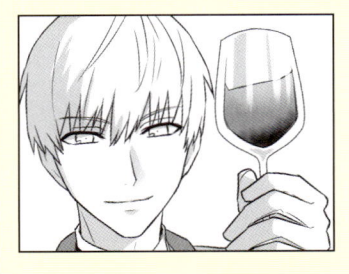

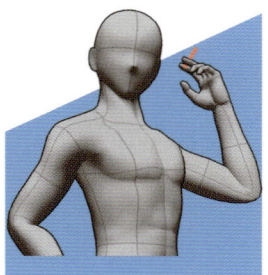

GUILTY PLEASURES
Smoking

Items like cigarettes and alcohol, which are only allowed for adults, are often used to create or suggest a more mature atmosphere. Pairing them with relaxed poses are common, showing characters in their leisure moments.

FOR A WILD CHARACTER

A wide stance, such as spreading the arms out, can express a wild character.

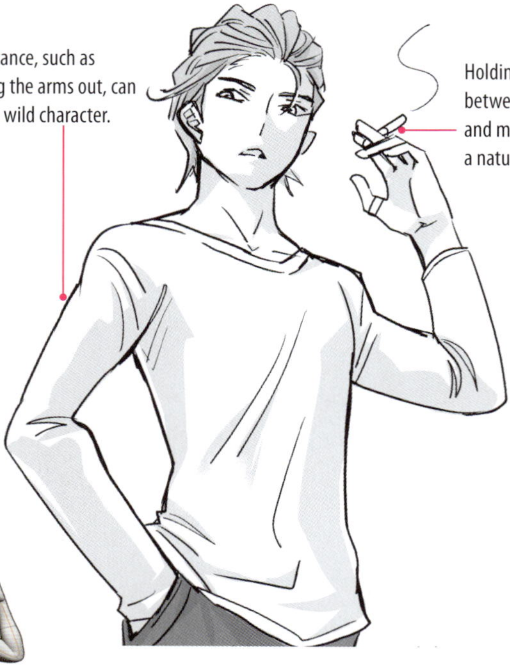

Holding the cigarette between the index and middle fingers is a natural way.

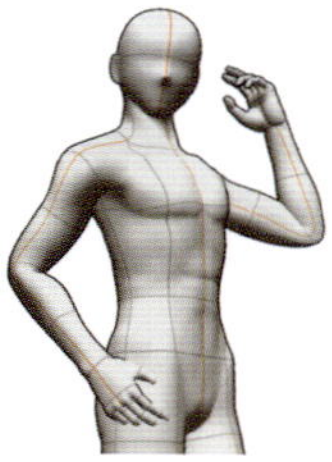

ANGLES
A low angle makes the character appear larger, emphasizing their confident posture.

EVERYDAY GESTURE

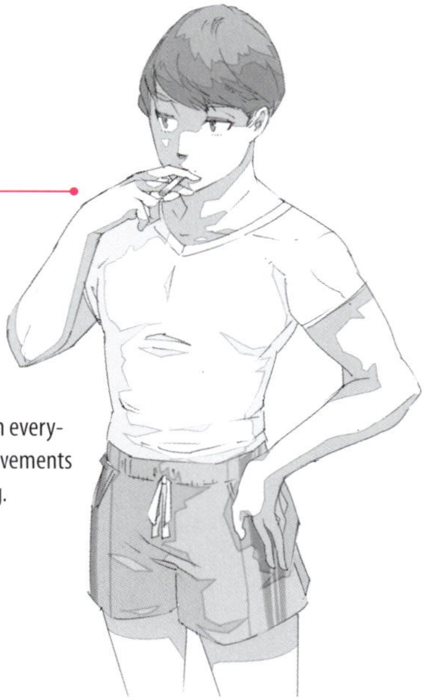

To depict a scene from everyday life, use small movements for the act of smoking.

CONVEYING MELANCHOLY

A profile view, gazing into the distance, conveys a sense of melancholy.

Lower the shoulders to suggest the relaxed state.

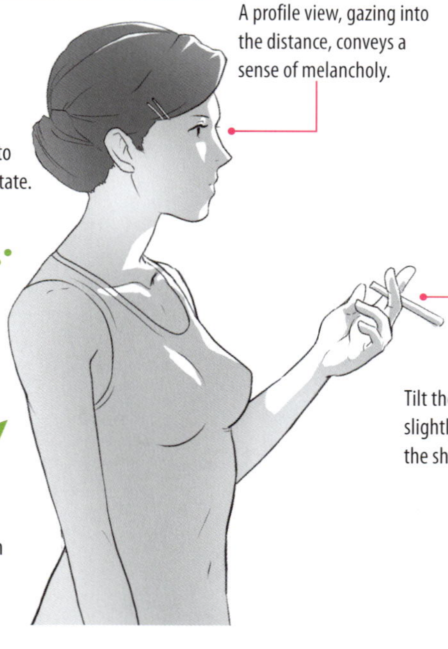

Tilt the tip of the cigarette slightly downward to match the shape of the fingers.

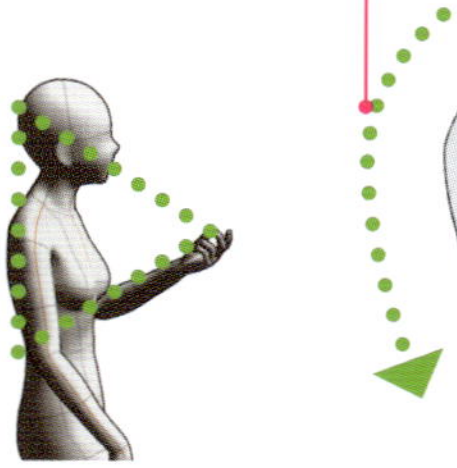

ANGLES
An angle that forms a triangle with the torso, head, and arm positions creates a sense of balance.

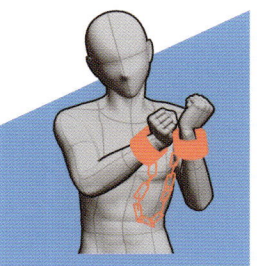

RESTRICTING MOVEMENT
Wearing Handcuffs

When creating poses with handcuffs, remember that the range of arm movements will be restricted. Or the handcuffs can be used as a playful accessory, dangling off an extended fingertip.

SHOWING OFF HANDCUFFS

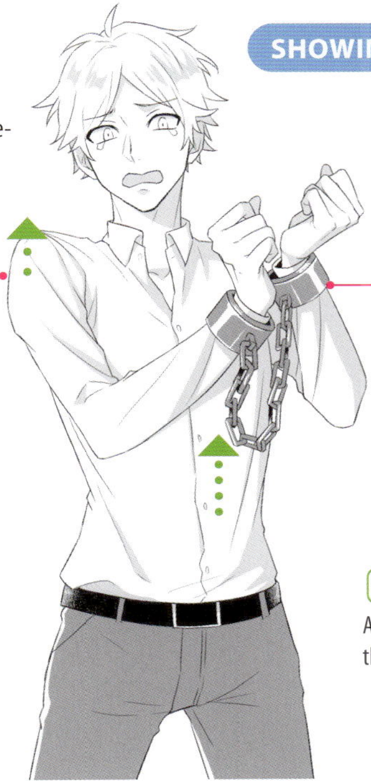

Raise the shoulders along with the movement of the hands.

This pose involves lifting the handcuffed hands to show them off.

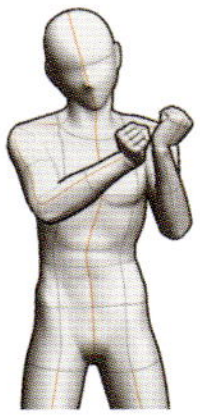

ANGLES
A front angle clearly shows the handcuffs on the wrists.

PLAYING WITH HANDCUFFS

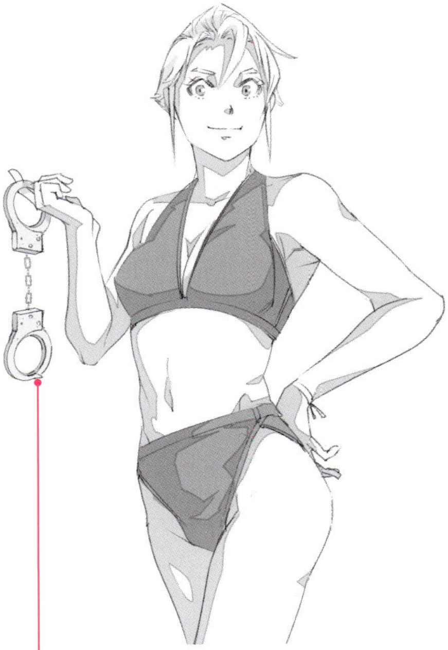

The character hooks a finger through the handcuffs. Treating the handcuffs like a toy expresses the character's sense of ease.

SHOWING BODY LINES

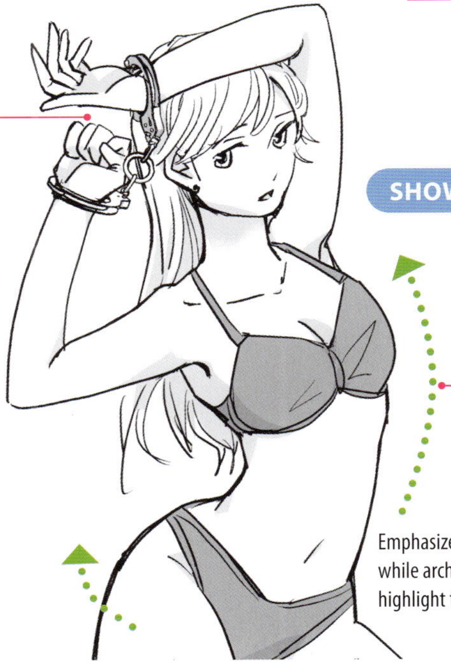

Raise the arms high to display the handcuffs. Ensure the face is not obscured.

Emphasize the handcuffs while arching the body to highlight the body's lines.

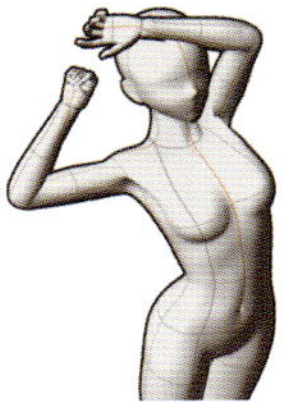

ANGLES
Use a slightly high angle to bring the handcuffs to the forefront and emphasize them.

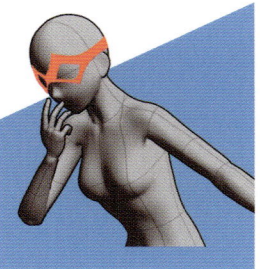

HIDING THE CHARACTER'S IDENTITY
Using a Mask

Are your characters concealing their identites? Consider poses where the character touches or holds the mask, stripping it off in a dramatic reveal.

REMOVING THE MASK

For a pose showing the moment of removing the mask, imagine the trajectory of the mask and position the hands accordingly.

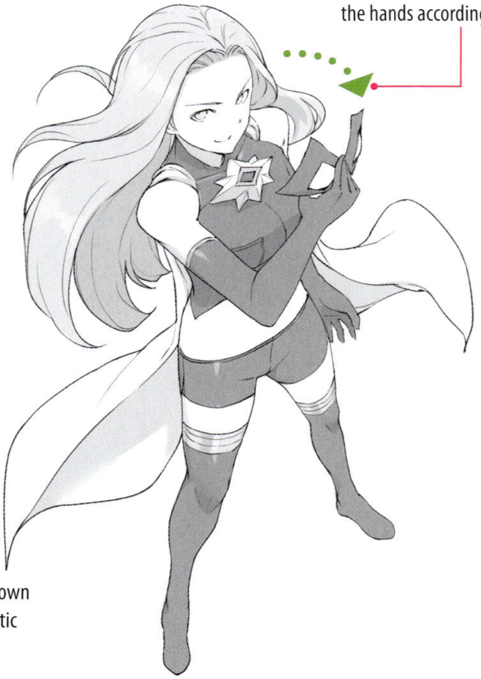

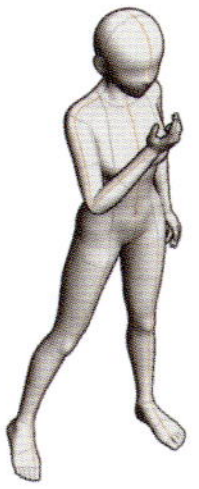

HUMAN FACE MASK

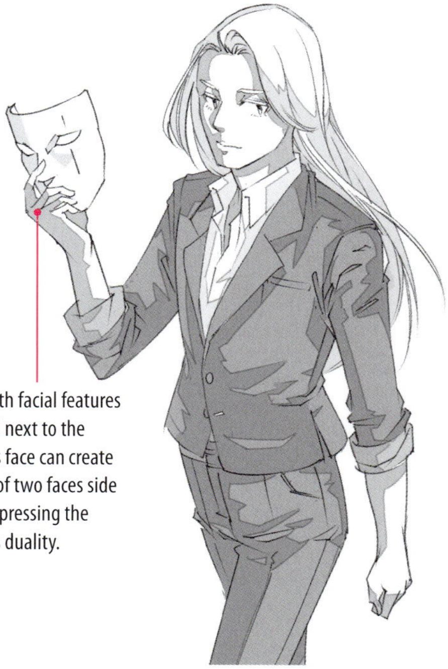

A mask with facial features positioned next to the character's face can create an image of two faces side by side, expressing the character's duality.

ANGLES
A high angle, as if peeking down at the character, adds dramatic perspective to a big reveal.

EMPHASIZING THE MASK

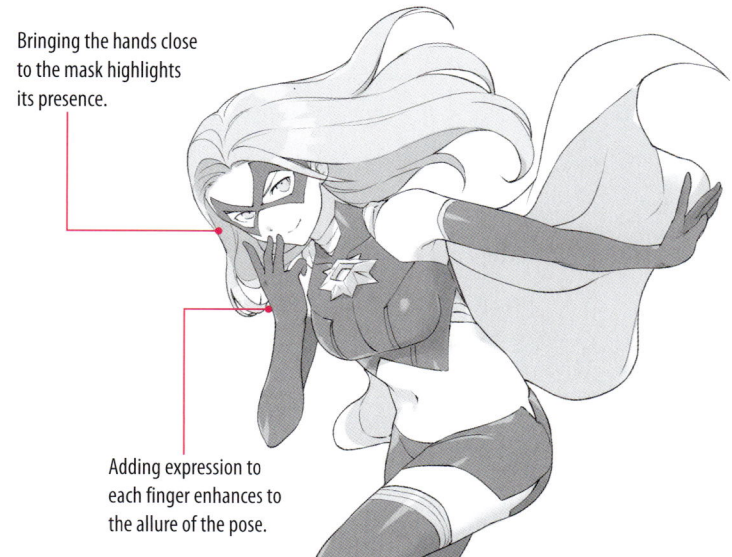

Bringing the hands close to the mask highlights its presence.

Adding expression to each finger enhances to the allure of the pose.

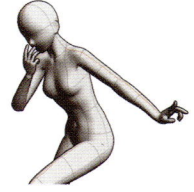

ANGLES
Use a slightly high, diagonal angle that showcases the arm and upper body lines elegantly to clearly display the hand near the mask and the expression of the face leaning forward.

MAKING A BOLD STATEMENT
Holding a Megaphone

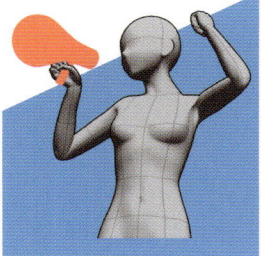

When using a megaphone, exaggerated gestures are key to matching the intensified volume. This item suits characters with assertive personalities who want to make their voices heard.

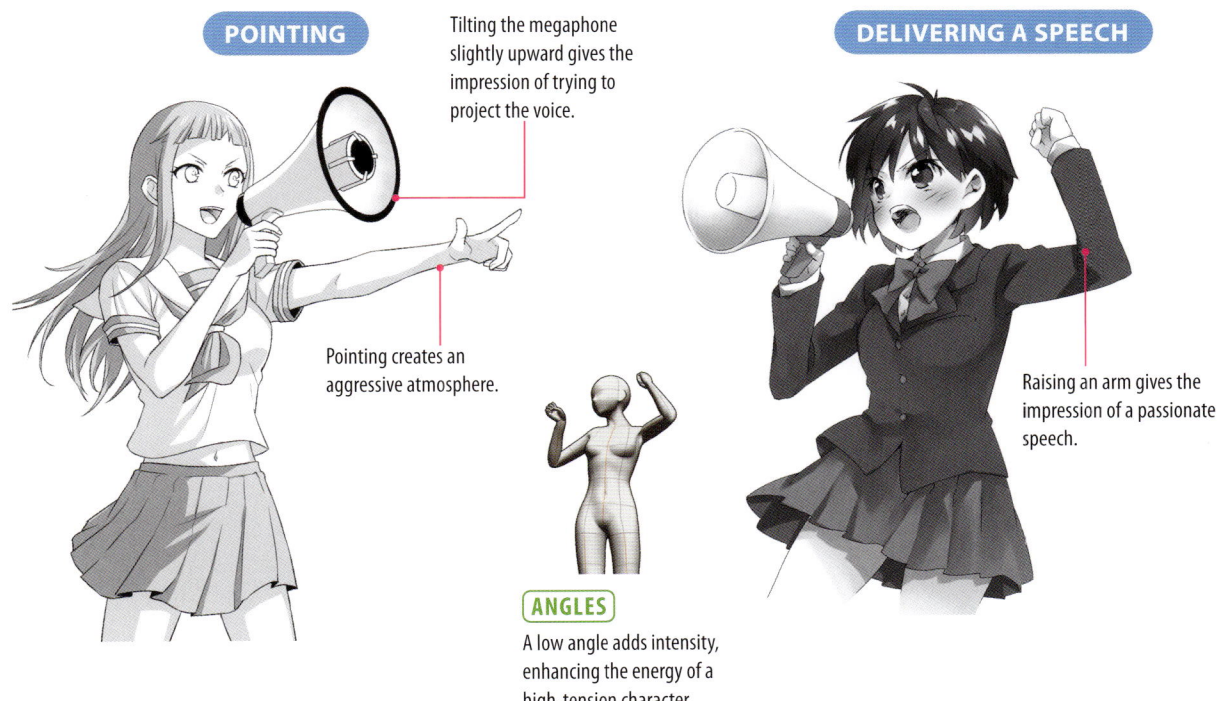

POINTING

Tilting the megaphone slightly upward gives the impression of trying to project the voice.

Pointing creates an aggressive atmosphere.

DELIVERING A SPEECH

Raising an arm gives the impression of a passionate speech.

ANGLES

A low angle adds intensity, enhancing the energy of a high-tension character.

REMOVING THE MEGAPHONE

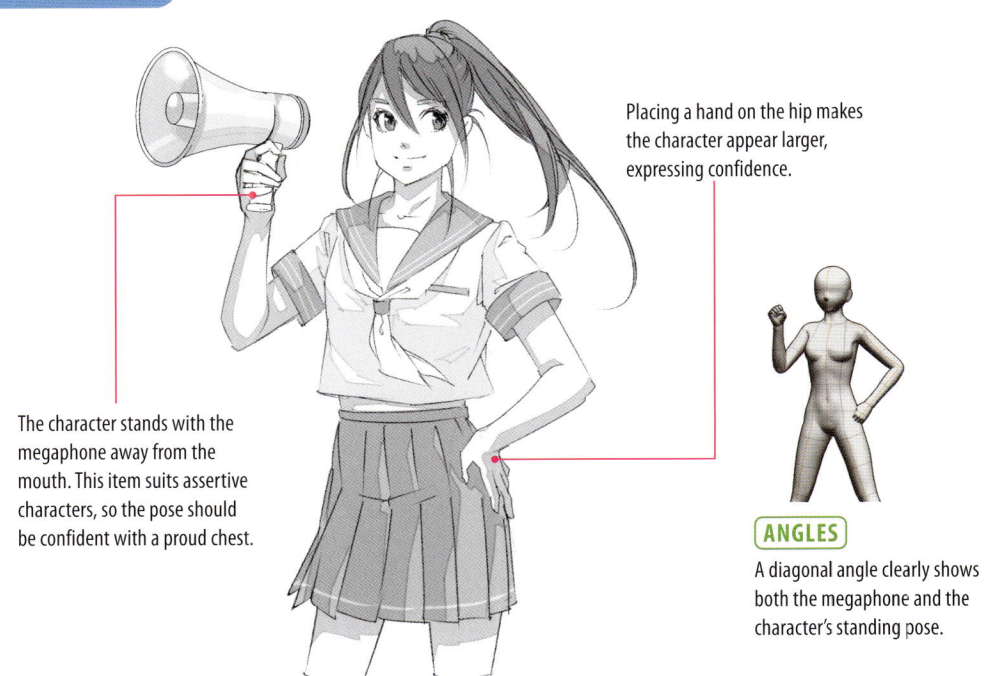

The character stands with the megaphone away from the mouth. This item suits assertive characters, so the pose should be confident with a proud chest.

Placing a hand on the hip makes the character appear larger, expressing confidence.

ANGLES

A diagonal angle clearly shows both the megaphone and the character's standing pose.

LEADING A PERFORMANCE
Conducting

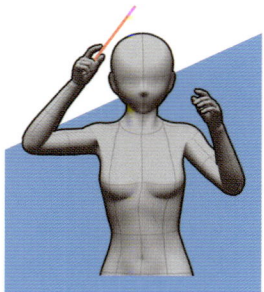

Posing a character as an orchestra conductor waving a baton can suggest dynamism, refinement or joyful freedom. When creating the pose, consider the type of music being conducted and the angle from which the character's being viewed.

RAISING HIGH

A pose with the baton raised high conveys a high-energy atmosphere, as if the performance is reaching its peak.

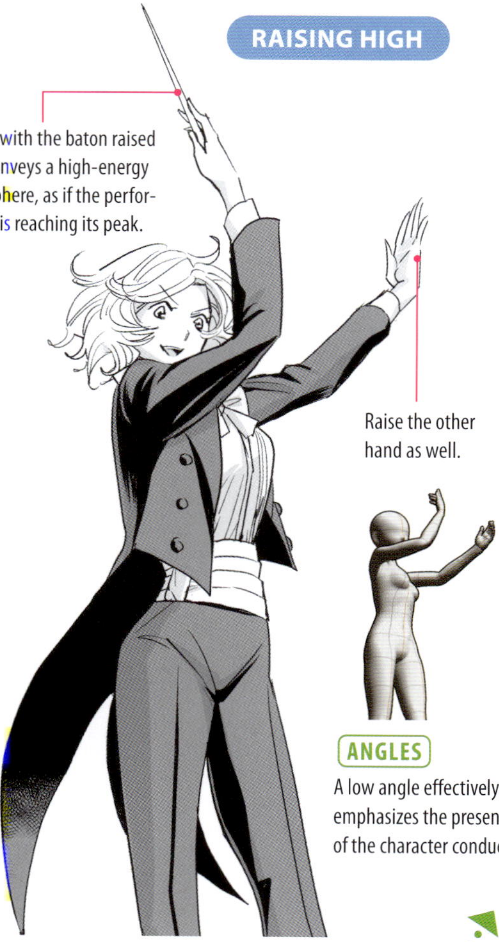

Raise the other hand as well.

ANGLES

A low angle effectively emphasizes the presence of the character conducting.

LOWERING THE BATON

When the baton is low, it suggests a quieter, more subdued piece of music.

Slightly raise the index finger.

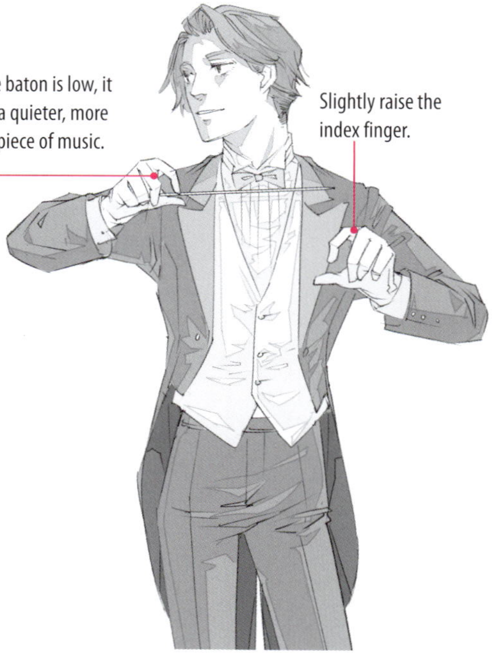

DRAWING STRAIGHT LINES

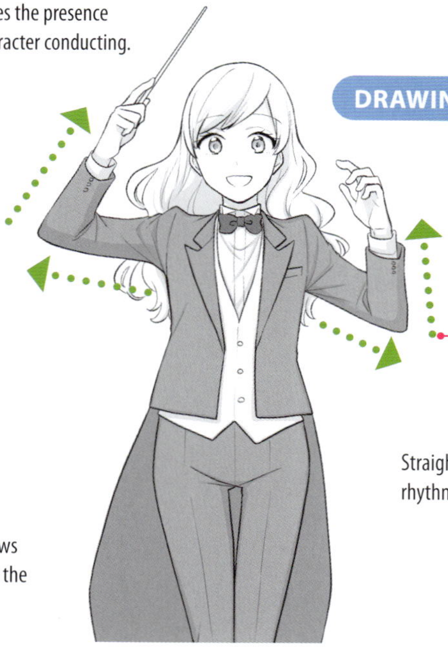

Straight arm poses create a rhythmic, fun atmosphere.

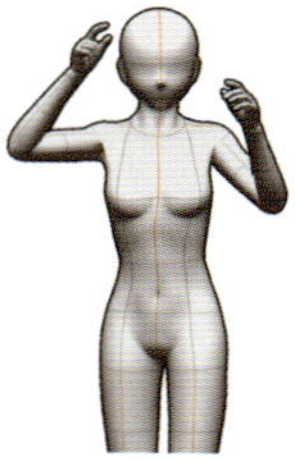

ANGLES

A front angle clearly shows the shape of the arms as the character conducts.

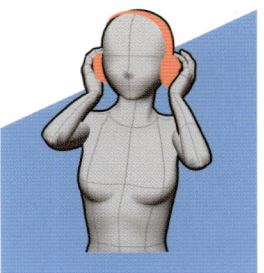

HEADPHONES AND EARBUDS
Listening to Music

Headphones and earbuds can be used to shut out the outside world, perfect for a quiet or introspective moment or for suggesting a shy character. Alternately, hanging them loosely around the neck adds a strong visual detail.

PLACING A HAND

Slightly tilting the posture conveys a sense of getting into the music.

Placing a hand on the headphones is a classic pose.

WEARING AROUND THE NECK

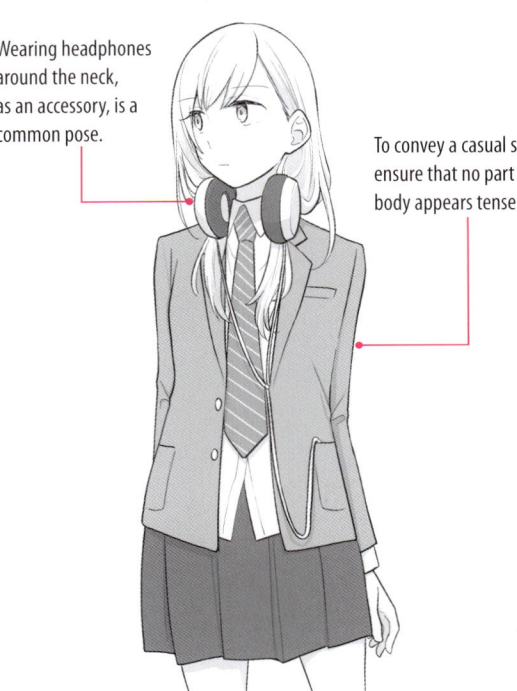

Wearing headphones around the neck, as an accessory, is a common pose.

To convey a casual stance, ensure that no part of the body appears tense.

ANGLES
Headphones are best viewed from a slight angle to clearly show their shape.

CLOSING EYES

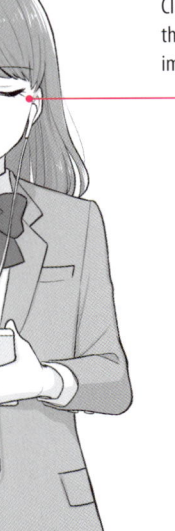

Closing the eyes gives the impression of being immersed in the music.

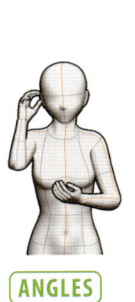

ANGLES
For earbuds, a front angle clearly shows them being worn.

Holding a music player or smartphone at mid-chest level creates a natural posture.

CROPPING Cutting the Headband is Fine

When cropping headphones, create a composition that highlights the ear pads. It's fine if the headband is cut out, as it doesn't cause any visual discomfort.

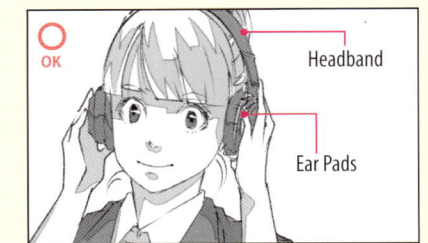

OK — Headband — Ear Pads

AN INSTRUMENT FOR EFFECT
Holding a Guitar

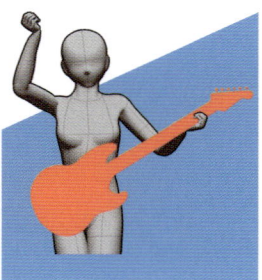

Guitars and basses make great props even if your character isn't playing them. The instrument is primarily supported by the shoulder with the strap. When not being played, it looks natural to hold the neck with the non-dominant hand.

HOLDING THE GUITAR AND LOOKING BACK

In a standing pose where the character looks back while holding a guitar, the guitar is positioned so it is visible behind them.

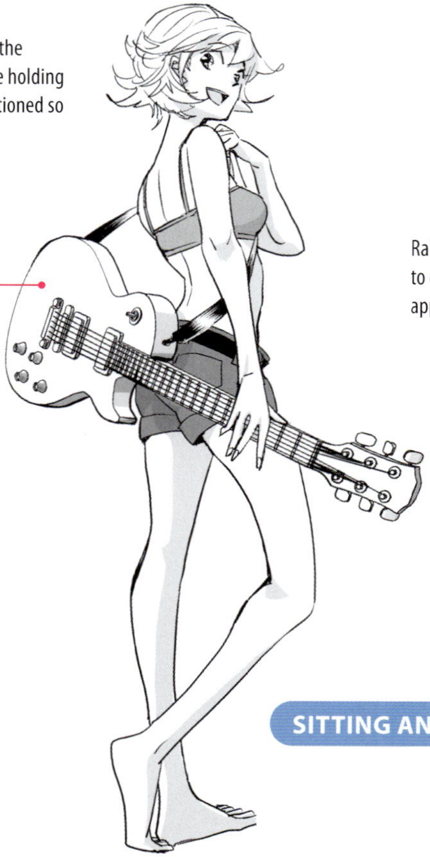

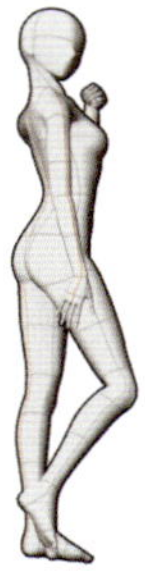

ANGLES
Choose an angle that showcases the guitar behind the character. To make the guitar stand out, find an angle that presents it in a three-dimensional manner.

PLAYING PASSIONATELY

The dominant hand holds a pick, which is commonly used for playing an electric guitar.

Raise the dominant hand to convey the impression of appealing to the audience.

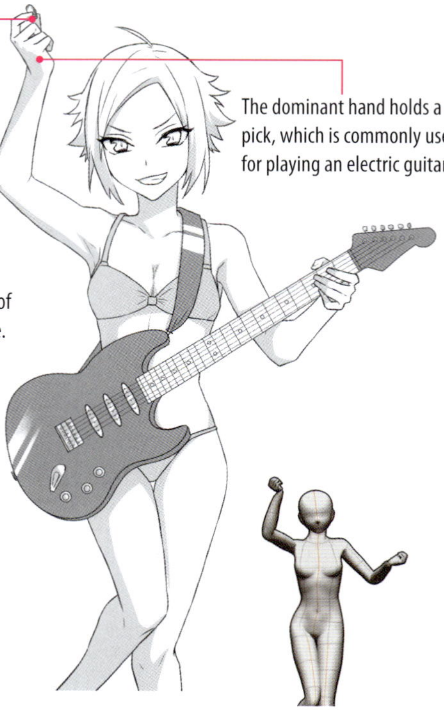

ANGLES
A front angle effectively highlights the character's expression, emphasizing their confident look.

SITTING AND HUGGING THE BASS

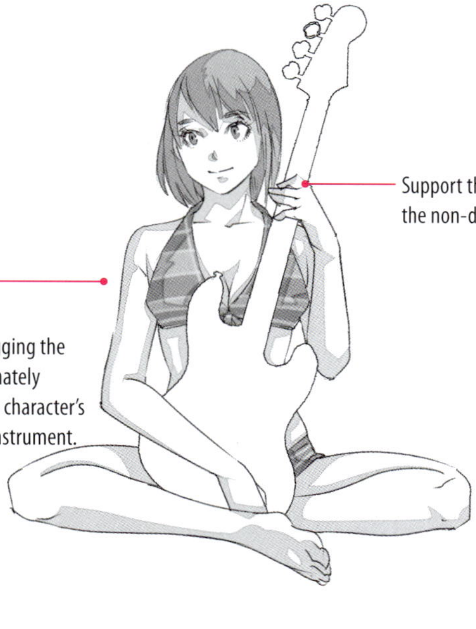

Support the neck with the non-dominant hand.

A pose of hugging the bass affectionately expresses the character's love for the instrument.

170

STANDING WITH THE GUITAR

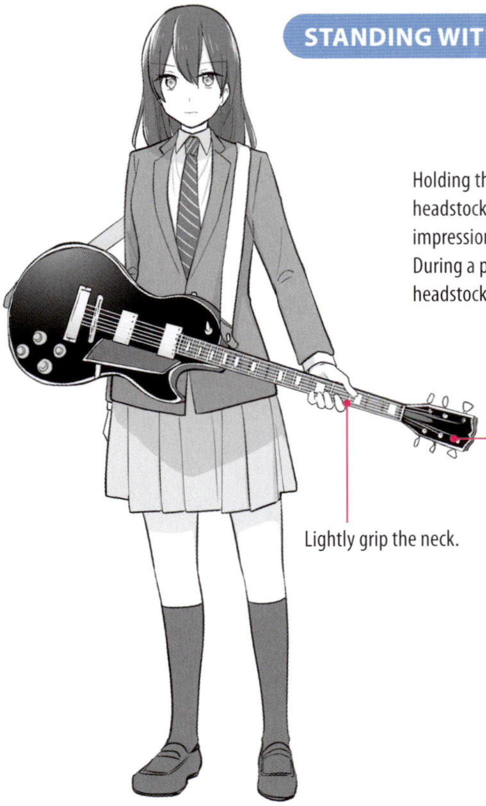

Holding the guitar with the headstock down gives the impression of taking a break. During a performance, the headstock is usually up.

Lightly grip the neck.

PLAYING WHILE LOOKING AT THE HANDS

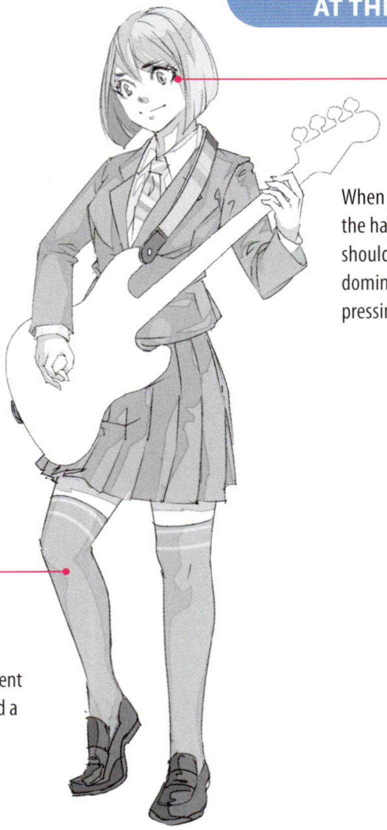

When playing while looking at the hands, the character's gaze should be directed either at the dominant hand or the hand pressing the strings.

Add some movement to the legs to avoid a stiff stance.

PLAYING WITHOUT A PICK

For bass, which handles the band's low end, playing without a pick is common, using the index and middle fingers instead.

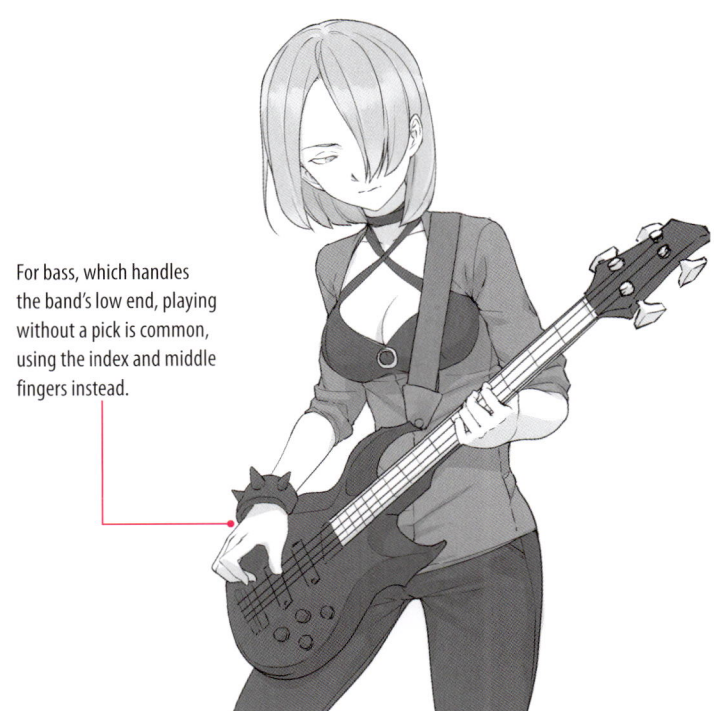

CROPPING — Leave the Headstock and Pickups Visible

When cropping, avoid cutting off too much of the guitar, making it unclear what the character is holding. Keeping part of the headstock and the area around the pickups in the frame will maintain the guitar's presence even when cropped.

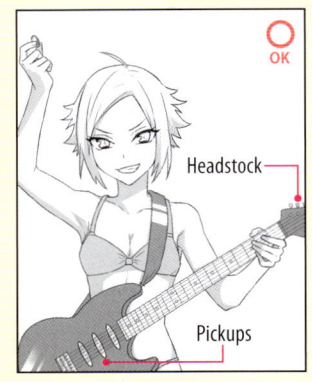

OK

Headstock

Pickups

CAPTIVATING PERFORMANCES
Singing

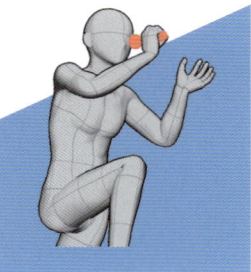

Is your character stealing the spotlight, singing a solo? To create captivating performance poses for the character, pay attention to the shape of the fingers holding the microphone.

SINGING WHILE DANCING

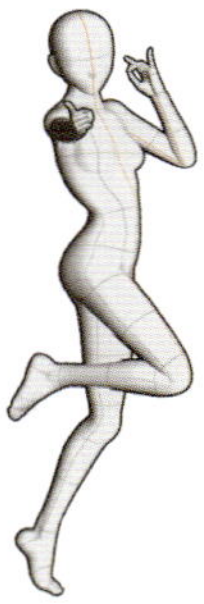

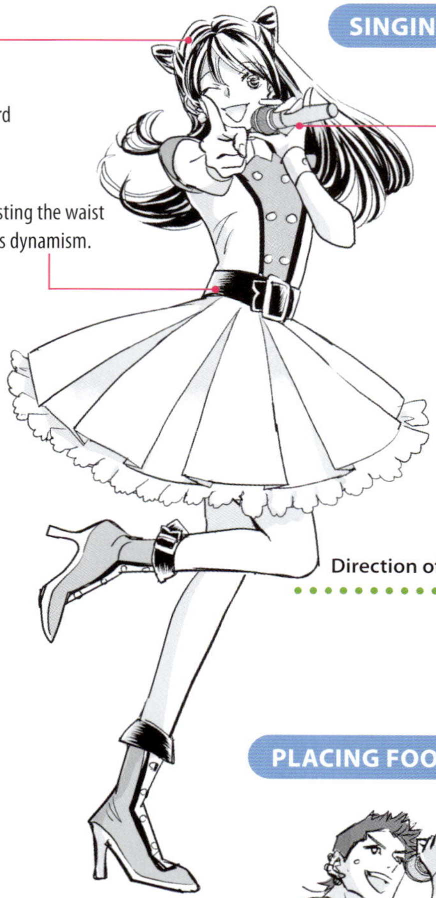

The character looks forward while moving sideways.

Adjust the way the character holds the microphone to suit their personality. Here, the character holds the pinky up.

Twisting the waist adds dynamism.

Direction of Movement

ANGLES

This angle captures the face looking directly at the camera while the body is angled and the legs face sideways, allowing the expression to be seen along with the body movement.

CALL AND RESPONSE

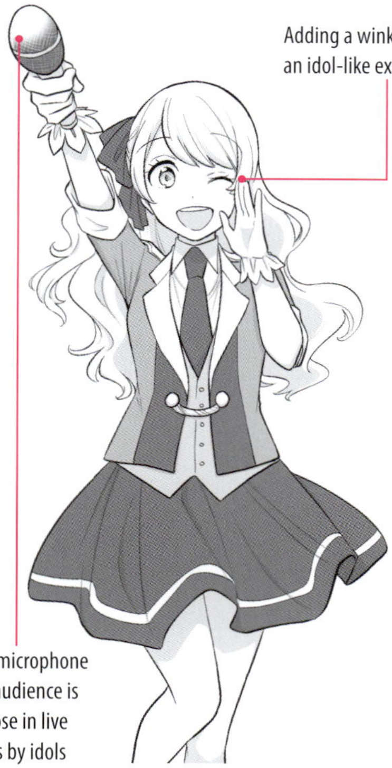

Adding a wink creates an idol-like expression.

Pointing the microphone towards the audience is a common pose in live performances by idols and musicians.

PLACING FOOT ON MONITOR

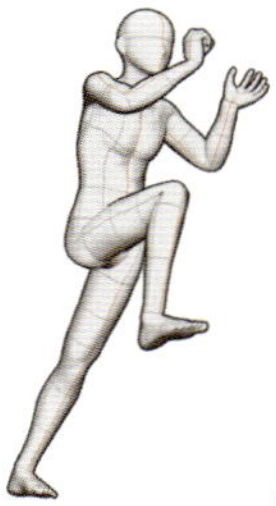

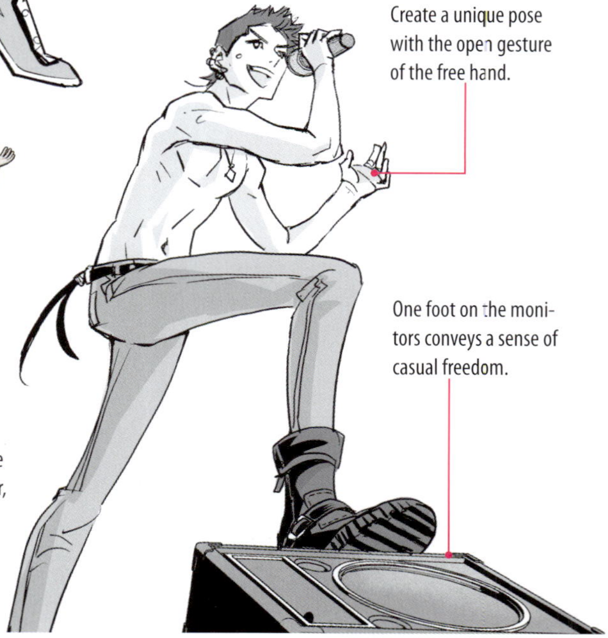

Create a unique pose with the open gesture of the free hand.

One foot on the monitors conveys a sense of casual freedom.

ANGLES

A low angle makes the foot placed on the monitor appear larger, enhancing the sense of action.

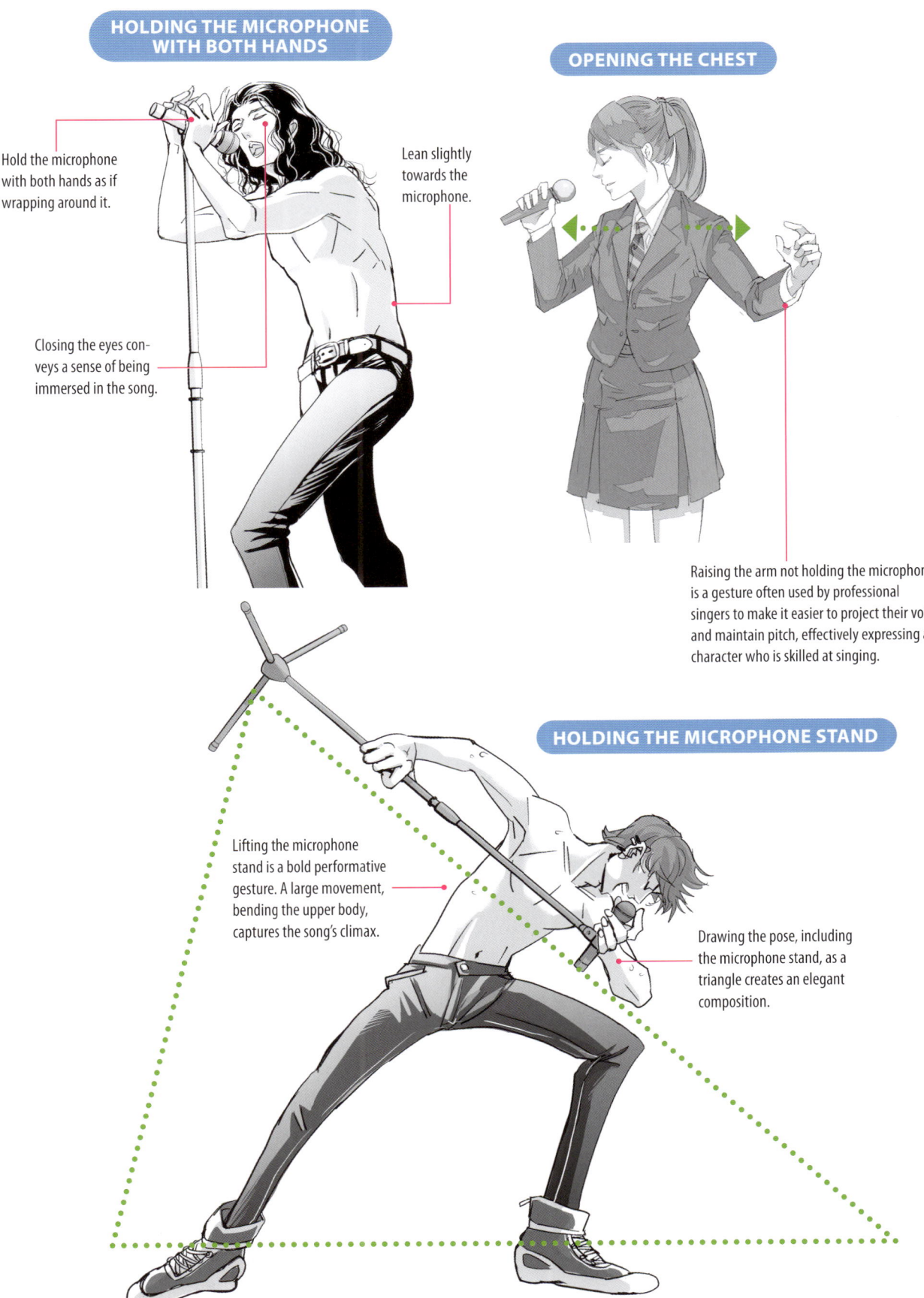

HOLDING THE MICROPHONE WITH BOTH HANDS

Hold the microphone with both hands as if wrapping around it.

Lean slightly towards the microphone.

Closing the eyes conveys a sense of being immersed in the song.

OPENING THE CHEST

Raising the arm not holding the microphone is a gesture often used by professional singers to make it easier to project their voice and maintain pitch, effectively expressing a character who is skilled at singing.

HOLDING THE MICROPHONE STAND

Lifting the microphone stand is a bold performative gesture. A large movement, bending the upper body, captures the song's climax.

Drawing the pose, including the microphone stand, as a triangle creates an elegant composition.

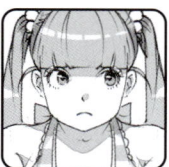
Uzuki
When giving a character a pose, pay attention to the movements of the fingertips and subtle gestures. This helps convey the character's personality more effectively.

- URL: http://xcqx.jakou.com
- Pixiv: 47662
- Twitter: @cq_zu

Eichi
My name is Eichi. I had fun illustrating various situations as part of a pose-themed guide. I have drawn various illustrations, including magical girls and idols. If you happen to come across my work, please take a look.

- URL: https://www.pixiv.net/fanbox/creator/356998
- Pixiv: 356998
- Twitter: @ech_

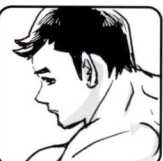
Kanyoko
I draw manga and illustrations. Most of my work involves educational and advertising projects, as well as adapting new books into manga. Drawing cool, striking poses was very enjoyable. Thank you very much!

- Twitter: @k3mangayou

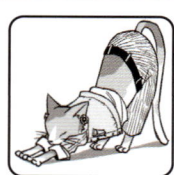
Genmai
I enjoyed drawing while considering the expressions and character qualities suggested by the poses!

- URL: http://haidoroxxx.blog.fc2.com/
- Pixiv: 17772
- Twitter: @gm_uu

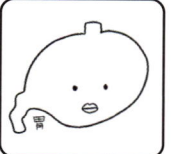
Yuko Kobara
I love drawing the female form, so I had a lot of fun working on this project. Thank you very much!

- URL: https://kobara-desu.tumblr.com/
- Pixiv: 1429333
- Twitter: @kobarayuuuuko

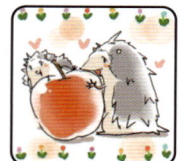
Kiyoshi Buregaku
When drawing the human body, I try to consider the skeleton, muscles, and center of gravity as much as possible. I will continue to strive for improvement, so please continue to support me!

- Pixiv: 3771155

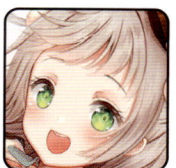
Fumufumu
This time, I drew various pose illustrations, and I was reminded of how challenging it is to come up with attractive poses. I hope I was able to help a little in thinking about poses.

- Pixiv: 3028080
- Twitter: @humuhumu28

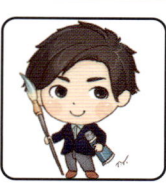
Takuya Yoshimura
When coming up with poses, I choose from several reference illustrations where the emphasized body part is most naturally highlighted, or I slightly modify the classic cool angles to add a bit of originality.

- Twitter: @takuyayoshimura

Books to Span the East and West

Tuttle Publishing was founded in 1832 in the small New England town of Rutland, Vermont [USA]. Our core values remain as strong today as they were then—to publish best-in-class books which bring people together one page at a time. In 1948, we established a publishing outpost in Japan—and Tuttle is now a leader in publishing English-language books about the arts, languages and cultures of Asia. The world has become a much smaller place today and Asia's economic and cultural influence has grown. Yet the need for meaningful dialogue and information about this diverse region has never been greater. Over the past seven decades, Tuttle has published thousands of books on subjects ranging from martial arts and paper crafts to language learning and literature—and our talented authors, illustrators, designers and photographers have won many prestigious awards. We welcome you to explore the wealth of information available on Asia at **www.tuttlepublishing.com**.

Published by Tuttle Publishing, an imprint of Periplus Editions (HK) Ltd.

www.tuttlepublishing.com

Digital Illust no Pose Mitsukaru Jiten
Copyright © 2020 Sideranch
Original Japanese edition published in 2020 by SB Creative Corp.
English translation rights arranged with SB Creative Corp., Tokyo through Japan UNI Agency, Inc., Tokyo

English translation copyright © 2025 Periplus Editions

Library of Congress Cataloging-in-Publication Data in process

ISBN 978-4-8053-1863-8

All rights reserved. No part of this publication may be reproduced or utilized in any form or by any means, electronic or mechanical, including photocopying, recording, or by any information storage and retrieval system, without prior written permission from the publisher.

27 26 25 24   10 9 8 7 6 5 4 3 2 1

Printed in China   2409EP

Distributed by
North America, Latin America & Europe
Tuttle Publishing
364 Innovation Drive
North Clarendon, VT 05759-9436 U.S.A.
Tel: 1 (802) 773-8930
Fax: 1 (802) 773-6993
info@tuttlepublishing.com
www.tuttlepublishing.com

Japan
Tuttle Publishing
Yaekari Building, 3rd Floor
5-4-12 Osaki
Shinagawa-ku
Tokyo 141 0032
Tel: (81) 3 5437-0171
Fax: (81) 3 5437-0755
tuttle-sales@gol.com

Asia Pacific
Berkeley Books Pte. Ltd.
3 Kallang Sector, #04-01
Singapore 349278
Tel: (65) 67412178
Fax: (65) 67412179
inquiries@periplus.com.sg
www.tuttlepublishing.com

TUTTLE PUBLISHING® is a registered trademark of Tuttle Publishing, a division of Periplus Editions (HK) Ltd.

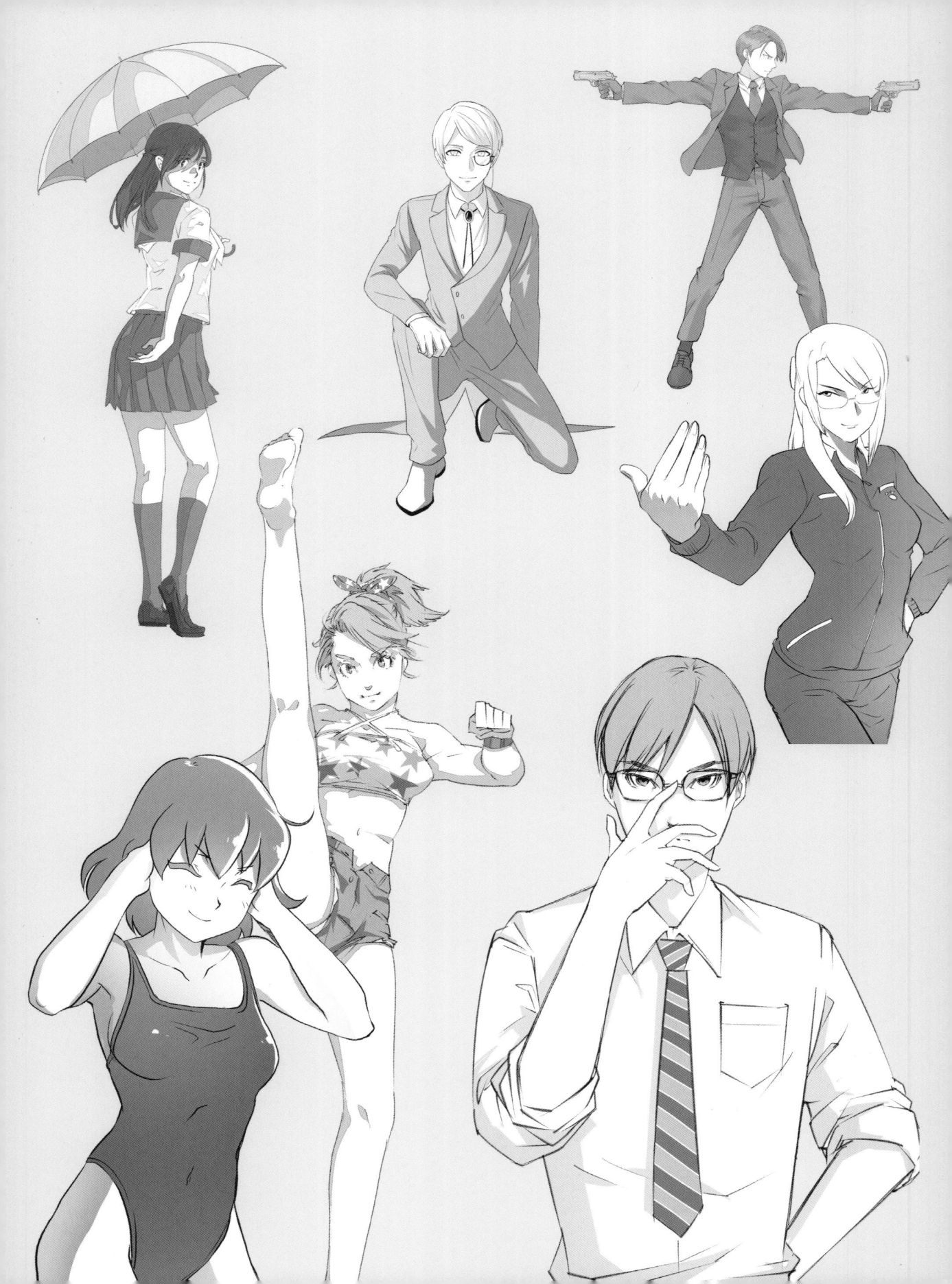